Steve McCoy

# Choice and Consequence

Steve Nelson

# Choice and Consequence

## Thomas C. Schelling

HARVARD UNIVERSITY PRESS
Cambridge, Massachusetts
and
London, England

**Library of Congress Cataloging in Publication Data**


Schelling, Thomas C., 1921–
    Choice and consequence.

    Bibliography: p.
    Includes index.
    1. Social sciences—Addresses, essays, lectures. 2. Economics—Addresses, essays, lectures. 3. Social problems—Addresses, essays, lectures. 4. Choice (Psychology)—Addresses, essays, lectures. I. Title.
H35.S335    1984          300          83-18332
ISBN 0-674-12770-6 (cloth)
ISBN 0-674-12771-4 (paper)

*To the memory of*
*William John Fellner*

# Preface

I ONCE RECEIVED an award in political economy and expected to be asked, What for? Instead I was asked, What is political economy?

I could think of two answers. They differ in emphasis. One is
economics in a context of policy, where the policy is more than economics but the "more" cannot be separated from the economics.
Nuclear energy is an example, or foreign aid, or the military draft.
The second is working on a problem area to which an economist
can bring a little insight that, without offering solutions, helps in
finding a solution or in facing an issue, even though the problems
themselves would not usually be identified as economics. In these
days of interdisciplinary committees there is rarely a problem that
doesn't appear to demand—in addition to lawyers and anthropol-
ogists and biologists—an economist. The economist is usually invited because of a perception that, whatever else may be
important, there are some important economics. The economist
who joins up usually finds the "whatever else" more engaging
than the economics; though he pays his entrance fee in economics, he gets his satisfaction from the whole problem.

I have been in studies of smoking and health; the intriguing
issues are not the economics of tobacco farming and tobacco
taxes. I have been in symposia on medical ethics, like the "right to
die," and it was not the rising costs of hospital care that held my
attention. I have helped with studies of biomedical technologies,

like selecting the sex of offspring, and the fascination is not in animal husbandry.

Recruitment is along networks that are sometimes invisible. I can usually deduce the connections by which I get asked to do something on nuclear terrorism; the historical sequence may have been almost Brownian in movement, but there is a trail to follow. I can guess how I got asked by a Committee on Life Sciences and Social Policy to join in assessing *in vitro* fertilization. But I have never figured out why I was chosen as the economist for the Committee on Substance Abuse and Habitual Behavior, or on Carbon Dioxide and Climate Change. Planets are so called from a Greek word meaning "wanderer," and maybe some of us are conspicuous for wandering and presumed willing to keep moving. I am not complaining. Still, when Arthur J. Rosenthal, Director of Harvard University Press, invited me to select about fifteen essays to be published together, I knew it would not be easy to find a title for the book.

Actually, just as the planets did not really wander but only appeared to, I have not wandered as much as may appear. In 1960 Harvard University Press published my *Strategy of Conflict*, a dozen essays in bargaining, conflict, and strategy. The applications were international—diplomacy, deterrence, arms control, foreign aid—but I looked for ideas in the ways people maneuvered in traffic jams, negotiated with children, confronted demands for ransom, filed suit, or designed agendas for meetings. And though for many years my principal policy concerns were with national security, I was easily attracted to other fields where similar principles seemed to be at work.

In 1966 I was asked to help the President's Crime Commission on the deterrence of income-tax evasion; I got diverted onto a task force on organized crime; the result was two of the essays in this book.

Coercing, cajoling, or constraining another's behavior had seemed to me, in writing that earlier book, to have something in common with constraining or controlling one's own behavior. (Devices to keep somebody else from firing a weapon in panic are not altogether different from devices to keep oneself from firing in panic.) After arguing that point for several years with colleagues on a Committee on Substance Abuse and Habitual Behavior, I was challenged to commit my thoughts to paper; ultimately two of these essays appeared.

The relations between physician and patient, especially a terminally ill or hopelessly wretched patient, involve negotiation, strategic withholding of information, a need to authenticate assertions, and conflict of interest within small groups. Two of these essays reflect that interest in the circumstances of dying.

In trying to say something intelligent about punishment, euthanasia, rescue, or the treatment of drug addicts, one needs a policy toward the ethical issues, real or alleged, that are bound to come up. One policy is to leave them alone, to recognize that they are there and are somebody else's business, but not mine. A second is to assume responsibility for resolving them in the hope that if I can resolve them to my own satisfaction, I will have satisfied my audience too. The third, which appeals to me, is to try to identify, to clarify, and if possible to dispose of the ethical issues in the belief that sometimes I actually can help, and if I can I ought to, and that sometimes, especially on matters wrapped up in economics, I may be able to unwrap the economics and disclose that the ethical issue was misplaced or misidentified. Trying doesn't always get me very far. The first two essays in this book were responses to invitations—one from the Hastings Center, Institute of Society, Ethics, and the Life Sciences, and one from the Brookings Institution—to deal with the ethics of policy head on.

Much of economics exploits the principle that in the phenomena we want to understand, people are behaving in purposive fashion, aware of their values and alert to their opportunities, knowledgeable about their environment and the constraints on what they may choose, and are able to match actions with objectives over time. This is sometimes referred to as the assumption that behavior is "rational." That assumption has to exclude some people, like the very young, the senile, those who hallucinate and those who panic, people who are intoxicated or suffering brain damage; but there are plenty of people left over to whom it is supposed to apply. It is a powerful tool of analysis, even if it applies only approximately most of the time and badly some of the time. It allows what, in one of these essays, I call "vicarious problem-solving." We figure out what a person might do by putting ourselves into his position, as best we understand that position, adopting for the purpose as much as we know about his own preferences and deciding what he ought to do. By "what he ought to do" we merely mean what he should decide in accordance with his own aims, values, and objectives, given the alternatives that he faces. Like most economists I am attracted to this model, at least as a benchmark, because when it works we get a lot of output from minimal input using a standard piece of intellectual machinery.

I have been intrigued by cases in which that model seems not to work well. The two essays on self-command and one on dying examine situations of choice and consequence in which that model leaves too much unexplained. Preoccupation with these intriguing special cases probably does not mean that I am any less loyal to economics than other economists of my age, but only that I am more tantalized by the unusual. The final essay is a somewhat playful attempt to recognize that our minds are not only problem-solving equipment but also the organ in which much of our consumption takes place.

In selecting these essays, written over a period of fifteen years, I relied on the judgment of Michael Aronson, General Editor of Harvard University Press, and got some decisive advice from Sidney G. Winter, Professor of Economics at Yale. It was Sid Winter who pointed out that the essays went nicely in pairs, though most of them had not been written that way. The exception is Chapter 15, the most recent one, and I have a superstitious feeling that I have not finished with its subject.

I have sometimes been annoyed in citing or assigning, or just rereading, somebody's article that had been stripped, updated, or expurgated for republication and no longer said what I thought it had said. And I have an uneasy feeling that it is cheating to purge predictions that did not come true and judgments I now think were unwise. So everything here is almost the same as when first published. The entire manuscript had one more round of tasteful copyediting by Ann Louise McLaughlin, Senior Editor at Harvard University Press. Some references no longer current were dropped and some quaint terminology, like "dope" for hard drugs, has been modernized. I resisted the temptation to inflate the "reasonable tip" for a parlor-car steward, letting it stand at fifty cents. And younger readers will be puzzled by a mysterious reference to laws against the sale of yellow margarine.

In a few places I have altered the tense of a verb or inserted a bracketed remark to orient the reader historically. Chapter 2 was written well into the era of airplane hijacking, but before introduction of the hand luggage inspection we now take for granted.

Chapter 7 was written an age ago in the legal history of abortion. What I wrote I still like, but the context may seem strange even when you make allowance for the passage of time, the upheaval having been so extensive, so rapid, and so little anticipated. Chapter 9 has an innocent charm in its treatment of the market for what used to be called "filthy pictures"; the few pages survive as a period piece. Occasionally a phenomenon waxes, wanes, and waxes again; if you are in phase your results may seem as pertinent—not still, but again—as when you wrote them. With ABM in mind I said ten years go, "It is anomalous that in the last few years the bargaining-chip idea became a subject of popular discussion precisely because the Executive Branch put forward positions that it explained at home to be bargaining-chips." I can say it again: different weapon, different president, same tactic.

There is no way I can thank the many people who offered me help or encouragement or opportunity, or whose influence I felt, during the long period in which these essays were originally composed. But as I write this preface I have just learned of the death of Willi Fellner; and I do know that his kindness to me and his influence are unsurpassed. Everyone who knew him will understand why I have dedicated this book to him.

*October 1983*                                                    T.C.S.

# Contents

# Choice and Consequence

# 1 | Economic Reasoning and the Ethics of Policy

**P**OLICY JUDGMENTS are easier to come by, the farther we are from our goals. If there are only two directions and we know which is forward, and there are limits to how fast we can go, no fine discrimination is needed. If aid to the poor is far too little, highway traffic far too fast, building codes far too lax, teachers' salaries far too low, or the rights of defendants far too little observed, we know what we need to know to get moving. We can worry about how much is enough when we get close, if we ever do. Meanwhile we can push on.

Knowing what to do is also easy if our capabilities are growing and our horizons receding, and yesterday's goals will be outgrown tomorrow. Like a family on a rising income, we needn't worry about overshooting: if we buy too big a house today, we'll afford it tomorrow.

I have often been glad that I wasn't in charge. It is easy enough to see plainly that there is too much inequality (or illiteracy, or ill health, or injustice) and to help to reduce it, knowing that despite all efforts too much will remain. But if it were up to me to decide *how much* inequality is not too much, or how much injustice, or how much disregard for the elderly or for future generations, I'd need more than a sense of direction.

Discomfort also arises when, intent on speeding toward an ever-receding goal, the goal suddenly stops receding and we threaten to overshoot. There appears to be a widespread belief that overshoot is what we've done.

Worse, there is retrospective disenchantment with the mood that motivated the effort and set the goals in the first place, back in the 1960s. There is chagrin at having been too enthusiastic about what could be accomplished. There is disaffection toward those whose demands are insatiable and whose gratitude is inconspicuous. Whatever the reason, there is a reexamination of policy, especially policy that reflects social obligation. There is retrenchment in the air and on the ballot, and second thoughts about what we can afford for ourselves and what we owe others.

It isn't all sour grapes. Our projection of the possible has shrunk. Our economy is not behaving. Growing income no longer promises to make light of our burdens in another decade or two. We do not know what has been depressing our productivity and can't be sure that, whatever it is, we shall recover soon. Inflation has a mind of its own. The demographics of the labor force are against us, and at the same time the rules of the game allow endless numbers of people from faraway places, once over the line, to touch base and be safe.

So it is not surprising that commitments are being reassessed, "tradeoffs" discussed, costs weighed anew against benefits, and even constitutional initiatives promoted to enforce a policy of containment. Techniques of policy analysis that recently were despised as mean spirited and stingy by people who preferred to base policy on vision and generosity are being superseded by what used to be called meat-axes and straitjackets.

These are not "hard times" in the old sense. In this country life is still good and getting better for most people. But it is not measuring up to expectations. They might better be called "difficult times": it is the problems, not the times, that are hard. And among the hard issues are some ethical ones. They may not be the hardest or the most important, but they are important and they are hard.

I have been asked how economic reasoning can help, or how it misleads, in facing, solving, or avoiding the ethical components of policy. Does economic reasoning itself represent a particular ethic; or, if not the reasoning, the people who use it?

## The Ethics of Policy

What I mean by the ethics of policy is the relevant ethics when we try to think *disinterestedly* about rent control, minimum wages, Medicaid, food stamps, safety regulations, cigarette taxes, or the financing of Social Security.

Farmers have an interest in price supports, laundry operators in minimum-wage laws, doctors in the financing of Medicare, and electric utilities in clean-air regulation; and until my youngest child is safely overage I shall have a personal interest in the draft. When people take sides on a leash law we don't expect them to argue it the way they discuss the space shuttle. I want to define the ethics of policy as what we try to bring to bear on *those issues in which we do not have a personal stake.*

It is hard to find issues that are absolutely unsoiled with personal interest. On abortion and capital punishment our personal ethics usually dominate. Food stamps affect us, whether we qualify or not, because they cost money. Someone meticulously interested in his own welfare could find at least a minuscule personal interest in a UN program for alphabet reform.

Still, most of us on many issues want to think and to talk as though we are not interested parties. We want to discuss welfare and national defense and school construction and unemployment benefits and automobile-mileage standards as though we were not personally involved. There will be an unmistakable element of social obligation; nobody can discuss income-tax rates or welfare levels without a participatory awareness that the poor, the unfortunate, the disadvantaged, and the otherwise deserving have some legitimate claim on those among us who can afford to help. But although few issues are without financial impact somewhere, and most big issues involve big amounts of money, we can often confine our personal stake to an aggregate and nonspecific social obligation. Our position in the income scale affects our conditioning as well as our reasoning, but beyond that we can try to be neutral, removed, vicarious, impartial, judicious.

Incidentally, I say this only because I expect this book to be read by a special set of people. Most people probably devote most of their policy interest to the things that concern themselves and do it with a clear conscience. They do not get drawn into ethical abstractions. They may have strong ethical views on a limited

number of subjects that do not flow from their stake in the outcome, but on matters called "bread and butter" they accept the
ethic that in politics it is fair to look out for your own interest, expecting others to look out for theirs. People who read or write
books like this one, though, usually try to take distributive issues
seriously but not personally. Students, for example, rebelling
against higher tuition are reluctant to say it is to save their own
money; they join the picket line in behalf of somebody poorer.
And professors concerned to protect their *own* salaries are thought
not to be playing the ethical game. But the tobacco farmer concerned solely with his own family's welfare is excused from schol-
arly disinterest.

## The Ethics of Pricing

My students always like gasoline rationing. They believe in it on
ethical principles. (They say they do, and they sound as if they
do.) Evidently the principles lie deeper than rationing itself; the
students must have some notion of what happens with rationing
and without it, or with some specific alternative, and they must
have a preference about the outcome. Students know that there
are gainers and losers; their ethics appear to relate to who gains,
who loses, and how much.

I can talk most of them out of it. It takes longer than fifty minutes, and I never try it if I have only a single class hour. They
probably distrust my ethical principles and think I do not care
about what they care about, or care as much. They very likely
think my ethics are "process oriented" and the free market enchants me, while they are "consequences oriented" and don't like
the results.

Time permitting, I accomplish their conversion in two stages. I
warn them in advance that I am going to show them that if they
like rationing there is something they should like better. I join
them in believing the free market needn't be let alone, but I do
propose what is sometimes called "rationing by the purse." I suggest we let the price of gasoline rise until there is no shortage, and
capture the price increase with a tax. Because that looks hard on
the poor my students do not like it.

The first step in subverting their ethical preference is to propose
that under any system of rationing that they might devise—and I
take a little while to show them that it is not easy to design a

"fair" system of rations—people should be encouraged to buy and sell ration coupons. This proposal has little appeal. The rich will obviously burn more than their share of gas, the poor being coerced by their very poverty into releasing coupons for the money they so desperately need. But eventually students recognize that the poor, *because* they are poor, would like the privilege of turning their coupons into money. Where gas coupons can only provide them gas at a discount, transferable coupons can buy milk at a discount. If it is unfair that the poor cannot drive as much as the rich, it is the poverty that is unfair, not the gasoline system.

That principle established, we observe that coupons are worth cash, whether you buy them, sell them, or merely turn in your own at the local service station. If gas at the pump is $1.25 and coupons sell for 75 cents, the net price of gasoline is $2.00; anyone who gets ten gallons' worth of coupons from the Department of Energy is getting a clumsy equivalent of $7.50 cash. The station that sells ten gallons receives $12.50 in money and $7.50 in coupons that could have been traded for cash. What we have is a 75-cent tax payable at the pump in special money, and a cash disbursement to motorists paid in this special money. We could just as well do it all without the coupons.

There is more to it than that, but the "more" usually does not involve much ethics. It isn't that we resolved an ethical issue. We merely lifted the veil of money and discovered that the ethical issue we thought was there was not. Or, perhaps better, the ethical issue that we associated with rationing was tangential to that procedure. Whatever the compensatory principle is that appeals to the students' sense of fairness, there are many procedures that can achieve it, some better than others, rationing neither worst nor best; and once it is all converted to money, it is easier to see what some of the alternatives are and whether they are ethically superior. Superficially it may seem wrong to give gas coupons to people who don't drive; but if the gasoline is taxed instead and the proceeds rebated to the public, we can judge the ethics of alternative distributions of the proceeds, not just those based on drivers' licenses and car registrations.

Persuasion is a little harder with rent control, partly because students do not like landlords. We try to see whether there might be something better, even in principle; whether people seeking apartments are losers under rent control; whether some nonevict-able tenants in rent-controlled apartments would like to cash in their precious property right but are locked in because their claim is to a specific apartment. Usually by the time we have identified all the interested parties and the likely magnitudes of their inter-ests, and have considered a few alternative ways to accomplish the things rent control is intended to accomplish, the liveliness of the issue is undiminished but the ethical loading has mostly evapo-rated.

I dislike "counting coup" over vanquished students in order to display, and to hope you are impressed with, some of the ways that economics can contribute to the clarification of ethical issues. But at least the claim for economics is modest: it often helps diag-nose misplaced identification of an ethical issue. And it does this solely by helping to identify what is happening. It is not clarifying ethics; it is only clarifying economics.

Let me give a few more examples. Minimum-wage laws are thought to have ethical content. But if their main effect, or even their purpose, is to keep the young and the old and the otherwise least valuable employees from working at all, the ethical issues may not be what the proponents thought they were. Making util-ities pay the full cost of smoke abatement seems eminently fair, unless the costs are borne by consumers of electricity and the clean air enjoyed by whoever lives downwind, in which case we may want to know who lives downwind and who buys the elec-tricity, the utility company not having much interest in the mat-ter. (Even if the electricity is procured mainly by business, we don't know yet who is paying until we know who buys the prod-ucts, or who will settle for lower wages when the other costs rise.) Even our feelings about people who evade the income tax by not declaring tips or typing fees or truck garden sales will depend on whether the system mainly lowers wages and prices in bars and restaurants and reduces the cost of lettuce or of getting theses typed.

### The Clash between Equity and Incentives

Policy issues are preponderantly concerned with helping, in com-pensatory fashion, the unfortunate and the disadvantaged. We have welfare for those who cannot work, unemployment benefits for people out of jobs, disability benefits for the disabled, hospital care for the injured and the ill, disaster relief for the victims of floods, income tax relief for the victims of accidental loss, and rescue services for people who find themselves in danger. Social Security is based on the premise that people will arrive at post-working age with inadequate savings to live on.

An unsympathetic way to restate this is that a preponderance of government policies have the purpose of rewarding people who get into difficulty. People are paid handsomely for losing their jobs; if you smash your car the IRS will share the cost of a new one; and if your injury requires hospitalization you can stay in an air-conditioned room as long as the doctor certifies that you will recover better if you don't go home. By treating the absence of a "man in the house" as a special grievance for a woman with dependent children, families have even received a bonus for fathers' leaving home.

There is no getting away from it. Almost any compensatory program directed toward a condition over which people have any kind of control, even remote and probabilistic control, reduces the incentive to stay out of that condition and detracts from the urgency of getting out of it. It is a rare ameliorative program that has no visible way, by its influence on behavior, to affect the likelihood or the duration or the severity of the circumstances it is intended to ameliorate. And most commonly—not always but most commonly—the effect on behavior is undesired and in the wrong direction.

To keep the issue in perspective we can observe that private insurance, even the informal kind that allows us to ask for help when we run out of gas, can have the same adverse influence on behavior. People more willingly drive on slippery roads the more nearly complete their collision coverage; back doors are unlocked if the homeowner's policy is liberal in its provisions for burglary. I am more indulgent of my sore throat if my employer provides an ample quota of sick days.

There is no use denying it in defense of social programs. As is usually the case with important issues, principles conflict. On the one hand, we want to treat unemployment as a collective liability, sustaining the family at public expense when working members lose their livelihoods. And on the other, we want not to induce people to get conveniently disemployed or to feel no need when unemployed to seek work vigorously. What helps toward one objective hurts toward the other. Offering 90 percent of normal pay can make unemployment irresistible for some, and even a net profit for those who can moonlight or work around the home. Providing only 40 percent over a protracted period makes living harsher than we want it to be. There is nothing to do but compromise. But a compromise that makes unemployment a grave hardship for some makes it a pleasant respite for others, and we cannot even be comfortable with the compromise.

Decent welfare in a high-income state is bound to be at a higher level than in a low-income state. It induces migration. Even if we favor migration, the state that finds more and more migrants on its welfare rolls did not intend to reduce the poverty of other states by helping any and all who could get up and move. But to provide an unattractive level of benefits would condemn the intended beneficiaries to a level of living below what their home state wanted to provide them. Again two principles conflict.

There are exceptions to this tendency of inducing the wrong behavior. Federal deposit insurance was designed in the 1930s to provide restitution to people whose bank deposits were lost; by generating confidence, the insurance reduced precisely the behavior that caused the problem. And a benefit strictly related to age in years, though it may reduce efforts to save, at least can have no effect on the speed with which people grow older. But the tendency is pervasive. It accounts for a good part of the escalation of medical costs.

I do not know whether one of the principles, helping the disadvantaged, should be considered ethical and the other, not letting them get away with it, not ethical. Much of the discussion about welfare rights, about not proportioning medical care to the ability to pay, and about not producing a "work ethic" by threatening the unemployed with their families' starvation, is in an ethical mode. To a lesser extent, ethical considerations are evoked over the encouragement of malingering, rewarding those who beat the system, or inducing dependence on the state. Once it is recognized, however, that two principles conflict, that two desiderata point in opposite directions and neither is so overwhelming that the other can be ignored, that both objectives have merit, and even that there is no ideal compromise because there is a diversified population at risk, the ethical contents of the principles begin to seem tangential to the inescapable problem of locating an acceptable compromise.

It is a universal problem. It won't go away. It can't be neglected. It isn't even unique to *public* policy. The word "compromise" has those two different meanings. Compromising *a* principle sounds wrong. Compromising *between* principles is all right.

## Valuing the Priceless

Among the poignant issues that policy has to face, explicitly or by default, are some that seem to pit finite cost against infinite value. What is it worth to save a life? How much to spend on fair trial to protect the innocent against false verdicts? What limits to put on the measures, some costly in money and some in anguish, to extend the lives of people who will die soon anyway or whose lives, in someone's judgment, are not worth preserving?

These issues are ubiquitous. They arise in designing a national health program. They are directly involved in decisions for traffic lights, airport safety, medical research, fire and Coast Guard protection, and the safety of government employees. They are implicitly involved in regulation for occupational safety or safe water supplies, in building codes and speed laws, even helmets for motorcyclists—because somebody has to pay the costs.

It is characteristic of policymakers, especially at the federal level, that they usually think of themselves as making decisions that affect others, not themselves. Hurricane and tornado warnings are for those living where hurricanes and tornados strike; mine safety is a responsibility of legislators and officials aboveground concerning the lives of people who work underground. Policies toward the senile, the comatose, the paralyzed, and the terminally ill are deliberated by people who are none of the above. Occasionally the legislator debating a 55-mile speed limit pauses to think whether the benefits in safety to his own family will be worth the added driving time, but if he or she is conscientious even that calculation may be surreptitious.

The situation is different when a small community considers a mobile cardiac unit or a new fire engine. The question then is not what we ought to spend to save someone else's life but what we can afford to make *our* lives safer. Spending or stinting on the lives of others invites moral contemplation; budgeting my expenditures for my own benefit, alone or with neighbors for the school safety program, is less a moral judgment than a consumer choice, a weighing of some reduction in risk against the other things that money will buy.

There is a suggestion here. Maybe we can reduce the unmanageable moral content of that paternalistic decision at the national level by making it more genuinely vicarious. Instead of asking what society's obligation to *them* is, we should ask how *they* would want *us* to spend *their* money. In deciding how much to require people to spend on their own seat belts, smoke alarms, fire extinguishers, and lightning rods, it is easier to be vicarious and it is legitimate to get our bearings by reflecting on how much we might reasonably spend on our own safety. The question still may not be easy, but it is less morally intimidating.

Surely, if we were all similarly at risk and in like economic circumstances, this would be the way to look at it, whether for the town bandstand or the town ambulance. On a national scale it is less transparently so, but nevertheless so, that we should want our appropriations committees to think of themselves as spending our money in our behalf. We want them neither to skimp where it really counts nor to go overboard to prepare at great expense— our expense—for the remotest of dangers. We want them to be thinking not about what concern the government owes its citizens for their safety but how much of our own money we taxpayers want spent for our safety.

With that perspective it is remarkable how quickly the issue, now collectively self-regarding instead of other-regarding, drops the ethical content that was only a construct of the initial formulation. We can still find ethical issues, but not the one that seemed so central.

We could call this the contractual approach to social obligation. In the absence of an understanding, I may owe you, in your extremity, unbounded attention and concern, comfort and livelihood, room and board, and the best medical attention in perpetuity, and feel guilty when I stop to wonder whether you are worth the burden you are putting on me. When it is my turn of course I'll expect the same from you (or from whoever has the corresponding responsibility toward me that I had toward you), feeling a little guilty perhaps but not enough to relinquish my claim. But if we could sit down together at an early age in good health and legislate our relation to each other, specifying the entitlements we wished to obtain between us, recognizing equal likelihood of being beneficiaries or benefactors, we could elect to eschew exorbitant claims. And it would not strike us as an ethical issue.

The contractual approach can help with some of those other tantalizing dilemmas, like which planeload of passengers to save, the big plane with lots of passengers or the one with mostly empty seats, if both are at risk and one at most can be saved. What I should do in the control tower if that Godlike decision were mine is an ethical dilemma that for some thoughtful people has no easy answer. But if I am an airline passenger answering a questionnaire for the FAA on what rule I want the control tower to follow in emergencies, the issue is neither ethical nor a dilemma.

I cheated a little in supposing that we were all similarly situated with respect to some risk and alike in our ability to afford protective measures. We usually are not. But the value of this conceptual approach, of considering what the safety is worth to the people who are safer, may still be salvaged. If you are more at risk than I—let's say you are at risk and I am not at all—and the rule is that we share the cost of reducing the risk and we are purely self-regarding, I shall find the measures worth nothing, while you find the measures twice as attractive as if you had to pay it all yourself. If you fly a plane and I do not, the new runway lights at the local airport will cost us each $1,000, and may be worth it to you but not to me. If they are worth more than $2,000 to you, they ought to be bought, at least if you'll pay for them. (Whether I ought to pay half is a separable issue.) But suppose you wouldn't pay more than $1,500 for the slight contribution the runway lights make to your safety. I propose that they shouldn't be bought.

Even though we divide on the issue of whether, paying $1,000 apiece, we ought to buy the lights, the economist in me formulates the problem this way: If, because your personal safety is involved, you are entitled to my contributing $1,000 toward the purchase of runway lights, and I acknowledge your claim and put up my money for your exclusive benefit, do you really want to buy the runway lights or would you rather take my $1,000 and keep it? I don't care. I may be annoyed at having to put up the money when you don't want the lights after all, but I might be more annoyed that you are spending my $1,000 on something that you didn't consider worth the cost. In fact, we could both be better off if instead of purchasing the lights I just gave you $750 and we forgot the lights.

For some among us that may not settle the issue. But I propose that it is nevertheless a useful perspective, a relevant consideration, and although other considerations are relevant too they may not be ethical ones, or if they are they are not the ethical question of whether our little two-person society put too low a value on *your* life in deciding not to buy the runway lights. (*You* may have put too low a value on your life, but I don't know why I should feel guilty about that. You may also need better lighting in your driveway.)

A harder question is what to do if you are poor and I am rich, and you use a cheap little airport and I use a better equipped one, and better runway lights are now available, and they are to be provided, if provided at all, out of a common fund for airport safety. If the lights will make as much difference to safety at your airport as at mine, and someone raises the question whether we should afford the same expensive lifesaving apparatus at your cheap airport as at my more lavish one, we really come up against the question: is your life worth as much as mine? (Leave aside the possibility that there are more of you to benefit from your lights, or fewer of you, compared with the traffic at my airport.)

Let's face the question. If you are poor and I am rich is your life worth less than mine? "Worth" refers here to how much might properly be spent to protect it from some specified risk. (Notice that "worth" is an arithmetical construct: If we are willing to spend $2,000 per capita, but not more than $2,000, to protect everybody from something that is fatal for one person in five hundred, we shall spend an average of $1,000,000 per life saved. In that respect and only in that respect have we "valued" each life at $1,000,000.) And when we ask what your life is worth, or what my life is worth, and whether your life is worth less than my life, it helps greatly in straightening out what we have in mind if we ask, worth to whom? And, who's to pay it?

If you are poorer than I, it is likely that *your* life is worth less to *you* in *your* money than *my* life is worth to *me* in *mine*. You cannot afford to pay as much for anything, including personal safety, as I can, precisely because you are poorer.

We expect the poor to invest less in home or auto safety than the well-to-do, because these goods are purchased at the expense of more urgent necessities. We expect a poor town to spend less on fire protection than a well-to-do town, because the poor town can afford less taxes and needs schools and streets as well as fire engines. But does this mean that a government air-safety program might properly decline to provide you those new runway lights, while my airport gets them at government expense?

The economist in me wants to say "yes." The policy adviser in me will go only as far as "maybe" or "it depends." It depends on who is ultimately putting up the money, and it depends on what the alternative is if you don't get the lights.

The affirmative argument contains something worth knowing. It runs as follows, in stages.

First, if the users of each runway had to pay for all the facilities at that runway, including safety facilities, we might find that the lower-income users of your airport did not consider the marginal addition to safety contributed by the new lights to be worth the money, while the well-to-do people at my airport considered the lights a good bargain. We may have feelings just like yours about life and death; but the expenditures we forego to pay for our lights are less important to us than if we were as poor as you. So one should not be surprised to find that our airport gets the lights and yours does not.

If now (stage two) a federal safety authority were to consider requiring those new lights, the lights still to be paid for by each airport's users, to require you to buy the lights they would have to believe that you had made a mistake. Assuming that you knew the cost of the lights, they would have to assume either that you did not know how much the lights would reduce the risks of landing and takeoff, or that you didn't know how to weigh your own safety against your own money. But notice that they would have to believe that you had made a mistake from your *own* point of view; and if they can ascertain that you did understand how much reduction in risk the lights would provide, they must now think that you undervalue your own life or overvalue the other things you have to buy out of your income. Maybe you do; but you may not see why federal air-safety authorities should have a better idea than you do of what your money is worth to you. You might reasonably protest the requirement that you equip your airport at your own expense with those expensive runway lights.

Now (stage three) let the authorities dispose of funds with which to provide safety equipment, including those new lights. They offer them to your airport at public expense. You may refuse them; but they will be free and, although they are worth less to you than what they cost, they are better than the old lights. Is the best outcome that you be provided those lights at public expense?

I try to teach my students when asked a question like that to ask in return, *what is the alternative?* If the alternative is tax reduction—your taxes—you are really paying for these lights, paying taxes while receiving the lights "free." You might elect lower taxes, a smaller public air-safety budget, and the old lights.

But maybe, being poor, you pay much less in taxes than we do who fly in and out of the other airport. If you decline the lights you will save *us* most of the cost. Your share of the cost, in the taxes you would save, may be less than what the lights are worth to you. Now should you take the lights with a clear conscience?

There is a final alternative. If the air-safety authorities give you the price of the lights and do not oblige you to spend it on lights—or if they give you the lights and you can sell them to somebody and keep the cash—you will probably choose the money. And I don't care. I'd rather have the money, the lower taxes, but if you are entitled to the money and would rather have money than lights, I'll get no satisfaction out of making you buy the lights. Maybe you will compromise, and settle for a little less in money than the lights would have cost, and save me a little in taxes.

I think that is a powerful argument in favor of the proposition that a government might properly spend less per capita to save the lives of poor people than to save the lives of people who are well-to-do. But notice that it is not an unconditional argument. It is only an argument that there is a better way to use the money— a better way from the perspective of the poor.

It is not a decisive argument. In some contexts it may be no help in resolving the issue. If the money is available only for those lights and you cannot have the money to spend as you prefer, if it is available only for air safety and not for reduced airport noise or better schools, if we who pay the taxes will respond to your appeal for comparable airport safety but will not give you other services or the equivalent in a reduction of your taxes—then your alternative to more runway safety is only less runway safety. The above line of reasoning will not help you get something better than runway lights.

But these qualifications, important as they are and decisive as they often will be, are more like political constraints on programming for safety than the ethical issue that initially seemed to arise in the question, should the lives of the poor as a matter of policy get less protection than the lives of the rich? Still, when a plane crashes at that airport with the obsolete lights we may find it hard to explain to our children why that little airport on the other side of the tracks was of less apparent concern to the safety authorities than our own airport. The authorities may have trouble explaining it to their children, too. There still are ethical issues, if not quite the one we first perceived.

## The "Something Better" Approach

What the reader will have noticed both with gas rationing and with airport safety is a technique that economics commonly employs in addressing whether a particular condition or policy or program has virtue. That technique is to explore whether, in respect of alternative outcomes or consequences, some alternative policy or condition or program technique is "better." And "better" has a particular definition: superior, as an outcome, for everyone involved or, somewhat less ambitiously, for all the identifiable interests. Of gasoline rationing we explore whether there is something better, something that meets whatever objectives rationing was supposed to fulfill and does a little more besides, or meets some of them more amply, or achieves the same results at lower costs to someone concerned. To find something better does not necessarily mean that rationing is not among the better policies, only that it is still inferior to some identifiable alternative. Sometimes, but not always, it is possible to measure or estimate a lower, or upper bound to the magnitude of the superiority. And sometimes if an alternative is better for not quite everybody and disadvantageous to some, we can find a way to estimate the extent of disadvantage, or put an upper bound on it.

The example of runway lights illustrates precisely what this reasoning accomplishes and some of its limitations. It is concerned only with outcomes, not with appearances, not with processes. Most important, the reasoning does not demonstrate that the superior policy or program technique is actually achievable. In particular, it may depend on institutions that do not exist or politics that are unacceptable or administrative determinations that are infeasible. I doubt whether many readers will be any more convinced than I am of the wisdom of publicly providing inferior airport safety at the airport utilized by lower-income passengers and crews, even though in principle a deal could be struck according to which they obtained instead something (money, for example) worth more to them in their own judgment than the uneconomically modest improvement in runway safety.

To explore the example further, I conjecture that if airport safety were a municipal rather than a federal responsibility we would not expect the same investment in lifesaving facilities at municipal airports used mainly by low-income people as we would expect at airports frequented by business executives and wealthier tourists. We might not feel obliged to tax the passengers at the wealthier airports and transfer the proceeds to the less favored cities. We might even expect people in search of economy fares to fly in and out of the less well-protected airports, taking advantage of lower fares reflecting lower airport fees reflecting lower-cost ground equipment. And if it were then proposed that the federal budget should subsidize ground equipment at the poorer municipal airports, there would appear competing claimants to argue that more good could be done or more lives could be saved by programs for nutrition, pest control, toxic waste disposal, or police and medical care downtown instead of runway lights out at the airport.

Let me close this part of the discussion by reiterating with emphasis two points. First, this line of reasoning attempts, when honestly done, to reshuffle the consequences by rearranging proposed programs and comparing alternatives, leaving intact the original weighting system by which the outcomes for different people, or different interests, were to be evaluated. It explores alternative consequences, assessing those consequences from the points of view of all the affected parties, to see whether, whatever the proposal is or the situation being evaluated, there is "something better." It is therefore of limited, but genuine, usefulness. And the second point is that there is no mystery, nothing that cannot be penetrated by a responsible policymaker, one who is willing to make some effort to discover whether indeed there is something better.

Unfortunately, economists use the term "efficiency" to describe this process, and often distinguish between considerations of "equity" and "efficiency." The word "efficiency" sounds more like engineering than human satisfaction; and if I tell you that it is not "efficient" to put the best runway lights at the poorer airport, you are likely to think you know exactly what I mean and not like it, perhaps also not liking me. If I tell you that "not efficient" merely means that I can think of something better—something potentially better from the points of view of all parties concerned—you can at least be excused for wondering why I use "efficient" in such an unaccustomed way. The only explanation I can think of is that economists talk mainly to each other.

### Escaping the Dilemma of Equity and Efficiency

Among the most divisive issues that policy deals with is the distribution of income and wealth. Taxation and tariffs, welfare and food stamps, rent control, farm price supports, the regulation of natural gas, minimum-wage laws, public housing, Social Security and its financing, electric rate regulation, and laws about labor relations and collective bargaining are mainly about the distribution of income. At least, controversies over those policies are controversies about the gains and costs to the farmers and the urban consumers and the unemployed and the landlords and the chronically ill and the healthy and the well-to-do. Freedom is an issue, but often what is fought over is freedom to pursue profit or livelihood. Rights are an issue, but they are often rights to welfare, rights to work, rights to lifepreserving medical attention, and the right to persist in a threatened occupation like fishing or farming, or the right to compete for jobs and markets.

Capital punishment, abortion, and preventive detention are issues that divide us and are not primarily concerned with the distribution of income. But even these are loaded with distributional significance. It was abortions at public expense that resurrected the controversy over the right to procure an abortion; capital punishment and the rights of defendants involve procedures that may be suspect precisely because they discriminate by income.

Ethics aside, we expect controversy along lines of economic interest. The auto industry wants protection against foreign automobiles, the steel industry against foreign steel, and the meat industry against foreign beef, and we expect both business and labor to couch their self-serving arguments in the most captivating moral terms they can think of; their political adversaries to do likewise. But for those among us who want to affect a disinterested stance and to judge right and wrong by reference to the public interest, with special concern for the ethical implications of particular policies or the overall distribution of income, what help can we get from economics?

On the relative virtues of different distributions of income, or on how much money a poor person has to get to justify an intervention that denies a dollar to somebody who is not poor, the answer is "not much." True to the somewhat ethically evasive character that I have been imputing to economics, economic reasoning is better at helping to choose among ways to accomplish a distributional objective than at helping to choose objectives. It can help in minimizing the cost to the rich of doing something for the poor. And in case that doesn't interest you, economic reasoning can help to point out that it ought to! There is more for the poor, at any given cost to the rich, if you do it in the least wasteful way. And often the way economics does this is simply by looking at two things at the same time.

Economics is often like a broker or mediator in a bargaining process, good at promoting "integrative bargaining." Integrative bargaining is searching for superior trades, finding ways to bring to the bargaining table those things that matter more to the beneficiary of a concession than to the party making the concession. If your coffee break costs me as much as an expanded medical program that you would rather have, trading coffee for medicine may make us both better off. But it requires bringing both topics to the table together.

Let me illustrate with another tantalizing proposition that I put to my students, who reject it, and to whom I then make it palatable by dealing with it in two dimensions rather than one. The income tax allows you to subtract, in going from gross income to taxable income, $1,000 per child. It allows it whether the child is an infant or a teenager, whether you have six or only one, and—what I want to focus on—whether your income is $20,000 or $120,000 per year. The question is, if at $20,000 per year $1,000 is allowed for each child, at $120,000 should the deduction still be $1,000? Let me propose, as I do to my students, that the figure ought to be larger than $1,000 per child at the higher income.

One way to make the case is that high-income families spend much more on children and the "cost" of raising their children is much more. There are counter-arguments. One is that the children of the rich are already so privileged that they don't need tax privileges, too, compared with poor children; it should not be official policy that rich children enjoy several thousand dollars of family income while poor children get along on $1,000. Another is that although the rich children do "cost" more than the poor and there is no need to begrudge them their superior life and environment, there is also no reason why taxpayers should collectively support well-to-do families with many children; there are other worthy causes that deserve tax relief more. It can also be argued that some wealthy couples like nice automobiles and expensive homes, some like pets, and some like children; and whether or not we approve of those who choose to spend their money on children, we should not have to share the cost with them, especially if we ourselves are not wealthy like them.

That is not an easy argument for my side to win. But to set the stage I point out an anomaly. The tax schedule that the Congress legislates is in two parts. First there is a schedule of taxes for a married couple without children; then there is a formula to adjust for family size. It is this family-size formula that allows the invariant $1,000 per child. To increase that allowance for the well-to-do would lower the taxes for well-to-do families with children, and reduce the total taxes paid by the well-to-do. But the Congress could just as well have legislated a tax schedule not for the childless couple but for the "typical" family, say a family with two children or three. Then the basic schedule needs an adjustment, because families without children can afford to pay more income tax. A "childless premium" might be attached; that could be done either by canceling some other deductions and exemptions, say $1,000 worth for the family that had one child and $2,000 for the family with no children, or by adding "virtual income" to the basic income in arriving at taxable income. Question: In raising the taxable income of the childless couple, compared with the base-rate family with two or three children, do we *add* the same amount of taxable income to the family with only $20,000 as we add to the family with $120,000?

Evidently the family earning $20,000 can pay somewhat more taxes if it has no children than if it has two or three, but not a lot more; the childless couple with $60,000 or $120,000 appears able to pay a good deal more. Just sending a child to college can cost $10,000 per year. If the object is to get all the taxes we can from the well-to-do families, once we have screwed the taxes as tightly as we can on families with three children, there ought to be a lot more still to be squeezed out of that childless couple living on $60,000 or $120,000 a year. It looks as though the adjustment for childlessness should be much larger for the family that has three or six times $20,000.

But that is simply the mathematical contradiction of the principle we worked out a moment ago! We originally found it difficult to argue that the taxable-income difference should be larger for the rich family than for the poor; now we find that the taxable-income difference ought to be larger for the rich family than for the poor. Since the same income tax can be formulated either as a base schedule for the childless couple with an adjustment for children, or as a base schedule for the family with children plus an adjustment for childlessness, it should not make any difference which way we do it. But by simply reformulating the same income tax we seem to have arrived at the opposite conclusion.

The students work it out by themselves if I give them a little time, but my pedagogical interest is not in the tax treatment of children in different families but in the proposition that two dimensions give you more freedom than one. So I resolve the issue for them.

We have a two-dimensional tax schedule. One dimension is income, the other is family size. We can manipulate them independently. True, with any given income schedule a larger deduction for children at high income levels reduces the taxes paid by the rich. If *your* ways and means subcommittee first sets the basic schedule for childless families and *my* subcommittee gets only to determine the size of the deduction for children, there is no way that I can enlarge the child differential at high incomes without forgiving some wealthy families some taxes. But if my subcommittee goes first, and we determine larger differentials for high-income families with children, you can set as progressive a schedule as you please, making sure that the rich pay the same amount of taxes you would have wanted them to pay if my subcommittee had treated children quite differently. Together we can have as wide a child-differential as we please at high income levels without providing any average tax advantage to the rich, by designing the schedule so that the childless rich pay more than they would have if the child differential were small.

In two dimensions we can have it both ways. We adjust the child differentials to conform to our notions at each income level of what difference children ought to make to the taxes paid at that income. And we design the basic income-tax schedule so that, compared with the poor, the well-to-do pay whatever we want them to pay. The income dimension and the family-size dimension allow us to meet both objectives.

The test of my success is not whether I have changed the minds of the students and they can go propose over lunch that the children of the rich should receive larger income tax deductions, and proceed to persuade their incredulous luncheon partners. The test is whether on the next issue that arises, maybe energy pricing, they understand the principle well enough to see how it applies there.

And how is that? Well, *that* is that rising energy prices during a time when energy costs are going up and shortages are becoming common do two things. They induce an "efficient" (sic!) response to the rising cost of energy. And they impose an income loss on consumers, a loss that may be quite disproportionate in its distribution, perhaps especially affecting the poor or at least the poor who live in cold climates or depend on transportation.

By an "efficient" response I mean (a) that people will use less fuel because it costs more in the other things that money will buy; (b) that those who have stronger needs for fuel will pay for more and burn it while those who have less urgent needs will save their money for other things; and (c) that the supply of fuels will be enhanced from sources that were not economical at lower prices, or through new technologies that are economical now that fuel savings are worth more. (Whether this is the same or a different use of the term "efficient" is a little intricate and needn't be resolved here.)

If the decision is whether to let the price of fuel go up or instead to impose price control, to subsidize imports, or to reduce demand by denying specific uses, we have a dilemma, a tradeoff. We can hurt the poor (and many others in all kinds of special categories that are especially dependent on fuel) by making them spend more for the fuel they need with less left over for other necessities, or we can spare them that hardship while pricing fuel in a way that encourages waste and discourages conservation and new supplies. Here we are again weighing "equity" against "efficiency." An inescapable dilemma? Nothing to do but compromise, with strongly divided interests in compromising between the energy-efficient end of the scale and the hardship-minimizing end?

To the rescue we bring the two-dimensional approach. We have two problems. We can call them the energy problem and the poverty problem. They may turn out to be an efficiency problem and an equity problem, but our object is to avoid that. Like a Supreme Court that shies from constitutional questions if it can settle a case on other merits, we try to resolve the competing claims of poverty and energy without choosing sides between equity and efficiency. The way we do this is to recognize that, although we have two objectives or criteria or competing claims, we also have two sets of instruments for coping. We have an energy problem and a poverty problem; we have an energy program and a poverty program. With two programs to work with, and two objectives to meet, we may be able to evade the ethical dilemma.

All we need technically is a way to identify the poor (and the otherwise deserving) who would suffer severely with higher fuel prices, estimate what they would lose in the higher prices, and give them an income subsidy. Not easy, but not terribly difficult. No program is perfect in targeting help to *all* of those and *only* those who are intended to receive it. But compared with holding down the price of natural gas—while fending off all the customers who want cheap gas but cannot be accommodated, and discouraging exploration for new supply, letting rich and poor alike enjoy the cheap gas as long as they are among those lucky enough to be old customers, with the rich getting proportionately more benefit because, being rich, they can buy more of everything including gas—a combination of higher gas prices and a separate compensatory program targeted on the not-rich, or on the poor, or on the very poor, can easily be a superior policy.

It will be opposed of course by those who benefit from cheap fuel who could not put forward a legitimate claim under a poverty program.

It will also be opposed by the poor or their representatives if they have learned through experience that the principle of splitting the problem into two parts is sometimes an excuse for relieving the one part from responsibility for what happens to the poor while neglecting the second part that was supposed to take care of them. (Having separate congressional committees deal with energy pricing and with programs that compensate the poor makes it appear that if the energy committee doesn't protect the poor there is no assurance that another committee will.)

But again we may have transformed an ethical problem into a political problem.

We may also have run up against another ethical problem. This one did not reveal itself in the original formulation. If we have money to compensate the poor, why compensate only the poor who are worse off on account of the rising prices of fuel? Specifically, suppose we put a 50-cent tax on gasoline and dedicate a fraction of the proceeds to offsetting the cost increases to families whose income is below the bottom quartile. As a way to buy off the poor's opposition to the tax, concentrating assistance on those and only those whose poverty will be aggravated by the tax can be shrewd politics. But once we have the tax and a source of revenue to help the poor in proportions determined by their dependence on fuel, somebody will propose that there are people in the bottom 10 percent who were *already* poorer, before the tax, than a lot of low-income people after the tax. The family with $8,000 that has burned eight gallons of gasoline per week stands to lose $200 a year from the 50-cent tax and fall to $7,800, while the elderly couple that has no car and lives on $6,000 qualifies for no gasoline bonus. The poor family that paints its modest home and finds the cost of paint up $200 might prefer that the gas tax revenue help all the disadvantaged, not just those who burn gasoline.

This looks like an ethical issue, and not the one we started with. It reflects our political system. Our system recognizes that there are some poor and otherwise disadvantaged and deserving people who should receive help. But instead of dealing with their needs in a unified way, deciding how much we want to help, we tend to help the poor a little in each of many different and uncoordinated things we do. We help with food stamps and medical care and subsidized housing, and we invoke hardship in programs to keep farm prices up and rents down. This piecemeal approach does not necessarily do a bad job, but it does create repeatedly that ethical dilemma that arose out of our compensatory programs for gasoline and heating fuel.

If a family loses its rent-controlled apartment, because rent controls are eliminated or because the apartment is eliminated, and if taxes are raised on all rental apartments and some of the proceeds set aside to help the disadvantaged, do we help only those disadvantaged by loss of rent-controlled apartments? Or do we help whoever is most in need of help?

### The Market Ethic

Nothing distinguishes economists from other people as much as a belief in the market system, or what some call the free market. A perennial difficulty in dealing with economics and policy is the inability of people who are not economists, and some who are, to ascertain how much of an economist's confidence in the way markets work is faith and how much is analysis and observation. How much is due to the economist's observing the way markets work and judging actual *outcomes,* and how much is a belief that the *process* is right and just? (Or right, if occasionally unjust; or right, and justice is indeterminate.)

The problem is compounded because some economists do identify markets with freedom of choice, or construe markets as processes that yield returns that are commensurate with an individual's deserts. A conclusion that arises in the analysis of a perfectly working competitive market is that people who work for hire are paid amounts equivalent to their marginal contributions to the total product, to the difference it makes if one's contribution is withdrawn while the rest of the system continues. An ethical question is whether one's marginal product constitutes an appropriate rate of remuneration. Critics of the theory, however, typically direct their energies toward the empirical issue, arguing that actual markets work differently. Nevertheless, there are economists who have given considerable thought to the matter who find that a system that distributes the fruits of economic activity in accordance with marginal contributions, be they contributions in effort or ideas or property, is ethically attractive, and others who have given considerable thought to it and find that such a system has great practical merit but little ethical claim. Most of these others believe there is a need for policies to readjust the results.

There is even an important socialist school of market economics, pioneered by Abba Lerner and Oscar Lange in the 1930s, that asserts that pricing in a socialist economy should mimic the pricing of a perfectly competitive free market, that such an economy would be least wasteful of resources, and that extramarket income transfers should compensate for any results that one does not like.

And there is a large body of professional opinion among economists, perhaps more among older than among younger ones, to the effect that markets left to themselves may turn in a pretty poor performance, but not nearly as poor when left alone as when tinkered with, especially when the tinkering is simplistically done or done cleverly to disguise the size and distribution of the costs or losses associated with some "innocuous" favoritism.

Whether or not an economist shares the ethic or the ideology that values the working of the market system for its own sake (or that identifies it not only *with* personal freedom but *as* personal freedom), most professional economists accept certain principles that others, if not the economists themselves, would recognize to have ethical content.

An example is incentives. Economists see economic incentives operating everywhere; they find nothing offensive or coercive about the responses of people to economic opportunities and sanctions; they have no interest in overcoming or opposing incentives for the sake of victory over an enemy; and they have a predilection toward tilting incentives and augmenting and dampening and restructuring incentives and even inventing incentives, to induce people to behave in ways that are collectively more rewarding or less frustrating. You can usually tell an economist from a noneconomist by asking whether at the peak season for tourism and camping there should be substantial entrance fees at the campgrounds of national parks.

A related touchstone of market economics is the idea that most people are better at spending their own money than somebody else is at spending it for them. Sometimes this is directly elevated into an ethical principle: the consumer's right to make his own mistakes. But usually it is simply that giving a poor family a shopping cart filled from the shelves of a supermarket is not as good as giving them the money and the cart and letting them do their own shopping. The idea is that *they* will get more for *your* money if *they* get to spend it. A given amount of your money will do more good for the family from the family's point of view if it is spent the way they want it spent.

Economists have a long checklist of exceptions to this principle, exceptions from the point of view of that family's welfare and from other points of view, but generally the economist thinks the burden of proof belongs on those who want to give food stamps or subway tokens or eyeglasses to the poor and the elderly, not money. Proof may not be hard to come by; but the burden, for most economists, should be on those who don't trust the efficacy of money. It often sounds like an ethical principle. Maybe it is.

There have recently been proposals to compensate poor families in cash for the exact amount by which their heating bills, at deregulated prices, exceed what the same amount of fuel would have cost at regulated prices. The question was raised why they shouldn't merely receive, unconditionally, an amount of money estimated in advance by that formula. The retort was that, being poor, they couldn't be trusted to spend the money on heating fuel. They might spend it on something else!

This is the point at which most economists can only shake their heads slowly.

# 2 | Command and Control

TRADITIONAL THEORY envisions the firm as a finely tuned machine controlled by an absolute master who not only knows what he wants, from a faultless calculation of what will maximize his profits, but can enforce his decision on the enterprise he commands. In practice, however, it is helpful to recall what President Truman said in the summer of 1952, contemplating the problems that General Eisenhower would have if he won the forthcoming election. According to Richard Neustadt's *Presidential Power,* "He'll sit here, and he'll say, 'Do this! Do that!' *And nothing will happen.* Poor Ike—it won't be a bit like the Army. He'll find it very frustrating." [1]

Is the President of the United States more impotent by an order of magnitude than the president of a telephone company, a hotel chain, or an airline? Had "Poor Ike" even found the Army as obedient as Truman thought he did? In September 1972 the Environmental Protection Agency reported that "high" officials of a major auto company, without the cognizance of "top" officials, had falsified the results of engine emission tests, while across town the Senate Armed Services Committee sought to determine whether or not the Commander of the Seventh Air Force had had the cognizance of his theater commander or of the Joint Chiefs of Staff in willfully violating what were believed to be the orders of his Commander-in-Chief in the bombing of North Viet Nam.

It is too bad that some of our Presidents did not become presidents of business firms after leaving public office, with analysts like Neustadt to chronicle their frustrations. Some of them might have expected that at last they could say, "Institute equal opportunity here! Eliminate noxious preservatives there! Don't spoil the quiet in that community!"—and have it done.

Part of the problem of "the social responsibility of business" is that captains of industry are hell-bent for profits or too beset by competition to indulge their social consciences. But another part is that the president of a telephone company may be no more able to institute equal rights for women than the president of a university or the director of a nonprofit hospital. He can't even fire people for disobeying his directives. And if he could, he might still be unable to devise a system that would monitor the way minority applicants were treated in a personnel office.

The problem arises in the small and in the large. The taxi company with a fleet of twenty or thirty drivers, all known by their first names to the owner-dispatcher, may be no better able to make passengers fasten their seat belts than a large conglomerate that owns cab companies in a dozen cities. The conglomerate, in turn, is like a "government" attempting to devise policies for the decentralized firms that it owns but that it controls only in a legal sense.

One should not too much disparage the effect of adding a consumer or minority-group representative to the board of directors of some huge corporation; the symbolism as well as the authority can make a difference. But the cartoonist's image of the captain of industry should not mislead us into supposing that even the whole board of directors can make policy and then sit back and see its will be done. Neither conscience nor the profit motive, at the level of business management, is likely to make a captain of industry like the captain of a ship. And even the captain of a ship may suffer some of the frustrations of President Truman once in a while.

For setting public policy with respect to business, two implications emerge. First, business, as a "black box" to be dealt with through government action, will not be instantly and effectively responsive either to the consciences of managers or to the market incentives—taxes and subsidies, property rights and liabilities—that may be designed as "proxies" for conscience. Second, in thinking about social responsibility, it may often be a mistake to think of "the company" as the unit of action. Business is not a population of unitary entities—"firms" in the private sector. On the contrary, it is a number of small societies comprising many people with different interests, opportunities, information, motivations, and group interests.

### Taking the Lid off the Black Box

For some purposes it will be necessary to disaggregate the firm and to deal with the social responsibility of subdivisions and individuals, applying incentives and sanctions directly on the people or the transactions that constitute the business and its activity, rather than to conceptualize the firm or the industry as the target of attention.

A clear-cut example would be to impose criminal liability on individuals for, say, activity contrary to the antitrust laws. One can apply sanctions on the firm; or one can make people individually liable for their actions as managers, supervisors, even salesmen. A city can attempt to hold taxi companies liable for the safe driving, courtesy, and traffic behavior of taxi drivers; or the city can make it a personal offense of the cabby to double-park or to refuse service to a member of some minority group. The government might even, though this is rarely done, attempt to influence the reward structure within the firm. Especially in matters of equal opportunity and nondiscrimination, there is developing some tendency toward disaggregating large organizations into the individuals who compose them (or at least directly scrutinizing and monitoring the policy directives and procedures). The concept of an affirmative action program for hiring members of minority groups is illustrative of not dealing with the industry as a population or with the firm as a black box but of getting inside the firm and monitoring the processes that govern it.

The Nuremberg trials developed the notion of war criminals, people who could not find legal defense merely in having been commanded to carry out the policies of higher authority. In some countries the acts of a functionary are immune to personal legal action, and a formal complaint has to be lodged with the government he represents; in others, individuals are liable for their actions and their uniforms do not make them immune even though they are cogs in a large machine. It is interesting that the Anglo-American legal tradition makes the policeman criminally responsible for what he does with a firearm, even when on duty and in uniform. There is apparently a corresponding distinction between the social responsibility *of* a business and the exercise of responsibility *in* a business.

It is useful to imagine how we would approach the problem of responsibility if we avoided altogether considering the "business" as an entity—as a corporate individual that could have cognizance of responsibility or that could be acted on through a centralized profit motive.

Take a few areas of social responsibility, like equal opportunity or consumer protection, and imagine that we conceptually disaggregate the firm into nonexistence or deny it legal recognition. Now we cannot act on profits and the profit motive. We cannot use taxes and subsidies on the *firm* as instruments of social control. We cannot direct our persuasion at boards of directors. We cannot work with a concept of administrative law that identifies an individual with the firm that employs him. Instead we have to motivate people who are earning individual livelihoods. For equal-opportunity purposes we have to appeal to, or work through, the personnel officers and clerks, the people who devise questionnaires, who deal politely or impolitely with applicants, and who make actual hiring decisions. We work directly on the chemist who recommends an additive to preserve the color in a jar of jelly and on the person who designs a cheap bumper that will not withstand impact. We work on the pilot of the plane who steers his craft at particular altitudes over noise-conscious population centers. We go after the navigator who brought that tanker too close to shore in bad weather and risked an oil spill.

That is, we should recall, the way we are supposed to deal with a policeman who fires his gun in a crowd.

I am drawing a distinction, not a conclusion. The question of *where* it is most efficacious to locate responsibility within the business is a complicated one. It is a convenience to government if policy can be directed toward the firm and not toward the people who work for it. But sometimes that won't work. Sometimes the firm is impotent. Sometimes the firm is a clumsy instrument to work with. Sometimes the firm has little control over the activities that the authorities wish to regulate. (Sometimes the firm can take refuge in its own impotence!) And even when the firm is the appropriate target for policy, it is difficult to identify the level of corporate decentralization or the mixture of stock holdings that determine just which entity is "the business."

## The Problem of Identification

Even legally it is sometimes difficult to identify just what a business is, or where it is. Especially for corporate business, one has to inquire whether it is the stockholder group, the board of directors, the management, or the entire social entity that engages in the business. For several decades it has been common to distinguish between ownership and control, especially in the modern corporation; and this distinction blurs the idea of responsibility. Add a union, and it becomes even harder to decide where the firm is governed. The "production" of rock-and-roll music and the "production" of telephone service include many parties to the transaction. Baseball and prizefighting are businesses; so are newspapers and taxis, insurance and automobile sales. From the point of view of social responsibility, it may be important to know who's in charge; and it may be as difficult as it is important.

Anyone who has shipped goods across country by moving van or across the ocean by freighter, or who has bought an automobile from a dealer or stopped at a chain restaurant on a turnpike, knows how difficult it is to find out just where responsibility is focused, who's in charge, what the "industry" is. If you like your Chevrolet or the meal at Howard Johnson's, where do you send your letter of appreciation? Many businesses are not only complex in the legality of their ownership but in the arrangements they have worked out with their laborers, distributors, even their customers. If you see a bad movie and would like to complain, to whom do you complain?

The typical commodity or transaction involves a diffusion of responsibility, and, when one wants to focus liability or obligation, blame or credit, it is typically not easy to locate the target. Furthermore, it cannot be expected that the business firm, as an entity, will be the institutional equivalent of the people who work for it or a simple reflection of them. The key people in an organization may be bold or timid, sensitive or callous, innovative or lacking in imagination, "responsible" or "irresponsible," without the business they work in having corresponding qualities or being the image of the managers and without the "business" being analyzable as the equivalent of a businessman. A bunch of timid people directing an enterprise do not necessarily make for a "timid" enterprise; everybody may lack the personal boldness to oppose a rash action. "Responsible" individuals may be so loyal to the organization that they acquiesce in policies that appear irresponsible. Responsibility may be so diluted within an enterprise that there is no one to blame when the organization seems blameworthy, no individual to reward when the organization behaves well. An organization, business or other, is a system of information, rules for decision, and incentives; its performance is different from the individual performances of the people in it. An organization can be negligent without any individual's being negligent. To expect an organization to reflect the qualities of the individuals who work for it or to impute to the individuals the qualities one sees in the organization is to commit what logicians call the "fallacy of composition." Fallacy isn't error of course, but it can be treacherous.

### A Universal Dilemma: Internalize or Decentralize

Many problems relating to the social responsibility of business that we are conscious of in our own country are problems also in other countries that do not share our business system. Marshall Goldman has persuasively illustrated the thesis that pollution in the Soviet Union is not only a serious problem but the same kind of problem as it is in the United States.[2] Part of our subject can best be thought of as "the social responsibility of large organizations" (or social responsibility *in* large organizations).

Comparing the Russian economy with the American gives some appreciation of what is meant by "internalizing" externalities. The ministry that controls pulp and paper in the Soviet Union apparently no more internalizes its impact on fish and wildlife in Russian lakes and streams than does a large corporation in the United States. Just as it is useful to compare the telephone company with Columbia University, for analyzing policy and its effectiveness with respect to the employment of women, it can be useful to compare an American firm with its counterpart in a socialist country.

What emerges from the comparison is a downgrading of the profit motive as a key to the behavior of the business system. Profits, as a motivating force, become rapidly attenuated as one moves down the chain of command or through the social network of decisions in the firm, away from those individuals who have a strong and direct interest in company profits or a lively sensation that their own behavior would make a noticeable difference. Profits are substantially "external" even to many individuals in top management. (It is helpful to recall that close-order drill in the army originated in the need to keep every infantryman within easy pistol range of his squad leader, to help that infantryman to "internalize" the objective of victory, and squad leaders within similar range of platoon leaders for similar reasons.)

A firm as large as General Motors apparently finds it worthwhile to decentralize management. So does a Soviet ministry. There are evidently limits to the effectiveness of hierarchical control. But there is no such thing, then, as internalizing all of the externalities if there are organizational limitations on the radius of responsibility. To decentralize in the interest of managerial incentives and effectiveness is to externalize the more diffuse responsibilities. Decentralization of incentives to the individual motels of a large chain will make the goodwill of the cross-country traveler more proximate but external to the motel manager who affects the goodwill. Centralization to the home office makes it internal but remote. The problem may be much the same for Intourist as for Holiday Inn. There is a sense in which the leaders of the Soviet Union are monopolists; but complete hierarchical control is beyond their means. And, whether decentralization is deliberate or ineluctable, it leads to many of the same problems we impute to the profit motive in the private sector in this country.

## Discipline and the Supportive Role of Government

Later I suggest that firms might, and sometimes do, submit voluntarily to "coercion" as a substitute or supplement for contract or compact, as a way of solving some of the problems of freeloaders, chiselers, and others who could not or would not join in internalizing the costs and benefits of more responsible policies. Firms have surely learned to place their activities under "outside" rules when their own security or profits, not the public interest, is at stake. The barbershops, for example, appreciate mandatory closing on Wednesday in Massachusetts, since it precludes competitors from staying open. No agency short of the federal government, to take another example, could possibly institute cotton acreage controls on a workable scale.

But there is another role that government might play in helping firms to do what they might wish they could do but cannot—or cannot as well as government, or cannot without the help of government. I earlier mentioned obstructions to command and control. It is interesting to note to what extent government may substitute for the firm's own management, or augment the firm's capability, or supplement the firm's efforts to enforce policy directives within the firm, and particularly policy directives that represent a social responsibility.

Let me begin with a few clear cases. Certain forms of personal violence and material sabotage are criminal offenses, and a company is also presumably helped by the police in enforcing the rules against prostitution, drug peddling, and gambling on company time. Similarly with theft and embezzlement. Certain regulations that reduce the hazards of fire and disease are more easily enforced within the firm if there are local ordinances that can be adverted to or if certain careless actions are violations of law as well as of company policy.

For a case that is a small step closer to the government's monitoring the activities of a firm's employees, consider a taxi company. The company may desire a reputation for courtesy and safety—it may even desire courtesy and safety. But it may be unable to enforce its regulations about seat belts, double-parking, illegal U-turns, or drinking on the job. The police, the Registry of Motor Vehicles, or other public authorities may have to do the monitoring. A taxi driver who refuses to take a black passenger from the airport to a black residential district at night may be more susceptible to the command of the state trooper at the airport than to any complaints phoned in to his dispatcher. And one of the functions of metered fares, established by an agency of government, is to keep drivers from engaging in pricing practices, or subterfuge about their earnings, or intimidation of passengers, in a way that a taxi company on its own might not be able to do.

The idea extends to a number of operations that occur outside the reach of a company, beyond the company's observation, and where the company's ability to spy and detect is inadequate. This could include fishing fleets, airlines, truck drivers, repairmen, and anyone who might cheat or steal or blackmail customers. The principle extends to customers as well as employees: the airlines, left to themselves, showed no eagerness to examine passengers' handbags; if they had to do it, they preferred to be required to do it, and probably they wanted the job to be done by customs officials.

It is worth noticing that the licensing both of airline pilots and of cab drivers is done by government. Though one may expect the airlines to demand higher standards of pilot competence than are prescribed by the regulations, there is no thought that the profit motive alone should be counted on to guarantee the competence of those airline employees to whom are entrusted the airborne mixed cargoes of people and kerosene.

Now, how does this bear on our subject? Business firms may indeed want government to help them police their employees or their customers, to help protect the firm itself—its profits, its reputation, its legal security. May it also need some direct intervention of government in the command-and-control process to meet some social responsibilities? What are the areas of social responsibility in which a firm might lack the discipline, the information, the incentives, or the moral authority to command performance or restraint on the part of everyone whose cooperation is required?

One possibility is that employees are personally irresponsible and out of laziness or for personal gain fail in their performance. Trash collectors leave debris in the gutters; fishing boats dump garbage in the harbor; sanitary regulations are neglected in a fruit-processing plant; nurses sleep and airline ground crews drink on duty; truck drivers make up for an extra-long lunch hour by driving through an off-limits tunnel with a dangerous cargo.

Another possibility is that employees oppose some "socially responsible" policy on moral or ideological grounds; or they suspect that top management is making a pretense at demanding performance but doesn't really want its orders heeded. Discrimination in hiring, promoting, firing, and job assignment comes quickly to mind. Someone may even out of kindness turn down a job applicant who, being male or being female, being old or young, being black or white, would be uncomfortable in a particular job but may not know it. Someone can subtly discourage job applicants through procrastination, can mislay documents, misrepresent the job, or pretend it has already been filled. The question is whether government efforts to demand nondiscriminatory performance, or even affirmative action to compensate groups that have been discriminated against, might not be better directed in some instances toward the performance of individuals rather than toward a statistical monitoring of the firm itself. Statistically based penalties and rewards may provide adequate motivation for top management. The question is whether this motivation on the part of those whose profits are at stake, whose reputations are in the limelight, or whose moral responsibilities are being tested and challenged can be transmitted throughout the organization to show up as personal motivation in a myriad of individuals whose compliance or cooperation is required.

Whether we have in mind criminal charges or damage suits, it will turn out in many cases that the government does best to make it an obligation of *people* in a firm, not of the firm as a profit-making entity, to behave properly. Just as the police can keep a delivery truck from double-parking even though the home office of the delivery truck may not be able to, the holding of individuals personally responsible for hazardous behavior in the plant, for violation of civil rights, misrepresentation of a product, or the destruction of beauty or quiet, can sometimes be more effectively managed by government directly than by government attempting to manipulate rewards and penalties on stockholder dividends.

The issue is one of comparative advantage. Technology may make it easier for the trucking firm than for the Registry of Motor Vehicles to monitor the emission of gaseous pollutants. Or it may not. Or it may be that large firms owning their own tractors can be centrally penalized and can enforce exhaust-pipe standards on their own fleet, while the driver-entrepreneur who owns a single tractor and will haul anybody's trailer is too small and too itinerant to be caught by the Environmental Protection Agency, and he enjoys such a competitive advantage that eventually the task of monitoring the regulations and inflicting the fines has to be a matter between the driver and the authorities. (The company's obligation then is not to reimburse its employees for the fines levied on them in line of duty.)

In some cases the firm's inability to control the behavior of individuals within the firm is not the result of a physical incapacity to monitor performance and to identify delinquents by name, but stems from some lack of moral authority to command behavior in other respects than those that go with a strict construction of job and job performance. Personal hygiene may be an example. An ordinance against spitting on the floor may work better than a company directive, either because the local authorities can enforce it or because it legitimizes a parallel injunction by the company itself. A company's efforts to test employees for communicable infections and to suspend those who are a hazard to the health of co-workers might meet resistance and malingering, whereas public health authorities could quarantine the plant until everybody had submitted and insist on treatment for the individuals who had contagious venereal and other diseases. Fire drills are carried out more seriously when attended by firemen in uniform.

### Moral Choice or Policy Choice

In discussing social responsibility there is a tendency to take for granted that more of it is a good thing. (Those who don't think so probably don't spend much time discussing it.) There may be limits to how much one would demand, but, if one thinks of a unidimensional scale—"responsibility" at one end and "irresponsibility" at the other—responsibility seems to be something we can always wish for more of.

At least, it does until somebody feels morally compelled to persuade us to his faith in some god or some food, or to protect us from books or card games, to make us salute the flag or refuse to salute the flag, to prohibit smoking in the cafeteria or to make us stop using the masculine pronoun in referring to everybody.

There are of course situations in which responsibility means considerateness, less selfishness, helping or supporting someone and offending no one. Flammable children's pajamas without warning labels, the clandestine dumping of garbage, and reset odometers on second-hand cars are not likely to cause any moral dilemmas. (Not so fast. The dealer who sold me my Mustang argued earnestly that, as a car buyer, I should oppose the unfair law against tampering with odometers, because it would lower the resale value of my automobile!) But at a time when, urged by the brother of two assassination victims, the Senate can barely muster a majority in moral support of suppression of the cheap and easily obtainable handguns known as "Saturday night specials"; when the town dog-catcher is still among the least-loved public servants; when abortions are construed by some as an inalienable freedom and by others as a sin to be publicly suppressed; when Academy Awards are won by pictures that couldn't have been shown when my children were young; when many black people are genuinely apprehensive about the dilution of their culture and the co-opting of their leaders by "integrationist" campaigns reflecting the best of intentions—at such a time responsibility is often not a quantity (something a person can have more or less of) but a *policy choice,* a choice among the alternative values that one can be responsible to.

There are dangers in urging business to let its responsibilities be defined by some subset of its customers, by the special interests of its employees, by whatever ethnic group in the community is most articulate or most threatening, by people who love dogs or by people who are allergic to dog hair. There is no need to be alarmist, but it is worthwhile to recall that, even in matters of business responsibility, especially social responsibility, there are always conflicts of interest to be found; and they often correspond to conflicts of responsibility. Protective tariffs, safety inspection of marginal coal mines, pets in apartment buildings, and of course the gun laws are reminders of this principle. Some of the issues may be strictly distributional: higher-cost low-sulphur fuels clean the air for the people who live downwind of the smokestacks; and use of these same fuels may add to the cost of electric power and other commodities, with an incidence that falls disproportionately on the poor. Pity the "responsible" refuse company that has to decide in which community to locate its dumping ground!

My purpose at this point is not to attack the idea of responsibility or to suggest that all efforts at responsibility are doomed to violate somebody's principles. It is just to point out that being responsible for a business firm is a little like being responsible as a senator or as a university president. Often the question is not "Do I want to do the right thing?" It arises in the form "What is the right thing to want to do?" The choice is not always between some selfish temptation and some obvious responsible course. The choice is often a policy decision.

What should a business do about drug addiction among its employees? What should it do about admitting men to jobs that have been traditionally women's—secretaries, receptionists, or file clerks? Or smoking on the job? Or eliminating some hazard in the product by producing it more expensively and selling it at a higher price? Or letting a black organization dictate policy toward blacks, letting a women's organization negotiate on behalf of women? Consider the business that is under pressure to discontinue operations in South Africa, throwing people out of work there. What is the right thing to do? To whom should the company defer in deciding the right thing to do? Is there a "right thing" in this case or just a choice between equally unsatisfactory options?

Many of today's issues in business responsibility are new. There is no easy answer to the question of whether the Sierra Club or a farm group speaks for the responsible position, and they may take opposite sides. One thing seems sure: on the issues that exercise people today, especially the issues of the social responsibility of business, there is often no source of reliable guidance, no acknowledged source of policy, no easy choice between the responsible and the selfish.

Not all problems of responsibility involve dilemmas of conscience. Ambiguity about what is right is no excuse for doing wrong. But we should usually be careful not to adopt the idea that it is easy to know what is right and responsible and that the choice is only between responsibility and irresponsibility. People in business who have the decisiveness to do the responsible thing will often be the people who, because they did something decisive, are accused of irresponsibility. Even the prejudiced employer may have trouble deciding whether or not his responsibility is to his community and its traditional values; it is the unprejudiced employer who may have the hardest time deciding how much of a handicap it is appropriate to give some disadvantaged minority.

### Irresponsible or Unresponsive

The vexed and ambiguous character of many modern problems of business responsibility has been exemplified, if in an exaggerated way, by the tantalizing problem of aircraft hijacking. In addition to the dramatic crisis of responsibility that is bound to occur when an actual hijacking is attempted or in process and perilous decisions of an unforeseen and often unique kind have to be reached in a hurry, a multitude of routine decisions with a bearing on hijacking remained on the agenda for a good many years without being settled.

There is, for example, the straightforward matter of baggage handling, about which nothing has been done. Maybe nothing should be done. Baggage in the cabin is evidently important, as evidenced by the search procedures that were initiated in early 1973. Until the early sixties we checked our bags; then, with the large-diameter fuselage that goes with jet airplanes, it became feasible to elevate the seats off the floor to accommodate overnight bags. Most baggage is apparently carried aboard for quick retrieval, not because anyone wants to shave or wear his bathrobe in flight. Maybe passengers could be induced to surrender their baggage or eventually to invest in specially designed aircraft luggage that yielded more readily to search.

Instead we have search procedures. Whatever their efficacy, one thing is certain: if it made sense to institute them in 1973, it would have made sense to institute them several years earlier. There were halfhearted efforts by some airlines. Eventually federal regulations made the procedures mandatory.

There were some procedures for screening passengers, by reference to "behavior profiles" of real and potential hijackers. It was apparently left to busy passenger agents, on their own responsibility and with no very clear system of penalties for either kind of mistake—overzealous and heavy-handed screening or laxity or laziness—to enforce or even to legitimize the procedure. Little or nothing was done about airport security or the design of aircraft or of loading facilities. Nothing noticeable was done about aircraft operating procedures, personnel selection, or restrictions on passenger seating and behavior in relation to hijacking.

The point in rehearsing this unimpressive early history of efforts to cope with the danger of hijacking is not to disparage what the airlines did, to give them low marks for responsibility, or to complain that solvable problems went unsolved. The point is rather to observe how difficult it may be to identify social responsibility.

In the first place, it was not clear just where primary responsibility rested. The matter involved criminal behavior and airline safety. While the federal government fumbled its own policies and failed to specify clearly where responsibility lay, an airline executive could only have been bewildered about even what responsibility would be allowed him if he were to assume it. It was by no means evident how jurisdiction was divided among agencies of the federal government or between levels of government.

Second, many of the measures that airlines might have considered depended largely on collective action, perhaps uniform arrangements common to all airlines. It may not have been clear how far the Civil Aeronautics Board or the Department of Justice would have let them go. And many changes in operating procedures would have required the active cooperation of air-terminal facilities, which for the most part the airlines neither owned nor controlled.

In the third place, it is not altogether clear toward whom the airlines ought to have felt responsible or whose interest the airlines should responsibly have tried to serve. Airline managers can feel responsible for the safety of their firm's own passengers, or for all passengers on all airlines, or more generally for helping to prevent an epidemic of violence. They could have a sense of obligation not to use ethnic data in the screening and selective search or interrogation of passengers. They could feel responsible for protecting passengers from illegal or improper search and seizure. Responsibility for the safety of employees is still another consideration, as well as a responsibility not to waste the stockholders' resources.

If a senior executive of an airline had resolved, as many of them may have done for all I know, to be guided by his sense of social responsibility on all matters relating to hijacking, it is not clear what he would have done. A responsible objective could have been to avoid unduly alarming passengers, to avoid making a dramatic and enticing game out of efforts to thwart hijackers, to avoid burdening passengers or crew with any sense of obligation to risk their lives in heroics, and of course to avoid any behavior that would so exaggerate the hazards of flying as to impair airline travel seriously, at high cost to passengers and stockholders alike.

Just as banks may be wise, individually and collectively, and responsible as well, not to do anything drastic to counter the threat of bank robbery, maybe the airlines were wise to keep their response to the hijacking threat within bounds. But there is no dearth of alternative hypotheses to explain the haphazard, desultory, and indecisive small efforts that punctuated the basic trend of nonresponse, nor any sign that the airlines responded as they did out of wisdom and self-discipline, forgoing the competitive public relations of individual action in the interest of a calm, collectively low-profile treatment of the problem.

And if a case can be made that the social responsibilities of the airlines with respect to the hijacking problem are complex and fraught with potential conflict, it should also be kept in mind that these are not naive little suburban taxi companies but large corporations engaged in high-technology interstate commerce, a line of business that from the outset was beset by dramatic hazards to life and property. If any business in America should be able to cope wth the prospect of armed, possibly crazed men and women taking customers hostage in a risky and unstable environment, it ought to be the airlines. A small soup company may not know how to cope wth botulism, but one might expect the major airlines to rise to the occasion when a new hazard confronts them.

But even more, one might have expected the federal government to rise to the occasion. In a matter involving airline safety, criminal activity under federal jurisdiction, and possibly airline costs and rate schedules, there is a presumption that the social responsibilities of the airline companies would be defined for them by some cognizant federal agency. At least, the auspices existed under which the airlines might have come together to arrive at collective policies and uniform practices.

One cannot easily make a case of *irresponsibility* against the airlines. What we had instead was simply a *lack* of any commanding sense of *responsibility,* of any initiative toward assumption of responsibility, of any leadership or collective action inspired by social responsibility. The lack seemed even more conspicuous on the part of federal agencies than on the part of private airlines. One of the differences between irresponsibility and lack of responsibility may be that conscience or legal liability can help to safeguard against the former, but some real initiative is required to overcome the latter. The diagnosis involves the organizational basis for behavior, not merely the private consciences of people. The discouragement of wrongdoing is different from the stimulation of something right.

### Immanence or Assignment

There are two different notions of responsibility. One is like the doctrine of immanence: the responsibility is there. Duty exists. It ought to be perceived and acted on by the responsible agent. It reflects some natural notion of justice, obligation, or legitimate expectation.

The other is that responsibility is something to be assigned or created or invented.

In matters of morality and conscience one typically assumes that responsibility is not manipulable. It exists and is to be recognized. But there is also the notion that responsibility is an assignable or allocable obligation, that the responsible persons or entities are the ones to whom responsibility has been delegated or imputed or otherwise affixed. Within an organization the assignment of responsibility—deciding who is supposed to look out for something, to be blamed or credited, to have the power of decision or to be morally cognizant of a decision—is part of skillful management. Judicial decisions often reflect the conflict between identifying, for retrospective justice, where responsibility naturally inheres and calculating, as a matter of policy, where responsibility can best be placed to be effective. *Legislative* cognizance of a problem usually has to do with where responsibility can most efficaciously be assigned.

The question arises with, say, accidents resulting from defective auto parts. If the problem is simply to do justice once an accident has occurred, there is a retrospective interest in who really failed to meet traditional expectations. Somebody was at fault and the problem is to decide who. But prospectively the situation is different. Prospectively, we usually want to assign responsibility in an effective way. We want to determine who is in a position to know what is defective and what to do about it. If we are concerned only about somebody who has already died because of a defective tie rod connecting the steering mechanism to the wheels, we have a very different problem from deciding where, in the future, we want to affix responsibility so that somebody knows that, if there is a fatal accident, he is going to be liable for damages.

There is usually some leeway. We can put somebody on notice that he is responsible and induce a legally enforceable sense of responsibility. We can tell the restaurateur that if somebody dies of food poisoning, he is liable. Or we can tell the meat wholesaler that if anybody dies of food poisoning after dining at a restaurant, the immediate source of the meat is responsible. Or we can tell the customer that he's supposed to learn how to tell healthy from unhealthy meat. Sometimes it is more important just to identify the responsibility than to identify it in the technically most accurate way; what matters is that the responsible person know that he is responsible. Other times it is important to see that legal responsibility be sensitively placed where it can be responded to.

We could decide that whoever last lubricated the automobile is responsible for failing to notice a defect; whether or not this is a smart way to assign responsibility is an empirical question. Is the person who lubricates the car in the best position to respond to incentives, to process information, to spot the defect and warn the motorist? Or is it the firm that assembled the car? Or the producer of the defective part?

To sum up, the question of the social responsibility of business is sometimes the question of who is or was responsible, legally or morally, as though responsibility were immanent in the situation. For policymaking, however, the question becomes that of assigning or identifying responsibility at the socially expedient point, so that cognizant parties are able and motivated to act responsibly.

### Business as an Agent of Government

Most discussion of the social responsibility of business is really about *irresponsibility*—how to redress it, penalize it, inoculate against it, compensate for it, or otherwise overcome it. We discuss pollution, equal opportunity employment, safety on the job, non-hazardous consumption goods, the need to internalize costs and benefits that are already "there" but external to the firm's accounting, and occasionally, going a little further, landscaping the buildings or helping to support a museum. When we look for more positive contributions, like developing a better contraceptive or a better washing machine or a substitute for having to make beds every morning, we have in mind *business as a system,* it not being the responsibility of any particular firm to accomplish what we would like at least one of them to achieve. But there are some matters of social policy that go beyond the normal business of the firm, beyond the ordinary responsibility that goes with being in business. They involve the business firm as an *agent* of social policy or social reform.

To make clear what I have in mind, let me use the analogy of the school system. Public schools are nominally supposed to teach children certain intellectual arts and skills, to make them better able to earn a living, to get along in the world, to meet the obligations of citizenship. Schooling is also expected to civilize them by teaching them to sit still, to be punctual, and to get along in a group. Schools often go further and try to teach children how to dress and to cut their hair, to teach them personal hygiene or the evils of tobacco and other stimulants, and sometimes how to pay their respects to God and country.

Most schools go further still and provide sports and contests. They often provide skin tests for tuberculosis, eye tests and hearing tests, and some inoculations. Some schools aim to improve the diet with hot lunches and fresh milk. Some try to teach children how to save money, through arrangements with local savings banks. Schools organize social activities and a variety of clubs and hobbies, to keep children off the streets, to separate the boys from the girls or to mix the boys with the girls, sometimes to make up deficiencies in the local community.

Which among these activities are the central purposes and which have been added on because school is where a child is conveniently captive for several hours five days a week and therefore a convenient place to give him his shots or to teach him how to clean his teeth? If the age groupings were just a little different, schools might become the locus of registration for voting, the draft, and social security cards.

Just as it is hard to draw the line between activities central to schooling and those added for social convenience, it is difficult to draw the line in business. But the effort can sensitize us to this kind of activity, making us alert both to opportunities and to possible dangers.

Let me cite a few activities in which business appears to be used as a *social instrument*—as a convenient organizational setting for getting things done that might otherwise be done elsewhere. An example is the withholding of income tax. Unlike an excise or sales tax, which is a tax on business activity, the withholding of income represents a drafting of the firm into the service of the Treasury. True, the income originates within the business; and one might construe the whole thing as the firm's rendering to Caesar what is Caesar's before turning the residue over to the employee as take-home pay. But a more practical interpretation is that the business firm can cheaply, conveniently, and reliably take care of the employees' periodic tax installments and is in a good position to police them on behalf of the Internal Revenue Service. (The employer could instead send periodic wage statements to the IRS, which could monitor the taxpayer directly: it would take more postage stamps.)

As a second example, there is a policy consensus that working people ought to put something aside for retirement. The organizations that employ people have been identified as the "chosen instruments" to make this easy, or even mandatory. (It is slightly reminiscent of savings-bank day when I was in sixth grade.) Just as we could pay our income tax installments by ourselves, we could save money on our own for our retirement years; if we didn't trust ourselves, we could do as the Christmas savings people do and buy annuities as we went along. But for most people it makes sense to relate the amount saved for retirement to the amount currently earned; a simple withholding formula at the source of the income takes care of it, and there are administrative savings in letting the employer do the paperwork. It is furthermore easier to have statutory safeguards if retirement plans are managed through large organizations, like the firms that hire many of us.

"Affirmative action programs" in the hiring and promotion of women and minorities are another example of business used as a social instrument. The responsibility of the firm might plausibly be construed as the absence of adverse discrimination and a little bending backward to avoid inadvertent discrimination. Going beyond that, to deliberately giving advantage to groups that are universally disadvantaged, to help solve a universal problem, is a social program using the firm as a social instrument. The conscious activity in making arrangements to give special attention to the disadvantaged, to avoid practices that *could* discriminate whether or not in fact they do, to avoid language that might offend, and so forth, has been and probably is intended to have an educational effect on people within the business, an effect that will carry over outside working hours and that may affect, and is intended to affect, customs, speech, and self-consciousness, in a manner not altogether different from what is attempted in the schools.

Health is another field in which business firms for adults, like schools for younger people, are uniquely convenient agents. I have in mind not programs oriented toward occupational hazards (such as are found in coal mines or factories that use radioactive materials) but the promotion of general health care, physical exams, tuberculosis tests, screening for heart disease, tests of eyesight and hearing, and programs to encourage the drinking of milk or the avoidance of alcohol. The Nixon administration proposed, in the Comprehensive Health Insurance Act of 1974, that employers be required to offer employees a private health insurance plan with comprehensive benefits (including eye examinations for children under thirteen). The plan would make the employing firm the chosen instrument for medical and hospital coverage, as it already is for retirement but without quite the same rationale.

A related development that could arise through governmental pressure or through the demands of employees or customers is the discouragement of smoking. Airlines reintroduced the no-smoking sections, and I detect an increase in the frequency of signs requesting that for the comfort of others and the health of everybody tobacco not be smoked. It is not out of the question that an emergency program for flu inoculation or the treatment of venereal disease would take advantage of the fact that most people have a regular place of work where they can be located and identified, that many work in places large enough to enjoy economies of scale in examination or administration of vaccine, and that business firms might be prevailed on to encourage or slightly to coerce their employees and to make time and space available.

Other possibilities are more controversial. Encouragement of patriotism and worship can go beyond good taste or the civil liberties of employees and customers (though I have not come across any objection to the chapels located in air terminals). Testing urinals for narcotics, educating people in the recognition of drug addicts or enemy agents, and coercing dress and hair styles would surely meet with objection. (The banning by some states of bare feet in retail establishments probably has more than a public health motivation.) Union and customer boycotts, not merely state, municipal, and federal programs, can sometimes be the motivating force.

Business is already expected to participate to some small extent in encouraging people to vote and in making it convenient for them to do so. More could be done, if it were thought appropriate, in connection with voter registration. Income tax advice is available in many business organizations; time off for daily prayer is a little more controversial.

In the United States it is probably nonbusiness organizations that engage most conspicuously, most self-consciously, and most paternalistically in social programs. The armed forces, the Job

Corps, and some prisons are examples. In other countries, especially underdeveloped countries, literacy, public health, and family planning have been encouraged or organized through the place of employment.

In America the history of business' own efforts to encourage or coerce conformity to "accepted" social standards does not command universal admiration. *The Organization Man* was an exposé of "business responsibility" as defined by business itself. A good deal of political power has been exercised by business firms, especially in local communities, under the heading—innocent or contrived and probably some of both—of "business responsibility." Some of the most criticized practices of real estate boards come readily to mind. A history of political reform and civil liberties in America is likely to devote a chapter to the repudiation of many responsibilities that business arrogated to itself.

It is one thing to exercise an acknowledged responsibility. It is quite another to define that responsibility. And business itself is only one of the contenders for defining it.

### The Two Faces of Regulation

It is hard to escape the impression that the original attitude of the airlines toward hijacking was about as zealous as the attitude of the automobile companies toward safety in the middle 1950s. There was, until the mandatory procedures of 1973, something so desultory in the inspection of briefcases and handbags, even the magnetic inspection that turned up keyrings and pocketknives, that the airlines almost appeared to be spoofing. (Pilots were concerned; but pilots have to fly.) The occasional intensive examination of passengers, with attendant congested queues and delayed departures, seemed intended to sabotage the campaign and to provoke passenger discontent.

Auto safety was for years apparently not "commercial" enough to feature in the advertisements. "Danger" being implied in concern over "safety," it was considered poor merchandising to call attention to the risks of motoring. Besides, focusing upon auto safety might have led to a more critical attitude on the part of car buyers toward the entire subject of auto engineering; and critical customers scrutinizing auto design were a less attractive prospect than happy motorists buying their machines uncritically.

A preoccupation with air safety must appear even more threatening, both to the airlines and to the aircraft manufacturers, because so many millions of people traditionally considered air an unstable substance on which to travel. Cocktails aloft helped, but airplane travel had an uphill struggle to eliminate the image of daring and danger.

Evidently to the airlines the greatest fear is fear itself—fear on the part of passengers. And newspaper accounts of hijacking, especially of hijacking not accompanied by violence, may inhibit flying less than the sight of pistoled, uniformed guards in the terminals and cabins.

So it may not be hard to understand why the airline companies were among the more silent of those involved. And when the question arose about who should foot the bill for protective measures, it was not immediately apparent who had the greatest interest in reducing the hazards of airline piracy. It is by no means clear that the interest is even confined to people who have any connection with flying.

Consider some alarming by-products of ordinary commercial activity. There is the dumping of noxious substances into rivers and lakes; there is strip mining; there is the production of electric power by combustion of cheap fuels that fill the air with sulphuric acid. It appears to be typical of producers that they resist being identified with the harms that they promulgate and being saddled with compulsory efforts to clean up or to change their technology. In some cases there is a transparent motive: fear that they will be put out of business by an aroused populace. In some cases there may be fear that the image of their product will be contaminated by association with noxious by-products. People may come to associate potato chips with dead fish or associate the harmful effects of insecticides with the foods protected by them, even though there is no physical connection between the harms and the foods.

But suppose all the barbers in Massachusetts were theatened with a law requiring everyone to get a shampoo with his haircut. Suppose all the building contractors in California were required by law to put external fire escapes on new three-story houses. How would we expect the barbers and the contractors to react?

The answer is not easy. It is not easy to guess; and it may not be easy for them to decide. The consequences depend on the elasticity of demand for the product, on the vertical integration of the industry, and on traditional pricing. Mandatory shampoos may so raise the price of haircuts that barbershop business declines, or it may double the activity of shops that install sinks and get twice as much per customer. Surely a law requiring everybody to get his hair regularly trimmed would not be viewed as an onerous interference in the barbering trade. Regulations on the sulphur content of fuels used in electric power production might be welcome or not to the power industry, according to whether the industry were so integrated that expensive production of fuels was internal to the industry.

Why did the automobile manufacturers not lobby for expensive antipollution devices on automobiles? Why—to go further—were the auto companies not demanding, in the early 1970s, abolition of the internal combustion engine by 1980?

I am not raising a question of responsibility, only trying to get at the question of what business motivation ought to be expected to be. One of the phrases popularized in the last decade is "built-in obsolescence." It is alleged that automobile companies and companies that produce television sets or electric freezers like to see this year's product become unacceptable to consumers next year or the year after. What could more reliably promise "built-in obsolescence" than a federal law prohibiting internal combustion engines in automobiles a decade hence?

Several hypotheses come to mind. One relates to the *elasticity of demand.* Just as painters may not benefit from a law restricting the width of brushes, nor barbers from a law requiring shampoos, people may not only buy fewer automobiles but spend less money altogether on automobiles if the cost of cars increases. The auto companies may worry that demand is price-elastic and that mandatory cost increases will lead to a reduced dollar amount.

A second hypothesis relates to the *vertical integration* of the industry. If the law requires that all cars be equipped with something not produced by the firms that produce cars, the industry that produces the item will be delighted but the auto producers will not. A law that required everybody who got a haircut to buy a bottle of shampoo at the nearest drugstore would raise the total cost of haircuts and do the barbershops no good; a law that required the internal fumigation of all houses painted on the outside would not help the painters unless they were simultaneously fumigators. Mandatory safety glass is most interesting to auto manufacturers if they produce glass.

A third possibility is that traditional firms fear the *entry* of new firms. If it were assured that external combustion engines could be produced only by Ford, General Motors, Chrysler, and American Motors and that cars would forever be produced by the firms that produce them now, mandatory obsolescence of the internal combustion engine might appear a splendid way of getting fifty million cars off the road in the near future. But suppose the ultimate technology of an external combustion engine (or of other alternatives to the internal combustion engine) is so different that it isn't clear whether producers of sewing machines or submarines are likely to get into the business. Then it will not be obvious to the auto manufacturers that they benefit from a technology that opens up the industry to new entrants.

I haven't the answer. There is even a fourth interesting possibility. It is that the auto manufacturers have not learned to think like painters and barbers and building contractors. They may be unaware that cost-increasing regulations are often good for the business.

There is of course a strong sentiment against antibusiness regulation. There is apprehension, not always unjustified, that when government intrudes into a field of production it bodes ill for the companies intruded on. This attitude may not have much to do with profits: people don't like, or pretend not to like, being told what to do. One is provoked to wonder, nevertheless, whether government regulation is quite as menacing as it is seen to be.

There is growing recognition that firms may acquiesce in standards that penalize them no more than their competitors. A "responsible" firm can wish to comply with some social standards but refuse to adopt them unilaterally while its competitors ignore them. My suggestion here is that the standards, once adopted by all, may not always turn out to be onerous. Often measures that perforce increase business costs (or internalize costs) turn out to be neutral or even beneficial in relation to business profits.

### The False Dichotomy of Voluntarism and Coercion

The question is sometimes posed where the line should be drawn between reliance on the voluntary assumption of responsibility by business and the coercion of "responsible" performance by government sanctions. So many techniques, instruments, and philosophies exist beyond or in addition to these two rather pure forms that that may be a poor way of posing a choice.

Posing the question in terms of drawing a line suggests gratuitously that what is needed is something business firms "ought" to have done voluntarily but did not, so that coercion is both corrective and punitive. It may also suggest, inadvertently and often wrongly, that business firms prefer (or naturally should prefer) public reliance on their voluntary assumption of responsibility and that coercion is what they always and naturally wish to avoid.

Taking off from that last point, an interesting alternative approach is that of permitting businesses *to coerce themselves.* "Mutual coercion, mutually agreed on," a term publicized by Garrett Hardin in connection with population policy, could appeal to firms that are prepared to incur costs but only on condition that competitors do also. The coercion could take the form of the government's responding to a plea to enforce a mandatory regulation. Alternatively, the government might allow, in the public interest, a voluntary contractual arrangement that would otherwise run afoul of the antitrust laws. As still another arrangement for the same purpose, there could be legislation that would make mandatory the application to all firms in an industry of an agreement that had been ratified by some substantial number. (Retail price maintenance in some states may be a near example.)

Sometimes what business may need is an ability to *concert on a uniform practice* or simply the information by which they could coordinate their activities. Heterogeneous phonograph speeds may not have been a sufficient nuisance to consumers to arouse a demand for regulatory action, but bumper heights are a different matter. The sheer power of suggestion could become almost coercive on domestic automobile manufacturers if a simple, identifiable, easily remembered standard could be impressed on consumers and insurance companies. The primary enforcement of daylight saving is merely the publicized announcement of the date for setting clocks forward or backward and everybody's expectation that, if they don't participate, they'll only confuse themselves and their friends.

Another alternative to the voluntarism-coercion dichotomy (one much discussed recently in the professional economics literature) is the *relocation of legal obligations.* Property rights and liabilities for damage are important ways of dealing with externalities. No-fault insurance is a current, dramatic example.

Still another approach is *leadership in the public sector.* In addition to setting an example, government purchasing power can often overcome the overhead costs of, say, redesign of a product; and government contracting has long been used as a way of enforcing, with at least some success, certain hiring practices. The government may reach an industry indirectly through its powers of regulation over suppliers to that industry. Both these techniques have affected automobile design: seat belts, direction signals, and bumper standards can be influenced by requiring police cars and other government vehicles, and taxis, to meet the new standards. (Now that legislation protecting pension plans has been enacted, the federal government can help reform retirement practices in private business by remodeling its own practices to set the example.)

*Changing the rules of the game* has been another important way that government has redefined and restructured the responsibility of business. The National Labor Relations Act is an example. Both legislatively and through the courts a similar shift of bargaining advantage may occur, or may now be occurring, with respect to multiple-tenant landlords.

Schemes that operate in the market can have an element both of the voluntary and of the coercive. A tax that is discretionary rather than prohibitive is a flexible kind of coercion. Subsidies are much the same, though harsh words like "coercion" are typically not used when the firm is, on balance, a beneficiary and not a victim. Tax relief and cost-sharing arrangements are somewhat less "coercive" than straightforward regulation.

Similarly, government-financed research and development and government provision of goods and services offer a way of bypassing the coercion-voluntarism issue.

Thus the coercive and the voluntary are not exhaustive alternatives. They are not even opposite ends of a scale, since many techniques have little to do with either category.

## The Marketplace Is No Excuse

It is sometimes argued, by economists as well as by businessmen accused of neglecting the public interest, that the business of business is just business. A firm is expected to compete for the consumer's dollar by ruthlessly cutting costs and single-mindedly attending to what the consumer will buy. When the firm tries to do some conscionable thing like planting trees or suppressing noise or designing automobiles that meet aesthetic standards that the car buyer is not interested in, the result is higher prices or lower wages or the squandering of potential dividends on things that, though usually harmless and often quite good, merely represent some executive's notion of what he'd appreciate if he were the public, or what he'd like to be remembered for. Even the beneficiaries would usually be better off with equivalent or less cash instead of "public goods" paternalistically provided.

The individual proprietor of course is free to spend his money as he pleases. If he wants to provide for his customers a higher-quality product than they'd be willing to spend their own money on, or play music for his employees, or subsidize some group by hiring them at wages they cannot earn, at least it's his own money he is spending, and only the Internal Revenue Service need wring its hands at the potential waste. But when the semiautonomous managers of a large, publicly owned corporation choose to invest in good works, so the argument goes, they are not only spending somebody else's money but indulging their personal whims in the process.

This argument, which begins by making fun, perhaps properly, of what businesses may actually accomplish when they try to do good, can easily be pushed to the point of proposing that all is fair in business and that a sufficient excuse for ruthlessness in competitive business is that the marketplace demands it. According to the hard line, if the firm that cuts corners didn't cut corners, it would lose ground to its competition and possibly become extinct. Business is business, and the fittest survive. Just as governments are often alleged to have a higher obligation to national survival than to any virtuous aspirations of the electorate, and just as the Constitution appears to many not to countenance philanthropy at the expense of some national interest, the corporation is expected to follow what people sometimes call the law of the jungle.

This view unduly depreciates the law of the jungle. Konrad Lorenz, in his widely read book *On Aggression*, gave numerous illustrations of how biological evolution reflects the survival needs of the species as well as of the individual. Time and again, modes of behavior are suppressed that, though advantageous for the individual, would be inefficacious for the larger community. The nervous system of the adult wolf makes it incapable of attacking the cub. If this restraint were not built into the wolf's nervous system, the adult wolf itself would never have survived as an infant, nor would its parents have survived to give it birth. The law of the jungle contains its own commandments. Without them, without nature's restraints, the species does not flourish. Lawlessness is not the way of the jungle.

A second difficulty with the notion that business should merely maximize profits, no matter what, is that it conflicts with what we expect of ordinary people. We would condemn doctors who promoted disease in the interest of selling their services more dearly. We don't expect the motorist with a disabled car to have to pay $10 to get a passing motorist to phone for help. We disparage the repairman who installs an expensive replacement part that the ignorant consumer doesn't need, and we disparage him because, if we were repairmen, we wouldn't want our children to know we did that. Some personal morality is an enormous social asset. It helps to keep us all from getting small personal advantage at large expense to each other, with a net loss all around. Trust and honesty are of great social worth. Lorenz may have had it backward when he characterized animal restraint as "behavioral analogies to morality." [3] Maybe our human morality is a necessary substitute for those instinctual commandments that beasts of the jungle are neurologically incapable of violating.

The question is whether the modern business corporation has to be thought of as a solvent within which personal morality becomes unstuck. Should human decency be considered incapable of surviving the sterile atmosphere of the business firm? Can we not demand of a large corporation—or, if not demand, wish for—the same decency that we think we have a right to expect from our paper boy?

It is asking too much to expect the profit-motivated pharmaceutical firm to share the ethics of our family physician. But we are not surprised when an ordinary person sacrifices earnings to do the decent thing. Individual people are allowed to be as sentimental as they please toward fellow human beings. If they combine to form a corporation, must they be denied the same sentimentality? May they not be encouraged, at least, to forgo profits, consciously and openly, in the interest of behaving, as a firm, the way they would all wish to behave as individuals? Shouldn't it be considered merely the decent thing for a firm to go to the wall competitively, perhaps to succumb and go out of business, rather than violate the spirit of the law or take deceitful advantage of somebody's ignorance?

The difficulty is one of diffusion of responsibility. Decisions are made by a multiplicity of individuals in a large organization. Ultimate liability is to a multiplicity of owners, stockholders who are unknown and unknowable. The sheer organizational process seems to be inhospitable to the softer sentiments that we appreciate so much in individuals or small organizations.

There is no sense in expecting a large organization—the organization itself, as distinct from the people within it—to have the corporate self-respect that we hope for in a person. An organization is not a person, and it will have neither the same strengths nor the same weaknesses. But maybe we could expect people in organizations to continue to be people, even though they are executives of large firms. Maybe the guideline for executives who want advice on what their social responsibilities are or ought to be might as a rough approximation be just to be themselves. The standard to which they should hold the organization is the standard they would set for themselves if they were in it alone.

# 3 | The Intimate Contest for Self-Command

*You will come first of all to the Sirens, who are enchanters of all mankind and whoever comes their way; and that man who unsuspecting approaches them, and listens to the Sirens singing, has no prospect of coming home and delighting his wife and little children as they stand about him in greeting, but the Sirens by the melody of their singing enchant him. They sit in their meadow, but the beach before it is piled with boneheaps of men now rotted away, and the skins shrivel upon them. You must drive straight on past, but melt down sweet wax of honey and with it stop your companions' ears, so none can listen; the rest, that is, but if you yourself are wanting to hear them, then have them tie you hand and foot on the fast ship, standing upright against the mast with the ropes' ends lashed around it, so that you can have joy in hearing the song of the Sirens; but if you supplicate your men and implore them to set you free, then they must tie you fast wth even more lashings.*

The Odyssey of Homer, Richmond Lattimore, translator,
Book XII, lines 39–54

I DO NOT KNOW whether more people watched football on New Year's than any other day of the season, but I am sure that more people quit smoking. Resolutions are not as popular as a generation ago, but some of us need all the help we can get and New Year's still seems propitious for a fresh start.

For many of us, "all the help we can get" is not enough, and January is a month for recidivism too. Still, more people succeed on the day they can discard the old calendar than on April Fool's. In economics—the nearest thing we have to a science of choice— both those facts invite attention. Why is it so hard for so many of us, on matters great and small—being kind to our families or to our fingernails, taking up exercise or giving up coffee, turning off the TV or settling down to write that article for *The Public Interest*—to do the things we already decided to do and to quit the things we decided to quit? And what is there about New Year's that offers support, even if not much? What are the other times and places and tactics and techniques that we use or avoid to keep our programs on track?

People also resolve, about that time of year, to lay money aside

57

regularly for the following Christmas. Some people are poor at saving, and a sophisticated arrangement is offered by your neighborhood bank to help overcome the problem. It is called "Christmas saving." In this plan you are committed to weekly deposits until a date in November when all the money is there, with interest, to spend for Christmas. Sometimes it doesn't earn quite as much interest as regular savings. People accept lower interest because the bank protects these funds better than ordinary savings. Ordinary savings are protected against robbery, embezzlement, and insolvency; and insurance takes care of what protection cannot. But there is one predator against whom the bank is impotent—you. For a Christmas account the bank creates ceremonial barriers to protect your account from yourself.

Some people cheat on the withholding-tax forms they fill out for their employers. They *understate* their dependents. The IRS takes more than it deserves all year—a free loan from the taxpayer—and in return the taxpayer gets a reduced shock, possibly a refund, the following April.

Many of us have little tricks we play on ourselves to make us do the things we ought to do or to keep us from the things we have foresworn. We place the alarm clock across the room so we cannot turn it off without getting out of bed. We put things out of sight or out of reach for the moment of temptation. We surrender authority to a trustworthy friend who will police our calories or our cigarettes. People who are chronically late set their watches ahead hoping to fool themselves. I heard of a corporate dining room where lunch orders are telephoned in at 9:30; no food is served except what was ordered at that time, not long after breakfast, when food was least tempting and resolve at its highest. A grimmer example is people who have their jaws wired shut.

People behave sometimes as if they had two selves, one who wants clean lungs and long life and another who adores tobacco, or one who wants a lean body and another who wants dessert, or one who yearns to improve himself by reading Adam Smith on self-command (in *The Theory of Moral Sentiments*) and another who would rather watch an old movie on television. The two are in continual contest for control.

As a boy I saw a movie about Admiral Byrd's Antarctic expedition and was impressed that as a boy he had gone outdoors in shirtsleeves to toughen himself against the cold. I resolved to go to bed at night with one blanket too few. That decision to go to bed minus one blanket was made by a warm boy. Another boy awoke cold in the night, too cold to retrieve the blanket, cursing the boy who had removed the blanket and resolving to restore it tomorrow. But the next bedtime it was the warm boy again, dreaming of Antarctica, who got to make the decision. And he always did it again.

How should we conceptualize this rational consumer whom all of us know and who some of us are, who in self-disgust grinds his cigarettes down the disposal swearing that this time he means never again to risk orphaning his children with lung cancer and is on the street three hours later looking for a store that's still open to buy cigarettes; who eats a high-calorie lunch knowing that he will regret it, does regret it, cannot understand how he lost control, resolves to compensate with a low-calorie dinner, eats a high-calorie dinner knowing he will regret it, and does regret it; who sits glued to the TV knowing that again tomorrow he'll wake early in a cold sweat unprepared for that morning meeting on which so much of his career depends; who spoils the trip to Disneyland by losing his temper when his children do what he knew they were going to do when he resolved not to lose his temper when they did it?

Does it matter, for theory or policy, whether we know how to characterize such behavior, even just to describe it in the language of preferences and values, choices and decisions, utility, welfare, and rationality? We could be interested in casting suspicion on the entire individualistic-utilitarian foundation of neoclassical economics by adding a large fraction of the literate adult population to that already large population disqualified by infancy, senility, or incompetence from being represented in our theory of the consumer. Alternatively, we could just be interested, as I am, in getting a better idea of what is going on and how much it matters when people behave in these apparently contradictory fashions. However we end up reconciling, if we do reconcile, these behaviors with the notion of a consumer's having reasonably stable values, knowing his values, and having the intellectual capacity to make choices that satisfy those values, there still seems to be for many among us a problem of self-management.

## The Non-Self-Governing Consumer

A striking characteristic of textbooks in economics is that the consumer is a single person. So are owners of businesses. A couple of decades ago theorists began to recognize that a board of directors or an executive staff of a corporation, not being a single person, might not make decisions like a single person, especially not like a single person who either owned the whole business or owned only a few shares of stock. Only recently has the family made an appearance. People who deal with income taxes and family welfare have always had to think of families as multiperson units, but theorists who deal with "social choice" have typically used as their model the political system, or a board of directors, rarely that ubiquitous small society, the family. The family is an income-sharing unit, a consumption-sharing unit, and a welfare-sharing unit; that is, they live off the same income, share the same bathroom, and care about each other. No wonder theory neglects the family; it complicates things enormously.

But maybe it isn't only the family that, on a close look, fails to behave like a single-minded individual because it isn't one. Maybe the ordinary man or woman also doesn't behave like a single-minded individual because he or she isn't one. Lewis Thomas, author of *The Lives of a Cell* and more recently *The Medusa and the Snail,* enchants us with the idea that private functions of our bodies are performed by autonomous one-celled creatures that don't know they are part of us and might resent it if told they were. Carl Sagan, in *The Dragons of Eden,* hints that the two hemispheres of our brains reflect different evolutionary paths, giving us two ways of perceiving our little universes.[1] I believe as I write this that I am awake, but science fiction suggests that I have no way of determining whether I am asleep and dreaming. Schizophrenia, hypnosis, amnesia, narcosis, and anesthesia suggest that anything as complicated as the human brain, especially if designed with redundancy for good measure and most assuredly if not designed at all but arising out of a continuous process that began before we were reptiles, should be capable of representing more than one "person." In fact, it must occasionally wire in a bit of memory that doesn't belong or signal for a change in the body's hormonal chemistry that makes us, at least momentarily, "somebody else." I am reminded of the tantalizing distinction that someone made when my wife had our first child after two hours on sodium pentathol: it doesn't make it hurt less, it just keeps you from remembering afterward. Strange that the prospect of pain can't scare me once I've seen that, when I become conscious, I won't remember!

So we should not be surprised that people can act as if they were not quite singular individuals with unique identities and values and tastes and memories and sensory perceptions that display smooth continuity over time. Maybe for some purposes each of us is like two or more different identities, not switching discontinuously as in amnesia or electric-shock therapy, but with enough oscillation to affect some of those decisions that are neither binding long-term commitments nor shorter commitments so synchronized with the command cycle that the same self—that brave warm boy who dreamed of Antarctica—is always in charge.

Sometimes, but not always, it is easy to know which is Jekyll and which is Hyde. The person who drinks and becomes vicious, or a bore, and is morose about it for days afterwards; the person who continually resolves to demand that increase in pay and never musters the courage; and the person who walks into a casino for a little sociable gambling, loses more than he intended, commits more to recover it, and emerges traumatized after blowing his bankroll, all seem to present an unequal pair, a "straight" *ego* and a wayward *alter*. But even if that assessment is a fair one, it isn't so easy to judge the person whose loss of control leads to impulsive if regrettable generosity, giving his overcoat to a shivering wino or emptying his wallet into the Salvation Army bucket. The person who on doctor's orders is holding to 2,000 calories for the sake of his heart who goes on a midnight binge, stuffing his mouth as if his warden or his conscience might step in momentarily and stop him, seems to be somebody who needs a better grip on himself; but the people who out of vanity resolve to starve themselves in order to be movie thin, who from time to time decide the hell with it and have a good meal in good company, don't make it so easy to choose whose side we are on. Many of us have tried to help someone escape from a regime of austerity that we thought not only ill-founded but stifling in its consequences. And I still don't know whether, if those Antarctic dreams had come true, I'd have been better able to stand the cold and *both* boys would have been glad that the command structure gave the decision to the boy who, feeling no pain himself, could inflict it on the other.

"The spirit is willing but the flesh is weak." That may be sufficient explanation for gluttony, some sexual incontinence, heroin addiction, or the scratching of hives. It doesn't as readily cover television or gambling, procrastination or loss of temper, or the plain lack of motivation to get on with some self-improvement re-gime like rapid reading or better posture or spending more time with the children. It furthermore misses the important point that the willingness of the spirit and the weakness of the flesh—or is it the weakness of the spirit and the strength of the flesh?—fre-quently alternate rather than coincide, and that the willing spirit, like a loving parent (or like a punitive one), can try to isolate or immobilize that mischievous self that periodically takes charge. Furthermore, the "flesh" often seems endowed with as ingenious an intelligence and command system as the allegedly stronger "spirit," in evading or overcoming the stratagems of the spirit. And maybe, memories of pain and discomfort being of no-toriously low fidelity, the "willingness" of the spirit to resolve on some arduous program is only a sign that it's easy to be brave when the danger is remote.

One model suggested for this ambivalence in choice would let the two selves—or the several—differ along a single dimension amenable to economic analysis. That is the dimension of time preference—of the discount rate to compare present with future, near future with far future, imminent with remote, or permanent with transient. The idea is that the person who takes that drink or lights that cigarette or digs into that hot fudge sundae is merely discounting the future with a high interest rate. Resolving in late December to begin running three miles before every breakfast in January is a future-oriented decision, especially if the benefits are reduced mortality two or three decades from now. The same is true with reducing weight. The person who then fails to get up some January morning to do that stint before breakfast, or who eats and drinks 3,500 calories at a party on January 10, has merely shifted gears in his discount system, undervaluing that sec-ond decade compared with tonight or this morning.

In a study of discounting that may be a good way to treat the person who lives, as they say, "like there was no tomorrow." It's the way we say, in an economics textbook, that you can always grow bananas in a submarine: the price would simply be so high that you may as well call it infinite. But the person who is simply not thinking of the future, who shuts his eyes to avoid it (espe-cially when the future is not a decade away but tomorrow, when he knows he'll suffer remorse and disgust and the disapproval of family and friends who witness the collapse of resolve), like the person who furiously scratches his hives, would have to be someone whose time discount is 100 percent per hour or per minute, compounding to an annual rate too large for my calculator. It is not clear whether the straight fellow who resolves to run three miles before breakfast enjoys such a far horizon that he can appreciate the benefits of elderly good health, or merely has such a short memory that he forgets how disagreeable it's going to be, every morning in perpetuity, to spend thirty minutes gasping for breath.

## The Art of Self-Management

"Economics" comes through the Latin *oeconomia* from the Greek *oikonomia,* meaning household management (*oikos,* house, and *nomos,* managing) and still has some of that meaning in its variant, "economical." My suggestion is to recognize a comparable art or science of "self-management" possibly as part of economics—or possibly not, but related. Maybe we could attach the Latin *ego* to the Greek *nomos,* and make *egonomics.* What scope such a discipline would have I don't know. I am interested only in the part that might be called *strategic egonomics,* consciously coping with one's own behavior, especially one's conscious behavior. As a motto, my colleague David Hemenway has suggested, "No Thyself!"

My suggestion is that we get help from comparing self-management with the way one tries to manage another, another who is in a special relation to one's self. Many of the skills and maxims and stratagems for coping with one's own behavior become less mystifying and more familiar if we can recognize them as the same principles and stratagems that apply to managing someone else— someone in a close relation, with a paternalist or senior-junior quality like that between parent and child, teacher and pupil, missionary and convert, master and apprentice, or guide and follower.

I don't intend anything mysterious or philosophically profound in this notion that some intriguing parts of strategic self-management are like coping with one's own behavior as though it were another's. To emphasize that I am dealing with mundane issues, familiar to us all, with no deep meanings intended and no necessary intention of questioning what the "self" is or offering an answer, let me begin with some cases remote from smoking, drinking, eating, gambling, jogging, and procrastinating, in which the question what one "really" wants does not intrude. What do you do with a child that scratches in its sleep?

Usually scratching is thought to be dysfunctional. Whether it is hives, chicken pox, mosquito bites, or poison ivy, doctors worry about infection; and most of us, especially parents, have observed that any momentary frenzied relief from scratching is followed almost instantly by enhanced itching. Many of us learn to resist the temptation to scratch. But not in our sleep.

Mittens are an answer. (Close-trimmed nails are another.) Suppose it's not a child but you: you are as likely to scratch as that kid, once you're asleep. I suggest mittens. If you don't think of it yourself, your doctor will; it beats having somebody tie your hands to the bedpost. (Even that's better than scratching if you haven't any mittens.) There doesn't seem to be much difference between tying mittens on a child's hands to make scratching innocuous and tying mittens on your own with the same intention. Either way there is "somebody" who in his sleep will lack the discipline or the awareness to do what "he" might have wished to do, namely to abstain from scratching. Treating your sometime self as though it were somebody else is a ubiquitous and familiar technique of self-management.

Where else do we find it unexceptionable? There's an endless list of occasions, some important, and once I start the list any reader can extend it. These are cases in which there is a genuine problem of managing one's own behavior, and in which the control process is such that the "manager" is not always in charge, especially not when management becomes a problem. And in such cases the ways that one attempts to cope, while in charge, with the problems that will arise when that other self is in charge (or when no one is in charge) are like—not identical with, but like—the ways one would manage another.

My interest is focused at the more conscious strategic end of the spectrum, where all but the most doctrinaire would describe behavior as voluntary and conscious. Usually, though not always, lighting a cigarette can be characterized as voluntary and conscious, or accepting a first drink, or ordering dessert, or buying an expensive piece of jewelry to please a salesperson, or agreeing to perform an onerous task when it keeps one from facing another that is more fearsome and more urgent. It is not quite so evident that flying into a rage is "voluntary" and "conscious." Or biting fingernails or slouching into an unattractive and unhealthful posture. Or turning off the alarm half asleep and failing to get out of bed. Or slamming on the brakes when the car skids on snow and braking is exactly the wrong thing and you know it. Averting one's gaze under interrogation may be conscious and voluntary, blushing perhaps not, and the electrical conductivity of the skin of one's palm may be impossible to control without training. My idea is that in the detached way that we can approach management problems near the unconscious or involuntary end of the scale, including some of those that involve physical and mechanical props as well as environmental manipulation, we can more casually approach those behaviors that are indubitably "voluntary," substantially conscious, and more than trivial.

Sleep has already been mentioned in some connections and there are more. I mentioned scratching during sleep; there is removing bandages, suffocating an infant, rolling off a ledge, snoring, talking (either noise or information), and, though it has gone out of vogue in the last forty years, sleepwalking. In some circumstances resisting interrogation is important while asleep. Then there is awakening—both hearing the alarm (or the baby's voice, or the intruder's footfall) and overcoming those sometimes overwhelming forces when the alarm goes off. And staying awake. Sentries have been shot, truckers burned, watchmen bypassed, babies neglected, and tasks unfinished when people—voluntarily? consciously?—let their lids droop or fell asleep with their eyes open or even lapsed only a few seconds from full awareness.

Panic is another. Public doors now have panic bars to open them; horses are blindfolded to be led out of a burning barn. Alcohol and other tranquilizers are regularly used to induce bravery on the battlefield and calm among airline passengers. Carl Sagan even proposes that sleep can insulate an organism from that awareness of danger that might cause it to panic and reveal itself, or to breathe harder and emit more telltale carbon dioxide.

For stagefright, I know people who use tranquilizers, both those sold at the drugstore and those served before dinner. Albert Edward Wiggam wrote *The Marks of an Educated Man,* which I read as a boy when I was trying to improve myself. He'd been inspired by William Jennings Bryan and wanted to be an orator as badly as I wanted to explore Antarctica. But when he faced an audience he blacked out. It lasted only a minute, but not many audiences would wait a minute. Wiggam memorized a story to begin every speech with, memorized it so well he could tell it in his sleep or while engaged at other things, and, he hoped, during the blackout that would occur as he walked on stage. He knew his career was secure at that glorious moment when, recovering consciousness while standing before an audience, he heard himself finishing the story just in time to enjoy the laughter that he had earned with such effort.

What about fear of heights? Although it won't work if you have to drive a mountain road, shutting your eyes helps. If I have to carry you piggyback over a chasm, I may blindfold you; if I don't think of it, you may tie your own blindfold. Odysseus' sailors could just as well have put the wax in their own ears.

Absent-mindedness is a funny one. Whether you tie that string on somebody else's finger or on your own, you do it for the same reason and with the same expectation. All of us have been at meetings where someone's wrist alarm or pocket beeper went off. Most people run out of gas while surrounded by service stations.

Anger is a condition in which we may on impulse do the wrong thing. "Count to ten" is a principle that can be applied in many ways, to oneself as well as to others. And a multitude of phobias invite management efforts to overcome some powerful immediate inhibition—diving off the high board for the first time, or getting fluid syringed out of one's knee with a four-inch needle.

Some of these problems of self-management are joint among two or more people. Consider giggling. If somebody sneezes at a lecture I'll exclude the sneeze from the "behavior" we're talking about, and if two people talk to each other I'll consider it bad manners rather than bad management; but if two children giggle every time they catch each other's eyes it can become painfully hysterical, beyond control once it starts. Not looking at each other helps, not sitting where they can see each other helps more, not going to the same event is still better. When I watched "The Death of Chuckles the Clown" on The Mary Tyler Moore Show with a group gathered to study a sample of programs, the twenty-minute spasm of uncontrollable giggling spread to many of us viewing it. I'm sure I would have kept my decorum if I'd seen it in private.

### Stark Cases

Science fiction can clarify principles by inventing stark cases. I propose two. The first involves pain. A person is to be subjected to intense pain that will last five minutes no matter what he does, and twenty-five more if he does nothing to stop it. He can stop it after the first five by banging his fist on a button. If he hits the button and stops the pain before thirty minutes are up, the process will be repeated the next day, and the next, forever until he endures thirty consecutive minutes. Any day he lets the pain go on for thirty minutes it will end; it's over forever and he's released. The pain is to be as severe as it can be without making him incapable of hitting the button or unmindful of the button, and if necessary he'll be trained to hit the button when he wants to stop the pain.

I offer three observations. First, there may well be people, possibly most of us, "shortsighted" you may call us (or "high discount"), who cannot endure the extra twenty-five minutes without hitting the button—ever.

Second, if I were the victim and you were my friend and you had an opportunity not to disconnect the pain but to disconnect the button, so that I could pound my fist for thirty minutes and never stop the pain, you would disconnect the button. And afterward I would thank you.

Third, if at any time during the interval I can disconnect that button myself, condemning myself to the full thirty minutes of pain, I expect that I would do so. I hope that I would. And only my worst enemy would reconnect it in time to insure the next pain session.

My second example is less artificial. It is deciding in advance on the circumstances in which one might wish to be dead though in danger of going on living. It is particularly poignant if carrying out the decision will require the help of someone whom I may then beseech to disregard what I earlier decided. I ask you in advance to see that I die if certain conditions befall me and to disregard any change of mind that the fear of imminent death may induce; if I become terrified of dying, you must not prolong my terror. We confront that question, which is the authentic "I"? There are two of me, one who was in command when I made the arrangements, gave the instructions, and warned you not to heed that other one who might surface and speak with my voice when it was time to die. How do we tell—how do you tell—whether this is the moment of truth or the moment of derangement?

This is the problem of authenticity that arises when someone addicted to alcohol, drugs, or cigarettes, or a compulsive over-eater, asks you under no circumstances to heed a plea for a smoke or a drink or a dose or another helping, even if he pleads with tears. Indeed, the more frantically he pleads, the more you may be enjoined to recognize what a horror you perpetuate, while momentarily relieving it if you accede.

Even if at that time I still want to die, I may need help. (I do not believe it possible to hold your breath and die; the urge to breathe overcomes the urge to die, however much you regret it once you've caught your breath.) So I propose this piece of technology. A specific contingency in which many people wish they would die is a massively disabling stroke, a stroke that leaves one bedridden, inarticulate, incapable of recognizing faces. Some of us may wish to die because of the horror or indignity, some to remove a penalty that no one would wish to inflict on the family. Suppose there were a diagnostic contrivance that could be implanted in the brain that, in the event of cerebral hemorrhage, would measure the severity, remaining inactive if the predicted paralysis were less than some limiting value but aggravating fatally any condition above that limit. With the device implanted, I needn't lift my hand to take my own life. You needn't help me, nor need you try to stop me. My doctor can't save me and needn't try. It is prearranged and automatic.

My conjecture is that the device would be attractive to many of us. Further, that it would be less attractive if it were designed so that it could be, and had to be, activated in the event by the victim.

### Management Skills or Moral Fiber

The situations I discussed, including the artificial ones, are background. They are to remind us that there is nothing strange or unfamiliar, let alone mysterious and inexplicable, about people's regarding themselves as problems of discipline, control, or motivation and taking measures: to insulate themselves against stimuli, to disable themselves with respect to actions, to change the rewards and penalties that attach to behaviors, to submit to the control of others, and to surrender the power to decide for themselves on occasions when, their internal mechanisms having changed or become susceptible to alteration, they would make a decision that now they deprecate. If someone can drink alcohol now to be braver in an hour, without straining our credulity that somebody could wish to distort his own perception of what is at stake in a decision he has to make shortly, then his declining a drink now, the better to appreciate what is at stake when he decides in an hour on the chocolate mousse or the cigarette that follows, needn't puzzle us either. It isn't much different from declining to offer a drink to a friend who is trying to quit smoking, when a little alcohol in the blood tends to shift his preferences toward nicotine and away from longevity. Leaving one's money at home in case of thieves on the road, or creditors, or friends in need of loans, is not altogether different, judged as plain financial management, from leaving it at home for fear of the temptation to spend it.

The advantage of looking at self-management in this light is a simple one. There are many tactics and techniques employed successfully or unsuccessfully to influence and constrain the behavior of others. We have some familiarity with them, in diverse areas ranging from child discipline to military discipline, school discipline and religious discipline, athletic training and the care of institutionalized patients, the managing of parolees and, somewhat vicariously through books and movies, the preparation of espionage agents who, for example, can't blurt out under painful interrogation the names of people whose names they do not know or cannot write a recognizable signature if they can arrange to crush a hand in a doorjamb.

What I'm talking about is different from what is usually thought of as self-control or self-discipline. I am not talking about the development of inner strength, character, or moral fiber, or the change in values that goes with religious conversion. Nor am I talking about education in the consequences of behavior—lung and heart disease from smoking, spoiled careers and families and livers from alcohol, higher mortality from abandonment of a medicinal regime for hypertension, or the self-aggravation of habits like card-playing or television.

## Some Distinguishing Characteristics

It is one thing to appreciate the general idea of tactics deployed to protect oneself from oneself, and the ubiquitousness of the problem. It is something quite different to focus on a specific problem, and to do so not to illuminate a general principle but to cope with the mischief at hand. For that we need a systematic way of analyzing the habit or weakness along relevant dimensions: the vulnerabilities of its victim, the environment in which it occurs, and the information, communication, and institutional commitments that can be brought to bear.

I do not know any taxonomy or analytical scheme for finding the similarities and highlighting the differences among the different habits or addictions and the targets they afflict. I can only illustrate the kinds of analytical dimensions I have in mind.

One relates to the timing or "time profile" of the habit or addiction. We can distinguish the afflictions, temptations, or habits that (1) occur at random, unpredictably, providing no free time or "time out" but which are not continuously present; (2) occur cyclically, on a schedule that is physiological or that reflects the daily or weekly pattern of living, or on some cycle autonomous to the habit itself, a cycle of onset and exhaustion and recovery; or (3) are continuous, ever-present, neither waning and waxing nor coming by surprise.

Another temporal dimension is the "time to indulgence," or "onset time." This is ambiguous and yields only an order of magnitude. It is the time from the moment of suggestion or temptation, or of yielding or decision, to the act that constitutes the offending event. It is how much time intervenes during which succumbing can be impeded or the victim dissuaded or a warning sounded or help mustered or some mode of rescue mobilized. For smoking the time is seconds or minutes, according to where the nearest cigarette is; for alcohol it is minutes to hours, according to whether one is at home or on the street, at work or on the tennis court, alone or with somebody, the time of day, and whether alcohol is handy. Scratching takes seconds; eating takes minutes or hours, again as with alcohol depending on whether one is driving on the freeway or sitting in his own kitchen. If only another piece of toast is at issue the time is in seconds.

Here is where abstaining and persevering are qualitatively different. A person can often quit exercising promptly—unless he is hiking a mountainside or rowing far from shore—but it may be possible to resume if you quit. Determined to run a couple of miles you can quit at a mile and a half, but after a few minutes get back on course, possibly doing a little extra for good measure with no irretrievable loss. Unsmoking a cigarette is harder.

Still another measure is "warning time." If there are early symptoms, harbingers of the motivational onset, or signals that precede the stimuli, there may be a period in which protective measures are still available to the victim or to others concerned.

There are physical characteristics by which to classify some substances or compulsive behaviors. Weight and bulk, portability and privacy, are significant. It is easier to carry cigarettes than a coffee pot. Pipe and tobacco are more easily carried in a sport jacket than a tuxedo. People whose addictions require poolrooms or swimming pools, slot machines or record players, television sets, chessboards, card tables, or a bed or bench are not as continuously and universally free to indulge their habits as the people who have their tics and fingernails and eczema always with them.

Money is important. Heroin is "artificially" costly on account of denial; anyone addicted to the best Beluga caviar or the rarest of perfumes has a different problem than someone addicted to chocolate. Indeed if cigarettes cost as much as Havana cigars, there would be little concern about smoking.

Visibility or detectability is important for habits whose indulgence is illicit or disapproved. A couple that cannot resist squabbling may wisely stay among company; lunching where no liquor is served avoids the risk that one can be cajoled into a first drink and thereby lubricated into a second. There is an interaction between legal or social status and visibility or detectability.

Another way to classify a habit or addiction is by the "damage function." Is the risk or damage a cumulative total, or geared to current activity? With smoking, the cumulative total determines lung cancer, and probably current absorption determines the monoxide damage. Behavioral dangers from alcohol—driving, fighting, and abusing children—are certainly current, while damage to liver, stomach, or throat is cumulative. Cumulative damage can be continuous and linear, or there can be some threshold below which the habit is harmless or a plateau beyond which all the harm is done. (This is the same issue that arises with risks of cancer from nuclear radiation or coal-burning emissions.)

With both current and cumulative damage there is the "decay rate." If a smoker quits at fifty, does the risk of cancer or heart disease diminish, relative to what it would have been with continued smoking, or is the damage irreversible? If it declines, does it diminish promptly or slowly, toward zero or some compromise level, and linearly, exponentially, or with what shape over time? Evidently calories, cholesterol, and tobacco are strikingly different in these respects: the distinction between cumulative and current shifts on a time scale of hours, minutes, weeks, or years. Momentary drunkenness is "current" in days but "cumulative" in quarter-hours: The decay rate of blood alcohol, and the tendency of alcohol to be neither imbibed nor assimilated instantaneously but over some fractions of hours, make the process current or cumulative according to our time perspective. Calories and weight are cumulative in the laws of thermodynamics and the time perspective of people gaining or losing; but a professional athlete who trains six months out of the year and relaxes the other six may think of abstinence and minimum weight as concurrent rather than cumulative.

Still another dimension is whether the habit is autonomous or self-aggravating. Is there feedback between indulgence and the ensuing intensity of the affliction? By most reports the withdrawal symptoms of tobacco, especially the craving, diminish but not always immediately, with a "half-life" measured in days for some and weeks or months for others, diminishing to zero for some but remaining above for others. An associated question is the speed with which the habit is reconstructed if the behavior is resumed. Some smokers, but not all, appear to revert virtually to where they were before they quit. It is never reported that a veteran smoker who quits and takes it up again smokes like a novice. So we distinguish, for those who quit some habit, the time scale on which withdrawal symptoms disappear and the (different) scale on which all effects disappear permanently—if they ever do. The controversies over "controlled drinking" for former alcoholics involve these different diagnostic time scales.

Another dimension is consciousness. This, too, is ambiguous. Nobody who smokes is unconscious that he smokes, but smokers do light cigarettes "unconsciously" and "awake" to wonder when they lit them or where they found the matches. But unlike the skin affliction that one can scratch unconsciously any time, cigarettes can at least be left behind or unpurchased so that one is unlikely to smoke unconsciously during a non-smoking campaign. Daydreaming is a debilitating habit for some people, and usually by its nature unconscious. So with posture, speech habits, and a multitude of cosmetic and other mannerisms that can be unconscious simply because they are always and everywhere on instant call. We need terminology to distinguish the person who is consciously losing his temper but unconscious that that is what he is doing. The person who, losing control, is accused of losing it, of overreacting to the occasion, and who answers that his behavior is precisely in accordance with what the situation demands—scolding the child or the waiter or the other driver, raising his voice, losing his temper, fighting the appliance he is trying to repair, or driving with too much abandon—might be said to be "conscious" of his behavior but not conscious of an incongruity of his behavior with its occasion.

## The Size of the Problem

If we think of our subject as part of or akin to economics, we ought, as economists do, to ask whether the problems here are big ones or little ones and how to measure their magnitude. Is it a trivial matter of two or three minutes wasted reading the comics, or of cuticle-picking and hair-twirling and other compulsive "grooming" that represent minor cosmetic ailments or major discomforts, but rank well below arthritis as a scourge? Or is it a substantial problem of health or productivity?

We can try smoking for size. The serious consequences of smoking are heart and lung fatalities. Estimating the social cost of early death from smoking usually leads to the result that the costs are large and fall on the smokers, or on the smokers and those who care about them. But they don't inflict a lot of cost on their fellow citizens, since the incidence of chronic, expensive illness among them—whether paid for publicly through Medicare and Medicaid or shared quasi-publicly through Blue Cross—is fairly low. There's nothing quite like a heart attack for wiping people off the Blue Cross and Medicaid rolls just before they begin to enter the expensive age; it tends also to knock them off just about when they've made most of their contributions to Social Security, but haven't collected much. They die when their children are grown, and don't leave families on welfare. And there's not much to do for lung cancer except ease the pain; it, too, hits at an age, at least historically among its male victims, that pretty nearly minimizes the costs or even maximizes the financial benefits to the rest of the population. So to appreciate the nature and magnitude of the problem that tobacco presents we should measure it for the people who smoke. (Some who do not smoke suffer from the carbon monoxide of those who do, and a few will be burned by hotel fires when a smoker falls asleep, but these do not add to enough to make smoking mainly a problem of "external damages.")

Surveys in the United States and in Britain indicate that most people who smoke—not everybody, but a majority—have tried to stop. The Surgeon General has been warning people for two decades that smoking is bad. Just about everybody knows it. If there were some way that cigarettes could be reliably put beyond reach, and people could vote on whether they would like that done, my guess is that a majority of smokers would elect to deny themselves the possibility of lighting another cigarette. How much might they pay for the opportunity?

Hardly anybody thinks it could be done, and neither alcohol in the 1920s nor marijuana in the 1960s makes the effort look promising. Those who didn't want the ban would offer a market for contraband cigarettes; nobody has an idea how to suppress such a market; and if the market is there the smokers who favored the ban will be little more able to resist cigarettes than they used to be. Even if the abolition were unanimously approved, people would know that if they could sneak in a few cigarettes people would buy them; there would be a black market, and people who wished the market did not exist would patronize it.

But suppose there were a reliable way to quit cigarettes—to quit even wanting them—without torment or suspense or loss of privacy or any restrictions on mobility or any physical side effects. What would it be worth to those fifty million smokers out there, and to some of those thirty million former smokers who may need help to keep from backsliding? Let's postulate an immediate market of thirty million customers for this painless and reliable way to stop smoking or, having stopped, never to return. If the people who wanted to quit smoked as much as those who wished to continue these thirty million would-be quitters would spend about ten billion dollars per year on cigarettes. If smokers expect—in the absence of relief—to smoke another fifteen or twenty years, and if they discount future savings at a "real" rate of interest (after adjustment for inflation) somewhere from 4 to 10 percent per year, and if at a minimum they would value relief from smoking the way they would value the fuel-oil savings from warmer weather, we can put a minimum valuation somewhere around $100 billion. "Minimum" means only the saved *expenditures*.

We can only guess what people would pay to be relieved of the nonfinancial costs associated with smoking—the cleaner teeth and cleaner ashtrays and freedom from a "habit," and especially better health and longer lives—and what people would pay to help spouses, children, parents, and friends be rid of a deplorable and dangerous addiction. We don't know, because they don't know. (Some of "us" are "them" and we still don't know.)

An alternative question is how much smokers would pay for something that, with little impairment of their smoking pleasure, would make the habit safe and so certified by that Surgeon General who otherwise tells us that smoking is dangerous.

My conjecture, which you may compare with your own, is that the worth of being free of smoking, or free of the consequences, is far greater than the financial savings on cigarette purchases. If that is so, the benefit from a suspense-free, torment-free, *reliable* method of quitting, discounted to the present for three-fifths of today's American smoking population, would be a sizable fraction of a trillion dollars. This is only the worth to people who already smoke and excludes our children who, not yet smoking or not yet wishing to quit, might be customers for that reliable self-management regime in another fifteen or twenty years.

I am not thinking of what the market would bear if I could monopolize a nicotine chewing gum that eliminated the need to smoke, merely trying to get some sense of whether there is a consumer problem here of real magnitude.

Smoking is only one of several addictive or habitual behaviors that people engage in, but it is the best example of one that is widespread, meets no known physical need (except for people who have already acquired the habit), is known to be harmful but only in the statistical long run, is hard to quit, and that most people might like to quit, especially if they could be relieved of withdrawal discomforts, *but very likely might like to quit even if they had to suffer withdrawal if only they could be assured of success.*

Going through a little more conjectural arithmetic, I find it easy to arrive at the conclusion that these problems of consumer self-management can easily be on the order of a trillion dollars (lump-sum, discounted value) for the current population of consumers. But it doesn't matter whether you come out with one-third of a trillion or three trillion. On an annual basis, again just for the purpose of suggesting order of magnitude, it is more like one hundred billion dollars per year than ten billion.

What does that make it as big as? These days one is tempted to say it's about the size of the energy problem, but that is a comparison only in gross magnitude and we don't need it if we've already got the magnitude. I propose that people concerned about consumer ignorance, about the inability of consumers to budget, the inability of shoppers, especially poor people, to spend money wisely, and about the consequences of misleading advertising—including the advertising that convinces people they feel bad or smell bad and need something that comes out of a spray can or a medicine bottle—all together add up to no more than the inadequacies of consumer self-management. In other words, if people could reliably do, or abstain from, the things that in their serious mode they resolved to do and to abstain from (or would resolve if they didn't give it up as hopeless), it would make as much difference in the aggregate as if all those other familiar problems of consumer ignorance and budget management could be dissolved away.

## Some Tactics of Control

Let's go back to that New Year's resolution. What is its appeal? Why does it sometimes work?

There is evidently some "investment" in a New Year's inauguration. Since the days of the Druids the midwinter solstice has been a time of new beginnings, not an occasion to be wasted. Fail this time around and you lose a year. Deciding earlier and waiting for the day the leaf is turned affords some psychological preparation. If there is any way that a person can persuade himself that he really means it this time, a birthday or a new year or the first day on a new job offers a discontinuity, a break with the past. There may even be a little magic about it. Doing it at New Year's, even writing it with lipstick on the bathroom mirror or carrying the printed resolution strapped to a wrist, one impresses oneself with the seriousness. It raises the stakes. More is threatened by failure than just the substance of the resolution: one's personal constitution is violated, confidence demoralized, and the whole year spoiled. At least one can try to make it so.

The mechanism is more obvious when one announces to family or carpool the renunciation of alcohol, tobacco, or potato chips—especially when several weeks are devoted to preparing everyone for the starting date. Shame is a deterrent.

Ideally, there might be legal arrangements. One goes to the town clerk and swears out a resolution, paying the cost of publication, posting a reward for evidence leading to one's own conviction for violating the terms of the oath just sworn. I suppose it would be unenforceable, there being neither damages nor a valid contract. But one might authorize "citizen's arrest"—a "Good Samaritan" immunity—inviting the use of all necessary force to keep the pledged party from cleaning out the dish of peanuts, with the prospect of a reward being volunteered in later gratitude. If the courts are closed at the times of day that one self might then sue for release from the involuntary bondage to which the other self has committed him, he successfully makes himself an outlaw for bounty hunters with respect to the particular transgression he forswears. And who can protect his rights if, forcibly prevented at midnight from violating his pledge, he is satisfied next morning with his involuntary salvation (like that boy who sent me to bed without a blanket) and turns down the importunate civil-liberties lawyer.

New Year's is also an answer to the question "When?" The question is especially in need of a firm answer when the correct answer is "already." It is comparatively easy, any old Thursday that one planned to begin getting up an hour early, to perceive clearly when the alarm rings that the weekend is a better time to initiate such things.

Walter Lippmann's "plate glass window" that deters the sidewalk thief—and characterized American troops in postwar Europe—is a useful principle for self-management. Clearly marked lines, unambiguous rules, straightforward principles that cannot be made ambiguous by even the most inspired casuistry, are the stuff with which "salami tactics" are rebuffed. Just as it may be easier to ban nuclear weapons from the battlefield *in toto* than through carefully graduated specifications on their use, zero is a more enforceable limit on cigarettes or chewing gum than some flexible quantitative ration. (There was a time when I allowed myself tobacco only after the "evening meal." It worked well but led to tortured reasoning Thanksgiving afternoon, or flying west across the Atlantic with perpetual afternoon, and it stimulated lots of token sandwiches on leaving the ski slopes to drive home.)

"Precautionary rules" can be effective. Many annoying and unsightly small habits, involving face and fingers, are associated with "precursor" explorations, touchings and fingerings that are resistible themselves but lead unawares to irresistible sequels. The victim is often unaware of the relation between innocuous, non-compulsive behavior, and the trap that it leads to. People who wish to quit smoking sometimes discover that, at the outset anyhow, it helps to give up alcohol too, it being easier to rationalize the after-dinner cigarette when one's thoughts have been clarified by a few glasses of wine. And those wonderful folks who brought us potato chips are so sure of themselves that they dare us on television to eat one and stop. Just as children are best kept away from the water if you don't want them to swim, and infants best taught never to open the cupboard where soaps and poisons are kept, avoiding the cue or stimulus or trigger is important in drug therapy and dietary regimes and in the treatment of gambling fever. I have often wished that for a small addition to my bill the hotel would disable the television in my room during my occupancy.

There is one family of tactics common in interpersonal relations that is peculiarly unavailable, or nearly so, in dealing with oneself. That is deceit. One can indeed throw a key into the darkness where it cannot be found until morning, putting the locked cabinet or the car's ignition beyond reach, but it is hard to hide something and forget where it was hidden, especially when it has to available for finding at some legitimate time.

It is also hard to motivate abstention by tricking oneself to believe that the risks have become truly prohibitive. It is reported by drug therapists to be a source of relief and reduced discomfort to an addict just to know, once the acute stage of withdrawal is past, that there simply is nothing available. Doctors report that when patients are flatly told that their condition makes it imperative they cease smoking at once, the patients quit not only more reliably than when they are left any choice, but far more comfortably. Continual indecision, or continual deciding or resisting temptation, aggravates both the discomfort and the temptation; and anyone who wishes to quit should wish to be told with finality that, though he is healthy in other respects, his next cigarette will kill him. Although his doctor could deceive him—probably won't, but could—he cannot deceive himself, and probably cannot credulously instruct his doctor to deceive him.

Parole systems offer an interesting model. So do the modern

technologies for medical monitoring, including the more fictional devices that ring a remote alarm or release a stupefying drug or electric current upon some kind of arousal in the monitored patient. The parolee who must show up once a day, or phone in every three hours, or stay in somebody's custody on pain of that person's being treated as an accomplice, may be physically able to escape surveillance but deterred by the certainty of apprehension. Whenever the foresworn activity is inherently visible, arranging for no escape from public places may be a sufficient way to incapacitate oneself.

For positive performance there are other tactics, some quite opposite to those for abstention. For example, breaking a large task, such as a Ph.D. thesis, into small pieces to make the goals more proximate and the magnitudes less intimidating, even setting time limits rather than piecework goals, works for some people. Kafka's "Great Wall of China" required motivating people toward a task that could not be completed in their lifetimes; learning a new language, or a new athletic game, eventually entails a long hike on a seemingly infinite plateau. Round-number targets help motivate the joggers; and if there is no unique distance between two miles and five to offer an intermediate goal some runners joyfully discover the metric system with its handy five-kilometer distance. Even the weakness that takes the form of discounting the future—actually, more like averting one's gaze from the future—can be turned to account: medium-distance deadlines look so unthreatening that people welcome them, even plead for them, knowing that without them "today never comes" and the promised task will never be done, perhaps never started.

I have come across an interesting case in which three "people" seem to be involved—three of me or three of you. It is the offering of modest rewards or punishments, and it goes like this. The person tells himself that he may sleep late and skip the exercise regime whenever he wishes but only on condition that he forego lunch, or a favorite program, or a weekend skiing; alternatively he promises himself that every day that he gets up early he can watch five innings of baseball on the tube. Now, this scheme works only on two conditions. First, that the reward or punishment be potent enough to induce the desired behavior; and second, that the "somebody" who wants to turn off his alarm with his eyes closed will believe that another "somebody" will later have the fortitude to administer the punishment or deny the reward, when "they" are really all the same person. People told me it worked; I tried it and found that it could. If A lacks the fortitude to get out of bed, B has the fortitude to do without baseball because C laid down the law at an earlier time. If I cannot directly make myself get up at the alarm, I can nevertheless make myself inflict some worse privation later, contemplating which I get up with the alarm! It sounds like something a decision theorist would describe as "intransitive."

Something similar is involved in a mandatory delay system. Imagine that monitoring device that will inflict pain the moment it detects nicotine in my blood, but that I can disable on three hours' notice. Desperate for a cigarette I throw the switch so that in three hours I can safely smoke. Any time within the three hours I may suffer a resurgence of resolve and reset the mechanism, setting the timer back to three hours. If I can never go three hours without losing control to that tyrant who wants me to quit, he'll get his innings and when he does he'll turn the timer back. But it works on the honor system too. There are people who can wait, but not forever; they allow themselves to smoke (or eat or drink or some other indulgence) whenever they wish, *with a specified delay.* In a moment of truth, realizing they should never have taken such an ill-conceived oath, they declare their abstinence at an end and have only to wait then the specified number of hours to be free. Just knowing that they are never more than three hours from a cigarette helps them avoid panic; they rarely invoke the escape clause, though, and when they do they almost always—before the waiting period is up—withdraw the notice they filed.

That comes close to deception. The patient might not submit to the discipline of waiting three hours if he knew that his petition would be challenged and withdrawn before the three hours were up—that that was the whole purpose of the scheme. Somehow it works, at least occcasionally. How to describe the collusion is beyond me. I have spoken to distance runners who, as exhaustion approaches, pick their stopping places a mile in advance with the rule that any place more distant can be picked at any time before they reach the current target, and once picked even by the most fleeting resolve it becomes controlling. I think I know whose side I'm on, and I'm sorry for him.

One of the central dilemmas of self-management is epitomized by titles like *You Can Stop*. You can, perhaps, if you believe you can, and *Maybe You Can Stop—You'll Never Know Until You Try* is an invitation to failure. Raising the stakes in the game, by investing one's self-respect in a campaign that is sure to try one's steadfastness, is a risky business. Failing in January is worse than failing in April if the New Year's launching was billed in advance as the ultimate test of one's worthiness. Once a threat of reprisal fails to induce the desired behavior and the punishment has to be inflicted, one can only regret the whole attempt. That is particularly true in coercing oneself, when both parties share the same values and feel the same remorse.

Furthermore, the suspense seems to be the worst of it. Continually resisting temptation, watching oneself anxiously, talking oneself to the brink of rebellion and painfully getting a grip, allegedly is itself what eventually becomes unendurable—the anxiety, not the withdrawal, or the anxiety and not the pain of continuing on course or up the mountain. Failure takes the form of a desperate dash to freedom. Not freedom from the pain of continuing, or from the hunger and privation, but freedom from suspense, freedom from indecision—or, better, from perpetual unfinished decision, freedom from intense and unremitting self-regard and responsibility. And in a few cases, such as becoming intoxicated, one escapes the ordeal and the remorse as well.

Ben Hur didn't have to make himself keep rowing. The man with the whip took care of that. Some people who run for exercise discover that the fear of quitting—not the fear of running painfully, but of quitting—becomes so severe that they are tempted to quit to get rid of the fear. Once they've run the course the mental agony is gone and the physical agony bearable; so they treat themselves at the end to a little extra when, anxiety gone and nothing at stake, they can at last run for the fun of it.

Building confidence is part of many regimes. Break a few easy habits before going on to the hard ones; quit a few to convince yourself you can; talk to people who succeeded, not who failed, and "psych yourself" into believing you'll inevitably do it. At least, that's the advice you get from those who want you to try, including those who will help you for money. It apparently enhances the likelihood of success. (Whether it makes failure more catastrophic we're usually not told.)

The empirical science of self-management is not much further developed than the theoretical egonomics. Still, there are grounds for optimism. Since the Surgeon General's findings were first made public, the number of cigarettes per capita stopped increasing and has decreased slightly. The tar content has declined markedly. In my own census group, males aged forty-five to sixty-five, the proportion that smokes is declining 4 percent per year, or one-third per decade, and among males that age who read this book—among males who wear neckties—the residue of smokers is diminishing with a half-life of a decade. (Not dying, just giving it up!) Old hotel employees remember when after an all-day professional meeting they emptied the ashtrays into wastebaskets; now they empty them into an ashtray.

# 4 | Ethics, Law, and the Exercise of Self-Command

A FEW YEARS AGO I saw again, after nearly fifty years, the original *Moby Dick,* an early talkie in black and white. Ahab, in a bunk below deck after his leg has been severed by the whale, watches the ship's blacksmith approach with a red-hot iron which, only slightly cooled by momentary immersion in a bucket of water, is to cauterize his stump. As three seamen hold him, he pleads not to be burnt, begging in horror as the blacksmith throws back the blanket. And as the iron touches his body he spews out the apple that he has been chewing, in the most awful scream that at age twelve I had ever heard.

Nobody doubts that the sailors who held him did what they had to do, and the blacksmith too. When the story resumes there is no sign he regrets having been cauterized or bears any grievance toward the men who, rather than defend him against the hot iron, held him at the blacksmith's mercy. They were not protecting him from an involuntary reflex. And he was not unaware of the medical consequences of an uncauterized wound. Until the iron touched him he knew exactly what was afoot. It was a moment of truth. He was unmistakably all there. He made his petition in clear and understandable language. They had neither personal interest nor legal obligation to subject him to torture. And they disregarded his plea.

When the iron struck he went out of his mind, still able,

though, to communicate with perfect fidelity that all he wanted was the pain to stop. While the iron was burning his body we might declare him to have been not fully present, but until that instant it is hard to claim that he didn't understand better than we do what the stakes were.

Ahab and his wound dramatize a phenomenon that, usually not so terrifying, all of us have observed in others and most have observed in ourselves. It is behaving as if two selves were alternately in command. A familiar example is someone who cannot get up when the alarm goes off. More poignant is someone who cannot commit suicide.

I say only that people act *as if* there were two selves alternately in command. I'd rather not commit myself on whether there really are two different selves or cognitive faculties or value centers that alternate and compete for control. But the ways that people cope, or try to cope, with loss of command within or over themselves are much like the ways that one exercises command over a second individual. Putting the alarm clock across the room is a familiar example. The varied behaviors and decisions that can display this quality range from merely troublesome to deadly serious:

smoking, drinking, drugs
gambling
scratching
eating
beating children while drunk
procrastinating
attempting suicide
exercising
diving off a high board
staying awake
panic
stage fright
spending binge
sexual arousal.

Let me try to be precise about what I have in mind. I shall state what it is and contrast it with some things that it is not.

What I have in mind is an act or decision that a person takes decisively at some particular point in time, about which the person's preferences differ at the time of action from what they were earlier, when the prospect was contemplated but the decision was still in the future. If the person could make the final decision about that action at the earlier time, precluding a later change in mind, he would make a different choice from what he knows will be his choice on that later occasion.

Specifically, if I could decide now not to eat dessert at dinner, not to smoke a cigarette with my coffee, not to have a second glass of wine, and not to watch the late movie after I get home, I would make those decisions because *now* I want *not* to do those things *then*. And I know that when the time arrives I shall want to do those things and will do them. I now prefer to frustrate my later preferences.

Finding ways to anticipate those decisions, to make them irreversibly with the preferences of this moment and not leave them to be made differently when other preferences reign, can be difficult or impossible. *Decision theory* is the science of choosing in accordance with one's existing preferences, maximizing the satisfaction of one's values. When the values that govern one's preferences are liable to be displaced by values that one deprecates, we need in addition something that we might call *command theory*—the theory of self-command, or self-management.

Let me be clear about what I do not have in mind. People can undergo changes in mood. They like different foods at breakfast and at dinner. There are times when they want to hear music, other times when they want to talk, to be alone, to play with children, to play golf, or to go to bed. One can be a warrior during the day and a romantic at night, or absorbed in a laboratory for days on end and then spend a weekend above the timberline. These are not unstable values. Even when someone is described as "a different person" in the evening from what he was during the day, or after a good night's sleep, the different persons are not in a quarrel with each other. If the warrior cannot savor during the heat of battle the gentler nocturnal sport that requires a different mood, he can remember it when he needs to, can appreciate it, and can be sure that when the time comes his mood will respond.

The alternate moods do not discredit each other. They do not deny each other's legitimacy. A conscientious adult is able to allocate resources among these alternating activities and to be considerate of one mood while in another. The fact that my interest in dinner is at a nadir after breakfast does not mean that, asked what I want for dinner, I shall give a negligent answer. Just as a parent can allocate benefits among children, one can be one's own manager or referee and maintain a long-run perspective on his own biorhythms, changing moods, and seasonal interests and not see the alternating moods and interests as contradictions. In economics this is the normal case. Decision theory treats people as able to mediate among points in time.

The contrast between this normal case and the case that I introduced with Ahab is that in deciding this morning what I would choose for this evening, or during summer whether to make reservations for a ski holiday eight months later, I normally want my preferences at that later time to be controlling. Those later preferences, as best I can anticipate them, are the ones that matter to me now. They may compete with the present, if my budget will cover only a seashore holiday this week or a ski holiday next winter, or if I cannot enjoy on Sunday a movie that I saw on Wednesday. But however much those anticipated future preferences about a future action compete for resources with my current preferences about current action, my *current* preferences about that *future* occasion are those future preferences as I foresee them and appreciate them now. There can be competition but there is no conflict.

In this normal case I know that I shall want to watch the movie on television tonight, and I make sure there is TV in my hotel room. In the other case I know that I shall want to watch the movie, and for that reason I ask for a room without television. (I would even pay extra for a room with the TV disconnected.)

The phenomenon that I want to deal with can be described as alternating preferences, or alternating values that are incompatible or uncompromisable. In the normal case there is a dynamic programming self that looks over wants and desires that continually change, anticipating preferences and attempting to satisfy them. It is as if there were a succession of momentary selves, each with its own wants and desires, all under the supervision of a timeless superself, an overall manager or referee who treats the transient selves evenhandedly.

In the case I want to discuss, that superself, that dynamically programming referee, does not exist. Instead, there is a succession or alternation of impermanent selves, each in command part of the time, each with its own needs and desires during the time it is in command but having—at least some of them—strong preferences about what is done during the period that another one is in command. One of us, the nicotine addict, wants to smoke when he is in command; the other, concerned about health and longevity, wants not to smoke ever, no matter who is in command, and therefore wants *now* not to smoke *then* when he will want to. In the normal case a person's sexual interests wax and wane and, subject to the difficulty of imagining or remembering the alternate appetites, one tries to accommodate them. The case that concerns me is the person who some of the time wants sexual satisfaction and the rest of the time wants to be a virgin.[1]

I have tried to describe a phenomenon that generates the problem of self-command, or self-management. Self-management is not unilateral. It occurs in a social environment. People are helped or hindered in their self-management by social arrangements. They have friends who offer cigarettes and friends who chide them when they smoke, hostesses who tempt them with chocolate and hostesses who cooperate with an earlier self by serving grapefruit, firms that advertise temptations and fraternities that support abstinence. There are prohibitions, taxes, regulations, and public education that impinge on self-management. Custom and etiquette are involved. Work environments make a difference. Even strangers can help.

The questions I want to call attention to are those of ethics and social policy. If somebody now wants our help later in constraining his later behavior against his own wishes at that later time, how do we decide which side we are on? If we promise now to frustrate him later, and he later releases us from the very promise that we were to honor despite his release, must we—may we—keep our promise against his express wishes? Should we rescue Ahab from his tormentors? Should people be able to surrender to a "fat farm" that legally may keep them, or legally must keep them, until their weight loss reaches the pounds they specified when they entered captivity? May a majority of the voting population ban dessert in the dining room, or outlaw cigarettes throughout the nation, not to keep others from eating or smoking but to discipline themselves?

In the cases that come quickly to mind, a conscientious by-stander has little difficulty deciding which side he is on, between the two rival selves that occur in a friend or stranger. We excuse or discount what is said or done in anger, under stress or the influence of alcohol. We are expected to protect a drunk person from excessively generous as well as destructive impulses, to impede any momentous and irreversible action like giving all his money away, joining the Foreign Legion, or quitting his job. When begged for a cigarette by someone who we know is trying to quit, or asked for his car keys by someone who is drunk when it's time to go home, we may comply but not without guilt. And we don't hesitate to be forceful with someone who will be late for work if he doesn't get out of bed!

But not all cases offer an easy choice. People trying to lose weight do not receive universal sympathy. A mother is expected to consider it unhealthy for a daughter to starve herself to be skinny, and she and her daughter may have different definitions of "skinny." When the fear of fat takes on the proportions of a phobia, as among anorexic girls who learned to control their food intake by vomiting and are unable now not to vomit, our usual sympathy for abstinence gets a challenge. The dilemma is most poignant in deciding one's obligation when an opportunity presents itself to frustrate an attempt at suicide.

Still, the frequent and familiar cases usually seem to be easy cases, not hard ones. It may be hard to decide how far our obligation extends to someone who asks us in advance to use all necessary force when he has drunk too much to see that he does not become too candid in public about his wife or his employer or his host, or to keep him from driving his own car, or to keep him from drinking any more. But whatever obligation we feel is usually to that earlier self that asked our help and elicited a promise, the one to whom we have to explain our own behavior tomorrow when he's sober, not the one who tells us to ignore the earlier inhibited sober self that never had the courage to speak out about his wife, his employer, or his host.

What are the familiar cases, and how do we decide them? How would we explain to ourselves why we just don't credit the person who refuses to get up in the morning? Why did nobody rescue Ahab, and why did I think that you would agree that anyone who loved Ahab, or even a conscientious stranger, should have held him down?

In some cases the person just doesn't seem to be all there. He is his usual self with something subtracted. The person who prefers not to get out of bed is thought to be not fully alert; his engine hasn't warmed up; he cannot remember or visualize the consequences of staying in bed or assess their importance. We may even believe that there are chemical inhibitors of brain activity that play a role in sleep, and until they have been washed or metabolized away his brain is not working. It is not a different *he,* just an incomplete one. The same may be thought of the person overtaken by fatigue or drowsiness, the person under sedation, and some of the people—the quieter ones—whose brains are awash with alcohol.

Then we have contrary cases, the people who are not only "all there"—but too much. They are overstimulated or exhilarated. There are drugs that will do it, but so will success. So will relief—from anxiety or fear or suspense. In contrast to the drowsy, these people need restraint, not arousal. They can suffer a transient selflessness and generosity, not withdrawal but hyperactivity. If the half-awake person can be described as somebody whose preference map is not fully illuminated, the overstimulated person is like one whose preference map, though illuminated everywhere, is too brightly lit in some places. The contrast has the same effect as partial darkness.

A third case is passion, or infatuation. We have the expression "marry in haste and repent at leisure," and some that convey the same thing more bluntly. But I include anger, patriotism, religious fervor, revenge, disgust, and all of those transient overwhelming moods that elevate certain values to absolute domination. Proposing marriage, joining the army, placing large wagers in support of one's opinion, abandoning one's family, and denouncing one's employer are among the things that may be done in haste and repented at leisure.

Next is capture, or captivation. It is being glued to TV, absorbed in a novel, caught in a mathematical puzzle, engrossed in a symphony, or absorbed in frustration trying to fix a recalcitrant piece of equipment. Fantasy belongs here; some of us are as readily captivated by daydreams as by that late movie or unfinished novel. A simple interruption will sometimes rescue the captive; other times he can still hear the siren song and may be as sneaky as an addict in getting back to that puzzle, story, or daydream.

My next set consists of phobias, panic, and extreme terror. The person who cannot dive off the high board or make the parachute jump, who cannot face an audience without an urge to flee, who suffers vertigo or claustrophobia, cannot make himself pick up a spider, and has to ask someone else to put a kitten to death. I saw a movie in which a Scottish fisherman had his thumb caught in a giant clamshell. The tide was rising. With his knife he severed the thumb. I've wondered whether I'd have drowned before I could remove mine. The friendlier illustration is a child's loose tooth; tying the tooth to a doorknob and slamming the door was the solution when I was a boy, and it illustrates how short the interval may be between the preference that the tooth be yanked and the succeeding preference that it not be.

Some of these are easy cases. But I mean easy to decide, not easy to cope with. If we've come across someone sitting in the winter woods freezing to death, drowsy and feeling no cold, and he refuses to jump to get warm, getting him to do it may be impossible; but deciding whether to obey his command to leave him alone should not be hard.

Some of these cases I no longer find easy. But there are at least some easy cases in every category I mentioned, and I tried to describe them with sufficiently prejudiced language to make you think of some easy cases. I have two more categories. The first is appetite. By that I mean food, drink, tobacco, and any substance that a person can eat or sniff or inject or rub on his skin that generates an addiction or habituation. (I could include here addictive activities, like gambling or golf or the morning newspaper; but they may be more at home in my earlier category of capture than here with nicotine and chocolate.) What keeps these appetites from being easy cases is that not everybody is more likable sober than drunk. Some of the addictive narcotics may be harmful only because they are disapproved and prohibited. And some attempts to quit cigarettes may be so doomed to failure, or to periodic relapse, that surrender is preferable to a fruitless pursuit of victory.

One more category is perseverance. Its obverse is procrastination, quitting. People who set themselves regimes of daily exercise, piano practice, or periodontal care often fall by the wayside. Joggers do not enjoy universal sympathy. Some good intentions abort for plain lack of serious dedication; and people who could bind themselves to a program might in the end find it a bore and regret it. I see all around me, and inside me, the occupational disease of procrastination. Many of us have to burden ourselves with deadlines or short-term goals to get anything written. Social controls play a role; the *Times Literary Supplement* for January 22, 1982, contained a splendid example, a review article by George Steiner on the life and work of the Hungarian radical Georg Lukacs. "When I first called on him, in the winter of 1957–8, in a house still pockmarked with shellbursts and grenade splinters, I stood speechless before the armada of his printed works, as it crowded the bookshelves. Lukacs seized on my puerile wonder and blazed out of his chair in a motion at once vulnerable and amused: 'You want to know how one gets work done? It's easy. House arrest, Steiner, house arrest!' "

Let me reexamine a few of these characterizations. The person who won't get up in the morning I said was not quite all there. Why does that count against him? Apparently because he cannot fully appreciate what it will be like to be late to work. But does the self who sets the alarm fully appreciate the discomfort of getting out of bed? My answer is yes. But notice: I am not in bed. I don't expect that to change your mind, but in more difficult cases I find it important to remind myself that when I think about these issues I am not impartial. I write only when I am awake, and the self that might prefer bed goes unrepresented.

In another respect we are not impartial. We have our own stake in the way people behave. For my comfort and convenience I prefer that people act civilized, drive carefully, not lose their tempers when I am around or beat their wives and children. I like them to get their work done. Now that I don't smoke, I prefer people near me not to. As long as we have laws against drug abuse, it would be easier all around if people didn't get hooked on something that makes them break the law. In the language of economics, these behaviors generate externalities and make us interested parties. Even if I believe that some poor inhibited creature's true self emerges only when he is drunk enough to admit that he despises his wife and children and gets satisfaction out of scaring them to death, I have my own reasons for cooperating with that repressed and inhibited self that petitions me to keep him sober if I can, to restrain him if he's drunk, or to keep his wife and children safely away from him.

And what about Ahab? When I first thought of mentioning him, I thought him a dramatic illustration of an easy case. If I were Ahab, I thought, I would thank you afterward for holding me down. But now I wonder what that proves.

If you hurt somebody so that I may live, my thanking you does not prove you did right. If I say that in Ahab's condition I would like to be cauterized, you will notice that I say it with a fearlessness that makes my decision suspect. It is hard to find a way to call my bluff. I'm not about to be burned. If I were, I'd behave like Ahab, and you would not credit me with now having a full appreciation of where my interest lay.

Suppose I were to be burned and Ahab in the next room were to be burned also. Would you, while disregarding my personal plea, ask my advice what do to about Ahab?

After you burn me and I recover and thank you, you give me the bad news: the other leg is infected and must be burned the same way to save my life, perhaps after a delay. Do I withdraw my thanks, for fear you'll think I want it done again? Does the delay matter?

How do we know whether an hour of extreme pain is more than life is worth? The conclusion that I reach tentatively is that we do not. At least I do not. The question entails the kind of undecidability that many economists attribute to the interpersonal comparison of utilities. Most economists believe we have no way of testing, or even defining, what we mean by whether one person gets greater joy or utility or satisfaction out of a meal or a holiday or a warm room than another person, or out of spending some amount of money, and whether my enjoying something at your expense, my pleasure and your pain, can be added algebraically. That means that if you must cauterize Ahab's leg to keep me from dying, there is no way to determine whether the little two-person society consisting of Ahab and me enjoys a net gain in utility when you spare him the pain and let me die.

The conclusion I come to is that I can no more decide this for myself, if it is I being burned and I dying, than I can decide for two other people.

Does it make it easier or harder if I imagine Ahab to be old, with only a few years of life to save at the cost of an hour's torture? You may well ask, if I have just alleged that a judgment is impossible, how it can then be easier or harder. What I have done is slip into the position that many economists take after acknowledging the impossibility in principle of that interpersonal comparison. It is to acknowledge that as a practical matter we do make decisions. We do not hesitate interminably over whether to favor some extra income for a poor person at the expense of a wealthy person, or whether to give our concert ticket to an enthusiast or to someone who merely likes music. Because we have to, we make such decisions.

So I must conclude that these decisions are not based on utility comparisons. What are they based on? In Ahab's case I think mine is taking sides. Which side am I on? Facing no pain, I seem to be on the side of the Ahab that wants to live. I do not think I know how to make the effort really to decide whether his life is worth the pain. When I try, I find myself succumbing to the pain, and to keep my resolve for Ahab's sake I abandon the effort at comparison.

This ambivalence makes a difference in welfare economics, social choice, and political philosophy. In economics there is a well-explored field of individual rational choice. There has also been an interesting field of social choice, in which the singular behavior of a rational individual is compared with a collective decision. We got used to the fact that in a collectivity there is no unanimous preference; we discovered that majority decision will not reliably point to a collective preference. And with continued work (of which Kenneth Arrow's is most widely cited) we have become convinced (some of us) that it is futile to model collective decision on the analogy of a single individual. I suggest that the ordinary human being is sometimes also not a *single* rational individual. Some of us, for some decisions, are more like a small collectivity than like the textbook consumer. Conflict occurs not only when two distinct human beings choose together but also within a single one; and individuals may not make decisions in accordance with the postulates of rationality, if by individuals we mean live people.

If we accept the idea of two selves of which usually only one is in charge at a time, or two value systems that are alternate rather than subject to simultaneous and integrated scrutiny, "rational decision" has to be replaced with something like collective choice. Two or more selves that alternately occupy the same individual, that have different goals and tastes, even if each self has some positive regard for the other (or one feels positively and the other does not reciprocate), have to be construed as engaged not in joint optimization but in a strategic game. There is no agreed weighting system for taking the alternate preferences simultaneously into account. And even the possibility of bargains and compromises is limited, if not precluded, by the absence of any internal mediator. It is hard for the different selves to negotiate if they cannot be simultaneously present. Not impossible, perhaps, but hard.

Jon Elster proposed, in discussing this essay, that typically one of the "selves" engages in forward planning and strategic behavior, making arrangements to constrain the other self's options, while the alternate self is preoccupied, when in command, only with the current episode. (He proposes that this asymmetry in strategic attitude might be a basis for choosing the authentic self.) In the perhaps rarer cases of reciprocal strategic behavior, each self might engage an attorney to represent it, empowering the attorney to reach an enforceable, jointly advantageous bargain. While this possibility has no legal standing, and, if it did, enforcement of the bargain might still not be manageable, it suggests a conceptual possibility of negotiation between two selves that never exist simultaneously.

So we should not expect a person's choices on those matters that give rise to alternating values to display the qualities typically imputed to rational decision, like transitivity, irrelevance of "irrelevant" alternatives, and short-run stability over time. We should expect the kinds of parliamentary strategies that go with small-group voting behavior, and the second-best choices that have to be made when rights and contracts are not enforceable. Depriving oneself of certain preferred opportunities—suppressing certain states that economists call "Pareto superior"—because the other self would abuse the opportunity becomes an expected tactic:

not keeping liquor (food, cigarettes) in the house
not keeping television in the house
not keeping sleeping pills in the house
not keeping a gun in the house
not keeping the car keys in the house

not keeping a telephone in the house
not keeping the children in the house.

Dramatic cases of a *latent* rather than a *regular* alternate self are the anticipation of a self that will emerge under torture, truth serum, or extreme privation. Less dramatic are anticipated somnambulism and talking in one's sleep, scratching or removing dressings while asleep, and social affairs at which one is likely to lose his temper. Other familiar instances are choosing a restaurant where desserts or liquor are not served or luncheon partners who do not drink, doing embarrassing business by telephone to avoid loss of poise, and leaving money at home to avoid a shopping binge.

There is even a possibility that within a single human body a nervous system and brain and body chemistry can alternately produce different "individuals," no one of which is uniquely *the* person or self. In science fiction a human body can be an arena in which several extraterrestrials play out their careers. When several aliens come to inhabit an Earthling's body, one of them may sleep during daytime and another nighttime, one may have access only to certain memories or sensory systems, and they compete to extend their spans of control over the Earthling body.

Is there anything like this among human beings? Maybe. Surgically an individual is changed into "another individual" through frontal lobotomy. Lobotomy is irreversible as it has been practiced; but in principle one can imagine an irreversible removal (lobectomy) and a reversible lobotomy. With the latter a person alternates between the self whose lobe is deactivated and the one whose lobe is functioning. The changes are described as dramatic enough to constitute a new personality. (The judicial system has had to decide, for purposes such as marriage annulment, whether it is the same person afterward.) Castration was an equivalently potent way of changing hormonally the value system of male human beings. It, too, is irreversible; but if we imagine castration accomplished chemically rather than surgically, it might be reversible.

Possibly the human being is not best modeled as a unique individual but as several alternates according to the contemporary body chemistry. Tuning in and tuning out perceptual and cognitive and affective characteristics is like choosing which "individual" will occupy this body and nervous system. When pressed, I insist only that people can usefully, for some purposes, be viewed *as if* they were two or more alternative rival selves, but the more I reflect on it the more I wonder whether there is any reason for excluding the literal possibility.

The law does not like to distinguish these different selves, or to differentiate an authentic self from impostors. In the United States I cannot go to a fat farm, a non-smoking resort, or an exercise camp and legally bind the management to hold me when I ask to get out. The management cannot claim that it has contracted with the authentic "me" to make me stay, even if my imposter self, the one that I went to the farm or camp to guard against, claims that "I" now want to get out. I can contract that they get no fee unless they succeed in keeping me; but the authentic I cannot sue them afterward for improper release if they let me go when the wrong "I" insists on leaving. And they cannot protect their investment by impeding my departure when that other self gets control and says he is leaving and to get out of his way.

The law does not permit me to write a will that I cannot change, nor promise a gift and be held to my promise. If I think I am potentially dangerous, to myself or to others, the law does not permit me to commit myself voluntarily to the custody or guardianship of an institution that may hold me captive. I have to demonstrate that I am so dangerous, to myself or to somebody else, that I qualify for involuntary commitment. Dr. Jekyll can ask to be locked up for his own good, but when Mr. Hyde says "let me out" they have to let him out.

There are ways of getting around the law, but they do not involve straightforward recognition of a person's right to bind himself against himself. If I think it would be good for me to change my habits and location, to be kept away from people and places I know, to learn discipline, I can enlist in the army. My enlistment is a contract in which the other party has an interest that can be legally protected against my defection. Legally the army is not conspiring with my authentic self to frustrate the other self when it wants to go AWOL.

But if I cannot prevent my imposter self from asserting his (my) rights when it is his turn to be in charge, cannot lock him up against his will or make it a legal offense to sell him liquor, can I nevertheless deny him legally certain faculties that he might exploit when he is in charge? Can I claim that he was impetuous when he made that gift, and I'd like it returned; that he enlisted in a fit of patriotism after seeing an inspiring movie, or as a heroic gesture after being turned down by the woman he loved? Can I claim that he married under the influence of passion or liquor or a biorhythmical euphoria, and the marriage vow should be void? Can I arrange with my bank not to honor his check if he fails to pass a diagnostic test that determines whether he is the authentic I or that imposter? The answer seems to be, not easily. Only very exceptionally. And usually only by claiming and demonstrating some recognized mode of mental incompetence. If I can be proved mentally impaired when I made a bequest, the bequest can be invalidated and you have to give it back; but if I was simply out of my mind with joy, and suffering one of my occasional fits of impulsive generosity, I cannot claim that it wasn't "I" and that the gift wasn't "his" to give.

There are statutory ways of guarding against certain actions that might be taken by one's wayward self. But the ways that I know of merely constitute denial of legal sanction for actions that might be taken impetuously or under duress. The political process itself guards against impetuous decisions by requiring two readings of a bill, time intervals between announcement of intent and consummation of some activity, public notice, and other dilatory procedures. The chief mechanism seems to be mandatory delay, or the requirement that certain things, like marriage licenses, be issued only during daytime hours. Mainly they can guard against decisions taken by an impetuous self that gains control long enough to do the business but not long enough to outlast the delay.

The law can try to help one self guard against the other by protecting private efforts of "third" parties to cooperate with one of them. Surgeons may be privileged to tranquilize the patient who, if his head were clear, would in mid-surgery overrule the surgeon's decision. That of course is taking sides. The law may protect me in restraining you from some impetuous or violent act against yourself, an act that your other self would ultimately deplore. The law may protect me if I restrain you from rushing into the burning building to recover your negotiable securities, the family dog, or one of your children, especially if I unquestionably did it believing it to be for your own good, and more especially if it is judged to have been to your benefit. But I probably cannot get away with kidnapping you to keep you from smoking or from getting tattooed, or to keep you a virgin, although your later recovery will probably protect me from your taking civil action. Recapturing you from a religious cult and washing out your brain is still in undecided legal status. The most serious cases are those that involve, one way or another, actively or passively, taking your own life—one of your selves taking the single life that you share.

Helping you die is not allowed. Attempts at suicide surely must often involve divided selves. The lesser acts that people seem incapable of making themselves perform, including those that involve a palpable phobia, suggest that taking one's own life, except in the most painful or utterly hopeless situations or where it constitutes a desperate act of heroism, is bound to be internally controversial. Two selves alternate in hoping for death or life. The law takes sides. In effect and in explicit intent, the law sides with the self that will not die. Someone who lives in perpetual terror of his own suicidal tendencies can welcome the law's sanctions against people who might be importuned to help with the suicide. People for whom life has become unbearable but cannot summon the resolve to end it have the law against them in their efforts to recruit accomplices. The self that wants to live, if there is one, has the law on its side.

There is a paradox. Full freedom entails the freedom to bind oneself, to incur obligation, to reduce one's range of choice. Specifically this is freedom of contract; and it works through expectations. The behavior of others depends on what they expect of me; by restricting my own freedom of choice I gain influence over the choices of others. The results can be called "cooperation," "immunity," "bargaining power," or even "coercion." A textbook on the legal attributes of corporations emphasizes not only the right to sue but the right to be sued. The *promise* is an instrument of great power, but only if it is believed that one has to keep the promise (or make restitution).

Charles Fried expresses it concisely. "In order that I be as free as possible, that my will have the greatest possible range consistent with the similar will of others, it is necessary that there be a way in which I may commit myself. It is necessary that I be able to make non-optional a course of conduct that would otherwise be optional for me. By doing this I can facilitate the projects of others, because I can make it possible for those others to count on my future conduct, and thus those others can pursue more intricate, more far-reaching projects. If it is my purpose, my will that others be able to count on me in the pursuit of their endeavor, it is essential that I be able to deliver myself into their hands more firmly than where they simply predict my future course."[2]

The law recognizes this principle as long as the promise—the commitment, the obligation, the impairment of one's own freedom of choice—has a reciprocal quality and is *to somebody*, somebody else. The promise requires an addressee. One may not contract with himself.

This is a stunning principle of social organization and legal philosophy. One cannot make a legally binding promise to oneself. Or perhaps we should say that the second party can always release the first from a promise; and if I can promise myself never to smoke a cigarette, I can legally release myself from that promise whenever I choose to smoke. It comes to the same thing.

Charles Fried provided me with the name for what has no standing at law—the *vow*. The vow has standing if directed to a deity, and is enforced by whatever authority the deity exercises. And the vow as an expression of intent can receive social and institutional support if it is recognized by an established church. Religious and fraternal orders differ from the common law in providing moral support, even coercive support, for vows like abstinence, celibacy, penury, and dedication to prayer, good works, and even heroism. But the vow has no standing at law.

People nevertheless seek to make binding decisions through physical constraints and informal social arrangements. People ingest chemical antagonists against alcohol to induce nausea upon drinking. If people cannot lock the refrigerator, they can wire their jaws shut. Devices can be implanted in people that will emit a signal to tell on them if they drink, or immobilize them if they do. Castration and lobotomy have been mentioned as surgical techniques for permanently changing motives and incentives, and there are tranquilizers and negative aphrodisiacs to keep certain fears and passions in check. I have mentioned tying the tooth to the doorknob; one can ask a friend to pull the string instead.

People avoid cues and precursors, the sights and smells that subvert their abstinent intentions; people dare not eat the first peanut, start an argument, begin the novel they can't afford to take the time to read, or turn on the TV because it is harder to turn off than merely not to turn on. The friend who will pull the string attached to the tooth, or extract a splinter, can also monitor calories and police cigarettes, or even push a person out of the airplane to help launch a skydiving hobby. But one can sometimes arrange a coercive environment, like offices in which smoking is not allowed or a job in an explosives factory, or make bets that are informally enforceable about weight control or cigarettes; and there are buddy systems, like Alcoholics Anonymous, whose moral support can be enlisted. We could invent some unconcealable testimony to one's dedication—dyed hair, or a tattooed forehead, imploring bartenders not to serve drinks and waiters not to serve desserts.

But nothing like contract law is available. I am not endorsing the idea that the law should be available to enforce unilateral vows. But there is little speculation about how the law might help and what the dangers and abuses might be.[3]

Actually, there is no a priori basis for confidence that enforceable contract is a generally good thing. People might just get themselves tied up with all kinds of regrettable contracts, and the custodians of legal wisdom might have decided that enforceable contract is a mischief. Suppose promises to second parties tended usually to get people into trouble, so that a wise legal tradition would readily excuse people from promises incurred in haste, or in passion, or in disgust. Duress is recognized; if impetuosity were a problem, legally binding contracts might require something like a second or third reading before acquiring status. It is an empirical question whether the freedom to enter contract, the freedom to make enforceable promises, or the freedom to emancipate oneself from a nicotine habit would prove generally to be a good thing. But the social utility of recognizing the vow, the unilateral promise, through social or legal innovation is not much discussed. It may therefore be worthwhile to imagine what form such legal innovation might take.

A possibility is that the state become an enforcer of commitments that people would voluntarily incur and submit to authority. How would the state enforce my commitment to give up smoking, reading the comics at breakfast, or terrorizing my children? A possibility is that I grant the state a perpetual search warrant: the authorities may enter my home or search my person at any time without warning or court order, confiscating anything they find that is authorized in my original disposition to be confiscated. Another would be to allow denunciation: any observer, or anybody on a list that I authorize, could have me locked up or examined or searched, even punished, I having relinquished rights of cross-examination or immunity. House arrest might be voluntarily incurred; I can be locked up, kept in my home that has been purified of television, alcohol, tobacco, or inventories of food. I can be incarcerated and denied things I want, or required to perform what I want to be required to perform—physical exercise, rapid reading, or writing this book. There could be a parole system: I oblige myself to report daily and be examined for weight, nicotine, heroin, or bloody cuticles. Curfews and placing gambling casinos or bars off-limits to me might be enforced by circulating my picture. I could be obliged to pay forfeit when caught in violation of my vow, giving up money or privileges or freedom; this would be like designing criminal law specifically for those who sign up to be subject to it. I could have license plates that do not permit me to drive at night or that authorize any policeman to stop me and check for alcohol without regard to the First or Fourth Amendments. Or I might legally submit to a guardian; this would be like power of attorney, but would give somebody authority to have me subdued, to command that I not be served, to sequester me without my consent, or to control my bank account and my car keys.

The state might enforce contracts that I entered into for purposes of self-restraint. I make a bet that I will not smoke. A bet is equivalent to a penalty on my smoking. I can already make a somewhat enforceable bet if I bring a friend into it, but if he or she is a real friend, what I commit is respect rather than money, and if he or she is not a real friend and the amount of money is large, I probably do not have to pay because the bet is not enforceable. (Surrendering the money to a third party could help.) Still, the social coercion of bets among friends, especially small groups of more than two, in losing weight or giving up cigarettes is impressive. Insurance contracts might help: that medical insurance should be cheaper for people who do not smoke, because they make fewer claims on their medical insurance, is an idea that has some appeal even though it may not have much logic. (Smoking may kill people less expensively than most ways of dying.) But as an incentive people might be allowed to enter insurance contracts that imposed heavy penalties on proven relapses from declarations of abstinence, if there were unambiguous tests like body weight or cigarette stains that would permit a person to incur a high price for delinquency.

There has recently been some attention to the liability of bartenders for serving drinks to people who were already drunk and subsequently suffered accidents. (There have been societies in which recognizable ethnic or racial types were ineligible for alcohol or other consumer goods—weapons, for example.) We can imagine a category of voluntary outlaws, people who have irreversibly chosen never again to be served liquor, the law cooperating by making it a misdemeanor to serve such a person in a public place or even in private, there being some form of identification to establish liability. There might even be "citizen's arrest" of anyone caught smoking or drinking in public who had voluntarily enrolled among those for whom it is forbidden to smoke or drink.

An innovation might permit people to make contracts from the terms of which they could not release the second party. We contract that you may and must expel me from the airplane if I am unable to make myself jump, when I have signed up for parachute instruction. Or you may keep me in a cell until I sober up, lose weight, or go thirty days without smoking. When I scream to be released there must be some provision for inspection to see what it is that I am screaming about; but when it becomes clear that I am screaming only for cigarettes or heroin, or complaining that they don't feed me enough, the authorities will certify that the contract is merely being enforced and that my screams needn't be attended to any further.

One proposal for a legally binding act of "self-paternalism" has received attention, most recently in an exhaustive analysis by Dr. Rebecca S. Dresser.[4] This is letting a patient give a psychiatrist authority to have the patient committed for treatment to an institution during an episode in which the psychiatrist prescribes such treatment and the patient refuses. In some ways the proposal is the epitome of our subject. It does, however, represent an extreme method, incarceration. All kinds of constitutional rights are impinged on, from the right to travel to the proscription of involuntary servitude. And it abuts the issue of involuntary commitment, which has a long civil-rights history. The careful analysis cited above demonstrates that concern for the merits of the case is only part of the matter; what might appear best for the rights and welfare of such patients could conflict with constitutional principles of much wider scope.

A difficulty with enforcing my vows is that there needs to be somebody with an interest in enforcing the rule on me. If you finance my business and I promise to return your investment, there is no need for the state to take any initiative; you take the initiative if I don't come through. But when I vow to do twenty push-ups before breakfast, even if there are techniques by which to establish whether or not I comply, there is no one to bother unless we make it in somebody's interest to spy on me and denounce me to the authorities. We might offer rewards to people who catch me overweight and bring me in for weighing; that means assimilating the self-directed promise to criminal rather than civil law, which I think is a strike against it.

When I contemplate the aloofness of the law and the needs that so many of us have for help, including legal help, in binding ourselves for our own good—as we can bind ourselves in contractual exchange—I see a gap in our legal institutions. The law has grasped the paradox that freedom should include the freedom to enter into enforceable contracts; it seems to overlook the need that people often have, and perhaps the right that they should have, to constrain their own behavior for their own good. And this could mean, as I have mentioned, either submitting oneself to a personal "criminal law" with rewards for private enforcement, or entering into contracts entailing reciprocal obligations from which one could not release the second party. But having identified an important legal right that seems to be missing, I have to ask myself whether I really think it would be a wise society that permitted me to make irrevocable decisions, or decisions that I could revoke only at a high and deterrent cost. Do I really wish that there were some magical way that I could put certain acts forever beyond reach? Do I really wish that I could swear out a warrant for my own arrest in the event I violate some pledge, offering a large reward and complete immunity for anyone who apprehends me?

It is ultimately an empirical question whether even the right to enter a contract is a good one. If people were continually entering contracts shortsightedly we might want to protect them by requiring every contract to be ratified three times with prescribed time intervals between, to avoid contracts entered in haste. We have laws that deny minors the right to borrow money. We forbid indentured labor. People may not assign their earnings. Involuntary servitude may not constitutionally be voluntarily incurred. One cannot offer a pound of flesh as collateral, even if there is no other security to offer and one is desperate for a loan. But except for some constitutional and paternalistic safeguards, enforceable contract is popular because it has proved itself. Would the legal power of unilateral determinism, of eliminating options, of entering an enforceable vow, prove to be a blessing or a curse?

I do not know; but we can identify some dangers. One is that the wrong self might get the jump and legally protect its power to beat up the kids, keep liquor in the office, get fat or get skinny—I forget which is the "wrong one" here—or never to go jogging again. It is one thing to ask the law to recognize an individual's right to become legally forbidden or legally obligated to engage in certain acts or to live a certain way; it is something quite different for the law to select the authentic or legitimate or socially approved self, and deny Mr. Hyde the right to oblige Dr. Jekyll to keep some of that stuff around that he drinks to become Mr. Hyde, or deny him the right to move away to where Mr. Hyde will have no place to play or people to play with when it is his turn to emerge.

Then, there is changing your mind. I have arranged to pay a forfeit if I am observed smoking, and my informer draws a reward from that forfeit. I later discover that I am terminally ill and may as well smoke; or harmless tobacco is developed; or new research discovers that not everybody is susceptible to the hazards of tobacco, and specifically that I am not, and I'd like to enjoy smoking again. Can we design procedures for backing out of a commitment that was skillfully designed to make it impossible to back out?

There will be unforeseen emergencies in which people who were never to lay eyes on their children again need to see them, people who wanted their licenses revoked need to drive, or people who wanted to be confined need to be released. Procedures that cannot be abused to undo the virtues of the original commitment would have to be devised.

I have heard expressions of concern that struggle builds character and the merchandising of "instant self-control" will weaken the human spirit. I acknowledge the possibility, but cannot help comparing the argument to a similar argument we used to hear against taking the pain out of childbirth.

We would want to avoid frivolous commitments—showing off, momentary demonstrations, excursions into martyrdom while under some kind of infatuation. (I conjecture that the tattoo has been popular among youngsters precisely because it is indelible; it is a permanent mutilation; it is an act of daring, precisely because it admits no change of mind, and shares if ever so slightly the finality of suicide or loss of virginity.)

As both law and medicine deprecate suicide, they both deprecate castration of children. Sterilization is allowed for adults, but I understand that psychiatrists are not at ease about sterilization that may be undertaken for convenience by people who haven't the maturity to appreciate how they may react at a later age. Children under the age of contract can probably be dismissed from these problems; but there is a slightly desperate quality to this whole subject that suggests that this legal opportunity would be of least interest to the people who could best claim sanity, adulthood, maturity, responsibility, and emotional stability.

The objection that appeals to me most strongly is that people may be coerced into "voluntary" self-denial, self-restriction, even self-removal. A Los Angeles judge offered probation to a welfare mother convicted of fraud, on condition that she let herself be sterilized, saving herself six months' incarceration. He was giving her a free option only if—which was doubtful—six months was the sentence he would have given her had her childbearing not been at issue. Employers, parole boards, judges and probation officers, even school admissions and spouses, not to mention various moral minorities in the electorate, may demand assurances of both good behavior and good intentions as conditions for what they can offer, once those assurances are publicly available. Certain rights, like early retirement (even early death), can come to carry some implied obligation. (Imagine an option, perhaps upon application for a marriage license, legally to forswear forever one's right to a divorce. Who could believe it was voluntary?) The "vow" itself, in its more traditional meaning as a profession of faith, was sometimes coerced by the vilest means. (Religious minorities have at least one advantage when the majority religion is one that a person must be born into—no coercive proselytizing.)[5]

Coercion shows up in two ways: the one I just mentioned and the direct act of enforcement. If the government itself is responsible for enforcing the sanctions one has voluntarily incurred, in the manner of criminal law, there is both unpleasantness and an enlargement of that domain of government, the manipulation or harassment of individuals, that many of us like least. Enforcement by a private party, in the manner of civil law, would probably be felt to involve a noticeably lesser governmental role in the coercive enforcement. If damages only, not actual performance, could be claimed, the arrangements might be less effective but less threatening to society. Finally, there is the question whether the government should void or deny or prohibit privately available means of binding ourselves. Thomas Nagel has remarked that few governments any longer make it easy to enter into a permanently indissoluble marriage. Governments might regulate measures that operate directly on the brain. The implantation of devices that monitor behavior, requiring the services of a surgeon, could be discouraged by several means. I tend to feel that the dangers in allowing long-term renunciations of freedom are least when they do not depend on the government for enforcement; that leaves open whether government should deny the freedom to impair freedom where enforcement of contract by the government is not involved.

I do not conclude that the dangers are so overwhelming that we should continue to deny any legitimacy to the demand for legal status for these unilateral self-commitments. But I also do not conclude that we should discover a new disadvantaged minority, those that need help in self-defense against themselves, and acknowledge their right to enlist the law in their behalf. I conclude instead that there are probably innovations along the lines I have suggested, and that with care there might be some tentative exploration, with adequate safeguards and the expectation that it may be years or generations before we converge on a reasonable legal philosophy. The law is still groping for how to cope with rights to life and rights to death, rights of children and rights of the unborn, rights of separated parents, the rights of the emotionally unstable or the mentally retarded, and the proper legal sanctions on drugs, adultery, contraceptive advice to minors, and the entrapment of drunken drivers. There should be no easy solution to this one.

I have spoken of the *legal* status of vows, but the issue could be more broadly formulated as one of social *policy*. The method could be legislative as well as judicial. Bartenders have been found liable for serving drinks to people who had already drunk too much and went on to get themselves destroyed by automobiles. The liability has been established by legislation as well as by judicial interpretation. There have been and are societies in which particular kinds of individuals may not be served alcohol; what would be new is the provision for voluntarily putting oneself, perhaps with some indelible mark like a tattoo on one's forehead, in the statutorily recognized category of persons who may not be served.

The law aside, there are difficult discriminations in determining the authenticity of a request for help in somebody's dying.

If your moral convictions never permit you to help someone die, or even to let someone die in the belief that that is what he wants, no authentication is necessary, no request being admissible no matter how authentic. But if you wish to credit a request to be allowed to die, or a request to be helped to die, authenticating the source of the request—which self it is that is in command and controls the decision to make the request—is certainly important and probably difficult.

It is hard to imagine there being no question of authenticity. Death is so complete, so final, so irreversible, that a self that controls the decision may be unable to command the action. Inability to produce one's own death does not seem to be reliable evidence that one "really" prefers to live, any more than inability to cut one's own thumb out of its socket testifies to one's preferring to drown. Even asking for help may be subject to inhibition, and only a transient surge of determination could galvanize it. And although the self that is created by that transient surge may be the one that deserves recognition, it is not the only self involved.

We are dealing with an even more unambiguously "divided self" when the requests vacillate. To plead in the night for the termination of an unbearable existence and to express relief at midday that one's gloomy night broodings were not taken seriously, to explain away the nighttime self in hopes of discrediting it, and then to plead again the next night for termination, creates an awesome dilemma.

How do we tell the authentic self? Maybe the nighttime self is in physical or mental agony and the daytime self has a short memory. Maybe the daytime self lives in terror of death and is condemned to perpetuate its terror, by frantically staying alive, suppressing both memory and anticipation of the more tangible horrors of the night. Or perhaps the nighttime self is overreacting to nocturnal gloom and depressed metabolism, trapped in a nightmare that it does not realize ends at dawn.

The search for a test of the authentic self may define the problem wrong. Both selves can be authentic. Like Siamese twins that live or die together but do not share pain, one pleads for life and the other for death—contradictory but inseparable pleas. If one of the twins sleeps when the other is awake, they are like the two selves that alternate between night and day.

That both selves are authentic does not eliminate the issue. We must still decide which request to grant. But if both selves deserve recognition, the issue is *distributive*, not one of *identification*. We can do cost-benefit analysis and try to maximize their joint utility. But it is *we* and not *they* who are concerned with joint utility. The need for commensurable utility, for adding the desires of the one and the desires of the other, is like the need, under the authenticity formulation, for assessing the probabilities and the severities of the two errors: wrongly crediting the plea to die and wrongly crediting the plea to live. If the nighttime self is authentic we commit error in heeding the daytime self; but also vice versa. In the absence of certainty about which self is authentic, we have something like the distributive issue of dealing fairly with two selves that have opposite needs.

In discussion I find that people's responses to a hypothetical ambivalence about wanting to live and wanting to die are sensitive to the way the alternative preferences are described. If the choices are presented symmetrically—a strong desire for life expressed at some times and a strong desire for death at others—people, while recognizing a grave conflict, elect to credit or defer to the voice in favor of life. But descriptions of actual patients who display the ambivalence often lend themselves to an alternative, nonsymmetrical formulation: a preference for *death* and a horror of *dying*. Death is the state; dying is the act, the transition. Dying is the terrifying, gruesome, violent, and possibly painful event.

Presented this way, the choice can be compared to Ahab's. Ahab can enjoy permanent relief—minus a leg, to be sure—only by undergoing a brief, horrifying interval of torture, much as the permanent relief of death can be achieved only through a brief, horrifying interval of possibly painful exit. Of course the person whose momentary preference is dominated by the terror of dying may not cooperate in making this discrimination for us. Indeed he or she may misrepresent, even to himself or herself, the terms of the choice, just as patients who face a frightening trip to doctor or dentist may misrepresent their symptoms. In somewhat the same way, the novice parachutist might be described as badly wanting *to have jumped* while frightened of *jumping*.

What about a promise made with certainty about the currently authentic self—authentic at the time the promise is made—to disregard the alternate self that may make an appearance? I ask you to promise to let me die, if necessary to help me, even to make me die, in certain gruesome and degrading circumstances that I specify in detail. Your promise is to disregard any countermand. No matter how much I plead to be left living, you are to honor your obligation. And I urge you to contemplate, if tempted to heed the countermand, that it may be the voice of a terrified self that is incapable even of letting its terror be terminated.

The worst happens, and I plead persuasively. I claim that the self that demanded my execution couldn't know what I know now.

The same dilemmas can arise for pain rather than death. But the miraculous progress of anesthesia in our society makes Ahab's predicament uncommon, while the miraculous progress in medical life support is increasing the concern with dying.

If I can get relief from chronic pain only through an interval of acute pain and I cannot be sufficiently anesthetized to keep me from screaming for relief and pleading that the surgery be discontinued, there arises the ethical question. Do you let me change my mind when I discover how painful the ordeal really is that I committed myself to before I could ever know what it felt like to be in such pain? Or do you take note on my behalf that pain is short and life is long—or that pain will be past and life will be ahead—and not bother even to measure my pain's intensity?

Dying, killing, and suicide are unlike pain, confinement, disablement, and even torture, which, however horrendous, have a finiteness that death lacks in our culture. Imagine a patient allergic to anesthesia solemnly signing a request before witnesses that the operation about to be embarked on proceed irrespective of the patient's vehemently expressed later wishes that the pain and the operation stop. I expect the surgical team to abide by the request, secure in the belief that no punitive action could be taken against them until the operation had been completed and the pain had subsided, by which time the patient's original self, the one that signed the request, would again be gratefully in charge. I can even more easily imagine the surgeon's assuring the patient that the operation requires confining his head so that no request could be voiced, and confining his head, whether it were necessary for the surgery or not. (The rule might be: anesthetize the tongue if you cannot anesthetize where it hurts.)

Our thinking on this may be affected by the observation that, at our ages, examples of unbearable pain are usually episodes, like surgery or cauterization. But when protracted intervals of pain are the lifetime price one pays for mobility or even for just living, doctors have to cope with patients who occasionally can't take it any more and who ask in desperation that the source of the pain, life itself, be removed.

We probably would not hesitate to deny the request if it were a child. (It may be easier to cope with adults, especially elderly adults, the more childlike they become when at the mercy of a physician.) I don't know whether that is because we assume that the child's current self has a poor appreciation of the future, and other successive selves may be grateful that the younger self was not allowed to make that decision before they came on the scene. How many later selves have to endorse that early decision before we count a quorum and let those who have now spoken have their way at last?

Pain is often the obverse of dying. Dying is just the back side of the coin, when removing the source of the pain means removing life from the body. There is no later grateful self to express satisfaction if the doctor withholds relief, and no self able to thank him if he complies.

For centuries people were terrified by Hell, a condition worse than life itself, one that awaited after death, an inescapable sequel to which self-destruction made one especially susceptible. Death was no escape. But the audience for these remarks probably believes that death is the end of pain, an exit, not the entrance to an eternity of horror. And whatever the morality of suicide, it is probably not thought by many in my audience to be punishable by eternal damnation.

But the medical ability to keep people alive, to keep them alive irrespective of their wishes or despite them, and the legal obligation or ethical compulsion to do so—the obstinate unwillingness to recognize a right to death as well as a right to life—may have recreated Hell. While science and enlightenment were emancipating us from Hell after death, medical technology has recreated Hell as an end-stage disease. And our social institutions have made it a fate not easy to escape.

But expressing a wish to die or to live, when circumstances are tragic enough to make the choice genuine, is subject to multifarious dimensions of authenticity. The preferences themselves may not be voiced. Just as a person may be incapable of the initiative to commit so awesome an act, a person may be incapable of speaking about it. If the decision requires moral support or intellectual guidance, if one needs advice or at least an opportunity to discuss it, there is no way to discuss it without engaging another person; and the other person will be an interested party, perhaps himself unable to identify or to authenticate an expressed preference. Anyone intimate enough to be asked for help, even in arriving at a decision, is likely to have a selfish interest in the outcome, one that may conflict with his interest in identifying the authentic wish of the person whose death is at issue.

If I am the unhappy patient, I may prefer to live but wish to die to stop being a burden to you. I may not want to burden you with guilt if I choose death or to suggest that I think you resent my living. I may not be able to ask you to help me die to relieve you of the burden of me. And if I wrongly think you will benefit from my death, how can you persuade me my belief is wrong?

If you genuinely believe I prefer death, how can you be sure your own preferences are not mingled in your judgment of what is best for me, or of what I think is best for me? How can you avoid being suspected, even by legal authorities, of excessive zeal in helping me to relieve you of me? May the legal availability of a right to invite death acquire the character of an obligation? How can you keep your willingness to help me reach a decision to die from being, or appearing to be, an effort to persuade me? And how do several interested parties—kin and medical attendants—participate in the decision when they are themselves in dispute about the death and about responsibility for it?

There is no graver issue for the coming century than how to recognize and authenticate the preferences of people for whom dying has become the issue that dominates their lives. This is the ultimate dilemma of authenticating the self, of discovering the legitimate sovereignty of the individual.

# 5 | The Life You Save May Be Your Own

**T**HIS IS A treacherous topic, and I must choose a nondescriptive title to avoid initial misunderstanding. It is not the worth of human life that I shall discuss, but of "life-saving," of preventing death. And it is not a particular death, but a statistical death. What is it worth to reduce the probability of death—the statistical frequency of death—within some identifiable group of people none of whom expects to die except eventually?

Worth to whom? Eventually I shall propose that it is to the people who may die, or who may lose somebody who matters to them. But the subject is surrounded by so much mystery, sentiment, moral consideration, husbandry, and paternalism that some of the fringe issues need to be discussed first, if only to identify what the subject is not. Some of these issues are exciting, more exciting than the economics of life expectancy. They involve the special qualities that make an individual's life unique and his death an awesome event, that make hangmen's wages a special market phenomenon and murder the only crime worth solving in a detective story.

The first part of this essay examines society's interest in life and death; the second surveys the economic impact of untimely death, viewing death more as a loss of livelihood than as a loss of life, seeing how the losses and any possible gains are distributed among taxpayers, insured policyholders, and others who have no personal connection with the deceased. The third part deals with the consumer's interest in reduced mortality and how that interest can be identified, expressed, or allowed for in government programs that, at some cost, can raise life expectancy. It is here that we recognize that life as well as livelihood is at stake. So is anxiety, and the life at risk concerns the consumer personally.

### Social Interest in Life and Death

"Pain, fear, and suffering," we are told, "are considered of great importance in a society that values human life and human welfare."[1] They are important, too, to ordinary people who do not like pain and suffering. We have been told that the value of a human life ought to be considered, at least partially, without regard to whether the person who might die is a producer or not, that this value should result from a collective decision concerning the "expense that the nation is willing—as a moral judgment—to undertake, to save one of its members."[2] Why a moral judgment? Why not a practical judgment—a consumer choice—by the members of society about what it is worth to reduce the risk of death? Is death so awesome, so frightening, and so remote, that in discussing its economics we must always suppose it is someone *else* who dies?

What is moral about wanting to live? People who do not care at all for each other, or for society, or for the value of human life, will take care to avoid pain and death. Why should it require a moral judgment for me to hire a policeman to protect my life, along with the lives of my neighbors who pay their share of his salary, but a purely economic judgment to hire him to protect my shop window, my payroll, or my automobile?

"For a variety of reasons it is beyond the competence of the economist to assign objective values to the losses suffered under [pain, fear, and suffering.]"[3] The same is true of cola and Novocain, one of which puts holes in children's teeth and the other takes the pain out of repairing them. If they were not for sale it would be beyond the competence of economists to put an objective value on them, at least until they took the trouble to ask people. Death is indeed different from most consumer events, and its avoidance different from most commodities. There is no sense in being insensitive about something that entails grief, anxiety, frustration, and mystery, as well as economic privation. But people have been dying for as long as they have been living; and where life and death are concerned we are all consumers. We nearly all want our lives extended and are probably willing to pay for it. It is worth while to remind ourselves that the people whose lives may be saved should have something to say about the value of the enterprise and that we who study the subject, however detached, are not immortal ourselves.

## INDIVIDUAL DEATH AND STATISTICAL DEATH

There is a distinction between individual life and a statistical life. Let a six-year-old girl with brown hair need thousands of dollars for an operation that will prolong her life until Christmas, and the post office will be swamped with nickels and dimes to save her. But let it be reported that without a sales tax the hospital facilities of Massachusetts will deteriorate and cause a barely perceptible increase in preventable deaths—not many will drop a tear or reach for their checkbooks. John Donne was partly right: the bell tolls for thee, usually, if thou didst send to know for whom it tolls, but most of us get used to the noise and go on about our business.

I am not going to talk about the worth of saving an identified individual's life. Amelia Earhart lost in the Pacific, a score of Illinois coal miners in a collapsed shaft, an astronaut on the tip of a rocket, or the little boy with pneumonia awaiting serum sent by dogsled—even the heretofore anonymous victims of a Yugoslavian earthquake—are part of ourselves, not a priceless part but a private part that we value in a different way, not just quantitatively but qualitatively, from the way we measure the incidence of death among a mass of unknown human beings, whether that population includes ourselves or not. If we know the people, we care. Half the entertainment industry and most great literature is built on this principle. But our concern in this essay will be statistical lives.

We must recognize, too, that the success of organized society depends on traditions, attitudes, beliefs, and rules that may appear extravagant or sentimental to a confirmed materialist (if there is one). The sinking of the *Titanic* illustrates the point. There were enough lifeboats for first class; steerage was expected to go down with the ship. We do not tolerate that any more. Those who want to risk their lives at sea and cannot afford a safe ship should perhaps not be denied the opportunity to entrust themselves to a cheaper ship without lifeboats; but if some people cannot afford the price of passage with lifeboats, and some people can, they should not travel on the same ship.

The death of an individual is a unique event. Even an atheist can wish he had been nicer to someone who recently died, as though the "someone" exists, which the atheist believes he does not. If death truly is final, it is only so for the person who dies. Whatever the source of the mystery, most of us have very special feelings about suicide and euthanasia, birth control and abortion, bloodsports and capital punishment, and there is no way to deny these feelings in the interest of "rationality" without denying most of what makes us human. We go to great lengths to recover dead bodies. We give a firing squad one blank cartridge so that every member can pretend he did not take a life.

*Responsibility* for death introduces special problems. A man can be sent on a mission or on repeated missions with small probability of survival, but sending a man to certain death is different. The "chance" makes the difference, apparently because people can hope—the people who go and the people who send them. Guilt is involved; one of the reasons for having a book of rules about when to run the risk and when not to—when to land the disabled aircraft and when to abandon it and take to parachute—is to relieve the man who gives the orders, the man in the control tower, of personal guilt for the instruction he gives. Safety regulations must be partly oriented toward guilt and responsibility. A window washer may smoke on the job until he gets lung cancer and it is no concern of his employer; but his safety belt must be in good condition.

To evaluate an individual death requires attention to special feelings. Most of these feelings, though, involve some connection between the person who dies and the person who has the feelings; a marginal change in mortality statistics is unlikely to evoke these sentiments. Programs that affect death statistically—whether they are safety regulations, programs for health and safety, or systems that ration risk among classes of people—need not evoke these personal, mysterious, superstitious, emotional, or religious qualities of life and death. These programs can probably be evaluated somewhat as we evaluate the commodities we spend our money on.

What is the alternative to death? It depends. For the paralytic it is a life of paralysis; for someone who escapes a highway accident it is the same life as before, unless the near miss changes his behavior. The type of risk that might be reduced is likely to be correlated with age, sex, income level, number of dependents, and life expectancy. Any program that reduces the risk of death will be discriminatory. Infant mortality affects infants and those who have them; motor accidents affect people who use the roads; starvation kills the poor; and a regulation that surrounds swimming pools with fences will affect different age groups according to the height of the fence. Even lightning is not random in its choice of victims—golfers are more at risk than coal miners—and any analysis that initially ignores the specific group affected has to be adaptable to the specific deaths that would be averted by a given program.

Where does the problem arise? It arises in disease, road accidents, industrial safety, flood control, the armed services, safety regulations, personal protection, and all the things that people do that affect their life expectancy. In the marketplace it arises in the choice of hazardous occupations, in home safety, in residential location and in risky everyday enterprises like diving and swimming. It is often hard to discern, though, or to separate, the things that people do to save their own lives or that governments do to save the lives of citizens, because mortality is so closely correlated with other things that concern people. We eat for satisfaction and avoid starvation, heat our homes to feel warm and avoid pneumonia; we buy fire and police protection to save economic loss, pain, embarrassment, and disorder, and in the process reduce the risks of death. When we ride in an airplane, death is about the only serious risk that we consider; but if we compare an advanced country with a backward one the difference in safety to life is correlated with so many comforts, amenities, and technological advances that it is hard to sort out life-saving and life-risking components. The impact on life expectancy of, say, the electric light, is so cumulative and indirect that it would hardly be worth sorting out if we could sort it out. The universal employment of snow-blowers would spare us all those heart attacks that the newspapers so faithfully report after a blizzard; but what number of us would eventually die younger for lack of exercise is not so readily estimated.

Who loses if a death occurs (or has to be anticipated)? First, the person who dies. Exactly what he loses we do not know. But, before it happens, people do not want to die and will go to some expense to avoid death. Beyond the privation that death causes the person who dies, there is the fear of death. The anxieties are visible and are real. Few who are sentenced to die, or have received the announcement that their deaths are inevitable, seem to consider those last few days or months the best of their lives. We may be in the grip of an instinct that has value for the race and not for the individual; but if we ask who is willing to make an economic sacrifice to prevent a death, in most societies there is at least one unequivocal answer: the person who is to die. By all the standards that economists take seriously, the prospective victim loses.

Second, death is an event—and the prevention of death a consumer good—that in our society inextricably involves the welfare of people close to the person who dies. Death is bereavement and disturbance of integral small societies—families—where people play roles that are often unique and always difficult for others to fill.

Finally, there is "society"—other people. They can lose money or save as a result of a death with which they have no personal connection. In a few dramatic cases—the inventor of a wonder drug, a poet, statesman, or a particularly predatory criminal—the impact of a death may be out of all proportion to the victim's personal economics—to his earnings, expenditures, taxes, and contributions, and to his exploitation of public programs and facilities. The rest of us, though, are known to the economy mainly by the money we earn and spend and the money that is spent upon us; and an accounting approach will uncover most of the impact.

Death is a comparatively private event. Society may be concerned but is not much affected. There is a social interest in schools and delinquency, discrimination and unrest, infection and pollution, noise and beauty, obscenity and corruption, justice and fair practices, and in the examples men set; but death is usually a very local event. The victim and his family have an intense interest; society may want to take that interest seriously, but it is hard to see that society has a further interest of its own unless, as in military service or public orphanages, there is an acknowledged public responsibility. Society's interest, moreover, may be more in whether reasonable efforts are made to conserve life than in whether those efforts succeed. A missing man has to be searched for, but whether or not he is found is usually of interest—intense interest, to be sure—to only a very few.

But the taxes we pay and the school lunches we eat have their impersonal ramifications and can motivate someone else to take an economic interest in our longevity. The accounting for those ramifications is the subject of the next section.

### Economic Interest in Lost Livelihoods

When we consider the costs of a death to society—the costs that might be decreased by a program that reduces deaths—it is as important to discover where the costs fall as to aggregate them. There is a convention that nations are the bases of aggregation, but costs can be local, regional, or national; they can fall on particular sectors of the economy, particular levels of income, particular groups of taxpayers or welfare recipients.

Especially if there is an opportunity to prevent the death—to reduce the incidence of death within some part of the population—there is as much interest in who would have borne the cost of the death as in what the total cost would be. First, interested parties may have to be identified, to persuade them that they should bear the cost of reducing some mortality rate. Moral judgments are fine, but in the end it may be airline passengers who want more air safety, parents who want children better protected, Oklahomans who want better tornado warning; it is worthwhile to identify the people who might care enough to do something about it. Second, if the losses are to be compensated, their location and size must be known. Third, if a sense of justice or social contract requires that the beneficiaries pay for the benefits, we want to know who benefits.

Someone may care about the effect of a death on the gross national product, though I doubt that anyone cares much. Still, the GNP is so often taken as the thing we care about that at least passing attention should be devoted to the aggregate effect of death and its postponement on the economy.

#### POPULATION ECONOMICS

At the GNP level, death is mainly a matter of population economics. Population has both a territorial and a national significance. The GNP was raised when Hawaii and Alaska were assimilated; it could be raised more by bringing Canada into the

United States. This is a purely "national" consideration, having to do with the virtues of being a big country.

There may be scale effects in efficiency or in the provision of public services, but it is hard to tell whether the United States is richer as it becomes more dense and more congested. Military considerations aside, it is not obvious that in a country like this the number of people makes much difference.

If it did, we would probably have a conscious policy of migration. We might also have a conscious policy of family incentives, subsidizing children or taxing their parents or designing social security programs to give incentives for larger or smaller families. It is hard to escape the conclusion that if people are what we want, programs to reduce mortality are a sluggish way to get them.

A question that has received some attention in efforts to put a wealth value on human life is how to calculate the worth of a child. There has been, it is often observed, some investment in the child, and, with accrued interest, this investment is lost if the child dies. Alternatively, the child will produce income in the future; and though the investment is sunk, the future income is lost if the child dies and his discounted net contribution, positive or negative, goes with him. This is complicated: if he lives he will produce and he will procreate; if he dies he may leave dependents of his own.

I doubt whether this kind of population economics is worth all the arithmetic. At best, it is the way a family will deal with the loss of a cow, not the loss of a collie. Though children are not pets, in the United States they are more like pets than like livestock, and it is doubtful whether the interests of any consumers are represented in a calculation that treats a child like an unfinished building or some expensive goods in process. At best, this would be relevant to a kind of replacement cost; but it tells little about the cost of replacement—whether a newborn baby is as good as a teenager if you cannot have the particular teenager whose death caused grief and loneliness.

No. Population economics is important, but if lifesaving deserves our attention, it is in some other context.

## ASSESSING THE COSTS OF A DEATH

If a lonely, self-sufficient hermit dies—a man who pays no taxes, supports no church, is too old for military service, and leaves no dependents, owning nothing but a burial plot and a prepaid funeral—there are no costs or benefits. Whatever he would have paid to make his life safer and to increase his life expectancy, he is dead now and no one knows the difference.

If a Harvard professor dies—a taxpaying man with a family, who contributes to the United Fund and owns twice his salary in life insurance, is eligible for social security, and has children who may go to college—the accounting of gains and losses is complicated.

The largest losses will fall on his family, and we should distinguish at once between his life and his livelihood. His family will miss him, and it will miss his earnings. We do not know which of the two in the end it will miss most, and if he died recently this is a disagreeable time to inquire. Let us for the moment leave aside the grief, the loneliness, the loss of direction or authority in the family, the emotional privation, and all the things the man represented except his income. The reason for leaving them out at this point is not that they are unmeasurable, or none of our business, but that they are nontransferable and nonmarketable, and there is no "accounting" way to estimate them. For the moment look at the material losses, and get the pure accounting out of the way.

How much of the loss of livelihood falls on the family depends on institutional and market arrangements. In an extremely communal society or an extremely individualist one, there may be a rule or tradition for sharing the loss: orphans may be supported by contributions, rotated among the neighbors, taken in by next of kin, absorbed in a communal orphanage, or otherwise supported at the expense of society at large or of a select responsible group. Alternatively, life insurance may accomplish somewhat the same thing. Whether a "protective benevolent society" is a genuinely fraternal institution or a modern insurance company with a quaint name, the effect is to share the costs.

It is somewhat arbitrary to say that the cost "really" falls on the family and the rest is redistribution, or the cost "really" falls on the committed members of the community, or on the policyholders whose premium payments will reflect the death. The family, the community, and the insurance market are all social institutions characterized by a system of enforceable or honored obligations; and it is a matter of social choice whether, in addition to identifying the child with its father, its consumption is identified with his earnings. The important question is who pays the costs or suffers the losses, not which losses are original and which are transferred.

Who pays the cost of the professor's insurance, and how much do they pay? Policyholders pay it, in proportions that reflect the sizes of their premiums and, if the man was in a preferred-risk or other special category, the actuarial correlation of his mortality class with theirs. The extent to which people share the burden of lost livelihoods in society is not altogether determined by social philosophy and legislation but can be determined by individual choices in an organized market where people can hedge against death somewhat the way they can hedge against crop failure, inflation, or fluctuating exchange rates.

As a matter of fact, policyholders all have quite a stake in each other. Through an impersonal market mechanism they have placed bets—each in his own way—on their lives and collectively have arranged to share some of the burdens of an individual death. There is no logical limit to this process, at least until pecuniary suicide, or homicide, becomes a problem and a limit must be placed on the bets. Up to the point where death becomes financially attractive, life insurance offers a straightforward way of identifying a group of people who have a financial interest in each other's longevity, and to whom the cash value of improved mortality has an unmistakable meaning. (Insurance-company campaigns to keep us from getting fat reflect this interest.)

### INSURANCE AND NATIONAL POLICY

In the United States there is no national policy on life insurance, as there is for retirement, unemployment, and certain kinds of medical care. (There is life insurance in Social Security, but it appears to be more a by-product of retirement than an explicit survivors' program.) There is, in some states, mandatory liability insurance for people who drive cars; there is not, except under Social Security, mandatory life insurance for people who bring children into the world. If you are hit by a car, your right to collect damages is recognized in some states by a law obliging the driver to have made financial provision in advance; if you are merely born, and have the bad luck to lose your father, the law has not obliged him to make financial provision for you.

If there were a national policy on life insurance, it could be interpreted as a national policy on sharing the financial losses that result from someone's death. (In fact, if there were mandatory life insurance in an amount determined by a person's income, life insurance could almost be dispensed with by merely revising the tax schedules. This is what, to a large extent, is done with retirement insurance.) If that were done, the cost of a person's death to the nation at large would be substantially reflected in the survivors' benefits paid out under the program, plus the lost taxes.

If one thinks that everybody with dependents ought to be "fully" insured—that his death should not affect the standard of living of his dependents—then one presumably believes that the full loss of a person's livelihood to his family is a proper burden for the nation and ought to be an actual burden for the nation. It should then be worth at least as much to society to keep the person alive as to replace his family's share in the livelihood he earns. (One also then presumably believes that the actuarial cost to the nation of a person's having children should be an actual cost to the person, in the form of taxes or mandatory premiums, though one can probably adduce other considerations for redistributing the taxes or premiums.)

One who believes instead that insurance is a private matter, not one for national policy or government intrusion, should concern himself with whether the market for life insurance is well organized and consumers are properly knowledgeable, and with how policyholders—the people who pay the premiums that are geared to mortality rates—get their interests represented, or could get their interests represented, in government or private programs that reduce the risk of death.

Policyholders constitute an enormous potential lobby with an interest in saving lives. And like the beneficiaries of any government programs—programs to prevent property damage, to reduce congestion, to improve communication or to reduce transport costs, to raise agricultural productivity or to preserve the fisheries—they are a biased sample of the population and cannot claim, any more than other groups can, that what is good for policyholders is good for the country.

NONCONTRACTUAL CLAIMS

Less contractual, but somewhat like insurance, are a variety of claims on relatives, friends, and welfare agencies. The family may cease to be a net contributor to a church, possibly become a beneficiary. The children's eventual claims for college scholarships will be enhanced, unless they are obliged to give up college altogether. The United Fund, the Girl Scout Cookie Drive, time volunteered to civic programs, and all the other informal taxes and transfer payments that people participate in will be affected. These are not trivial: there are crude data to suggest that the impact of voluntary "social security" and voluntary "taxes" are at least of the order of magnitude of, say, a fairly progressive state income tax.

It is interesting that some of the claims a person's dependents may make on others are themselves insurable, although brothers and sisters apparently do not insure each other's lives to protect themselves against having to care for each other's children at their own expense. Corporations insure the lives of employees, naming the survivors as beneficiaries, partly as a way—I have been told by a corporation executive who dealt with these matters—to minimize their vulnerability to the importunities of a person's dependents—to the claim of a widow, for example, that the corporation ought to give her a job. A large corporation can of course rely on self-insurance if these events occur with statistical regularity; but it may prefer the contractual formality of insurance, just as a person may want full collision coverage when he borrows a friend's car, to avoid the embarrassment of personal negotiation.

## TAXES

Turn now to the real taxes that a man or woman would have paid, had he or she lived, to the federal government, to the state he resided in or earned his living or spent his money in, and to the local community that his taxes helped to support. These taxes are a person's share in the overhead cost of government, in the provision of public goods and services that are not used up by the taxpayer himself. There are economies of scale in government; when a person dies he stops paying his share in the space program, and the rest have to make it up. Somebody loses transfer payments, or pays more taxes, when one of the net contributors disappears.

The person's taxes are positive or negative according to whether he is a net contributor or a net recipient, and according to how much cost his very presence in society imposes on government. Dead, he won't drive, steal, go to school, or leave unextinguished campfires; and various levels of government save an amount to offset against his taxes. (His death can be a gain to federal taxpayers and a loss to his city, or the other way around.)

These costs or losses, positive or negative, resulting from a person's death, could be approximately offset by replacing the person. In principle, selective immigration might compensate society for the person's death. There are societies in which immigration works in this fashion, or immigration policy reflects the loss of citizens through death. Without any policy, immigration works this way for local communities. Possibly with some conscious though indirect policy behind it, it works that way for the state of Alaska, and has worked for frontier societies and developing nations.

The main reason why immigration could not in principle handle the problem is that there is one obligation of citizenship that the immigrant is unlikely to assume. That is the family obligation of the man or woman who dies. There have been frontier societies that imported wives, even husbands. But to achieve a genuine economic replacement for the taxpaying father who dies, one would have to find bachelors and widowers seeking ready-made families to marry into; this is undoubtedly asking more than either the free market or individually negotiated immigration could manage. Most income-taxpayers probably spend more to support families than to support their government, and that contribution is a hard one to replace.

What are the taxes to be accounted for, and how are they to be accounted for? The person's property taxes can be excluded; the taxes will go on being paid by whoever owns the property—his family or whoever buys the house or automobile. (There will be a slight change of interest to local governments, a tendency for property assessments to change with the turnover of real estate, or for values to be depressed by an increment in the supply of houses—a matter of elasticity estimates, not of accounting.) The issues mainly concern federal and state income taxes, employment taxes, excise and sales taxes, net of the costs of collecting them and net of transfer receipts; and the subject of inquiry is the difference between the taxes (net of transfers) that the deceased and his family would have paid had he not died and the taxes they go on paying, and the person's (or the child's) utilization of government benefits, valued at marginal cost.

The difficult problems relate to the income tax, or to the income tax as well as to other taxes; if the income tax is examined, probably most of the interesting problems will have been discussed. One set of problems relates to how taxable incomes are; this depends on source of income, the jurisdiction a person lives in, and what constitutes taxable income. Another set relates to the distribution of taxable income in an economy like ours. What happens to taxable income when the Harvard professor dies? Is there merely a subtraction from the tax rolls of one income in a fairly high bracket? Or are there economic laws that impose a shape on the distribution of income independently of who dies? The professor will be replaced, by someone who in turn may be replaced by the institution he or she left to go to Harvard. Even if marginal productivity theory states that the GNP goes down by approximately what the professor was being paid, it will not say that taxable income goes down accordingly. If there is a loss to the economy because the deceased is replaced by a marginally less competent person at the same salary, this would show up as quality depreciation of Harvard's product and would be of interest to the Internal Revenue Service only as it influences future tax rates.

If one takes the extreme position that the distribution of taxable income is unaffected by the particular incidence of death by tax brackets, the reduction in income tax would be proportionate to the person's income, not to the taxes he paid. Thus, if the Harvard professor has twice the income of a high school teacher and pays four times the income tax, the impact on income tax revenues of his disappearance from the tax base is only twice that of the high school teacher, not four times. The alternative bench mark is the hypothesis that the remaining distribution of income is unchanged—there is just a little nick in the frequency distribution at the income of the professor who died and a little cusp at the new level of income for his family—and everybody else's tax return goes on being just what it would have been. I doubt whether the state of economic analysis permits us to identify which of these two hypotheses is the more plausible or what compromise is most valid.

### Consumer Interest in Reduced Risk

The avoidance of a particular death—the death of a named individual—cannot be treated straightforwardly as a consumer choice. It involves anxiety and sentiment, guilt and awe, responsibility and religion. If the individuals are identified, there are many of us who cannot even answer whether one should die that two may live. And when half of the children in a hospital ward are to get the serum that may save their lives, half a placebo to help test the serum, the doctor who divides them at random and keeps their identities secret is not exclusively interested in experimental design. He does not want personally to select them or to know who has been selected. But most of this awesomeness disappears when we deal with statistical deaths, with small increments in a mortality rate in a large population.

Suppose a program to save lives has been identified and we want to know its worth. Suppose the population whose vulnerability is to be reduced is a large one, and approximately identifiable. The dimensions of the risk to be reduced are fairly well known, as is the reduction to be achieved. Suppose also that this risk is small to begin with, not a source of anxiety or guilt.

Surely it is sensible to ask the question, What is it worth to the people who stand to benefit from it? If a scheme can be devised for collecting the cost from them, perhaps in a manner reflecting their relative gains if their benefits are dissimilar, it surely should be their privilege to have the program if they are collectively willing to bear the cost. If they are not willing, perhaps it would be a mistake to ask anybody else to bear the cost for them; they, the beneficiaries, prefer to have the money or some alternative benefits that the money could buy. There are reasons why this argument has to be qualified, but there is no obvious reason why a program that reduces mortality cannot be handled by letting the beneficiaries decide whether it is worth the cost, if the cost falls on them.

There are two main ways of finding out whether some economic benefits are worth the costs. One is to use the price system as a test of what something is worth to the people who have to pay for it. It is possible to see what people are willing to pay for the privilege of sitting at tables rather than counters in a restaurant, what they are willing to pay to use library books or to save an elm tree in the front yard. Sometimes the market is poor; sometimes analysis is confused by joint products; sometimes consumer behavior is subject to inertia and the information is needed before the market adjusts. But at least we can try to observe what people will pay for something.

Another way of discovering what the benefits are worth is to ask people. This can be done by election, interview, or questionnaire; the more common way is to let people volunteer the information, through lobby organizations, letters to congressmen or to the newspapers, and rallies. There may be something a little like a price system here if people are allowed to show the trouble they will go to, or the expense they will incur, to lobby for or against something. Like the price system, these methods may be ambiguous.

It is sometimes argued that asking people is a poor way to find out, because they have no incentive to tell the truth. That is an important point, but hardly decisive. It is also argued, and validly, that people are poor at answering hypothetical questions, especially about important events—that the mood and motive of actual choice are hard to simulate. While this argument casts suspicion on what one finds out by asking questions, it casts suspicion, too, on those market decisions that involve remote and improbable events. Unexpected death has a hypothetical quality whether it is merely being talked about or money is being spent to prevent it. Asked whether he would buy trip insurance if it were available at the airport (or would decline to fly in an aircraft that had a statistically higher accident rate than another if it would save an overnight stop), a person may not give verbally the same answer as his actions in the airport would reveal. He still might not feel that his actual decision was authoritative evidence of his values or that, had mood and circumstance been different—even had the amount of time for consultation and decision been different—his action might not have been different too. This problem of coping, as a consumer, with increments in the risk of unexpected death is very much the problem of coping with hypothetical questions, whether in response to survey research or to the man who sells lightning-rod attachments for the TV antenna. If consumers regularly retained professional consultants in coping with such decisions, there might be a good source of information.

In any case, relying exclusively on market valuations and denying the value of direct inquiry in the determination of government programs (or even the programs of nongovernmental organizations) would depend on there being, for every potential government service, a close substitute available in the market at a comparable price. It would be hard to deduce from first principles that there is bound to be. Voting behavior is probably to be classed somewhere between a purchase and a questionnaire: an individual's vote is indecisive, while the election as a whole is conclusive.

## SMALL PROBABILITY OF LARGE EVENTS

A difficulty about death, especially a minor risk of death, is that people have to deal with a minute probability of an awesome event, and may be poor at finding a way—by intellect, imagination, or analogy—to explore what the saving is worth to them. This is true whether they are confronted by a questionnaire or a market decision, a survey researcher or a salesman. It may even matter whether the figures are presented to them in percentage terms or as odds, whether charts are drawn on arithmetic or logarithmic scales, and whether people are familiar with the simple arithmetic of probability.

The smallness of the probability is itself a hard thing to come to grips with, especially when the increment in question is even smaller than the original risk. At the same time, the death itself is a large event, and until a person has some way of comparing death with other losses it is difficult or impossible to do anything with it probabilistically, even if one is quite willing to manipulate probabilities.

What it would be like to grow old without a companion, to rear a family without a mother or father in the house, to endure bereavement, is something that most of us have no direct knowledge of; and those who have some knowledge may not yet know the full effects over time. Many of us think about it only when we make a will or buy life insurance, suffer a medical false alarm or witness the bereavement of a friend or neighbor.

As consumers we can investigate the subject. It may be no harder to cope with than choosing a career, nor more painful than some of the medical decisions we actually have to take. But most of us have not investigated; the cost of doing so is high, and there is not much fun in it. In a program of interrogation, even a sales effort, some people will just not cooperate. Others, if they have to make a decision, would rather make a hasty one that may be wrong than a more painful or embarrassing decision that is more nearly right. Some of the reluctance may be unconscious, with a resulting bias that is hard to identify.

Furthermore, this is, more than most decisions, a family one, not an individual one. Nearly every death involves at least two major participants, typically the immediate family. It is not even clear who it is that has the greater stake in a person's not dying—

himself, his spouse if he has one, his children if he is a parent, or his parents if he is a child—and the subject is undoubtedly a delicate one for the members of the consuming unit to discuss with each other. Whatever the motives of a respondent when being interviewed alone about a safety program or a hazardous occupation, his motives are surely complex when he talks to his wife about how much he would miss her or she would miss him, the likelihood of a happy remarriage, or which of them would suffer more if one of the children died.

### DEATH VERSUS ANXIETY

The problem is even harder if the risk to be attenuated is large enough, or vivid enough, to cause anxiety. In fact, the pain associated with the awareness of risk—with the prospect of death—is probably often commensurate with the costs of death itself. A person who sooner or later must undergo an operation that carries a moderate risk of being fatal will apparently sometimes choose to have the operation now, raising the stakes against himself in the gamble, in order to avoid the suspense. Wives of men in hazardous duty suffer; and most of us have sat beside someone on an airplane who suffered more with anxiety than if he had been drilled by a dentist without Novocain and who would have paid a fairly handsome price for the Novocain. Let me conjecture that if one among forty men had been mistakenly injected with a substance that would kill him at the end of five years, and the forty were known to the doctor who did not know which among them had the fatal injection, and if the men did not know it yet, the doctor would do more harm by telling them what he had done than he had already done with the injection.

This anxiety is separate from the impact of death itself. It applies equally to those who do not die and to those who do, to people who exaggerate the risk of death as much as if their estimates were true. It counts, and is part of the consumer interest in reducing the risk of death. It is not, or usually not, any kind of double counting to bring it into the calculation. But it is—except where knowledge of risk permits people to make better economic decisions, or exaggerations of risk lead them to hedge excessively and uneconomically—almost entirely psychic or social. Relief from anxiety is a strange kind of consumer good. What the consumer buys is a state of mind, a picture in his imagination, a sensation.

And he must decide to do so by using the same brain that is itself the source of his discomfort or pleasure. However much "rationality" we impute to our consumer, we must never forget that the one thing he cannot control is his own imagination. (He can try though; this accounts for the business in tranquilizers, and for the readiness of airlines to serve their passengers alcoholic beverages.)

CONSUMER CHOICES AND POLICY DECISIONS

These, then, are some of the reasons why it is hard for our consumer to tell us intelligently what it is worth to him to reduce the risk of death, why it may even be hard to get him to make a proper try. These are also reasons why the consumer may be poor at making ordinary choices about death in the marketplace. He may not do much better in buying life insurance or seat belts, using or avoiding airplanes, flying separately or together with his wife when they leave the children behind, selecting cigarettes with or without filters, driving under the influence of liquor when he could have taken a taxi, or installing a fire detector over the basement furnace. Some of his marketplace decisions may be more casual (perhaps out of evading his responsibilities, not meeting them), but they may be no better evidence than the answers he would give to questions he might be asked.

Many parents try not to fly on the same plane (although they usually drive home together on New Year's Eve). I took for granted that this was sensible, though extravagant—a matter of the nuisance one would incur to reduce the risk of leaving the children without any parent at all, until Richard Zeckhauser suggested I think it over. Should a person double the risk of losing one parent to eliminate the risk of losing two? I decided then that the answer was hard to be sure of and probably sensitive to the number of children and their ages, even if only the welfare of the children is taken into account, and more so of course when the parents' welfare is considered as well. (Evidently, happily married childless couples should travel on the same plane, not just for company but to eliminate the risk of bereavement.) The point is not that I am right, now, where I was wrong before, but that I hadn't thought it through. Also that, now that I come to think about it, I'm not sure; and I still do not intend to discuss it with my wife, especially [this was written when they were still young] in the presence of the children.

Consumers apparently do often evade these questions when they have a chance. In matters of life and death doctors are not merely operations analysts who formulate the choice for the executive; they are professional decisionmakers, who not only diagnose but decide for the consumer, because they decide with less pain, less regret, cooler nerves, and a mind less flooded with alternating hopes and fears.

Still, in dealing with death-reducing programs, these are the kinds of decisions that somebody has to make. We can do it democratically, by letting the consumers decide for themselves through any of the marketplace or direct-inquiry techniques that we can think of. Or we can do it vicariously, paternalistically, perhaps professionally, by making some of these highly introspective and imaginative decisions for them, briefing ourselves on the facts as best we can, or perhaps hiring out the decisions to people who have professional knowledge about the consequences of death in the family.

If then it turns out that the safety device or health program is a public good and not everybody wants it at the price, or that the tax system will not distribute the costs where the benefits fall, so that we are collectively deciding on a program in which some of us have a strong interest, some a weak interest, and some a negative interest, that makes it rather like any other budgetary decision that the government takes. We need not get all wound up about the "pricelessness" of human life nor think it strange that the rich will pay more for longevity than the poor, or that the rich prefer programs that help the rich and the poor those that help the poor. There may be good reasons why the poor should not be allowed to fly in second-class aircraft that are more dangerous, or people in a hurry should not be allowed to pay a bonus to the pilot who will waive the safety regulations; but these reasons ought to be explicitly adduced as qualifications to a principle that makes economic sense, rather than as "first principles" that transcend economics.

## SOME QUANTITATIVE DETERMINANTS

What results should we anticipate if we engage in the kind of inquiry I have described, or if we survey the market evidence of what people will pay to avoid their own deaths or the deaths of the people who matter to them? Is there any a priori line of reasoning that will help us to establish an order of magnitude, an upper or lower limit, a bench mark, or some ideal accounting magnitude that ought to represent the worth, to a reflective and arithmetically sophisticated consumer, of a reduction in some mortality rate? Is there some good indicator—life insurance, lightning rods, hazardous-duty pay—that will give us some basis for estimate? Is there some scale factor, like a person's income, to which the ideal figure should be proportionate or of which it should be some function? And to what extent should our estimate be expected to depend on social and economic institutions?

At the outset, we can conjecture that any estimate based on market evidence will at best let us know to within a factor of 2 or 3 (perhaps only 5 or 10) what the reflective individual would decide after thoughtful, intensive inquiry and good professional advice. This conjecture is based on the observation that most of the market decisions people make relate to contingencies for which the probabilities themselves are ill-known to the consumer, sometimes barely available to the person who seeks statistics, invariably applicable in only rough degree, and mixed with joint products that make the evidence ambiguous. What will somebody pay for a babysitter who, in case of fire, will probably save the children or some of them? With a little research one can find out the likelihood of fire or other catastrophe during the time that one is away from home, the likelihood that they would be saved if a babysitter were on guard, and the likelihood that they would save themselves or otherwise be saved if no one were home; an upper or lower limit of "worth" may be manifested in the price that one pays or refuses to pay to a babysitter. It would take a good deal more research to relate this to the age and type of furnace, the shape and composition of the house and the location of roofs and windows, the performance of babysitters of different ages and sexes, the ages and personalities of the children, the season of the year, the quality of the fire department, the alertness of neighbors, and the hour of day or night that one is going to be away. In addition, babysitters perform other services: they help get the children to bed, soothe the child that awakes from a bad dream, telephone the parents or doctor in case of sickness, let the dog out, guard against burglary, and sometimes even clean the dishes. (Readers with small children will appreciate that this is a theoretical paper.) What the family pays for the babysitter will depend, furthermore, on whether it is the husband or the wife who decides, on what the local custom is, and on what vivid experience some acquaintance had in recent years. The evidential value of this "market test" will barely give us an estimate to within a factor of 2 or 3.

*Worth as a function of income.*  Is there some expectable or rational relation between what a person earns and what he would spend, or willingly be taxed, to increase the likelihood of his own survival or the survival of one of his family? Specifically, is there any close *accounting* connection between what he might spend and what he can hope to earn in the future, or what he owns?

So many examinations of the worth of saving a life are concerned with the fraction of a person's income that he in some way contributes, that there may be a presumption that the outside limit of the worth of saving his life is the entirety of his expected future earnings. It does seem that if we ask ourselves the worth of saving somebody else's life, and he is somebody who personally makes no difference to us, his net contribution to total production may be the outside limit to what we can interest ourselves in. But when we ask the question, What is it worth to him to increase the likelihood of his own survival (or to us, our own survival)?, it is hard to see that his (our) future lifetime earnings provide either an upper or lower limit.

There is no reason to suppose that what a person would pay to eliminate some specific probability, $P,$ of his own death is more than, less than, or equal to, $P$ times his discounted expected earnings. In fact there is no reason to suppose that a person's future earnings, discounted in any pertinent fashion, bear any particular relation to what he would pay to reduce some likelihood of his own death.

I am not saying that a person's expected lifetime income is irrelevant to an estimate of what he would pay to reduce fatalities in his age group. But discounted lifetime earnings are relevant only in the way that they are relevant to ordinary decisions about consumption, saving, quitting a job, or buying a house. They are part of the income and wealth data that go into the decisions. Their connection is a functional one, not an accounting one. What a person would pay to avoid death, to avoid pain, or to modernize his kitchen is a function of present and expected income but need bear no particular adding-up relation.

People get hung up sometimes on the apparent anomaly that if a person would yield 2 percent of his lifetime income to eliminate a 1-percent risk of death, he'd have to give up twice his entire lifetime income to save his own life—which he cannot do if his creditors are on their toes. But he doesn't have to. I'd pay my dentist an hour's income to avoid a minute's intense pain—even to prevent somebody else's pain—without having to know what I'd do if confronted with a lifetime of intense pain. This is why the "worth of saving a life" is but a mathematical construct when applied to an individual's decision on the reduction of small risks; it has literal meaning only if we mean that a hundred people would give up the equivalent of two lifetime incomes to save one (unidentified) life among them. [After this was written I found a helpful analogy. In counting work force the FTE (full-time equivalent) has come into common use; so we might refer to this lifesaving construct as FLE, or "full-life equivalent." If we'd each pay, on average, 2 percent of a year's income to eliminate a 1-percent risk of dying—that is, we'd pay together two annual incomes to eliminate one expected death among the hundred of us—we can say that the worth of one FLE is two years' income.]

Let me guess. If we ask people what it is worth to them to reduce by a certain number of percentage points over some period the likelihood that they will die, they will find it worth more than that percentage of the discounted value of their expected lifetime income. Arithmetically, if we tell a man that the likelihood of his accidental death over the next three years is 9 percent and we can reduce this to 6 percent by some measure we propose, and ask him what it is worth to reduce the probability of his death by 3 percent over this period (with no change in his mortality table after that period), my conjecture is it is worth to him a permanent reduction of perhaps 5 percent, possibly 10 percent, in his income.

This is conjecture. It is based on conversational inquiry among a score of respondents, and relates to fathers in professional income classes. The reader can add himself to my sample by examining what his own answer to the query would be.

*Death itself versus anxiety.* In conducting this inquiry it is important to make the distinction mentioned earlier between death itself and anxiety about death. If asked, for example, what it is worth to eliminate the fatality of certain childhood diseases (or—taking for illustration a problem that is commensurate with the problem of death—to reduce the danger of congenital defects and foetal injuries that cause infant deformities), one may discover that he is as preoccupied with the anxiety that goes with the risk as with the low-probability event itself.

A special difficulty of evaluating the anxiety and the event together is that they probably do not occur in fixed proportions. That is, their quantitative connection with the reduction of risk may be quite dissimilar. To be specific, there are good reasons for considering the worth of risk-reduction to be proportionate to the absolute reduction of risk, for considering a reduction from 10 percent to 9 percent about equivalent to a reduction from 5 percent to 4 percent. There is no reason for the anxiety to follow any such rational rule. Even a cool-headed consumer who rationally examines his own or his family's anxiety will probably have to recognize that anxiety and obsession are psychological phenomena that cannot be brought under any such rational control. If they could be, through an act of judgment, an act of self-hypnosis, a ban on disquieting conversations, or the avoidance of factual and fictional stimuli, through surgery or through drugs, the anxiety could perhaps be wholly disposed of. A family that lives with a "high" low probability of death in the family, high enough to cause anxiety but low enough to make it unlikely, may benefit as much from relief as from longevity if the risk can be eliminated.

The anxiety may depend on the absolute level of risk and the frequency and vividness of stimuli. There may be thresholds below which the risk is ignored and above which it is a preoccupation. It may depend on whether the risk is routine and continuous or concentrated in episodes. It undoubtedly depends on what people believe about risks and has no direct connection with what the risks truly are. The existence of one source of risk may affect the psychological reaction to another source of risk. Furthermore, the anxiety will be related to the duration of suspense and can even be inversely correlated with the risk of death itself.

In other words, decision theory, probability theory, and a rational calculus of risks and values will be pertinent—not compelling, but surely pertinent—to the avoidance of the event of death, but may have little or no relevance to choices involving fear, anxiety, and relief. People may, however, by engaging in enough sophisticated analysis of risk, change their sensitivity to the perception of risk, possibly but not surely bringing the discomfort into a more nearly proportionate relation to the risk itself.

There is a special reason why it is hard to separate the anxiety from the event itself. A person is unlikely to have pure or raw preferences involving small risks of serious events. He does not know what the elimination of a 0.0002 chance of death is worth to himself unless he can find some way of comparing it with the other terms of his choice, of making it commensurate with the other things that money can buy. One can hardly have a feeling about a 0.0002 chance of death quite the way one has a feeling about pain in the dental chair, the loss of an hour in a traffic jam, or even the loss of a favorite tree in the yard. It takes a little arithmetic even to remember that 1 chance in 5,000 is 1/50th of 1 chance in 100, 20 times 1 chance in 100,000. A person may have to explore until he finds a magnitude of risk about which he has, or can imagine his way into, a feeling of the kind we associate with preferences and tastes. The risk may have to be brought above some threshold where the size has some feel or familiarity, where the intensity of his feeling is too strong to escape his efforts to respond to it. If he can find a favorite level of risk, a familiar bench mark, a degree of risk that he can in some way perceive directly rather than through pencil and paper, there may then be a possibility of scaling the risk and its worth to find a proper or rational valuation of smaller or larger risks. The anxiety associated with the risk, though, may be quite unamenable to any such scaling.

## SCALING OF RISKS

There is a good case—not necessarily persuasive—for scaling risks. It is illustrated as follows.[4] A person is asked what risk of death is equivalent to certain blindness—at what risk of death he would prefer certain blindness, at what risk of death he would rather run the risk than be surely blind—and his point of indifference between the two is found. Since this is a decision that can arise, it is presumed that a person can answer the question—not offhand, but after some study and advice. Suppose he says that certain blindness balances out at about a 1/10 chance of death; he would run the risk of death to avoid blindness if it were less than 1/10, not if it were more than 1/10. He is then informed that a 1/10 chance of blindness must be equivalent to 1 chance in 100 of death. If he denies this, insisting that what holds for large probabilities does not hold for small ones, or that certainty is different from risk, the first question is rephrased as follows: If he had to choose between sure blindness and some risk of death, what risk of death would be equivalent to certain blindness? He may say he does not know and cannot find out because a hypothetical question will not motivate a meaningful answer. To make it meaningful, he is told that it may be necessary to incur some fatal risk to avoid blindness; there is, for instance, a surgical operation that cures certain kinds of blindness but involves a certain risk of death; there is some likelihood that this person will prove upon further diagnosis to be faced with that choice and he must make his decision now in case the contingency arises. If he can answer this contingent question—if he can say for the event that he must choose between certain blindness and some risk of death, an event with a yet unspecified probability, what risk of death he is just willing to incur to avoid otherwise certain blindness—then he has in effect chosen between some (unspecified) probability of blindness and a probability of death equal to that same probability multiplied by the contingent risk he said he was just willing to incur. He is now told that there is a 50-50 chance, or that there is 1 chance in 20, that the diagnosis will make his contingent answer relevant; if he lets his answer stand, he has in effect stated his indifference between a 0.5 chance of blindness and a 0.05 chance of death, and also between a 0.05 chance of blindness and a 0.005 chance of death.

The argument may not be compelling, but it helps in establishing at least a presumption in favor of a scaling principle that, at first glance, might have appeared implausible.

What has been said about anxiety, though, could interfere. It will probably not interfere much if the outcome is to be known soon; the discomfort of suspense probably depends on the duration, and ought to be negligible if the man will know the outcome the next day. It could be considerable if he will not know for a year or two and if he cannot keep his family from knowing the kind of risk he has accepted.

*An illustrative application.*    Imperfect as it is, this argument can be a tool for helping some people think about unfamiliar probabilities. A person who cannot come to grips with 1 chance in 1,000 of death may be able to come to grips with 1 chance in 10, or vice versa. He is asked, for example, what reduction in income after taxes he would incur in perpetuity to avoid a 10 percent chance of death (of himself or of somebody he cares about). Suppose he says that he will give up one-third of his income to avoid an immediate 10 percent chance of dying. How can it be calculated from this what he might give up to avoid 1 chance in 1,000 of dying? Rather, how can he tell from the answer he has given what his answer ought to be to the question containing the 0.001 risk? Dividing both figures by 100, he would give 1/300 of his income. But if successive increments of income lost are of progressively larger concern to a man, a loss of 0.33 percent of income will not look one-hundredth as bad to him as the loss of 33 percent of his income. He might, however, be asked what fraction of his income he would give up to avoid a one-tenth chance of losing one-third of his income. This is an ordinary insurance decision, which he can presumably make (and he may be expected to give an answer that exceeds one-thirtieth of his income). The process could be repeated for a one-hundredth chance of losing a third of his income, but possibly it is not necessary when it is a question of dealing with increments on the order of a few percent. Suppose he says that he would give up 5 percent of his income to avoid a 1/10 chance of losing 33 percent. Is he willing to give up about 0.5 percent to avoid a 10 percent chance of losing 5 percent? Not exactly; he may say approximately, perhaps somewhat more—say 0.6 percent. There is now a series of statements about bets he would place, suggesting that he considers the loss of 0.6 percent of his income (after taxes) in perpetuity about equivalent to 1 chance in 1,000 of immediate death.[5]

Let it be assumed that the person is in his early forties, with expected lifetime earnings to accrue on a rising scale over twenty-five more years. Discounting this income at something like the mortgage rate of interest—lower than the rate on consumer credit, higher than the earnings on conservative retirement plans, say, 7 percent—its capitalized value would be about ten times a year's income; 0.6 percent of that is about 6 percent of a year's income.

If similar answers were obtained from a thousand men and women of similar incomes and ages, it could be concluded that they would together rather give up the equivalent of six discounted lifetime incomes than suffer one immediate accidental death. ("Accidental death" is used to keep the arithmetic simple; the idea is to leave the population unchanged in its life expectancy.) In the age group of our people, that turns out to be about sixty annual incomes. Does this look high? Does it look low? It is up to the reader what figure he finds plausible, either for himself or for someone interviewed at random at the airport. (It is up to the reader both as an analytical reader and as a consumer of life-saving programs.) It is also up to the reader, or to the passenger at the airport, whether it is of any help to break the decision into a series of comparisons like this.

Try now a comparison. Turn the choice around and ask the person what compensation he demands for running some additional risk. Should there be for small increments the same figure of worth? Would he run an additional chance in a thousand for a bonus equal to 6 percent of a year's income? Should the answer be symmetrical? Probably not for the anxiety, not for the superstitious element in gambling, not for any special sense of regret that might ensue if the death could actually be identified—in case it occurred—with his choice to incur it. Otherwise, although symmetry cannot be demanded, it should probably be expected, or at least be treated as one more test.

As a check—after the price has been set by examining small increments in a small risk—the sample of a thousand men and women could be asked whether they would in the end rather take the cash as compensation. Rather than pay six lifetime incomes in total to avert one death among the thousand, might they prefer to run the risk and put the proceeds into life insurance? That would compensate the bereaved family with a sixfold rise in its income.

Or they might want to split the difference: to pay half the price they originally decided on, leave the risk intact, and triple the income of the family of the person who dies. If so, their best buy is life insurance; they gave a wrong answer in haste, and the exercise should be repeated. (If they retort that they are already insured up to that level, the inference is that their original answer was a financial calculation of what it was worth to save the cost of insurance.)

This line of reasoning leads to a distasteful question—one, though, that may be worth asking along with all the others in the attempt to help a person identify his own preferences. Is there some level of adequate compensation for the family? It is distasteful to ask how much monetary compensation a family needs in order to suffer no long-term loss in welfare when a member of the family dies; and an answer that makes a person priceless cannot be rejected. Symmetry cannot be adduced to prove that an infinite "selling" price would mean an infinite "buying" price. That is, a family that would not give up all its income to save one member can nevertheless refuse to consider any economic compensation adequate for the loss of a member.

But a person can run a risk for cash. And he may prefer, if he runs the risk, to trade the cash for some still larger amount invested in life insurance, that is, for a greater "expected value" correlated with death itself. If so, compensation tends to be commensurable with life-saving at the margin of small risks, and provides a helpful check on the consistency of a series of choices.

At this point, reexamination of both the life-saving decision and the life-insurance decision may be needed; apparent inconsistency can mean that either decision was out of line. (Both in introspection and in conversation I have been surprised, while writing this, at how far life insurance can go toward meeting the demand of middle-aged fathers for their own mortality reduction, if they do a little sustained reflection on the matter.)

Inquiry suggests that, to earners of income in college-professor brackets, saving one among their lives may be worth anywhere from 10 to 100 times a year's income. Or, to put it in absolute terms, professional people with earnings in the range from $40,000 to $80,000, which would include senior officials of government, professors at major universities, successful engineers, doctors, and lawyers, might value a life to be chosen at random among themselves at something like two million dollars. In crude numbers this could mean that a Boeing 707 full of professional business people might value their own lives in a way that would make prevention of the fatal crash of a (yet unidentified) full airplane worth about $250 million. This is but an order of magnitude; any figure between $100 million and $750 million would fit the crude data. The reader is invited to supply his own figure for his class of passengers.

*Discriminating for wealth.* A special matter of policy is bound to arise here. If a government is to initiate programs that may save the lives of the poor or the rich, is it worth more to save the rich than to save the poor? The answer is evidently yes if the question means, is it worth more to the rich to reduce the risk to their own lives than it is to the poor to reduce the risk to their own lives. Just as the rich will pay more to avoid wasting an hour in traffic or five hours on a train, it is worth more to them to reduce the risk of their own death or the death of somebody they care about. It is worth more because they are richer than the poor. A hospital that can save either of two lives, but not both, has no reason to save the richer of the two on these grounds; but an expensive athletic club can afford better safety equipment than a cheap gymnasium; the rich can afford safer stoves in their homes than the poor; and a rich country can spend more to save lives than a poor one.

*Other members of the family.* Most of this discussion has been focused on the person who supports the family. To deal comprehensively with the subject, the problem should be calculated from the point of view of the husband, putting wife or child at risk, and from the point of view of the wife, putting at risk her own life or her husband's or that of one of the children. (To get a proper feel for the subject, the children might be given a chance to express their views; their immaturity should not offhand make what they say irrelevant.)

There is a qualification about families and children: the values placed on lives by members of the family, as well as the costs to society involved in somebody's death, are not additive within the family. If death takes a mother, a father, and two children, each from a different family, the consequences are different from the death of a family of four in a single accident. This is true both of the costs to society, because of the differential impact of dependents' care, and of the personal valuations within the family.

If a family of four *must* fly, and has a choice among four aircraft, of which it is known that one is defective but not known which one, it should be possible to persuade them to fly together. The prospects for each individual's survival are the same, no matter how they divide themselves among the aircraft, but the prospects for bereavement are nearly eliminated through the "correlation" of their prospects. "Society's" interest, in support of the family's interest, should be to see that they are permitted and encouraged to take the same plane together. (Society's economic interest will coincide.)

## Conclusion

We have looked now at several ways to approach the worth of saving a statistical life. We have had to distinguish between the life and the livelihood that goes with it. We have had to distinguish between the loss of that livelihood to the consuming unit—the family—and the loss of the share that went to other members of the economy—the taxpayers, insurance policyholders, and kin. We have considered some of the ways that reduction of the risk of death differs from other commodities and services that consumers buy.

To recapitulate: (1) Death is an awesome and indivisible event that goes but one to a customer in a single large size. (2) For many people it is a low-probability event except on special occasions when the momentary likelihood becomes serious. (3) Its effect on a family is something that many consumers have little direct acquaintance with. (4) In an already advanced economy many of the ways of reducing the risk of death are necessarily public programs, budgetary or regulatory. (5) Reduction of risk is often a by-product of other programs that lead to health, comfort, or the security of property, though there are some identifiable programs of which the saving of lives is the main result. (6) Death is an insurable event. (7) Death is more of a family event than most other casualties that one might like to avert; its analysis requires more than perfunctory recognition that the family is the consuming unit, the income-sharing unit, and the welfare-sharing unit.

Still, though these characteristics are important, they do not necessarily make the avoidance of death a wholly different kind of objective from others to promote the general welfare. Although it is important to be aware of how the avoidance of death differs from other programs, it is equally important to keep in mind in what respects it is similar. Society may indeed sometimes express its profoundest moral values in the way it deals with life and death, but in a good many programs to reduce fatalities society merely expresses the amount of trouble people will go to, or the money people will spend, to reduce the risks they run. There is enough mystery already about death, not to exaggerate the mystery.

A good part of society's interest in the livelihood that may be lost is no different from its interest in saving a man's barn or his drugstore. What are the costs of a fire that burns property? Everything that was said about taxes, saving, insurance, and contributions to the United Fund is equally pertinent to this case. The fact that an appraiser can value the barn more readily than a vocational analyst can appraise a person's livelihood simplifies the problem in only one dimension: estimating the value of the barn is only a point of departure for tracing out society's interest. As a statistical aggregate, the national wealth goes down if I lose my home and furniture, but who cares except me? If my bank cares, or my insurance company, or the taxing authorities of my town, we are on the track of some interests that matter. But society has no direct interest in the national wealth. It is not owned collectively—not in the United States.

What makes the barn or shop easier to evaluate than a life (not livelihood) is that it is less difficult to guess what it is worth to the man who owns it. Its replacement cost sets an upper limit. Even that, though, does not directly tell the worth of a small increment in a small probability of material destruction; it is the insurability of the structure, with a policy that pays off in the same currency with which one buys replacement, that makes it possible to estimate the worth to someone of an incremental change in the risk of fire, collision, or windstorm.

The difficult part of the problem is not evaluating the worth of a person's livelihood to the different people who have an interest in it, but the worth of his life to himself or to whoever will pay to prolong it. This is what is not insurable in terms that permit replacement. This is the consumer interest in a unique and irreplaceable good. His livelihood he can usually insure, not exactly but approximately, sharing the loss and making it a matter of diffuse economic interest; it is valuing his life that poses the problem.

And the difficulty is not just that, as with so many government budgetary and regulatory programs, the government has to weigh the divergent interests of various beneficiaries and taxpayers. Nor is it that, as with so many government programs, the government has to investigate how much the program is worth to people. The main problem is that people have difficulty knowing what it is worth to themselves, cannot easily answer questions about it, and may object to being asked. Market evidence is unlikely to reveal much.

Dealing with small changes in small risks makes the evaluation more casual and takes the pricelessness and the pretentiousness out of a potentially awesome choice. The question is whether the consumer, at this more casual level of straightforward risk reduction, has any sovereign tastes (or thinks he has) and can be induced to place his bets as calmly as he would fasten a seat belt or buy a lock for his door. If it appears upon inquiry—an inquiry that the consumer participates in—that he has been casually deceiving himself that his decisions are the right ones, it is necessary to decide whether that is his privilege and he wants it respected, or he should be goaded into an agonizing reappraisal or the reappraisal should be made for him. Scaring people is usually bad, and the airlines can hardly be expected to cooperate—or their passengers either—in a survey that quickens a passenger's appreciation of danger at the moment he settles into his seat.

In the end there may be a philosophical question whether government should try to adapt itself to what consumer tastes would be if the consumers could be induced to have those tastes and to articulate them. There may be a strong temptation to do the consumer's thinking for him and to come out with a different answer. Should one try to be guided by what the consumer would choose, when in fact the consumer may refuse to make the choice at all? If a doctor is asked to make a grave medical decision that a patient, or a patient's spouse, declines to make for himself, is the doctor supposed to guess what the patient, or the patient's spouse, would have decided if he'd had to decide for himself? Or is the doctor to decide as he thinks he would himself decide if he were in the patient's position? Or is he to make a welfare decision for the whole family or some other small society? Should the doctor ask the patient which among these criteria he wants the doctor to use, or does that merely upset the patient and lead to the doctor's having to decide how to decide on the criterion?

The gravity of decisions about lifesaving can be dispelled by letting the consumer (taxpayer, lobbyist, questionnaire respondent) express himself on the comparatively unexciting subject of small increments in small risks, acting as though he has preferences even if in fact he does not. People do it for life insurance; they could do it for lifesaving. The fact that they may not do it well, or may not quite know what they are doing as they make the decision, may not bother them and need not disfranchise them in the exercise of consumer-taxpayer sovereignty.

As an economist I have to keep reminding myself that consumer sovereignty is not just a metaphor and is not justified solely by reference to the unseen hand. It derives with even greater authority from another principle of about the same vintage: "no taxation without representation." Welfare economics establishes the convenience of consumer sovereignty and its compatibility with economic efficiency; the sovereignty itself is typically established by arms, martyrdom, boycott, or some principles held to be self-evident. And it includes the inalienable right of the consumer to make his own mistakes.

Still, if it is a government program, not a market competition between buses and airplanes or electric and gas furnaces, the decisions will be made vicariously, with perhaps some attention to evidence of consumer tastes, but only some.

Maybe a sample of civil servants or legislators can be induced to take the plunge, explore their values, and share their wisdom. But if they can, what is wanted is not their evaluation of other people's lives, nor an expression of their responsibility for the lives of their constituents. They must speak for themselves, or for themselves and others like them, when it is their own lives that are at risk. And they must not be in a mood to save lives but in a mood to change risks, usually small risks. We often know who died for lack of safety; we rarely know who lived because of it. What the government buys, if it buys health and safety, is a reduction in individual risks. The lives saved are usually a mathematical construct, a statistical equivalent to what, at the level of the individual, is expressible as a longevity estimate but not a finite extension of life.

# 6 | Strategic Relationships in Dying

OME YEARS AGO I had occasion to address the question, What is it worth to save a life? Many expensive government programs have as their purpose, or include among their consequences, the saving of lives. But except for dramatic rescues, most programs that save lives do so by reducing some statistical likelihood of death among some part of the population. Deaths are reduced in the aggregate, but we may never know who would have died, but didn't, because of some improvement in safety or reduction in risk. Even when it is known afterward whose death was averted, it wasn't known when the program was decided on who the beneficiaries would be.

Not knowing yet who will benefit, perhaps never knowing who did benefit, we can approach the issues less dramatically and more straightforwardly. It is distasteful to count costs when deciding whether a rescue crew should keep drilling in a collapsed mine where it is known there are survivors; but it is easy to count costs, and we always do, in deciding whether to install traffic lights, to take the sulfur out of the coal we burn, or to enlarge the local fire department.

Not knowing who it is that may benefit from a statistically life-saving or mortality-reducing expenditure changes the decision in another way. When we decide what it is worth to save a particular life, the life is always somebody else's. But when we reduce in small measure some widespread risk to the population—reducing air pollution or producing a flu vaccine—we who discuss the value of the lifesaving, even those among us who participate in the decision, are part of the population at risk. We are not ourselves immortal; we are all consumers when risks are reduced and life expectancy lengthened. We cannot confine ourselves to the moralistic question, What is it worth to us to extend somebody else's life expectancy? or even to the legislative question, How much should some be taxed that others may have their life expectancies lengthened? Instead we share the question, What is it worth *to us* to reduce the risks that afflict *us*, to increase *our* life expectancy, to save some among us—we've no way of knowing who they will be—who might otherwise die? There is nothing inspirational in deciding whether it is worth the cost to install a lightning rod on the roof of my own house; and there is nothing wrong with self-interest in voting on whether to increase my town's expenditure on libraries, tennis courts, traffic controls, or fire equipment.

This question, What is it worth to me to reduce the risks to my own life?, or, What is it worth to my family to reduce the risks to my family?, is not the only point of view from which to enlighten the issues involved in public programs to save lives. But it is one point of view, an important one, sometimes the right one, and a refreshing check on the valuations one may arrive at by supposing vicariously that it is always "they" who die and "we" who make the decisions.

For what I wrote back then (in this book, the preceding chapter) I chose as title a familiar slogan: "The Life You Save May Be Your Own." Now I want the reader to join me in supposing that the "right to die" we are talking about is our right, not somebody else's. Most of the people who deal professionally with the subject are concerned with the dying—ministering to them, defending their rights, providing them help or protection, designing institutions for their comfort and dignity. I do not professionally deal with the dying; I do not represent them or advise them or treat them, nor do I deal with their families or their physicians or their attorneys, or their hospitals and nursing homes. I also am not myself dying, as far as I know; so I do not speak for "them" nor do I have a particular plea on behalf of a particular group of victims.

I represent the consumer. I am somebody who, like everybody else, is going to die. Like most of us, I am going to die but do not know how or in what circumstances, whether suddenly or after protracted illness, conscious or unknowing, expensively or cheaply, mute or articulate, in dignity or in defilement, a comfort or a burden to my family, or without any family at all.

## A Social Compact

And I ask myself what institutional arrangements I would like to govern my dying. What rules or traditions or practices would I like to be established? What rights and privileges and obligations would I like to govern my dying and the dying of others, recognizing that I shall share in the expense of the things that cost money, that I shall share in obligations to the dying just as I enjoy the obligations of others when I am the dying, and that the claims I would like to make when it is my turn to die will be the claims that the dying make on me when I am not yet dying?

From this point of view the issue is not the asymetrical one of my moral obligation to the dying, or their moral obligations to us, or what I shall want from you when it is my turn to be the dying. It is the more practical question—terribly important, but properly self-centered—of the arrangements for dying under which I would prefer to live *and* die.

For concreteness let me suppose that the various legal, ethical, financial, and professional arrangements that govern dying were determined within the individual states and that each among the fifty states had different traditions and practices and laws and institutions with respect to dying and death. Suppose that different states have different "rights to die" and "rights to live," different divisions of authority among physicians, hospital directors, public officials, spouses, and parents and guardians, different ways to allocate scarce medical resources or to apportion the costs of caring for the dying, different rules of privacy and immunity, different laws about suicide and malpractice and insurance claims, different rules for clergy, ombudsmen, and the judiciary. In which state would I prefer to live and die?

Having invited you to look at the issues from this standpoint, I am now going to disappoint you. This may be the right way to look at the subject, or at least one useful way, but it is not one that makes the subject any easier. From this point of view the subject is less loaded with morality, duty, and right and wrong; but it may be intellectually easier to identify one's duty in a particular situation than to identify that complex of rights and obligations with which one would choose to surround oneself if one had to do the choosing.

But a few of the issues do become a little easier to manage from this point of view. First, we can now disagree, even disagree sharply, about the regimes for dying that we prefer, without having to acknowledge that if one of us is right the other must be wrong, and especially without having to conclude that if one of us is morally correct the other must be morally wrong. Those among us who can differ about the lifestyles we choose, but who can respect each other because lifestyle is a matter of taste, may now differ in the deathstyles we prefer. The way of dying that appeals to me may not be the one that appeals to you, but, then, ways of living that appeal to me may not appeal to you. The amenities that I would sacrifice to avoid discomfort at dying may not be the amenities that you would sacrifice to avoid particular discomforts at dying, but, then, we differ about the trades we make every day in where and how we live and work and divide our time between earning money and enjoying leisure, or the way we trade sociability for solitude. So in choosing, from the point of view of dying, the state we want to live in, there is no need to feel that anything fundamental is necessarily wrong if we choose differently among the states.

The consumer point of view is also helpful in thinking about how great the sacrifices are that we should want to make for the dying, or to keep people from dying, and what the limits are to the time and trouble and money we should devote to the dying and to those who may die. Because from this point of view it is not what we owe them and ought to do for them, or what others owe us and ought to do for us; it is where we would choose to set the balance when it is both our time and trouble and money when they are dying, and their time and trouble and money when we are dying. The question is what bargain I want to make. How far do I want to impair my joy in living to relieve the discomfort of dying? How much do I want to be obliged to help others in their distress so that they are obliged to help me in mine? How much of the burden of my dying do I want others to accept if I must in like measure share the burden of their dying?

To withhold anything that might prolong a comfortable life may seem a dereliction when viewed unilaterally, and give rise to feelings of guilt; but to agree ahead of time that you don't have to do it for me if I don't have to do it for you may be a sensible bargain. If I choose a regime in which a spouse is not to be indefinitely enslaved to a helpless partner, you cannot easily dismiss me as heartless and selfish if we don't yet know which of the two partners I am going to be.

This question of the "rights of the dying" is different from that of the "right to die," but they are related. The right to die is occasionally the right to relieve loved ones of a physical and financial and emotional burden; and the "right to die" may include the right to relinquish certain claims for living that, viewed as reciprocal obligations, make a poor bargain.

But to recognize this principle does not mean it can be implemented. Let me go back to that question of saving lives with which I opened this essay. People who go to sea in boats may all agree that it is uneconomical to search more than one day for somebody lost at sea. While further search is not hopeless and people are occasionally rescued after the first day's effort, it is enormously expensive; and all who stand to benefit have to pay the cost of trying to rescue each other, and find it a cost not worth paying. Having agreed to that, you are lost at sea and at the end of a day we haven't found you. It will not be easy to curtail the rescue. Especially if the community is small and we know you and must live with the thought that had we tried one more day we might have saved you, and if we must face your family. One more day and another and another may be irresistible, though we damn ourselves for wasting our resources, not at all reconciled by the thought that, when it is our own turn to be lost at sea, others will waste their time and money in a fruitless search for us.

But if search beyond a certain distance requires aircraft and we agree not to acquire the aircraft, we cannot mount the extra search and there will be neither guilt nor a coerced waste of resources. We took the decision together—the one who is lost having shared in the decision—and each took the decision knowing that the person lost at sea could be himself. Any agreement not to waste resources taking care of each other in extremity, however sound the bargain that it represents, will be hard to enforce unless we can deny ourselves the ability.

### Make Me . . .

That situation is at one extremity of the spectrum of the "right to die." Let me divide the spectrum arbitrarily into three segments.

The three correspond to the demands "Let me die," "Help me die," and "Make me die." The third, "Make me die," involves at least two very different concepts. One is unilateral: make me die for my sake; I ought to die but can't (and can't even want to). The second is the reciprocal bargain discussed a moment ago: make me die because that's what I contracted for. This second, stronger case, not "Please make me die" but "Go ahead and make me, that's the bargain," is not what people usually have in mind in discussing rights rather than obligations. But it is worth including here because the right to be held to a bargain is usually a prerequisite to making the bargain.

The "right to be sued" for breach of contract sounds paradoxical, but if one cannot be sued for breach of contract one cannot find anybody to enter the contract. The right to have my mortgage foreclosed is part of the right to borrow money. The right to enter an enforceable contract is one of those important rights that we grant to corporations and that we withhold from children until they reach eighteen or twenty-one. If they can't repossess your car, they won't sell you the car on credit; if they can't hold you to your guarantee, they won't buy your merchandise. And the "right to forego" excessive claims for medical support will be part of the right to avoid excessive reciprocal obligations.

The more poignant case and more philosophically troubling is the demand "Make me die for my sake." Not "Let me" but "Make me." Make me, despite my wish to go on living, despite my pleading to be kept alive, despite my most desperate efforts to hang onto life. How does this situation arise, and what are the principles we should want to govern the response?

It arises of course when I have asked you in advance to see that I die if certain conditions befall me and to disregard any change of mind that the fear of imminent death may seem to induce. I have asked you not to heed my pleas when I become so deranged that I won't go through with it. I have commanded you not to let me live in such condition, and if I should become terrified of dying you must not prolong my terror.

We confront the question, Which is the authentic "I" in that crisis? There are probably two of me, one who was in command when I made anticipatory arrangements, contemplated the alternatives, and gave my instructions and warned you not to heed that other one who would surface and speak with my voice when it was time to die. Is that crisis the moment of truth or the moment of derangement?

A similar problem of authenticity arises in many contexts, though not often with quite the finality of this decision to heed or not to heed the plea to rescind the earlier instruction. Someone addicted to alcohol, drugs, or cigarettes, or a compulsive overeater, may ask you under no circumstances to heed a plea for a smoke or a drink or a dose or another helping, even if he pleads or screams with tears in his eyes. Indeed, the more frantically he pleads the more you may be enjoined to recognize what a horror you perpetuate, while momentarily relieving it, if you accede. I am told that people who are determined to try parachuting are sometimes incapable of leaping from the aircraft and may need and want and request to be forcibly expelled in the event they freeze at the last minute. Which is the authentic individual, the one who grips the door frame until his knuckles turn white, desperately resisting the foot against his back, or the one who said, on the ground a few minutes earlier, to use all the strength you need to get him out and not to mistake his phobia for himself?

I do not believe it is possible to hold your breath and die; before you die your urge to breathe will overcome your urge to die, however much you regret it once you've caught your breath. If someone is to help you, he must not interpret your struggle for breath as a reversal of your decision.

But these considerations do not settle the question; they merely create it. It is profoundly important to recognize that to let somebody live who previously chose to die can be as heartless and irresponsible as giving a second helping to the person whose doctor prescribed diet. But how do you know the person isn't starving, and how do you know the one who earlier elected to die hasn't really seen at last what he never saw before and has genuinely changed his mind? I am arguing only for the legitimacy of the problem, not for any particular solution.

### Let Me . . .

"Let me die" at the other end of the spectrum raises tortuous issues, even for those for whom no divine laws are involved. Before mentioning some of the complications that most trouble me, let me point out that the let-help-make division is itself ambiguous: unplugging my respirator does all three. "Let" implies that I want you to; "Make" may imply that I shall not want you to; but the difference is in the motive rather than the action. And the difference between letting and helping will often depend just on what the norm is: not removing the medicine with which I can overdose myself is "letting" if the custom is to let me be custodian of my own medicine, "helping" if the custom is to keep it out of reach.

Letting me die can take a number of forms. There is the physical one of allowing me the means to end my life. There is also relieving me of any moral obligation to stay alive, or of guilt, or legal sanctions; providing moral support; helping to avert the shame or disgrace of people to whom my death will be a reproach or a scandal.

At first glance I like the idea of being allowed to die. It isn't asking you to become an accessory by helping; it isn't asking you to overrule my pleas if I change my mind. It is not a right that I exercise against you, a claim that places a duty on you; it only asks you not to interfere or to impose hindrance or penalty.

But some rights bring responsibilities and verge on obligations. The "right" of a seventeen-year-old to volunteer in wartime can subject him to a sense of obligation. The right to early retirement can be construed as an obligation to get out and clear the way for others. The right to depart this world at least raises the question whether the decent thing wouldn't be to discontinue being a burden, an annoyance, an expense, and a source of anxiety to the people in whose care a dying person finds himself. My disability is a burden we share as long as no alternative is available; it is a burden of which I can relieve you if the option of dying is known to be available. And it is an option that can preoccupy us whether or not there is any immediate intention of taking advantage of it.

If I could die and relieve you of the burden and the expense, how could you persuade me you truly wanted me to live? Telling me so repeatedly will only demonstrate your awareness of my option, remind me of it, and remind me that I cannot take it for granted. And how do you discuss it behind my back? If my surviving gains me a few years of life of exceedingly low quality and condemns my spouse to the same when she could have been free of me had I exercised my right to go, and you feel this keenly, just how do you perceive your obligation to her, including your obligation to respect what she believes to be her obligations, and how do you mediate your obligations to her and your obligations to me? How do I manage my guilt upon awaking every morning, knowing I am spoiling another day of her life; and how do I evaluate the guilt she will feel if I take my life for her sake?

These are rhetorical questions as I pose them now, to remind us that freedom of choice is not always welcome and that more choice can mean more conflict, that rights may entail the obligation to exercise them. In the actual event they would be not rhetorical questions but real ones. I raise these unhappy questions not to suggest that they are unanswerable and that the right to die would bring more grief than it would remove. My purpose is only to illustrate how hard it is to anticipate how much freedom we should want and what kinds of constraints and safeguards may be needed.

## Help Me . . .

"Help me die" is even more laden with potential anxiety, conflict and misunderstanding, suspicion, guilt, and mistrust. Help can mean anything from "Let me—just don't intervene, when intervening to stop me would be your normal response" to "Do it for me, I can't do it myself; without your help I am doomed to live and suffer." And there are at least two important ways that I can be unable to do it for myself; I may be physically unable or, like that parachutist, I may be unable to make myself act.

The right to your help is the right to make you an accessory. If someone will help and someone won't, the first appears guilty of complicity. And if you volunteer your help—if I need your help even in raising the subject—how am I to interpret your suggestion that, with your help, I can accomplish my own removal? When I ask your help in dying are you to interpret that as a plea to be talked out of it, especially if I say I want to die to unburden others? What witnesses shall we need to allay my fears that you may "help me" when I don't want the help, or that you misunderstand me? What witnesses shall we need to protect you from the suspicion that you were a little too ready with your help? And if I continually change my mind, asking help in the morning and rescinding my request in the evening, begging to live and then begging to die, which of the two is my authentic self to whom you are responsible?

"Help" can mean many things, only one of which is being instrumental in some lethal process. It can mean comfort and moral support as I take a critical step myself. It can mean phoning the physician or the attorney or making legal arrangements, or helping me go where I can solve the problem myself or find professional help for the terminal process. It can even mean defending me from those who would intervene to prevent my dying. Most of all it may mean helping me to reach the right decision, whichever decision that is, sharing the anxiety and the uncertainty and the moral burden, even while being yourself an interested party.

The least burdensome kind of help and the least divisive would probably be participation in the arrangements we might make together, while death is still remote and hypothetical, for a decent death in certain contingencies. Let me propose a piece of technology out of science fiction, which I imagine is actually feasible. A particular contingency in which many people appear willing to hope they would die is a severely disabling stroke, a stroke that leaves one bedridden and inarticulate. Some of us may wish to die because of the horror and indignity of being unable to feed ourselves and unable even to smile if we should recognize our visitors; some of us want to remove a penalty that no one would dream of inflicting on the family, and a gratuitous expense for which no value is received. Now suppose there were available a diagnostic contrivance that could be implanted in the brain that, in the event of cerebral hemorrhage, would measure the severity, remaining inactive if the predicted paralysis were below some limiting value but fatally aggravating the condition above that limit. My conjecture is that the principle would be attractive to many of us.

In line with the consumer point of view that I am urging, I can also conjecture that it would be unattractive to many of us. I should be surprised, however, if even among those who would deprecate such mechanical contingent suicide, or automatic euthanasia, it wouldn't be considered superior to a contractual arrangement to provide an equivalent result by human hand.

### Who?

I've said nothing about the physician's role. I doubt whether it is good to give the physician much of a role, beyond a diagnostic and analytical role, in the decisions to let or to help or to make a patient die. It must be hard enough to be a good physician without being lawyer, clergyman, ombudsman, referee, and family counsellor or family arbiter, and it may help both patient and physician and their relation to each other to have the physician unambiguously devoted to the patient's life and comfort. But because the choice of treatment is often a trade of life expectancy for quality of life, the physician cannot always exempt himself from a role in the decisions to shorten or lengthen life. If the physician's role has typically been a dominant one, that may be because no other profession, at least no other lay profession, has been rash enough to seek aggressively an important role for itself.

As a consumer who is not yet a patient, I am attracted to the notion that an attorney is closer than a physician to the kind of profession that may need to be involved in exercising the right to die. It is, after all, attorneys who deal with many of the consequences of death, drawing wills and serving as executors when decisions must be made about the custody of children or the distribution of wealth. The issues in the right to die involve conflict of interest, enforcement of contract, and the maintenance of legal proprieties without which the whole arrangement could degenerate into something quite barbarian. Something like an ombudsman or executor may be needed, especially if that person could be chosen well in advance of the contingency, the way some of us choose the executors named in our wills.

I am not ready to choose which among fifty variegated regimes for dying I might wish to live in. If they actually existed in great diversity, we should have experience that would make the choice a more informed one, perhaps an easier one. The whole subject is in dispute, but not in great enough dispute, not enough to generate widespread imaginative exploration and critical evaluation of competing alternatives.

# 7 | Economics and Criminal Enterprise

A T THE LEVEL of national policy, if not always of local practice, the dominant approach to organized crime is through indictment and conviction. This is in striking contrast to the enforcement of antitrust or food-and-drug laws or the policing of public utilities, which work through regulation, accommodation, and the restructuring of markets. For some decades antitrust problems have received the sustained professional attention of economists concerned with the structure of markets, the organization of business enterprise, and the incentives toward collusion or price-cutting. Racketeering and the provision of illegal goods (like gambling) have been conspicuously neglected by economists. (There exists no analysis of the liquor industry under Prohibition that begins to compare with the best available studies of the aluminum or steel industries, air transport, milk distribution, or public-utility pricing.) Yet a good many economic and business principles that operate in the "upperworld" must, with suitable modification for change in environment, operate in the underworld as well—just as a good many economic principles that operate in an advanced competitive economy operate as well in a socialist or a primitive economy.

In addition to the sheer satisfaction of curiosity there are good policy reasons for encouraging a "strategic" analysis of the criminal underworld. Such an analysis, in contrast to "tactical" intelligence aimed at the apprehension of individual criminals, could help in identifying the incentives and disincentives to organize crime, in evaluating the costs and losses due to criminal enterprises, and in restructuring laws and programs to minimize the costs, wastes, and injustices that crime entails.

What market characteristics determine whether a criminal activity becomes "organized"? Gambling, by all accounts, invites organization; abortion, by all accounts, did not. In the upperworld, automobile manufacture is characterized by large firms but not machine-tool production; collusive price-fixing occurs in the electrical-machinery industry but not in the distribution of fruits and vegetables. The reasons for these differences are not entirely understood, but they are amenable to study. The same should not be impossible for gambling, extortion, and contraband cigarettes.

How much does organized crime depend on at least one major market in which the advantages of large scale are great enough to support a dominant monopoly firm or cartel? Not all businesses lend themselves to centralized organization; some do, and these may provide the nucleus of capital and entrepreneurial talent for extension into other businesses that would not, alone, support or give rise to an organized monopoly or cartel. Do a few "core" criminal markets provide the organizational stimulus for organized crime? If the answer turns out to be yes, then a critical question is whether the particular market so essential for the "economic development" of the underworld is a "black market," whose existence is dependent on the prohibition of legal competition, or instead is an inherently criminal activity. Black markets always offer to the policymaker, in principle, the option of restructuring the market—of increasing legal competition, of compromising the original prohibition, of selectively relaxing either the law itself or the way it is enforced. If, alternatively, that central criminal enterprise is one that rests on violence, relaxation of the law is likely to be both ineffectual and unappealing.

Since one of the interesting questions is why some underworld business becomes organized and some not, and another, what *kinds* of organization should be expected, a classification of these enterprises has to cover more than just "organized crime" and to distinguish types of organization. A tentative typology of underworld business might be as follows.

### Black Markets

A large part of organized crime is the selling of commodities and services contrary to law. In what we usually consider the underworld this includes drugs, prostitution, gambling, liquor (under Prohibition), abortions and pornography until recently, and contraband or stolen goods. Most of these are consumer goods.

In what is not usually considered the underworld, black markets include gold, contraceptives in some states, rationed commodities and coupons in wartime, loans and rentals above controlled prices, theater tickets in New York, and a good many similar commodities that, though not illegal per se, are handled outside legitimate markets or diverted from subsidized uses.

In some cases the law bans the commodity from all consumers; in others (cigarettes), some consumers are legitimate and some (minors) not. In some cases what is illegal is that the tax or duty has not been paid; in others, it is the price of the transaction that makes it illegal. In some (child labor, illegal immigrant labor), buying the commodity, not selling it, is proscribed.

### Racketeering

Racketeering includes two kinds of business, both based on intimidation. One is criminal monopoly, the other extortion.

"Criminal monopoly" means the use of criminal means to destroy competition. Whether a competitor is actually destroyed or just threatened with violence to make him go out of business, the object is to get protection from competition when the law will not provide it (by franchise or tariff protection) and when it cannot be legally achieved (through price wars, control of patents, or preclusive contracts).

We can distinguish altogether three kinds of "monopoly": those achieved through legal means; those achieved through means that are illegal only because of antitrust and other laws intended to make monopoly difficult; and monopolies achieved through means that are criminal by any standards—means that would be criminal whether or not they were aimed at monopolizing a business. It is also useful to distinguish between firms that, in an excess of zeal or deficiency of scruple, engage when necessary in ruthless and illegal competition, and the more strictly "racketeering" firms whose profitable monopoly rests entirely on criminal violence. The object of law enforcement in the former case is not to destroy the firm but to curtail its illegal practices. If the whole basis of success in business, though, is strong-arm methods that keep competition destroyed or scare it away, it is a pure "racket."

"Extortion" means living off somebody else's business by the threat of violence or of criminal competition. A protection racket lives off its victims, letting them operate and pay tribute. If one establishes a chain of restaurants and destroys competitors or scares them out of business, that is "monopoly"; if one merely threatens to destroy people's restaurant business, taking part of their profits as the price for leaving them alone, he is an extortionist and likes to see them prosper so that his share will be greater.

For several reasons it is difficult to distinguish "extortion" that, like a parasite, wants a healthy host, from "criminal monopoly" that is dedicated to the elimination of competitors. First, one means of extortion is to threaten to cut off the supply of a monopolized commodity—labor on a construction site, trucking, or some illegal commodity provided through the black market. That is to say, one can use a monopoly at one stage for extortionate leverage at the next. Second, extortion itself can be used to secure a monopoly privilege: instead of taking tribute in cash, for example, a victim signs a contract for the high-priced delivery of beer or linen supplies. The result looks like monopoly, but arose out of extortion.

It is evident that extortion can be organized or not, but in important cases it has to be. Vulnerable victims, after all, have to be protected from other extortionists. A monopolistic laundry service, deriving from a threat to harm the business that does not subscribe, has to destroy or to intimidate not only competing legitimate laundry services but other racketeers who would muscle in on the same victim. Thus, while criminal monopoly may not depend on extortion, organized extortion always needs an element of monopoly.

## Black-Market Monopoly

Any successful black marketeer enjoys a "protected" market in the way a domestic industry is protected by a tariff or butter is protected by a law against margarine. The black marketeer gets protection from the law against all competitors unwilling to pursue a criminal career. But there is a difference between a "protected industry" and a "monopolized industry." Abortion was a black-market commodity but not a monopoly; a labor racket is a local monopoly but not a black-market one; a monopoly in illicit drugs has both elements—it is a "black-market monopoly."

### Cartel

A "conspiracy in restraint of trade" that does not lead to single-firm monopoly but to collusive price-fixing, and that maintains itself by criminal action, gives rise to a cartel that is not in, but depends on, the underworld. If the garment trade eliminates competition by an agreement on prices and wages, hiring thugs to enforce the agreement, it is different from the monopoly racket just discussed. If the government would make such agreements legally enforceable (as it does with retail-price-maintenance laws in some states), the business would be in no need of criminally enforcing discipline on itself. Similarly, a labor union can use criminal means to discipline its members, even to the presumed benefit of its members, who may be better off working as a bloc rather than as competing individuals. If the law permits enforceable closed-shop agreements, the criminal means become unnecessary.

### Organized Criminal Services

A characteristic of the businesses listed above is that they usually involve relations between the underworld and the upperworld. But as businesses in the upperworld need legal services, financial advice, credit, enforcement of contract, places to conduct their business, and communication facilities, so in the underworld there has to be a variety of business services that are "domestic" to the underworld itself. These can be organized or unorganized. They are *in* the underworld, but not because they exploit the underworld as the underworld exploits the legitimate world.

### The Incentives to Criminal Organization

The simplest explanation of a large-scale firm, in the underworld or anywhere else, is high overhead costs or some other element of technology that makes small-scale operation more costly than large-scale. The need to keep equipment or specialized personnel fully utilized often explains at least the lower limit to the size of the firm.

A second explanation is the prospect of monopolistic prices. If most of the business can be cornered by a single firm, it can raise the price at which it sells its illegal services. Like any business, it does this at some sacrifice in size of the market; but if the demand is inelastic, the increase in profit margin will more than compensate for the reduction in output. Of course, decentralized individual firms would have as much to gain by pushing up the price, but without discipline it will not work; each will undercut its competitors. Where entry can be denied to newcomers, centralized price-setting will yield monopoly rewards to whoever can organize the market. With discipline a cartel can do it; in the absence of discipline a merger may do it; but intimidation, too, can lead to the elimination of competition and the conquest of a monopoly position by a single firm.

Third, the larger the firm, and especially the larger its share of the whole market, the more will formerly "external" costs become costs internal to the firm. "External costs" are those that fall on competitors, customers, bystanders, and others outside the firm itself. Collection of all the business within a single firm causes the costs that individual firms used to inflict on each other to show up as costs (or losses) to the larger centralized firm now doing the business. This is an advantage. The costs were originally there but disregarded; now there is an incentive to take them into account.

Violence is one such external cost. Racketeers have a collective interest in restricting violence, so as to avoid trouble with the public and the police; but the individual racketeer has little or no incentive to reduce the violence connected with his own crime. There is an analogy here with the whaling industry, which has a collective interest in not killing off the whales although an individual whaler has no incentive to consider what he is doing to the future of the industry when he maximizes his own catch. A large organization can afford to impose discipline, holding down violence if the business is crime, holding down the slaughter of females if the business is whaling.

There are also "external economies" that can become internalized, to the advantage of the centralized firm. Lobbying has this character, as does cultivating relations with the police. No small bookie can afford to spend money to influence gambling legislation, but an organized trade association or monopoly among those who live off illegal gambling can. Similarly with labor discipline: the small firm cannot afford to teach a lesson to the labor force of the industry, since most of the lesson is lost on other people's employees, but a single large firm can expect the full benefit of its labor policy. Similarly with cultivating the market: if one cultivates the market for illegal drugs, by hooking some customers, or cultivates a market for gambling in a territory where the demand is still latent, he cannot expect much of a return on his investment if opportunistic competitors will take advantage of the market he creates. Anything that requires a long investment in cultivating a consumer interest, a labor market, ancillary institutions, or relations with the police can be undertaken only by a fairly large firm that has reason to expect that it can enjoy most of the market and get a satisfactory return on the investment.

Finally, there is the attraction of not only monopolizing a market but achieving a dominant position in the underworld itself and participating in its governing. To the extent that large criminal business firms provide a governmental structure to the underworld, helping to maintain peace, setting rules, arbitrating disputes, and enforcing discipline, they are in a position to set up their own businesses and exclude competition. Constituting a "corporate state," they can give themselves the franchise for various "state-sponsored monopolies." They can do this either by denying the benefits of underworld government to their competitors or by using the equivalent of their "police power" to prevent competition.

### Market Structure

In evaluating crime, an accounting approach gives at best a bench mark as to magnitudes, and not even that for the distribution of economic and social gains and losses. The problem is like that of estimating the comparative incidence of profits taxes and excise taxes, or the impact of a minimum-wage law on wage differentials. Especially if we want to know who bears the cost, or to compare the costs to society with the gains to the criminals, an analysis of *market adjustments* is required. Even the pricing practices of organized crime need to be studied.

Consider the illegal wire-service syndicate in Miami that received attention from Senator Kefauver's committee in the 1950s. The magnitude that received explicit attention was the loss of state revenues as a result of the diversion of gambling from legal racetracks, which were taxable, to illegal bookmakers, whose turnover was not taxable. No accounting approach would yield this magnitude; it depended (as was pointed out in testimony) on what economists call the "elasticity of substitution" between the two services—on the fraction of potential racetrack business that patronized bookmakers.

Similar analysis is required to determine *at whose expense* the syndicate operated, or what the economic consequences of the syndicate's removal would have been. The provision of wire service was of small economic significance. It accounted on a cost basis for less than 5 percent of the net income of bookmakers (of which the syndicate took approximately 50 percent). And cheaper wire service to the bookies might have been available in the absence of the syndicate, whose function was not to provide wire service but to eliminate wire-service competitors.

The essential business of the syndicate was to practice *extortion against bookmakers*. It demanded half their earnings, against the threat of reprisals. The syndicate operated like a taxing authority (as well as providing some reinsurance on large bets); it apparently did not limit the number of bookmakers so long as they paid their "taxes."

How much of this tax was passed along to the customer (on the analogy of a gasoline or a sales tax) and how much was borne by the bookie (on the analogy of an income or profits tax) is hard to determine. If we assume (1) that bookmakers' earnings are approximately proportionate to the volume of turnover, (2) that their customers, though sensitive to the comparative odds of different bookmakers, are not sensitive to the profit margin, and (3) that they tend, consciously or implicitly, to budget their total bets and not their rate of loss, we can conclude that the tax is substantially passed along to the customer. In that case the bookmaker, though nominally the victim of extortion, is victimized only into raising the price to his customers, somewhat like a filling station that must pay a tax on every gallon sold. The bookmaker is thus an intermediary between an extortionate syndicate and a customer who pays his tribute voluntarily on the price he is willing to pay for his bets.

The syndicate in Miami relied on the police as their favorite instrument of intimidation. It could have been the other way around, with the police using the syndicate as their agency to negotiate and collect from the bookmakers; and if the police had been organized and disciplined as a monopoly, it would have been the police, not the syndicate, that we should put at the top of our organizational pyramid. From the testimony, though, it is evident that the initiative and entrepreneurship came from the syndicate, which had the talent and organization for this kind of business, and that the police lacked the centralized authority for exploiting to their own benefit the power they had over the book-makers. Presumably—though there were few hints of this in the hearings—the syndicate could have mobilized other techniques for intimidating the bookmakers; the police were the chosen in-strument only so long as the police share in the proceeds was com-petitive with alternative executors of the intimidating threats.

Any attempt to estimate the long-term effect on police salaries would have to take into account how widespread and nondis-criminatory the police participation was, especially by rank and seniority in service. Recruiting would be unaffected if police re-cruits were unaware of the illegal earnings that might accrue to them; senior members of the force who might otherwise have quit the service or lobbied harder for pay increases would agitate less vigorously for high wages if their salaries were augmented by the racket. One cannot easily infer that part of the "tax" paid by the bookmaker's customer subsidized the police force to the benefit of non-betting taxpayers; mainly they supported a more discrimina-tory and irregular earnings pattern among the police—besides contributing, unwittingly, to a demoralization of the police that would have made it a bad bargain for the taxpayer anyway.

This is just a sketch, based on the skimpy evidence available, of the rather complex structure of "organized gambling" in one city. (It is not of course the gambling that is organized; the organiza-tion is an extortionate monopoly that nominally provides a wire service but actually imposes a tribute on middlemen who pass most of the cost along to their voluntary customers.) Similar anal-ysis would be required to identify the incidence of costs and losses (and gains of course) of protection rackets everywhere (such as monopoly-priced beer deliveries to bars or restaurants or vending machines installed in bars and restaurants under pain of damage or nuisance).

## Institutional Practices

Institutional practices in the underworld need to be better under-stood. What, for example, is the effect of the tax laws on extor-tion? Why does an extortionist put cigarette machines in a restaurant or provide linen service? Do the tax laws make it difficult to disguise the payment of tribute in cash but easy to disguise it (and make it tax deductible) if the tribute takes the form of a concession or the purchase of high-priced services? Why does a gambling syndicate bother to provide "wire service" when evidently its primary economic function is to shake down bookies by the threat of hurting their businesses or their persons, possibly with the collusion of the police?

The Kefauver hearings indicate that the wire-service syndicate in Miami took a standard 50 percent from the bookies. The symmetry of the 50 percent figure is itself remarkable. Equally remarkable is that the figure was uniform. But most remarkable of all is that the syndicate went through the motions of providing a wire service when it perfectly well could have taken cash tribute instead. There is an analogy here with the car salesman who refuses to negotiate the price of a new car but is willing to negotiate quite freely the "allowance" on the used car that one turns in. The underworld seems to need institutions, conventions, traditions, and recognizable standard practices much like the upperworld of business. A better understanding of these practices might lead not only to a better evaluation of crime but also to a better understanding of the role of tax laws and regulatory laws on the operation of criminal business.

The role of vending machines, for example, appears to be that they provide a tax-deductible, nondiscriminatory, and "respectable" way of paying tribute. Pinball and slot machines installed by a gang in somebody's small store may be only half characterized when identified as "illegal gambling"; they are equally a conventionalized medium for the exaction of tribute from the store owner. Effective enforcement of a ban on the machines will take care of the "gambling" part of the enterprise; what happens to the extortion racket depends then on how readily some other lucrative concession, some exclusive delivery contract, or some direct cash tribute can be imposed on the store owner.

Even the resistance to crime would be affected by measures designed to change the cost structure. Economists make an important distinction between a lump-sum tax, a profits tax, and a specific or ad valorem tax on the commodity an enterprise sells. The manner in which a criminal monopolist or extortionist prices his service, or demands his tribute, should have a good deal to do with whether the cost is borne by the victim or passed along to the customer. The "tax" levied by the racketeer uniformly on all his customers—monopoly-priced beer or linen supplies—may just be passed along in turn to their customers, with little loss to the immediate victims, if the demand in their own market is inelastic. A bar that has to pay an extortionate price for its beer can seek relief in either of two ways. It can try to avoid paying the extortionate or monopolized price; alternatively, it can insist that its supplier achieve similar concessions from all competing bars, to avoid a competitive disadvantage. An individual bar suffers little if the price of wholesale beer goes up; it suffers when competitors' prices do not go up.

Similarly, legal arrangements that make it difficult to disguise illegal transactions and that make it a punishable offense to pay tribute might help to change the incentives. In a few cases the deliberate stimulation of competing enterprises could be in the public interest: loan-sharking, for example, might be somewhat mitigated by the deliberate creation of new and specialized lending enterprises. Loan-sharking appears to involve several elements, only one of which is the somewhat outmoded notion —outmoded by a few centuries—that people so much in need of cash that they'd pay high interest rates should be protected from "usury" even if it means that they are protected by being denied any access to credit at all. A second element is that, now that debtors' prison has been liberally abolished, people who cannot post collateral have no ready way to assure their own motivation to repay—attachment of wages has also been liberally made illegal—so that those without assets who need cash must pledge life and limb in the underworld. Thus, when the law has no way of enforcing contract, the underworld provides it: a man submits to the prospect of personal violence as the last resort in contract enforcement. Finally, the borrower whose prospects of repayment are so poor that even the threat of violence cannot hold him to repayment is enticed into an arrangement that makes him a victim of perpetual extortion, one who cannot go to the law because he is already party to a criminal transaction. Evidently there is some part of this racket that thrives on a void in our legal and financial institutions.

### Evaluating Costs and Losses

Crime is bad, as cancer is bad; but even for cancer, one can distinguish among death, pain, anxiety, the cost of treatment, the loss of earnings, the effects on the victim, and the effects on his family. Similarly with crime. It is offensive to society that the law be violated. But crime can involve a transfer of wealth from the victim to the criminal, a net social loss from the inefficient mode of transfer, the creation of fear and anxiety, violence from which nobody profits, the corruption of the police and other public officials, costs of law enforcement and private protection, high prices to customers, unfairness of competition, loss of revenue to the state, and even loss of earnings to the criminals themselves, who in some cases may be ill-suited to their trade.

There are important tradeoffs among these different costs and losses resulting from crime, and in the different ways that government can approach the problem of crime. There will be choices between reducing the incidence of crime and reducing the consequences of crime, and other choices that require a more explicit identification and evaluation of the magnitude and distribution of the gains and losses.

If there were but one way to wage war against crime, and the only question how vigorously to do it, there would be no need to identify the different objectives (costs and consequences) in devising the campaign. But if this is a continual campaign to cope with some pretty definite evils, without any real expectation of total victory or unconditional surrender, resources have to be allocated and deployed in a way that maximizes the value of a compromise.

In the black markets it is especially hard to identify just what the evils are. In the first place, a law-abiding citizen is not obliged to consider the procurement and consumption of illegal commodities inherently sinful. We have constitutional procedures for legislating prohibitions; the out-voted minority is bound to abide by the law, but not necessarily to agree with it, and can even campaign to become a majority and legalize liquor after a decade of Prohibition, or legalize contraceptives in states where they have been prohibited. Even those who vote to ban gambling or saloons or narcotics can do so, not because they consider the consumption sinful but because *some* of the consequences are bad; and if it is infeasible to prohibit the sale of alcohol only to alcoholics, or gambling only to minors, we have to forbid all of it to forbid the part we want to forbid.

The only reason for rehearsing these arguments is to remind ourselves that the evil of gambling, drinking, or illicit drugs is not necessarily proportionate to how much of it goes on. The evil can be greater or less than suggested by any such figure. One might, for example, conclude that the consumption of narcotics that actually occurs is precisely the consumption that one wanted to prevent and that it is the more harmless consumption that has been eliminated; or one might conclude that the gambling laws eliminate the worst of gambling, that what filters through the laws is fairly innocuous (or would be, if its being illegal per se were not harmful to society), and that gambling laws thus serve the purpose of selective discrimination in their enforcement if not in their enactment.

The alleged evils of abortion are particularly difficult to evaluate, especially because it is everybody's privilege to attach his own moral value to the commodity. [This essay was written—not a long time ago—when abortion was criminal in fifty states. The issues it exemplifies still need to be understood, even if many among us hope abortion never again becomes associated with crime. Leaving the essay as I wrote it, except for occasionally changing the tense of a verb, helps to dramatize the transient nature of some prohibitions. Gambling, pornography, and contraceptives have also changed in relation to criminal law and its enforcement, as has marijuana.] Are the disgust, anxiety, humiliation, and physical danger incurred by the abortionists' customers part of the "net cost" to society, or are they positively valued as punishment for the wicked? If a woman gets an abortion, do we prefer she pay a high price or a low one? Is the black-market price a cost to society, a proper penalty inflicted on the woman, or an economic waste? If a woman gets a safe cheap abortion abroad, is this a legitimate bit of "international trade," raising the national income like any gainful trade, or is it even worse than her getting an expensive, more disagreeable, more dangerous abortion at home, because she evaded the punishment and the sense of guilt?

These are not academic questions. There are issues of policy in identifying what it is we dislike about criminal activity, especially in deciding where and how to compromise. The case of prostitution is a familiar example. Granting the illegality of prostitution, and efforts to enforce the law against it, one may still discover that one particular evil of prostitution is a hazard to health—the spread of venereal disease, a spread that is not confined to the customers but transmitted even to those who had no connection with the illicit commodity. Yet there is some incompatibility between a campaign to eradicate venereal disease and a campaign to eradicate prostitution, and one may prefer to legislate a public health service for prostitutes and their customers, even at the expense of "diplomatic recognition" of the enemy. The point is that a hard choice can arise and ideology gives no answer. If two of the primary evils connected with a criminal activity are negatively correlated, one has to distinguish them, separately evaluate them, and then make up one's mind.

Similarly with abortion. At the very least, one can propose clinical help to women seeking abortion for the limited purpose of eliminating from the market those who are actually *not* pregnant, providing them the diagnosis that an abortionist might have neglected or preferred to withhold. Going a step further, one may want to provide reliable advice about postabortion symptoms to women who may become infected or who may hemorrhage or otherwise suffer from ignorance. Still a step further, one may like to provide even abortionists with a degree of immunity, so that if a woman needs emergency treatment he can call for it without danger of self-incrimination. None of these suggestions compromises the principle of illegality; they merely apply to abortion some of the principles that would ordinarily be applied to hit-and-run driving or to an armed robber who inadvertently hurt his victim and preferred to call an ambulance.

One has to go a step further, though, on the analogy with contraception and ask about the positive or negative value of scientific discovery, or research and development, in the field of abortion itself. Cheap, safe, and reliable contraceptives are now considered a stupendous boon to mankind. What is the worth of a cheap, safe, and reliable technique of abortion, one that involves no surgery, no harmful or addicting drugs, no infection, and preferably not even reliance on a professional abortionist? Suppose some of the new techniques developed in Eastern Europe and elsewhere for performing safer and more convenient abortions become technically available to abortionists in this country, with the consequence that fewer patients suffer—but also with the consequence that more abortions are procured? How do we weigh these consequences against each other? Each of us may have his own answer, and a political or judicial decision is required if we want an official answer. But the questions cannot be ignored.

The same questions arise in the field of firearm technology. Do we hope that nonlethal weapons become available to criminals, so that they kill and damage fewer victims, or would we deplore it on the ground that any technological improvement available to criminal enterprise is against the public interest? Do we hope to see less damaging narcotics become available, perhaps cheaply available through production and marketing techniques that do not lend themselves to criminal monopoly, to compete with the criminally monopolized and more deleterious narcotics? Or is this a "compromise" with crime?

### Should Crime Be Organized or Disorganized?

It is usually implied, if not asserted, that organized crime is a menace and has to be fought. But if the alternative is "disorganized crime"—if the criminals and their opportunities will remain, but with a lesser degree of organization than before—the choice is not an easy one.

There is one argument for favoring the "organization" of crime. It is that organization would "internalize" some of the costs that fall on the underworld itself but go unnoticed, or ignored, if criminal activity is decentralized. The individual hijacker may be tempted to kill a truck driver to destroy a potential witness—to the dismay of the underworld, which suffers from public outrage and the heightened activity of the police. A monopoly or a trade association could impose discipline. This is not a decisive argument, nor does it apply to all criminal industries if it applies to a few; but it is important.

If abortion, for example, will not be legalized and cannot be eliminated, one can wish it were better organized. A large organization could not afford to mutilate so many women. It could impose higher standards. It would have an interest in quality control and the protection of its "goodwill" that the petty abortionist is unlikely to have. As it is, the costs external to the enterprise—the costs that fall not on the abortionist but on the customer or on the reputation of other abortionists—are of little concern to him and he has no incentive to minimize them. By all accounts, criminal abortion is conducted more incompetently and more irresponsibly than illegal gambling.

### Compromising with Organized Crime

It is customary to deplore the accommodation that the underworld reaches, sometimes, with the forces of law and order, with the police, with the prosecutors, with the courts. Undoubtedly there is corruption of public officials, bad not only because it frustrates justice but also because it lowers standards of morality. On the other hand, officials concerned with law enforcement are inevitably in the front line of diplomacy between the legitimate world and the underworld. Aside from the approved negotiations by which criminals are induced to testify, to plead guilty, to surrender themselves, or to tip off the police, there is always a degree of accommodation between the police and the criminals—tacit or explicit understandings analogous to what in military affairs would be called the limitation of war, the control of armament, and the delineation of spheres of influence.

In criminal activity by legitimate firms—such as conspiracy in restraint of trade, tax evasion, illegal labor practices, or the marketing of dangerous drugs—regulatory agencies can deal specifically with the harmful practices. One does not have to declare war on the industry itself, only on the illegal practices. Regulation, even negotiation, are recognized techniques for coping with those practices. But when the business itself is criminal, it is harder to have an acknowledged policy of regulation and negotiation. For this involves a kind of "diplomatic recognition."

In the international field, one can cold-bloodedly limit warfare and come to an understanding about the kinds of violence that will be resisted or punished, the activities that will be considered nonaggressive, and the areas within the other side's sphere of influence. Maybe the same approach is necessary in dealing with crime. And if we cannot acknowledge it at the legislative level, it may have to be accomplished in an unauthorized or unacknowledged way by the people whose business—law enforcement—requires it of them.

### The Relation of Organized Crime to Enforcement

We have to distinguish the "black market monopolies," dealing in forbidden goods—gambling, drugs, smuggling, prostitution—from the racketeering enterprises. It is the black-market monopolies that depend on the law itself. Without the law and some degree of enforcement there is no presumption that the organization can survive competition—or, if it could survive competition once it is established, that the organization could have arisen in the first place in the face of competition.

There must be an "optimum degree of enforcement" from the point of view of the criminal monopoly. With no enforcement—either because enforcement is not attempted or because enforcement is not feasible—the black market could not be profitable enough to invite criminal monopoly (at least not any more than any other market, legitimate or criminal). With wholly effective enforcement, and no collusion with the police, the business would be destroyed. Between these extremes, there may be an attractive black market profitable enough to invite monopoly.

Organized crime could not, for example, possibly corner the market on cigarette sales to minors. Every twenty-one-year-old is a potential source of supply. No organization, legal or illegal, could keep a multitude of twenty-one-year-olds from buying cigarettes and passing them along to persons under twenty-one. No black-market price differential, great enough to make organized sale to minors profitable, could survive the competition. And no organization, legal or illegal, could so intimidate every adult that he would not be a source of supply to the youngsters. Without there being any way to enforce the law, organized crime would get no more out of selling cigarettes to children than out of selling them soft drinks.

The same is true of contraceptives in those states where their sale is nominally illegal. If the law is not enforced, there is no scarcity out of which to make profits. And if one is going to try to intimidate every drugstore that sells contraceptives, in the hope of monopolizing the business, he may as well monopolize toothpaste, which would be more profitable. The intervention of the law is needed to intimidate the druggists with respect to the one commodity that organized crime is trying to monopolize.

What about abortion? Why is it not "organized"? The answer is not easy, and there may be too many special characteristics of this market to permit a selection of the critical one. The consumer and the product have unusual characteristics. Nobody is a "regular" consumer the way a person may regularly gamble, drink, or use drugs. (A woman may repeatedly need the services of an abortionist, but each occasion is once-for-all.) The consumers are more secret about dealing with this black market, secret among intimate friends and relations, than are the consumers of most banned commodities. It is a dirty business and too many of the customers die; and while organized crime might drastically reduce fatalities, it may be afraid of getting involved with anything that kills and maims so many customers in a way that could be blamed on the criminal himself rather than just on the commodity that is sold.

## Black Markets and Competition

I have emphasized that a difference between black-market crimes and most others, like racketeering and robbery, is that they are "crimes" only because we have legislated against the commodity they provide. We single out certain goods and services as harmful or sinful; for reasons of history and tradition, and for other reasons, we forbid heroin but not tobacco, gambling in casinos but not on the stock market, extramarital sex but not gluttony, erotic stories but not mystery stories. We do all this for reasons different from those behind the laws against robbery and tax evasion.

It is policy that determines the black markets. Cigarettes and firearms are borderline cases. We can, as a matter of policy, make the sale of guns and cigarettes illegal. We can also, as a matter of policy, make contraceptives and abortion illegal. Times change, policies change, and what was banned yesterday can become legitimate today; what was freely available yesterday, can be banned tomorrow. Evidently there are changes under way in policy on birth control; there may be changes on abortion and homosexuality, and there may be legislation restricting the sale of firearms.

The pure black markets reflect some moral tastes, economic principles, paternalistic interests, and notions of personal freedom in a way that the rackets do not. And these tastes and principles change. We can revise our policy on birth control (and we are changing it) in a way that we could not change our policy on armed robbery. The usury laws may to some extent be a holdover from medieval economics; and some of the laws on prostitution, abortion, and contraception were products of the Victorian era and reflect the political power of various church groups. One cannot even deduce from the existence of abortion laws that a majority of the voters, even a majority of enlightened voters, oppose abortion; and the wise money would probably bet that the things that we shall be forbidding in fifty years will differ substantially from the things we forbid now.

What happens when a forbidden industry is subjected to legitimate competition? Legalized gambling is a good example. What has happened to Las Vegas is hardly reassuring. On the other hand, the legalization of liquor in the early 1930s swamped the criminal liquor industry with competition. Criminals are alleged to have moved into church bingo, but they have never got much of a hold on the stock market. Evidently criminals cannot always survive competition, evidently sometimes they can.

The question is important in the field of narcotics. We could easily put insulin and antibiotics into the hands of organized crime by forbidding their sale; we could do the same with a dentist's Novocain. (We could, that is, if we could sufficiently enforce the prohibition. If we cannot enforce it, the black market would be too competitive for any organized monopoly to arise.) If narcotics were not illegal, there could be no black market and no monopoly profits; the interest in "pushing" it would not be much greater than the pharmaceutical interest in pills to reduce the symptoms of common colds. This argument cannot by itself settle the question of whether (and which) narcotics (or other evil commodities) ought to be banned, but it is an important consideration.

The greatest gambling enterprise in the United States has not been significantly touched by organized crime. That is the stock market. (There has been criminal activity in the stock market, but not monopoly by what we usually call "organized crime.") Nor has organized crime succeeded in controlling the foreign currency black markets around the world. The reason is that the market works too well. Federal control over the stock market, designed mainly to keep it honest and informative and aimed at maximizing the competitiveness of the market and the information of the consumer, makes it a hard market to tamper with.

Ordinary gambling ought to be one of the hardest industries to monopolize. Almost anybody can compete, whether in taking bets or providing cards, dice, or racing information. "Wire services" could not stand the ordinary competition of radio and Western Union; bookmakers could not be intimidated if the police were not available to intimidate them. If ordinary brokerage firms were encouraged to take horse-racing accounts, and buy and sell bets by telephone for their customers, it is hard to see how racketeers could get any kind of grip on the business. And when any restaurant, bar, country club, or fraternity house can provide tables and sell fresh decks of cards, it is hard to see how gambling can be mönopolized any more than the soft-drink or television business, or any other.

We can still think gambling is a sin, and try to eliminate it; but we should probably try not to use the argument that it would remain in the hands of criminals if we legalized it. Both reason and evidence seem to indicate the contrary.

The decisive question is whether the goal of somewhat reducing the consumption of narcotics, gambling, prostitution, abortion, or anything else that is forced by law into the black market, is or is not outweighed by the costs to society of creating a criminal industry. The costs to society of creating these black markets are several.

First, it gives the criminal the same kind of protection that a tariff gives to a domestic monopoly. It guarantees the absence of competition from people who are unwilling to be criminal, and an advantage to those whose skill is in evading the law.

Second, it provides a special incentive to corrupt the police, because the police not only may be susceptible to being bought off but can even be used to eliminate competition.

Third, a large number of consumers who are probably not ordinary criminals—the conventioneers who visit prostitutes, the housewives who bet on horses, the women who seek abortions—are taught contempt, even enmity, for the law by being obliged to purchase particular commodities and services from criminals in an illegal transaction.

Fourth, drug addiction may so aggravate poverty for certain desperate people that they are induced to commit crimes, or can be urged to commit crimes, because the law arranges that the only (or main) source for what they desperately demand will be a criminal (high-priced) source.

Fifth, these big black markets may guarantee enough incentive and enough profit for organized crime so that large-scale criminal organization comes into being and maintains itself. It may be—this is an important question for research—that without these important black markets, crime would be substantially decentralized, lacking the kind of organization that makes it enterprising, safe, and able to corrupt public officials. In economic-development terms, these black markets may provide the central core (or "infrastructure") of underworld business.

A good economic history of Prohibition in the 1920s has never been attempted, so far as I know. By all accounts, though, Prohibition was a mistake. It merely turned the liquor industry over to organized crime. In the end we gave up, probably because not everybody agreed drinking was bad (or, if it was bad, that it was anybody's political business), but also because the attempt was an evident failure and a costly one in its social by-products. It may have propelled underworld business in the United States into what economic developers call the "take-off" into self-sustained growth.

# 8 | What Is the Business of Organized Crime?

I T IS BECOMING widely accepted that the business of organized crime is to provide the public with illicit goods and services like bets, narcotics, sex out of wedlock, and unregulated loans. Federal law even *defines* organized crime as those unlawful activities in which a highly organized, disciplined association supplies illegal goods and services. The appendix on organized crime in the Staff Report to the Commission on Violence states, "It is well known that organized crime exists and thrives because it provides services the public demands," and "Organized crime depends not on victims, but on customers."[1]

And the Task Force on Organized Crime of the 1967 President's Commission opened its report with the assertion, "The core of organized crime activity is the supplying of illegal goods and services—gambling, loansharking, narcotics, and other forms of vice—to countless numbers of citizen customers."[2]

This conception of organized crime corresponds to part of the image, although only a part, of the gangs that thrived when liquor was nationally prohibited in the 1920s and early 1930s. (Supplying liquor was the quieter part; suppressing rival supply was the part that made Chicago famous.)

This is in contrast to what may appear, at first glance, as a quite different line of business that, at different times and particularly in the later 1930s, appeared to characterize the organized

179

racketeers. This was extortion, based on the threat of damage, together with occasional efforts to monopolize "legitimate" lines of business by physically destroying or intimidating competition.

The Task Force Report gave lesser emphasis—nevertheless some emphasis—to the use by organized crime of "illegitimate methods" in connection with legitimate business and labor unions. These illegitimate methods were identified as "monopolization, terrorism, extortion, tax evasion." The contrast seems to be that in the "core" activities the racketeers are busy providing illicit goods and services, whereas, when they turn to legitimate business, they terrorize, blackmail, and monopolize.

In his appendix to that report, Donald Cressey, one of the outstanding investigators of this subject, draws a "basic distinction" between ordinary criminals and "organized criminals": the former are wholly predatory, and the latter offer "a return to the respectable members of society." Nobody will miss the burglars if they suddenly disappear. "But if the confederation of men employed in illicit businesses were suddenly abolished, it would be sorely missed because it performs services for which there is a great public demand."

And all are agreed that, as the Task Force stated, "To carry on its many activities secure from governmental interference, organized crime corrupts public officials." Further, some investigators, like the Kefauver committee, found that corruption procured not only immunity from the law but also employment of the police to enforce the mob's authority.

My purpose is to dissent from this widespread interpretation of what "organized crime" is engaged in. Mine will not be a disagreement with the facts, fragmentary as they are, from which most of the authors and commissions and lawmakers and law enforcers start. The difference will be one of analysis, of interpretation of what is going on. But, before dissenting, let me try to state in a purely descriptive, not analytical, way, what it is we all seem to be talking about when we speak of "organized crime."

Evidently we do not mean simply "crime that is organized." The term *organized crime* is not composed merely of two words in the English language that have their ordinary meanings when coupled in this fashion. Donald Cressey does not mean, I am sure, that burglars are never organized. If it should suit their purpose to work in small gangs, to share the take as a partnership, to vote new members into the club, to insure each other against accident or arrest and to maintain a common retirement fund, to have exclusive contracts with merchants who dispose of their goods and to regularize their relations with the police, to have a research staff, a retained lawyer, and a technological consultant, and to divide the labor among scouts, lookouts, breakers and enterers, and disposers of merchandise, they deserve to be called "organized" in the ordinary English-language sense of the word. But theirs would be a different kind of "organized crime" from what I am discussing, which is *organized crime*.

Exactly what is the difference? It can be described not only in the definitional language of the law, as being highly organized and disciplined—there may be highly organized and well-disciplined groups of burglars, or counterfeiters, or bank robbers, or embezzlers, or charlatans, or agitators—but as "a society that seeks to operate outside the control of the American people and their governments." Burglars may be *in* the underworld, but they do not apparently seek to govern it; they are not captains of underworld industry; they are not robber barons or monopolists; and they are not associated with ideas of power, control, and underworld "society."

Still, while it may be easy to say what we do not mean by *organized crime*, it is not easy to tell from the professional literature exactly what we should mean. There is no problem of course if we can simply point to a unique organization. There is no problem in defining what we mean by a "religious organization" if there is only one church, or by a "political party" if there is only one party. If there is a single "Mafia" that either governs and operates everywhere or has no counterpart in those places where it has no operations, we can give *organized crime* a proper name and call it "Mafia" with a capital M, "La Cosa Nostra" with capital letters, or "The Organization"—just as some people refer to "The Establishment" in relation to overworld society—and need not define the species because it has but a single member. But if we take that route we are committed to a particular hypothesis, one that is limited to a particular time and place, and one that precludes comparative analysis because the definition precludes comparison.

There is, I believe, a characteristic of *organized crime* that is consistent with all of these definitions and characterizations, even the one that treats "organized crime" as a proper noun, and that is consistent with most of the prevailing images of racketeers, whether based on stories of Chicago in the 1920s, New York in the 1930s, Miami in the 1940s, or any of these places in the 1960s. This key characteristic is suggested by the term, "society." But "society" is too broad and too loose for my purpose. "Government" would come closer to what I have in mind. The characteristic is *exclusivity,* or, to use a more focused term, *monopoly.* From all accounts, organized crime does not just extend itself broadly, but brooks no competition. It seeks not only influence, but exclusive influence. In the overworld its counterpart would be not just organized business, but monopoly. And we can apply to it some of the adjectives that are often associated with monopoly—ruthless, unscrupulous, greedy, exploitative, unprincipled.

Now it is clear that governments have to have an element of monopoly. We cannot all be obeying two conflicting sets of laws, two competing sets of traffic lights, or two contradictory building codes, and paying taxes to maintain duplicate street systems or armies. If there are several governments, they must work out jurisdictional or territorial arrangements, the way towns and counties and states and port authorities and the federal government do. So if an organization seeks governing authority in the underworld, we should expect it to seek exclusive authority, or at least to seek stable jurisdictional sharing with other authorities so that, all together, they constitute a hierarchy without competition.

That is what we should expect them to seek. We should not be surprised when civil war breaks out.

We now have a hint of what to look for when we ask about the business of organized crime. Part of my argument will be that organized crime is usually monopolized crime. What distinguishes the burglars from the loan sharks or the gambling syndicate is not only that one steals what we have and the other sells what we want. It is also that burglars are never reported to be fighting each other in gangs for exclusive control over their hunting grounds. Burglars are busy about their burglary, not staking claims and fighting off other burglars. It is when a gang of burglars begins to police its territory against the invasion of other gangs of burglars, and makes interloping burglars join up and share their loot or get out of town, collectively negotiating with the police not only for its own security but to enlist the police in the war against rival burglar gangs or nonjoining mavericks, that we should, I believe, begin to identify the burglary gang as "organized crime." Until then we should use a different term, like "organized burglary."

We can ask at this point why burglars are not "organized" in the more ambitious way I just described. More generally, why are some kinds of crime apparently "organized" in exclusivist monopoly fashion, and characterized by occasional gang wars and truces and market-sharing arrangements, while other kinds of crime are more like competitive business, the individual criminal or the criminal organization going about its business without a major effort to destroy or intimidate competition and obtain exclusive control?

There is probably no single or simple answer. The same question can be asked about business enterprise in the overworld. And there we find that some businesses lend themselves more than others to monopolization. And if we examine the businesses that seem rarely to be monopolized, or rarely to stay monopolized, and those that show a universal tendency to become monopolized, we may discover characteristics of the technology, the market, the consumer demand, the personnel requirements, or the financial and legal requirements that determine whether a business is ineluctably monopolized, sometimes monopolized, or hardly susceptible to monopolization. We can then turn to the underworld and see whether some corresponding principles apply.

In a purely descriptive sense this tendency toward monopolization surely seems to characterize organized crime. We have to keep in mind that rival claimants to monopoly position sometimes find it cheaper to merge than to make war, or cheaper to stabilize their boundaries than to fight over them, and that even war may lead to surrender and empire rather than to total destruction or massive retaliation. Where there is no governmental authority that can exert itself, or where a government is sympathetic or subservient to business, broad cartel arrangements may provide a framework for comparatively nonviolent resolution of competitive conflict.

It is worthwhile remembering that the Chicago gangster deaths of the 1920s, like the alleged Boston gangster deaths of the 1960s, were usually characterized, if not identified, as arising out of gang rivalry. Pickpockets and burglars and car thieves, embezzlers and people who cheat on their income taxes, shoplifters and muggers and bank robbers, usually don't go around killing each other.

There's nothing in it for them. Two bank robbers who pick the same day for the same bank may have to fight for the privilege if they arrive at the same time, and two purse-snatchers who grab the same purse may fight for possession; but these are rare instances, and the man who embezzles from the bank he works for has neither the knowledge nor the interest that would motivate him to make war on other embezzlers at other banks. But evidently the people in what the Crime Commission Task Force called "the core of organized crime"—the people in illegal gambling and loansharking—like the people who delivered illegal beer and gin in the days of the Untouchables, fought like the devil for the market, and patched up truces and imposed hierarchical empires that were continually susceptible to breakdown, defection and challenge.

One could of course give a particularist explanation of this. The big gangs have power and are greedy for more; the urge to exclusivity is natural, and when they get around to taking over burglary as they may have taken over the protection rackets and loansharking, we'll find burglary displaying these monopolistic tendencies. But I think that would be wrong. An alternative hypothesis is that we find "organized crime" in the lines of business that lend themselves to monopoly. The reason we don't find it in burglary may be that burglary is hard to monopolize.

It may be useful to remind ourselves of how many illegal goods and services are provided competitively rather than by monopoly organizations of the underworld. An ideal example for my purpose is the sale of cigarettes to those below the legal age. Why is this market not monopolized? If it could be, there might be several hundred million dollars of monopoly profits in it. But obviously it can't be. Nobody can keep a nineteen-year-old from buying a pack of cigarettes for a seventeen-year-old; the competition is everywhere. There is just no room for a black-market differential, because the law itself is virtually impossible to enforce. If you can't control the market and police it against competition, excluding competitors or making them pay for the franchise, you cannot do any more than sell cigarettes to minors, and that's not an occupation in which a criminal, organized or not, could make a living.

Monopolize shoplifting? Try it: if you succeed, department stores may hire you as a security guard, because you can presumably spot your competition better than the store detectives, and you may have a competitive advantage on the side of law and order.

At this point it might appear that we've reached the question Why does illegal gambling so readily lend itself to monopolization? Why is it that it not only occurs, as burglary and shoplifting occur, but is the object of monopolistic enterprise as those other criminal trades are not? But I'm going to ask a different question. What is the relation of organized crime to illegal gambling, at least as it shows up in investigations such as those of Senator Kefauver's committee?

## Organized Crime as Extortion

The interpretation I suggest is that *organized crime* does have a victim. The victim is the bookmaker—the man who sells illicit services to the public. And the crime of which he is the victim is the crime of extortion. He pays to stay in business. Nominally he may seem to procure a "wire service" or occasionally to borrow money or to use the clearinghouse facilities of the extortionate monopoly organization. But basically he is in a very simple business, one that needs no such organization; and he could do without The Organization. He might find organization useful, as many small businessmen find trade associations and lobbies and even public relations offices useful. But he does not need The Organization. It needs him. It lives off him. It lives off him the way it lives off anyone else, in the underworld or the overworld, who buys "protection."

And it is easier to see why extortion has to be monopolized than to see why gambling itself would have to be monopolized. Large-scale systematic extortion cannot really stand competition any more than can a local taxing authority; I cannot take half the bookie's earnings if you took it before I got there. We can divide the bookies between us, territorially or otherwise, but if nine different mobs are demanding half his earnings, all ten of them are in trouble. "Protection" is primarily against the one who offers it, but it has to include protection against rival taxing authorities.

And if the nominal basis for the extortion is the sale of a wire service or something of the sort, then evidently there will be an apparent monopoly of wire service in the underworld, but as a by-product of the monopolization of the protection racket.

We come now to the central question in this whole line of investigation. If the business of organized crime is extortion, in the underworld as well as in the overworld, why is the "core" of organized crime activity in the underworld itself? That is, why is the biggest victim of organized crime an illegal business rather than some legal business? (It may not be, but the traditional estimates as published, say, by the President's Commission in 1967 use figures between five and ten billion dollars as the gross earnings of the illegal gambling business, and impute the larger part of it to the profits of "organized crime.")

It is worthwhile to pause a moment and notice a certain anomaly. Making book may be a "crime without a victim," to use the name that Edwin Schur gave these activities,[3] but is itself victimized by organized crime. The victims of most crimes are not in the underworld. A department store may violate some laws and regulations, cheat its customers or the taxing authorities, or otherwise commit occasional crimes, but basically a department store is a "legitimate activity," and is the target of shoplifters. Shoplifters and pickpockets and burglars and embezzlers do not typically pick their victims in the underworld. Even if their victims are not altogether pure, they nevertheless do not usually have underworld careers. But what is generally referred to as the primary target of organized crime is itself an underworld activity. It is criminals who are victimized, if we accept my interpretation of the business of organized crime as that of extortion.

Should we be surprised? Can we identify characteristics of illegal bookmaking that make it a prime target for organized extortion? Can we possibly then look at other activities, legitimate activities and underworld activities, and infer which among them may be easy targets for organized extortion?

A first criterion for target selection by organized extortionists is that the victims should be poor at protecting themselves. In particular, one would like victims who have no ready access to the law. Criminals would therefore usually be ideal victims. The attractiveness of underworld victims is even greater if the police can actually be used as an instrument; if harassment can take the form of vigorous law enforcement by the police, the extortionists may not even need to engage in illegal violence to keep their victims in line.

Second, the extortionist wants a victim who cannot hide from him. Burglary is a very private affair, and the burglar has no need to advertise himself and his business and his location. Bookmakers and prostitutes who were as hard to locate and to identify as a burglar might well escape the racketeer, but they would lose their customers. If a customer can find a bookie when he wants to place a bet, the racketeer can find him. Those who sell illicit services to the public are therefore more visible, more easily located and identified, than embezzlers, pickpockets, shoplifters, car thieves, and people who cheat on their income tax. All criminals may be susceptible to blackmail, but those who cannot hide without losing their businesses are especially vulnerable.

Third, it is probably important to be able to monitor the victim's activity and his earnings. Those who operate in the open, dealing with a standard commodity, one that has a face value in money and few complicated costs, are probably those with whom an extortionist can reach an enforceable contract. Even if one can find and recognize an embezzler or jewel thief, one would have a hard time going shares with him, because the embezzler can fool the extortionist if he can fool the firm he embezzles from, and the jewel thief needn't put his best prizes on display. A bookmaker may get away with some business on the side, and avoid taxation by the extortionist organization, but his business is basically simpler and more public than most criminal activities.

Fourth, it helps if the victim has a regular business that he cannot carry away in an attempt to escape extortion. A bookmaker or prostitute or loan shark has to have a place of business; his chief business assets are goodwill, personal acquaintance, knowledge of the customers and their credit ratings, trust, access to a grapevine communication system, and perhaps personal relations with the police. A bookmaker or prostitute can probably always escape, but cannot then continue to do business within the jurisdiction of The Organization.

Fifth, all of this may work best if it works smoothly and regularly. The victim has to be treated "fairly." He has to know that he is treated like other victims. The business has to be depersonalized. Rules of the game are needed so that the victim knows where he stands. He has to compare his situation with that of others in the same business. There probably has to be a set of simple and fairly uniform arrangements. The bookmaker has the choice of paying or not paying; it might burden the system too much if each had to negotiate his own unique arrangement with The Organization, and renegotiate it month by month.

Consider, for example, the sharing arrangement that Senator Kefauver's committee turned up in Miami. The "syndicate" took

50 percent of the bookmaker's proceeds. This was a standardized percentage. Furthermore, it was not 40 percent or 55 percent or 29 percent or 83 percent. It was a nice round number, the nicest and roundest there is, an even 50–50. Oil-producing countries in the Middle East tend to converge on standard royalty arrangements with the Western companies they deal with. A king or a shah or a sultan or a sheik cannot explain to himself or to his constituents a lesser percentage share than the country next door receives, and he cannot persuasively hold out for a much more favorable share. So it may be that the very standardized nature and visibility of bookmaking lends itself to standardized, visible and institutionalized arrangements, known to all and applied without much discrimination.

Bookmakers probably can compare notes and tell whether they are receiving equal treatment far more readily than my neighbor and I can compare assessed valuations on our houses.

Perhaps another characteristic is that bookmaking, like prostitution, is a fairly petty activity, especially when it is illegal. That is, it can be a one-person job, or at least the retail organizations can be pretty small and decentralized. The bookmaker is probably his own bookkeeper, and he cannot readily plead inability when asked to pay. An officer of a bank would have to be a first-rate embezzler to pay large and regular amounts of blackmail out of the bank's resources without its becoming known to anybody else in the bank. In large organizations too many people have to sign the checks, initial the vouchers, audit the books, scrutinize budgets, take inventory, and otherwise tangle things up in red tape. The small independent entrepreneur, whether in the underworld or the overworld, may be more able to meet the demands than a complex organization would be.

These are only suggestions. There may be other characteristics of illegal bookmaking that I have missed, that are even more important in determining why it is such an attractive target for extortion. If we knew more about these activities in cities of different sizes, on the insides of large organizations as well as on the streets, and in different parts of the country, and particularly if we compared them with such activities in other countries, we could learn more. My conjectures may at least help to alert investigators to what they should be looking for; unless one raises the right questions, no amount of hearings and inquiries and investigations will turn up the pertinent answers.

It may be equally useful to look at the many black markets that are immune to organized crime. There have been elaborate black markets in foreign currency and gold, but while those engaged may occasionally have been subject to blackmail, there is no sign that it has been at the hands of large extortionate organizations. There is apparently an enormous black market in drugs, if one is willing to construe all the abuses of prescriptioning procedures as part of the black market, and apparently organized crime gets its hands on at most a small portion of it. If firearms should ever be banned in the United States, there will probably be an extensive black market, but the chances are overwhelmingly against its ever being monopolized by a criminal organization. I leave it to the reader to make his own list of the reasons why.

### Extortion in the Overworld

When we turn to the overworld we can similarly ask, What characteristics of a business would tend to make it an attractive target for organized extortion? An equally interesting and important question may be, What forms should we expect the tribute to take? It is of some interest that even in dealing with the petty bookmaker, The Organization sometimes goes through the motion of providing a wire service, or otherwise pretending that it offers something more than sheer brutal "protection." That may explain why organized crime is so widely alleged to have been engaged in businesses like the provision of laundry service. The reason for selecting laundry may not lie so much with the laundry business as with the nature of the customer. Restaurants may be comparatively easy targets for racketeers. They are so easily harassed, because their business is really rather fragile. Noises and bad odors and startling events can spoil the clientele, and even physical damage cannot be guarded against. Furthermore, restaurants do a great deal of business in cash, are often small proprietorships or partnerships, and are therefore financially capable of meeting the demands for tribute. But why not demand cash, then, rather than take it as a monopoly profit on a high-priced laundry service?

Or, to take another familiar example, why is it so often alleged that vending machines as well as pinball machines and slot machines are often "organized" by organized crime? Maybe organized crime likes gambling, and pinball machines are a little like slot machines, and then once you're in the machine business you may as well deal in cigarettes, too. Or maybe the machines are attractive for some other reason.

My conjecture is that the machines, like the laundry service, meet certain criteria that make them attractive means both of exacting tribute and of paying it. Again, if we were attempting organized extortion against restaurateurs in a city, planning to hit them all and to protect them all from rival extortionists, in what medium would we want them to pay us?

One criterion is that it should be tax deductible. There is no sense imposing a cost that is greater than what we get, when we could find a form in which we get everything that the victim loses. The high-priced laundry service is a deductible expense; profits from the cigarette machine are excludable income, as long as the concessionaire receives them, not the restaurateur.

Second, the victim wants to be able to keep books without showing that he pays tribute. He does not want creditors, revenue agents, or grand juries to be able to identify the tribute he pays, especially if it is illegal.

Third, the victim may want a manner of payment that minimizes embarrassment and the loss of self-respect. He may prefer to feel himself the victim of a monopoly linen service, and to complain to his wife and his employees about how the linen industry has been victimized and he is indirectly suffering, rather than to remind himself periodically that he is simply paying cash for protection. He may even be able to feel that the vending machines are monopolized, not that he is providing rent-free space for somebody else's vending machine in return for "protection."

Indeed, from most accounts, gambling machines were used for this purpose in the 1930s and perhaps were still so used in the 1960s. A gambling machine in a neighborhood store may represent two kinds of criminal activity. One is illicit gambling; the other is extortion. It tends to get listed under the heading of gambling; but the more brutal crime is that some poor store owner is being shaken down by a protection racketeer. And his tribute takes the form of having machines put in his store. He may despise the machines and make nothing off them; but that's the price he pays. If the laws against gambling were properly enforced, the "crime without a victim" might disappear, but the extortion might continue with payment taking another guise. It may hurt the extortionist somewhat to be denied his favorite medium of tribute; but we miss the point if we suppose that the only crime we're dealing with is gambling.

The machines and the laundry services and the other ostensible businesses that are used by the racketeers may also meet another need. That is the need for institutionalized practices, uniform arrangements, nondiscrimination, et cetera. If each victim privately pays cash, he has no way of knowing how his treatment compares with that of other victims; but if they all get their linen or beer or meat from the same monopolistic provider, or all provide their vestibules for similar kinds of machinery concessions, they know that they're getting standard treatment.

Incidentally, if news vendors, neighborhood store owners, or barbershops became universal victims of organized extortion, perhaps sharing their earnings and nominally receiving some services in return, perhaps paying extortionate prices for supplies or rent on their buildings, we would probably not describe haircuts and magazines and chewing gum as the businesses that organized crime was engaged in. We'd describe them as the victimized trades. We would distinguish the barbers and the news vendors from the personnel of organized crime. Even if The Organization helped to enforce union membership, uniform prices, and uniform closing days; lobbied for legislation favorable to barbers, occasionally intervened on their behalf with their landlords, lent them money, and occasionally got them barbershop space in new hotels, we still wouldn't consider the barber a criminal or consider organized crime to be in the business of providing haircuts. We would not be afraid that a successful crackdown on organized crime would close up the barbershops and leave us no place to get our hair trimmed. We'd expect instead that prices might fall, just as if a heavy tax on haircuts had just been repealed.

This thought may put illegal gambling back into better perspective. It is undoubtedly true that, as Donald Cressey said in the passage quoted earlier, "if the confederation of men employed in illicit businesses were suddenly abolished, it would be sorely missed because it performs services for which there is a great public demand." But it is only true if we take the "confederation" to include the bookmakers as well as the racketeers who prey on them. Even then it is true only if we permit no newcomers to enter the business in replacement of the abolished "confederation." Even if the customer wants his bookie, he has no use for the organization that restricts competition in the betting industry.

## Some Organization Theory

I must at this point offer two qualifications, one substantive and the other a point of view. The substantive one is this. Maybe bookmakers, prostitutes, loan sharks, and drug peddlers, if left alone by the racketeers, would be unable to come to proper terms with the police and unable to engage in their businesses. Maybe corruption is best handled collectively, and an illicit trade consisting only of individualist competitors could not buy off the public officials. Perhaps they would be unable to form their own organization: nobody likes to pay dues, people may drift in and out of the business, some may have satisfactory arrangements and no need for the union. In that case it might be worth a fairly high price to have discipline and organization imposed from outside. The Organization may levy a high tax once it imposes its own governance on the gambling business, but a high tax may be better than no governance at all.

Conceivably, then, bookmakers gain by being victims of a predatory organization; without it they would have no organization. Furthermore, much of the tax, perhaps most of it, may be passed along to the customer. Gasoline stations do not suffer enormously when gasoline taxes go up a nickel; they suffer only to the extent that motorists reduce their driving because of the higher price of gasoline, and on the whole the tax gets passed along to the buyer. Thus the direct victim of extortion is the bookmaker or prostitute, or the barber or the restaurateur; but if the tax is uniformly levied on all bookmakers or restaurateurs, and if it is a tax on transactions and not on residual profits, it probably is passed along so that the one who "pays" the tribute is the customer, not the nominal taxpayer. Just as the tenants in apartment houses "pay" the property tax, although the landlord forwards the check to the tax collector, the person who places the bet receives less favorable odds than if bookmaking were a purely competitive and "untaxed" consumer service.

The second qualification is that any organization can be viewed in different ways. It is possible to say with some truth that General Motors does not produce automobiles; the Chevrolet and

Pontiac divisions do. Many businesses, small and large, are decentralized; General Motors may deliberately allow the Chevrolet division a good deal of autonomy, just as Chevrolet grants its sales agents so much autonomy that they are considered to be "authorized dealers," dealing in their own names, rather than branches of Chevrolet. Many firms let their salesmen work on commission; farm owners often prefer going shares with a tenant rather than hiring him for a wage. Many hotel and restaurant chains lay down architectural and other standards, but do not directly manage the individual establishments that bear their names.

By analogy, one could say that organized crime is in the gambling business but finds it expedient to run that business by licensing individual bookmakers rather than by hiring them as employees. It may even do it on an "open shop" basis, according to which anybody can get into the business so long as he pays the franchise tax. A specific test might be whether The Organization could move into a locale where there was no offtrack betting and establish a bookmaking business, and if so whether it would own and operate the business or instead set it up in the familiar pattern, inviting independent operators to operate under the "protection" of the racketeering organization, which would protect them from molestation either by police or by rival organizations. If it did the latter, we'd have to admit that, although the arrangement has all the characteristics of extortion, and may often arise directly out of extortion, it can also be construed as a monopolized business in which independent operators are allowed on condition that they pay standardized tribute to the licensing organization.

All of this has some bearing on the question, If gambling were made legal, would it continue to attract racketeers? It is often alleged that organized crime is so skilled and experienced in the gambling business that it would have an edge over "legitimate" entrepreneurs and would not only entrench itself in legitimized gambling but enjoy the greater profits that would go with enlarged business. My argument suggests that The Organization is not really skilled and experienced in the provision of gambling services. It is skilled and experienced in the *suppression* of rival gambling services, especially in suppressing rival *illegal* gambling by collusion with the police. Its success, with or without the police, is appreciably dependent on the inability of the bookmaker to seek the protection of the law. It is also a result of the inability of the bookmaker to protect himself through corporate organization, trade association, and all the other ways that modern business protects itself from crude and petty interlopers, chiselers, and even racketeers.

Thus, the important question is not whether the *bookmakers* would show up as the sellers of legal bets if offtrack betting were made legal. The question is whether The Organization could get a monopolized extortionist grip on the industry. That may not be an easy question to answer, but it is at least clear that some of the characteristics of offtrack betting that presently make it an ideal target for monopolized extortion would not be present if it were made as legal to bet in front of a television screen as it is to bet in the presence of the horses themselves. The history of Prohibition and its aftermath in the liquor business strongly suggests that *organized crime* may not thrive or survive in the face of legal competition.

In any event, those among us who are so hypocritical as to want offtrack betting illegal, prostitution abolished, and the credit laws enforced, but still want to place their bets, visit the bawdy houses, and borrow on the side to preserve their credit ratings, needn't be afraid of a crackdown on organized crime. They may suffer, as Donald Cressey suggests they will, from a crackdown on gambling, prostitution and loansharking; they can benefit, though, from a crackdown on organized crime, just as the consumer always hopes to benefit from trust-busting.

The purpose of monopoly has always been to suppress, not to enlarge, supply. People who like monopoly prices and punitive taxes on the naughty activities may be pleased that the long arm of organized crime reaches out and levies a tax on the retailer that is passed on to the consumer.

The consumers will prefer to see the activities become more freely competitive, whether by being released from illegality, or released from the grip of organized crime. So will those who dislike corruption, especially when it is centralized and regularized by large monopoly organizations that can build corruption directly into our institutions, rather than leave it to gnaw away at the edges.

# 9 | Strategic Analysis and Social Problems

I WAS INVITED to talk about strategic aspects of social problems. I asked what that meant. I was told it meant whatever I meant. So, with the uneasy feeling that it had just been used on me, I set out to characterize the "strategic approach." Let me illustrate what I have in mind.

First consider a jury that must unanimously find a man guilty of murder or acquit him, and may unanimously recommend clemency if they find him guilty. It matters which vote comes first. If twelve find him guilty and only six then vote for clemency, some among the six may wish they had held out for acquittal. If they knew they would lose the second vote they might hold out for acquittal on the first vote, setting free a man they'd rather see in jail. If the clemency vote is taken first, the result to be applied in case they later find him guilty, some who oppose clemency may vote for it to secure unanimity when it's time to find him guilty. If the rules do not permit clemency to be taken up before a man is found guilty, some jurors may announce themselves for clemency to induce a unanimous vote of guilty. And if clemency then requires only a majority vote, an open ballot rather than a secret one may make such promises more enforceable by at least letting it be seen whether they are kept.

Next consider the recent announcement that a special mail-drop was being set up in New York for drug addicts who wanted medical advice; it was to be inaccessible to police officers and the Bureau of Narcotics, which might prosecute with the information. In Vietnam and other areas of insurgency, people who want to give intelligence to the authorities need either privacy or protection, some safe way to avoid reprisal if they inform. The Department of Justice has a similar problem in getting blacks to testify that their right to vote has been abused by authorities in Southern states; privacy cannot be observed since evidence, not just information, is needed. Counterinsurgent forces often coerce the behavior they want, not because the citizen is personally reluctant but he needs an "alibi" for cooperating. Florida hotel owners were reported needful of federal coercion to integrate, to avoid being accused of doing it voluntarily and subjecting themselves to reprisal. "Immunity" is a quality that cuts across integration, insurgency, and addiction; it can even be used to relieve a reluctant witness from an excuse under the Fifth Amendment and give him a protection he'd prefer to renounce. The hit-and-run driver is a special case: should drunken drivers be excused whenever they hit a pedestrian, to make sure they've no motive to flee before calling an ambulance?

Third, consider the blacks who not too long ago chained and padlocked themselves across a thoroughfare. It was reported that German machine gunners were sometimes chained to their guns in the First World War. There is a similarity; and if the German in fact is chained to his gun it helps him if the enemy knows it: someone who hopes to scare him away by charging may seek another target if he knows the machine gunner cannot escape. Xenophon explained the principle 2,000 years ago. Some of his men were worried about fighting with a gulley at their backs and no way of retreat. "As for the argument that by crossing over we are putting a difficult ravine in our rear just when we are going to fight, is not this really something that we ought to jump at: I should like the enemy to think it is easy-going in every direction for him to retreat; but we ought to learn from the very position in which we are placed that there is no safety for us except in victory."[1]

If gulleys and chains are unavailable, discipline may do it. Xenophon refers to a particular general who "exacted complete obedience from all who were put under his command . . . Once they began to win victories with him, one could see how important were the factors which made his men into good soldiers.

They had the advantage of being confident in the face of the enemy, and they were disciplined because they were afraid of his punishments." Singing hymns during the advance to display confidence and determination is as old as the Greeks and as new as integration. The soldier quelling a riot wears a mask not only to keep out tear gas but to hide the fear in his face; the Teutonic Knights took similar advantage of their helmets a thousand years ago.

Next look for a moment at some well-known techniques of nonviolence. In India people are reported to have staged hunger strikes on the doorsteps of people against whom they had complaints. Landlords know that the safest way to evict a tenant is to turn off the water and electricity, relying on the cumulative pressure of unflushed toilets and uncooked food. Against unarmed rioters, the United States Army has learned to protect its tanks and their armament by installing a mildly electric fence as a front bumper. The Soviets have used aerial "maneuvers" in the Berlin Corridor to hold up traffic, and invented the "stall-in" on the Autobahn long before it was used to blockade the New York World's Fair. "Over my dead body" are sometimes the heroic last words of the dedicated martyr, but more often the phrase is a deterrent threat shrewdly adapted to an adversary's fears and desires; Harvard students regularly cross against the lights with impunity, stopping trucks a hundred times their weight. The unarmed pilot of the U-2 reconnaissance plane over Cuba is in somewhat the same exposed position as the driver of a carload of black children on their way to a newly integrated school in a hostile city. Most "brinkmanship," in the Cuban crisis or a school-integration crisis, has the character of coercive "nonviolence," exploiting someone's fear of violence or reluctance to initiate it; the construction-site integrationists who lay down before bulldozers had their own version of massive retaliation.

As a final instance, concealed weapons are usually harmless, as is loitering near an integrated school or payroll truck. So is assembling in groups of five or six in a town susceptible to riot. But the authorities may forbid groups of four, disperse loiterers, confiscate concealed weapons if they find them, and keep a record of whom they were found on. One reason is that certain actions are hard to prevent or to deter once preparations are made, but the preparations themselves can be blocked or deterred. What is worrisome about the group of six is that it may grow to a mob of sixty, and is easier to disperse when it is small. It is likewise easier on the faculty to give an unsatisfactory midterm grade, denying a student athletic privileges until he pulls his average up, than to fail him abruptly at the end of the year and deny him his degree. These are "precautionary rules." Parents use them in confining children to their rooms to keep them from fighting each other, prohibiting possession of matches, or spanking a baby's hands when it opens the cabinet where soaps and bleaches are stored.

I have given a series of illustrations and now the question is, What do they illustrate? They are all situations or tactics that lend themselves to what I call "strategic analysis." To characterize them, let me emphasize that it is *situations*, not personalities. They are situations involving two or more participants, each trying to influence, to outguess, or to adapt to the decisions or lines of behavior that others have just adopted or are expected to adopt.

In all the examples, people have choices to make and must weigh the consequences. The structure of the situation can affect what those consequences are; and often one or both parties are trying to *restructure* the situation, often to restructure it in terms of *their own expected behavior.* The gulley permits Xenophon's Greek soldier to fight confident that his buddies will stick with him; and if it is visible to the attackers it can deny them any hope of inducing retreat and disorder by a bold attack. Each person, together with the courses of action that he can be expected to take, is part of the other person's environment, and a part that is relevant to his choice.

Not only can the situations be analyzed separately from the individuals and their personalities, but they have no close connection with virtue or evil, our side or their side, good guys or bad guys. "Salami tactics" can be used by blacks in Alabama, Russians in Europe, children against parental rules, or the PTA against a school committee. Destroying trust within the Mafia and creating it in a Vietnamese village may depend on much the same kind of analysis.

There are two reasons why "strategic analysis" tends to be neutral, even cold-blooded, toward the parties in a situation. One is that the analysis is usually about the situation, not the individuals—about the structure of incentives, of information and communication, the choices available, and the tactics that can be employed. There is little about the abstract situation that tells the analyst which side he ought to be on. Xenophon on the defensive against a superior force, as we saw, liked a gulley at his back; when attacking a smaller force on a hill, however, "they did not attack from every direction but left the enemy a way of escape, if he wanted to run away." Same principle, positions reversed.[2]

The second reason why strategic analysis seems disinterested is that it cannot proceed from the point of view of a single favored participant. It deals with situations in which one party has to think about how the others are going to reach their decisions. Even if we take sides with the jurors who prefer guilty with clemency, in deciding how to vote or to negotiate we have to think how the others will vote, what tactics they can use, what bargains will appeal to them, how we can make them trust us, what they know about *our* own preferences and how we can reveal or disguise those preferences—in short, how the situation looks from their side. The one juror cannot solve his own strategic problem without solving everybody else's at the same time. Analogies with games are treacherous, but for this point a comparison can be made with the chess player examining the board to decide what move to make, who must think about the next move his opponent will make, trying to figure out what his opponent thinks he himself will do next after that, and ends up playing chess with himself for a few moves to decide what to do next. If he does it carefully he is momentarily about as well-equipped to walk around the table and play the other color as to stay on his own side.

Let me use an example from the unparalleled classic in strategic analysis, Thucydides' *Peloponnesian War*. The people of Camarina, some hundred miles along the coast from Syracuse, were being urged by the Athenians to join against Syracuse. The Syracusans had argued that the Athenians disarmed their allies at home, exacted tribute from them, sometimes enslaved them, and would do the same to Camarina once Syracuse were defeated. The Athenians had to appeal to the Camarinaean interest and, to do this, analyzed for the Camarinaeans their own interests and capabilities. "No one must imagine," they said, "that the interest which we take in you has nothing to do with ourselves. You have only to reflect that so long as you are safe and strong enough to hold your own against Syracuse, the Syracusans will not find it so easy to do us harm by sending a force to help the Peloponnesians ... On the same principle, it is perfectly reasonable for us to restore their independence to the people of [Sicily] and ... to see that they are as powerful as possible ... When the Syracusan representative says that it is illogical for us to enslave Chalcideans in Hellas and liberate them in Sicily, he should remember that it is to our interest that in Hellas they should be unarmed and should merely contribute money, but here in Sicily we should like to see both the people of Leontini and all our friends as independent as possible ... The aim of the Syracusans is to rule over you, and their policy is to make you unite on the basis of your suspicions of us, and then to take over the empire of Sicily themselves either by force or, when we have retired without achieving anything, because there will be no one to dispute it with them. This is bound to happen if you do unite with them, since so great a combined force would no longer be easy for us to deal with, and, once we had disappeared from the scene, they would be quite strong enough to take their measures against you ... We for our part cannot stay here without your support, and even if we were so base as to deprive you of your independence, we could not keep you under our control because of the length of the voyage and the difficulty of garrisoning large cities armed on the lines of continental powers."[3] I urge you to read the entire passage, which is too long to quote in full—in fact the entire book—because I know of no modern work in any field of strategy that compares in lucidity with the words that Thucydides puts in the mouths of his Greeks. The art of looking at the problem from the other person's point of view, identifying his opportunities and his interests, an art that has traditionally been practiced by diplomats, lawyers, and chess players, is at the center of strategic analysis.

In calling it "strategic analysis," I have borrowed a word from *theory of games,* in which a game of "strategy" is one in which decisions are interdependent—the best action for each person depending on which actions the others take. "Theory of games" has come to denote the mathematical exploration of the frontier of our subject; and there is no conventional term for the activity of those who cultivate the territory—often virgin territory—that is within the frontier and is some part of social science (including law), not a branch of mathematics. "Strategic" of course has plenty of other meanings in both ordinary and professional language.

Though strategic analysis tends to be cold-blooded, it can encompass personal elements like conscience and affection. Herodotus reports that two kings were persuaded to have their children marry, "knowing that treaties seldom remain intact without powerful sanctions." Affection was also used as a strategic device to elicit honest estimates from people whose motives might be questionable. Xerxes received much encouragement to march on the Greeks but one loyal adviser, under pain of disapproval, cautioned against it, challenging one sycophant: "You and I will then stake our children on the issue, and you can start the venture with the men you want and as big an army as you please. Now for the wager: if the king prospers as you say he will, then I consent that my sons should be killed, and myself with them; if my own prediction is fulfilled, your sons forfeit their lives—and you too—if you ever get home." Solomon is reported to have used a similar tactic to get at what economists call "revealed preference" from two claimants to a baby; and state authorities use a similar ploy, involving cash rather than sentimental value, when they offer compensation to people whose houses are to be torn down for a throughway. Anyone who claims that his house is worth more than the compensation may have his bluff called with a gentle threat: the authorities will be happy to move his house instead, at state expense, if he really likes the house that much.

Affection of course is the basis for a good many disciplinary threats. About whether the Ionians could be trusted on the march into Attica, Xerxes was unworried. "For is it conceivable that they will wreck our cause, when they have left their wives, children, and property in our country?" And among those who would try to weigh "blood against money," translating human affection into a material equivalent, none goes at it in a more practical way than the kidnapper setting his price for return of the child, or a king setting ransom for another.

Lynn Montross puts it nicely. "All accounts make it plain that ransom played a leading part in medieval warfare, influencing both causes and tactics. As a result, men of quality were all but immune from the usual hazards to life and limb; and it could truthfully be said that friend and foe alike mourned their death."[4]

Even the gods play a strategic role, and are subject to what economists call "comparative advantage." Conscience and divine sanction may be scarce resources, and should not be wasted on rules of conduct that are easily enforced by other means. In classical Greece, "Certain offenses which human law could not punish or men detect were placed under divine sanction . . . Perjury is an offense which it may be impossible to prove; therefore, it is one which is peculiarly abhorrent to the gods."[5] And Julius Caesar noted of the Druids in Gaul, anticipating Kamikaze by two millennia: "A lesson which they take particular pains to inculcate is that the soul does not perish, but after death passes from one body to another; they think that this is the best incentive to bravery, because it teaches men to disregard the terrors of death."[6]

Gods and glands can work together in structuring the incentives of primitive people. "The multitude of dances and other pre-combat rites were devices to insure the proper glandular activity enabling warriors to walk into probable death."[7] Charms, amulets, and other magical devices helped to give the warrior confidence. "Magic may be tactical . . . A man, feeling himself invulnerable and sure of success, could afford to be brave, daring, and valiant, so such mass mutual excitement might actually have had value in the field." And by letting soothsayers determine, through signs, omens, and other rituals, whether the gods were favorable, "Fear could be repressed by entering only those battles the favorable outcome of which was assured."[8]

Drug addiction, hostages, chains and padlocks, the wrath of the gods, and in more civilized societies the injunction and the damage suit, are techniques for structuring incentives to assure compliance. And when trust or confidence is essential to an enterprise, the hostages may be given voluntarily. "Cross my heart and hope to die," is typically a voluntary pledge and these days not very persuasive, but swearing with a hand on the Bible incurs real commitment for many people. The procedure may be demanded or volunteered; when volunteered, it is not altogether different from the voluntary jeopardy that people incur when they post bail or pawn a camera.

If we do not like the enterprise that depends on the contract, we try to make the commitments unenforceable. Insurance companies are not permitted to insure us against traffic fines or time lost in jail. Threats as well as contracts may be against the interest of those who structure the situation: we *make* people vote in secret so that they cannot comply with a bribe or a threat. Neil Hickey, reformed jewel thief, describes an enterprise that depended on trust. The best customers for stolen jewels were the insurance companies that insured them, the thieves and various go-betweens being satisfied with a total ransom less than the face of the policy. It required face-to-face exchange of jewels for cash by the thief and an agent, the latter making his own deal with the company, which had no way of knowing what he actually paid for the jewels. The process required identification of a trustworthy go-between, preliminary communication, a safe meeting and no testimony afterward. The thief liked it, it gave him a market; the police liked it, it recovered the jewels; the lady liked it, she got her jewels back; and the go-between had a good business. The insurance company liked it when some jewels were outstanding; it was cheaper than paying off on the policy. But the whole procedure made the theft profitable. The lady's husband paid a higher premium because of the incentive for theft that the scheme provided, and the police and insurance companies had an uneasy feeling that the whole system of recovery made theft profitable. At times the police waged a campaign to discredit or remove the crucial individual whose personal reputation made the transaction possible.[9]

Strategic analysis typically involves a small number of interacting decision units. If the number is large, any individual's influence is so small that he needn't take account of what people expect him to do. The farmer who sells wheat needn't worry about whether to withhold part of his crop to push the price up. But numbers alone do not always protect one from having to put himself in somebody else's place and figure out what others will do. In a stock market prices may be largely set by expectations, and if people think prices are going to decline drastically, they will sell, and prices will decline. If everybody just thinks everybody else thinks prices are going to fall, everybody will think everybody else will sell, so he must sell too and he does, and—since he is everybody—prices fall. The statement can be further compounded.

Here the result is so little determined by objective considerations, so much by expectations about others' expectations, that one must look for "jointly expectable" results. Harvard students on the first warm night in spring may desire to engage in group action, to form a mob just for the fun of it, and each may be confident that the same thought is in the minds of the rest. But to form a mob they must assemble at some point, a point whose main qualification is that everyone can expect everybody else to recognize it. It may be a square, a bridge, or the president's house, but it must have some quality that demands attention, some capacity to signal itself, and a uniqueness to dispel ambiguity. Freedom of choice is what spoils the effort to concert, and if there are too many competing "obvious" places for a student to expect to meet his fellows on a warm night, they will find themselves divided among the eligible places, or perhaps not even bother because they can see there is no single "obvious" place to expect each other.

In using the word "mob" I did not mean to judge the students. Rescue organization in a disaster poses the same problem: in the absence of a plan, where do volunteers assemble to be of help? If we deplore the mob we can try to deny it a focus for their expectations, just as we might try to destroy the communications of an organization we oppose. To assure the stability of a group, to solidify rather than to disperse it, we may help to create or discover a unique focus for their expectations about where to meet, or whom to follow. Pascal pointed to an important application. "The most unreasonable things in the world become more reasonable, because of the unruliness of men. What is less reasonable than to choose the eldest son of a queen to rule a state? We do not choose as captain of a ship the passenger who is of the best family. This law would be absurd and unjust; but because men are so themselves, and always will be so, it becomes reasonable and just. For whom will men choose, as the most virtuous and able? We at once come to blows as each claims to be the most virtuous and able. Let us then attach this quality to something undisputable. This is the king's eldest son. That is clear, and there is no dispute. Reason can do no better, for civil war is the greatest of evils."[10]

Let me raise a final point about "strategic analysis," one that is methodologically important and often raised as an objection in relation to peace and war. This is whether strategic analysis always assumes, or must assume, that everybody involved is fully

rational and knows everybody else to be rational. In an important
sense the answer is yes. It usually does assume that parties com-
prehend the situation, are aware of the alternatives, know their
own values, are in command of themselves when they make their
choices, and can even put themselves in somebody else's shoes to
evaluate the other person's choice.

Whether the process has to be subtle, refined, and self-conscious
or crudely approximate and semi-conscious depends on whether
the situation is complex and calls for refined analysis, as in parliamentary strategy, or involves simple choices, as when a child pretends not to hear a command or when a person is asked to pick his
own night to come to dinner so that he cannot excuse himself
by being "busy" that night. The practical question of whether
rationality assumes a mental giant with nerves of steel is purely a
question of how exact a discrimination is needed, a question that
arises in chemistry, economics, and I suppose sociology, all the
time, and gets a practical answer in each instance. Solon shrewdly
went traveling, according to Herodotus, to avoid the necessity of
repealing the laws that he had made; the Athenians could not re-
peal his laws without him because they had sworn to give them a
ten years' trial. But a prison gatekeeper not renowned for his political judgment invoked the same principle on the spur of the
moment, throwing his key out the bars of the gate when he saw
some armed escapees approaching.[11]

The critical question is not whether a person is "rational" according to any particular definition, perfectionist or merely approximate, but whether his choice is determined in large part by
the situation he is in and by what we can guess about his values.
You see, strategic analysis is vicarious problem-solving. We figure
out what a person might do by putting ourselves into his position,
adopting for the purpose as much as we know about his preferences, and deciding what he ought to do or what we would do if
we were he. By "what he ought to do" we merely mean what he
should decide in accordance with his own aims, values, and objectives, given the alternatives that he faces. The supposition is that
he has a choice to make, can reflect on that choice taking into account things that we perceive or infer, and will decide not in a
haphazard way and not under the dominance of some unrevealed
drives but in a way that suits his apparent purposes. If we have
some clue to what his purposes are, and some appreciation of the

alternatives he faces, we anticipate his choice by figuring out what one would do in that situation with those aims and values.

In its pure form, this is cheap theory. We rely on empirical information about a man's objectives and what alternatives are available to him; but from there on we just imagine ourselves in his position, see how we should proceed if we were he, and conclude that he may go ahead and do just that.

And we may be wrong. We can misconceive his situation or the values by which he abides. He may not have the sense to perceive what he ought to do. Maybe he just doesn't go about deciding in that fashion—he may respond to some inarticulate urges, rationalize a choice motivated by unrevealed prejudices, or adhere to some maxims, superstitions, or rules of calculation that we failed to perceive as constraints on his choice. Still, we get a bench mark; and surely if we have no other way to predict his behavior, but must design his environment or choose an action to influence him and are going to put ourselves in his shoes to guess how he will react, the least we can do is to be systematic.

The hit-and-run driver, the juror, the policeman confronting a protest marcher, or the parolee who may jump bond may not be mainly guided by the factors that our strategic analysis is able to take into account. But if we are trying to design a voting system for the jury, penalties and amnesties, a protest march or a parole system, we may as well think seriously about the factors that *are* under our control. The important thing is then not to put too much confidence in our prediction or exaggerated emphasis on the elements that we happen to comprise in our analysis.

Economics, I should mention, produces a lot of theory of this sort. Economists want to know what will happen to the price of butter or cattle feed if legal restrictions on margarine are removed. It is hard to find evidence, so one tries to figure it out. If housewives are saved the nuisance of mixing yellow color into a lardlike substance they will buy more margarine and less butter unless the price of butter falls; if the price of butter falls, some dairying operations may become unprofitable and farmers will divert cream into other products, or cut back dairying in favor of beef, or pay less for feed grains. Or they will lobby for a tariff on butter, to find protection in another direction. Economists do not do badly, probably better with producers than consumers because there are fewer intangibles. Economists often have the advantage of dealing with large numbers and need only to be sure that a large fraction will behave as they anticipate or that there are forces of selection that in the long run will dispose of producers who regularly make unprofitable decisions. In other fields, where the variables are less quantitative or the elements less visible than price quotations or where political groupings make the decisions, one's expectations about the success of a deductive, vicarious-problem-solving theory must be more modest.

There is something more to be said: irrationality is not hard to work into the analysis if it is identifiable and systematic. If decisionmakers err in predictable ways—call them irrational ways—because of faulty evaluation, bad memory, random error, predictable loss of control, or some known obstacle to purposive decision, this can often be allowed for. In fact, one can rationally devise techniques to safeguard against irrationality, as in the rule about counting to ten before speaking in anger, requiring a second reading of a bill in Parliament, demanding two witnesses to a crime or two participants in the firing of a weapon, or inviting a man to take a few drinks before you break bad news to him. People who try to make themselves stop smoking and people who try to forestall the inadvertent outbreak of war must devise systems to accommodate foreseeable lapses of "rationality."

As a matter of fact, "self-control" is one of the most interesting dimensions of rationality, and safeguards against loss of control are often amenable to strategic analysis. Erving Goffman, one of the most creative strategists, has discussed techniques for controlling embarrassment. Embarrassment shares an important quality with certain kinds of fear and nervousness, romantic excitement, giggling and even military mobilization, namely, one's own embarrassment causes embarrassment to someone who is face to face with him, and the latter's induced embarrassment reinforces the embarrassment of the first in a feedback cycle. Goffman uses the term "poise" to refer to the capacity to suppress or conceal any tendency to become shamefaced during encounters, and thus to damp the feedback and minimize amplification. "Poise is one important type of face-work, for through poise the person controls his embarrassment and hence the embarrassment that he and others might have over his embarrassment."[12] Lacking poise, one has recourse to liquor or tranquilizers, or does his business on the telephone to minimize visual stimulation.

One can also promote loss of control to obtain advantage. A

splendid example is in a story of a man whose son was kidnapped, who was informed that the first installment of ransom should be 5,000 pound notes in a sack on a park bench. Caring more for his son than for the money and doubting the gang's intent to return the boy, he devised a campaign of rescue, the first step of which was to disrupt the gang's internal organization and self-confidence. He put in a bag not 5,000, but 10,000 pound notes, knowing this contingency was one the gang was not prepared for and would overload its collective capacity for decision. The scheme worked, but I cannot tell you the rest of the story here. (Look for it in one of the Hilton Hotel *Bedside Books*.)

Goffman has vividly described the techniques used by institutions—mental hospitals, boys' schools, military organizations, and nunneries—to disrupt the internal organization of individuals, to confuse their sense of identity, to deny them poise, and to disrupt the signals and conventions by which inmates can establish counterorganization. Shaved heads, ugly uniforms, no pockets, no cosmetics, even nakedness and no place to sit down, destroy poise and make difficult the development of cadres, leaders, and communication systems, and the development of discipline and esprit among subjects. The technique goes back at least to Croesus, who advised Cyrus to forgive the Lydians for their revolt, "But at the same time, if you want to keep them loyal and prevent any danger from them in the future, I suggest you put a veto on their possession of arms. Make them wear tunics under their cloaks, and high boots, and tell them to teach their sons to play the zither and harp, and to start shopkeeping. If you do that, my lord, you will soon see them turn into women instead of men, and there will not be any more danger of their rebelling against you." The tactic was undoubtedly aimed partly at habits and motivations, but at the same time would deny the development of expectations and confidence on the basis of which discipline and leadership would depend.[13]

Anatol Rapoport, author of *Fights, Games and Debates* and, more recently, *Strategy and Conscience*,[14] has been particularly exercised by those mischievous situations—and they occur everywhere—that are characterized by subversive incentives. In these situations people are *individually* motivated to behave in such ways that they *all* could have been better off if they all had behaved differently. During a water shortage nobody benefits by repairing his own leaky faucets; if everyone cuts wastage, everyone can have more water pressure, but even if everyone else fixes his faucets a person still has no individual incentive to fix his own. Rapoport has emphasized the incompatibility between a definition of rationality that attends only to individual incentives and the "collective rationality" that might lead people to choose in violation of individual incentives and jointly benefit in consequence.

He points out that a pair of cold-blooded rational individuals will in these situations come off worse than a pair of people *both* of whom are too obtuse to perceive their own incentives or two people *both* bound in conscience to behave the way they would like to be behaved toward. (The fact that a cold-blooded partner of a warm-hearted one comes off best of all, and the latter's virtue goes unrewarded, does not contradict the fact that two conscience-bound individuals fare better than two who are free to pursue separate gains.) These are the situations in which enforceable agreements should appeal to all participants, but no enforcement is available. For reasons relating to an anecdote, this predicament has become known in the trade as "prisoners' dilemma."*

If everyone behaved in these situations as they would like to be behaved toward—just because that is the way to behave or because one expects supernatural rewards or believes he intangibly influences others by behaving that way, or for that matter because he is being snooped on—everyone can benefit. And when individually rational observers subversively point out that each of the participants might have gained by breaking ranks and playing for individual gain, they can be offered the usual retort, "If you are so smart, why aren't you rich?"

As we saw, Xenophon supplemented, with a gulley at his soldiers' backs, the ultimate comradeship that might have kept any man from deserting his fellows in the heat of battle. Rousseau

---

* A typical version of the story goes like this. Two suspects are apprehended and separately interrogated. If neither confesses to the major crime they were apprehended for, both will be charged with minor crimes and convicted. If both confess, both will be convicted of the major crime with a recommendation of leniency. If one confesses while the other does not, the squealer will receive a suspended sentence; the other will be convicted and receive a full sentence. The idea is that an individual prisoner is better off confessing, whether the other confesses or not, but both are worse off when both confess than if they both had refused to talk. (Logically it is not a "dilemma," but by now the term has become a proper name.) There is also what could be called "martyrs' dilemma," in which each wants the pleasure of sacrificing his own gratification for the other's, the sacrifices outweighing the benefits, both frustrated in their aspirations.

proposed a social contract, which can be interpreted as the implicit promise that conscience makes one keep, as well as the basis of damage suits. The fact that Xenophon's enemies were defending their homeland against Greek invaders—and we are on Xenophon's side only because it is *his* book we are reading—does not detract from the collective advantage his 10,000 Greeks enjoyed from their discipline, whether that discipline arose from conscience and comradeship, fear of punishment, or an impassable gulley. In fact the Greeks and the Romans, like the Mohammedans and the Swiss later still, were successful in battle precisely because they had a collective "solution" to the multiperson prisoners' dilemma and did not break ranks. Conscience, religion, fear of punishment, and habit all contributed to the solution. Their enemies sometimes resorted to chains; and "whippers" were the Persian equivalent of a Spartan wife's tongue, which could lash her husband into preferring death to retreat.

One has only to consider the enormous frustration of conducting foreign aid in an underdeveloped country, or getting a business established there, to realize what an extraordinary economic asset is a population of honest conscientious people. Simple honesty is even sometimes the price of freedom; what a nuisance it would be for us at a university if we could not be counted on to meet our obligations and had to solve our collective prisoners' dilemma with supervisors, time clocks, or company spies.

The striking thing is how much conscience (or whatever we call it) does determine behavior in the societies we consider orderly and advanced, and in some that we call primitive. It even keeps people from selling their homes to "undesirable elements" and is part of the basis for segregated housing where formal covenants have been outlawed. Voltaire is reported to have found his servants' religion a great convenience, as employers both business and domestic have found for centuries; but whether his servants' conscience was of social value depends on what Voltaire was up to. The prisoners in the original dilemma need only be interpreted as purveyors of filthy pictures to juveniles, and we can not only hope that conscience is not available to bind their conspiracy but even doubt whether it is.

We often think of trust, reliable communication, and enforceable contract as good things. We like people to overcome distrust, confusion, and competing interests and reach an outcome beneficial to both. In the literature of social psychology I notice a greater interest in building trust than in collapsing it, in promoting cooperation than in frustrating it. But when we turn to the Ku Klux Klan, corruption in the police force, extortion in the junior high schools, or the silent conspiracy that keeps non-Aryans out of a medical school or an oil company, our concern is to spoil communication, to create distrust and suspicion, to make agreements unenforceable, to undermine tradition, to reduce solidarity, to discredit leadership, and to sever any moral bond that holds the conspirators together.

The mail-order filthy pictures market used to display a number of interesting strategic characteristics. [This quaint passage was written in 1965, an era ago. I have recast it in the past tense. The analysis still intrigues me.] It depended on a communication channel that enjoyed privacy at both ends; it could be managed by first-class mail but not telegraph or postcard. Prior to communication there was a need for identification; seller or buyer had to seek out and identify the other in a way that a diligent third party could not detect. One had to reveal himself in a noncommittal way; and in the transaction they had to avoid the production of incriminating evidence. Check, money order, and registered letter were not as good as cash. There was sometimes a need for blind communication, the customer not wanting his true identity known; by inadvertence or design the seller might let it be known, and he might try blackmail. The initial identification had to be by a broadcast system, and there had to be conventions about where to look for advertisements and how to read them, or else ways that the seller could recognize a potential customer by his participation in a more innocuous mail-order business.

There was no enforcement of contract, and thus a special problem of trust, as buyer and seller were separated by distance and could not engage in instantaneous exchange. Either the buyer trusted the seller, sending advance payment, or the seller trusted the buyer and sold on credit. In the absence of credit, the customer had not only to trust the seller with his money but to worry about blackmail.

I am told that there were special techniques for enforcing the bargain. Not only did a customer have to prove good faith by investing in second-rate stuff before he saw the most interesting merchandise, but he sometimes was asked to describe in his own words, in writing, the things he most wanted to buy, thus providing the seller protection in the form of incriminating evidence against the buyer.

Although the direct communication was private, the advertising was not; either side of the market was subject to masquerade. Seller and buyer could both be simulated, and there was no reliable technique of authentication. For the same reason there might be no reliable way to segregate markets; if, as with liquor, legality depended on the age of the customer, the seller could not distinguish legal from illegal transactions except at the expense of the customer's privacy.

Finally, although conscience and good faith may actually abide in such a market, it is not entirely satisfying to solve the game for the participants by harnessing the merchant's conscience to his business in the hope that youngsters would send cash in advance. If the purveyor of pornography had had that much conscience he might not have been in the business to begin with. The moral values here are complex; whatever our attitude toward the merchant was, and however much we might have wanted to spoil the market, we can hardly characterize his customer exclusively by participation in the enterprise, even by the community moral standards prevailing in the 1960s, since the customer might have been the same boy that played first base on the junior high school team.

As a social problem, compared with war and peace and racial integration, mail-order pornography, even in the 1960s, was well down the list. As an exercise in strategic analysis, however, it is good for that reason: the investigator is less committed than if it were the Ku Klux Klan or, in those days, a movement for Panamanian recovery of the Canal Zone; the principles are less buried in emotion and concern. I would not pretend that a strategic analysis of the situation, whether of the filthy pictures market or the Ku Klux Klan, discovers cheap and easy tactics for solving our problems. I do suggest that in many of these enterprises there are strategic aspects that can be brought under systematic analysis and can help us identify critical requirements and vulnerabilities in the enterprise. Depending on the enterprise, we can then try to support or collapse it, tilt the advantage to one side or the other, exploit it for our own benefit, or just understand what makes it work.

# 10 | What Is Game Theory?

**Y**OU ARE on the station platform, ready to board the train, and meet an old friend who has reserved a seat in a different car from yours. You agree to meet in the diner. After you board the train a steward comes through making reservations, and you discover that there is a first-class diner and a second-class buffet car. You'd somewhat rather eat in first class, you suspect that your friend would prefer the buffet car, but mainly you want to make a reservation that coincides with his. Do you elect the diner or the buffet car?

Again you are on the platform and meet a friend you are trying to avoid; he is going to coax you onto some committee. Your reservations are in different cars, but he suggests meeting in the diner. When the steward comes through you discover to your relief that there are two diners, first-class and buffet, and if you choose correctly you may "innocently" miss your friend. You have to be careful; he can guess that you'll evade him if you can. Normally you'd dine first class and he knows it. For which car do you make your lunch reservation?

Once again, you are on the train without a reserved seat. You find a seat but a few passengers are left standing. When the steward announces lunch, the standing passengers watch eagerly to see who will vacate a seat in favor of lunch. If you go to the diner you will have no claim to your seat when you return. If you do not vacate your seat you cannot eat; if you do not eat nobody gets your seat, not even for the time you would like to be in the diner. What arrangement can you work out?

Finally, you are in your air-conditioned parlor car when the steward gives you your ballot. Passengers are asked whether they wish smoking to be permitted in these cars. You suspect it will be a close vote. A second item on the ballot asks whether, if smoking is permitted in response to the passengers' wishes, it should be confined to cigarettes. You'd love a cigar, which is all you ever smoke, would evidently answer no to the second question, but suspect that all nonsmokers and some cigarette smokers would vote to exclude cigars. How do you vote? Can you make a deal with someone?

As you leave your parlor car at the station, the steward stands expecting his tip. Fifty cents would be a reasonable tip, but the steward disposes of enough favors to make it worth some small expense to be among his favorites. You suspect that some of the other regular commuters try to tip a little above average. You'd like to tip a little above average. How much do you give the steward?

### Interdependent Decisions

*Game Theory* is the formal study of rational decision in situations like these. Two or more individuals have choices to make, preferences regarding the outcomes, and some knowledge of the choices available to each other and of each other's preferences. The outcome depends on the choices that both of them make, or all of them if there are more than two. There is no independently "best" choice that one can make; it depends on what the others do.

For some problems, like choosing the route that minimizes distance from home to office, you can reach a solution without solving anybody else's problem at the same time. To drive through an intersection, though, you want to know what the other driver is going to do—to stop, slow down, speed up, or just keep going—and you know that a main element in his decision is what he thinks you are going to do. Any "solution" of a problem like this is necessarily a solution for *both* participants. Each must try to see the problem from the other's point of view, but when he does he sees himself trying to reach a decision.

What game theory did was to identify this class of situations as one of practical importance and intellectual challenge, and to propose that any satisfactory solution for rational participants ought to be a solution for them jointly. Each must base a decision on his expectations. Unless we are willing to suppose one or more among them merely to expect wrong—and then we have to decide *ad hominem* who is going to be wrong—there must be some consistency, not only of their choices with their expectations but among their expectations of each other. Game theory is the formal study of the rational, consistent expectations that participants can have about each other's choices.

It is, though, abstract and deductive, not the empirical study of how people make decisions but a deductive theory about the conditions that their decisions would have to meet in order to be considered "rational," "consistent," or "noncontradictory." Of course defining "rational," "consistent," or "noncontradictory" for interdependent decisions is itself part of the business of game theory. Take the case of the man whom we do not want to meet in the diner: could there be a theory that tells us unequivocally which diner to choose in order not to meet him? Only if we deny our opponent access to the theory. If logic could tell us which diner to choose, the same logic could tell him which diner we would choose, and as von Neumann and Morgenstern said in the monumental work that launched game theory nearly four decades ago, we can hardly be satisfied with the generality of any theory whose success depends on its not becoming known!

Strictly speaking, this kind of theory is not predictive. It is what is sometimes called "normative" theory in contrast to predictive or explanatory theory. Still, it is doubtful whether theorists would put forth so much energy and receive so much attention if their deductions were not felt to provide some bench mark for the analysis of actual behavior. This method, which might be called "vicarious problem-solving," has been traditional in economics; for the study of how business firms maximize profits, even for the study of whether they try to, it is helpful to know how they would behave if they actually tried and succeeded.[1]

### Solving the Problem

Let us look at how the problems that began this chapter are approached through game theory. First, with an exception to be noted later, from the point of view of game theory none of these problems involves dining cars. The dining cars are merely an interpretation; the man I did not want to meet in the diner could as well be a disarmament inspector along whose route I do not want to leave evidence of violation, or a submarine commander about to fire a torpedo in the direction he thinks my ship will go. Second, the problem does not involve particular individuals; game theory eschews solutions based on personal idiosyncrasy or the ability of one individual to outguess another. Third, in game theory one does not care why the one individual wants to meet the other and the second wants to avoid the first; they are treated as "rational" in the way they try to achieve their goals, but their goals are *their* business, and game theory takes them as data.

In the case of *opposed interests,* if either of us has to make his choice first, in a way that the other can see, the solution is easy: the first loses, however he chooses, and the second wins. This result is trivial but its implications are not. It points to the value of postponing decision, of gaining intelligence about the choice another has already made and denying intelligence in case one has to move first.

This dining-car case is simplified by the occurrence of only two possible outcomes, *meet* and *don't meet,* and using S and F for success and failure, the problem can be depicted in a 2 × 2 matrix (Figure 1). In the lower left corner of each cell is the outcome from my point of view, I being the one whose decision corresponds to

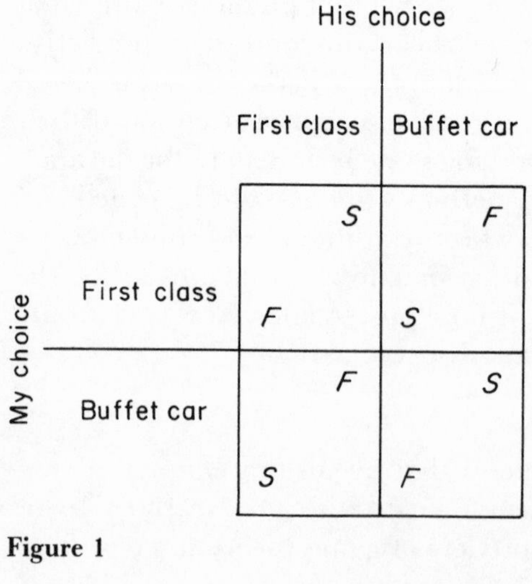

Figure 1

choosing the upper or lower row; and in the upper right corner of each cell is the outcome from his point of view, his decision corresponding to the choice of the left or right column. We can make the problem look somewhat quantitative by using numerical scores in place of $S$ and $F$—a 1 for success and a 0 for failure, or perhaps a $-1$ for failure, choosing numbers for sheer mnemonic and typographic convenience, just remembering that the larger of the two numbers means success. We may as well use the same pair of numbers for both players, although this again is just for convenience. We can now say that each player tries "to maximize his score," but this merely means that he tries to achieve success or to maximize his chances of success.

This is one of the situations that in game theory is known as "zero-sum." It is often described as a situation in which he loses what I gain and vice versa, but actually in game theory the scoring systems of the two individuals are invariably treated as incommensurate. If two feudal noblemen play a game of cards, one to lose his thumb if he loses and the other to lose his eyesight, the game is "zero-sum" (as long as neither cares about the other's loss) though nobody's loss is the other's gain and there may be no way of comparing what they risk losing. It is precisely *because* their value systems are incommensurable that, if their interests are strictly opposed, we can arbitrarily represent them by scales of value that make the scores or payoffs add up in every cell to zero. Visually it is often more convenient to use positive numbers and zeros; the sum then will be some positive number.

What, now, does game theory say about this dining-car or disarmament-inspection or torpedo-target problem that is abstractly represented in our matrix? The reader can probably guess: it says that each participant should have a fifty-fifty chance of succeeding. Why? Because the positions are symmetrical, and in game theory we agree not to pick favorites. Is it quite true that their positions are symmetrical, when one wants to meet and the other wants not to meet? Yes, the same situation arises in matching pennies; one wants both coins heads or tails and the other wants a head and a tail, but if we match a nickel against a penny it is arbitrary whether we call the Indian or the buffalo "head." So we not only eliminate the dining car, we eliminate the concept of "meeting." We can interchange columns in the matrix and get another that is superficially changed but essentially the same;

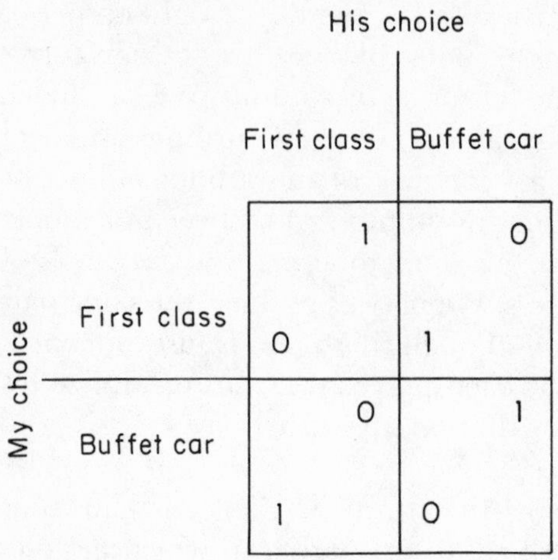

His choice

First class | Buffet car

**Figure 2**

"meet" and "not meet" are only labels, and in game theory we ignore the labels unless there are special reasons for using labels as part of the communication process.

We might say that it is a "toss-up" who wins this game and indeed one may as well flip a coin. But I can flip the coin for either of two reasons: because I just don't care and, like a person who doesn't know which shoe to put on first, want some arbitrary way to decide; or alternatively because if I deliberately flip a coin you cannot guess what I will do, any better than you can guess the toss of a coin. In game theory it is discovered that some games of wits (usually, "zero-sum" games of pure conflict) can be converted into games of chance by appropriate randomization of one's decision.

There is a consistency here: if I flip a coin you can have no better than a fifty-fifty chance at meeting me, and if you flip a coin I can have no better than a fifty-fifty chance of avoiding you. In game theory this fifty-fifty chance of success or failure for each participant is considered the "value of the game," and the "solution." This does not quite say that a person should flip a coin. What it says is that two rational participants, in this situation with alternative outcomes, cannot rationally expect more than a fifty-fifty chance of success unless there are special reasons for supposing that one of the opponents just does not understand the game. If you can think of any line of reasoning by which to choose one car or the other with a better than fifty-fifty chance of meeting me, I can spoil your strategy by flipping a coin. No mediator could talk the two of us into any scheme that gave odds of less than, or more than, a fifty-fifty chance of meeting, because one of us could always do better by flipping a coin.

Where is all the mathematics? The mathematics is of two sorts. One relates to logical generalization: it is interesting to know whether every problem of this kind has this kind of solution, and what kinds may not. Second, if we complicate the problem it may take some practical mathematics to figure out what kind of coin to flip. Suppose for example that there is one dining car in which your acquaintance is bound to find you but another in which he has only a fifty-fifty chance even if you both go to that car. The latter is like two dining cars coupled together, and to decide where to go you must choose among the equivalent of three dining cars, rolling dice to determine which of the three to go to. He then has one chance in three of finding you, and could himself guarantee one chance in three by choosing one or the other dining car with odds of two to one. Complicate the problem all you please, the principle remains the same; complicate it all you please, and the services of a mathematician or a computer become necessary. The intellectual achievement is in recognizing which complicated problems of disarmament inspection, torpedo fire control, and dining-car selection can be reduced to the general principle of flipping a coin or using random numbers. For generations people presumably chose safe combinations at random in order not to be outguessed by burglars, but it was game theory that saw the same principle (with the odds suitably chosen) in the allocation of a quota of on-site disarmament inspections among the months of a year or the sections of a territory.

Notice that communication is of no significance in this strictly adversary relation. The submarine commander and the captain of the target ship can have no rational interest in sending each other messages; any message worth sending is not worth reading, unless somebody thinks that he is a little smarter than his adversary and can think one step further in a game of mutual deceit.

### Alternative Solutions

Now turn to the two friends who want to meet in the same dining car. They succeed or fail together. (If we want symmetrical terminology we can call the situation a "zero-difference game" in exactly the same sense as the pure-conflict situation is called a "zero-sum game.") Their choices are represented in the matrix depicted in Figure 3. Their problem is an "embarrassment of solutions." There are two, and they do not know which to choose. If

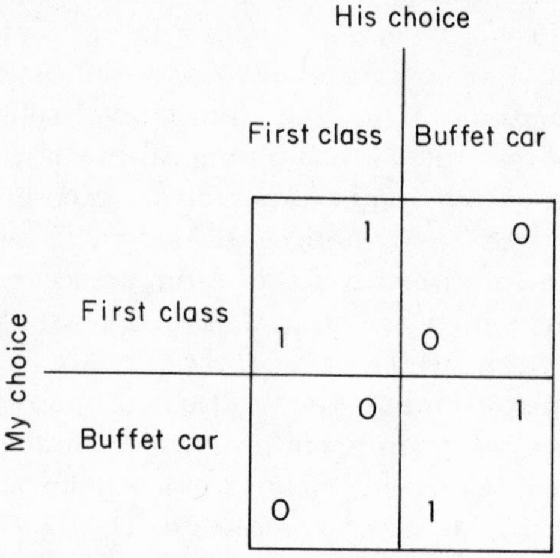

His choice

| | First class | Buffet car |
|---|---|---|
| **First class** | 1 / 1 | 0 / 0 |
| **Buffet car** | 0 / 0 | 1 / 1 |

My choice

**Figure 3**

either can move first, letting the other follow, the situation is trivially easy. This is a "team" situation and it takes only one-way communication, or a leader-follower relation, or a "rule" known to both participants, to solve their problem. If they flip coins, they guarantee the same fifty-fifty chance that the adversaries did. What they might do is search for clues; a clue is a kind of signal that each can recognize as an arbitrary instruction worth following in the interest of getting together. Here is the place where "labels" can make a difference, but only as a kind of surrogate for an instruction or a communication. If one dining car is named "The Rendezvous" and the other "Solitaire," they may agree tacitly that they have the signal they need. Members of a squad separated in combat, two people with a lunch date who failed to mention where to meet, or two cars keeping to opposite sides of the road need such clues and signals. Communication makes the problem trivial, but communication is not always available. What is interesting conceptually about this problem is that there are too many "solutions," posing a problem.

Consider now the man who will lose his seat if he goes to the diner. His interest, and that of the man who wants his seat, are neither strictly opposed nor wholly coincident. Both will be better off if the man can reclaim his seat when he returns, because if he can he will eat, and the other will get to sit down for a while. The "solution," if the man would rather sit than eat and has no way of reclaiming his seat, is an *inefficient* one: he goes without lunch, the other stands up all the way. What is needed is a one-way promise that the man who sits down will get up, or an enforceable contract, or a scheme to rearrange the incentives of the man who takes the seat (such as his going to the dining car second, not first, and being hungry enough to vacate his seat when the first returns). Game theory helps to discover some of these "inefficient" situations; it can also try to discover some rules or procedures, legal arrangements, or enlargement of the range of strategies available, to achieve better outcomes for both participants. Game theory also provides a framework for studying the bargaining that then occurs if there are two or more such outcomes and they discriminate differently among the participants.

## A Framework for Analysis

So far I have mentioned only some rudiments of game theory, and none of the subtle or elaborate analysis that has attracted the attention of mathematics. But what may be of most interest to a social scientist is these rudiments. The rudiments can help him to make his own theory, and make it in relation to the particular problems that interest him. One of the first things that strike a social scientist when he begins to experiment with illustrative matrices is how rich in variety the relationships can be even between two individuals, and how many different meanings there are for such simple notions as "threat," "agreement," and "conflict." He is struck by how many configurations of information and misinformation there are, how many different communication systems, and what a variety of alternative "legal" constraints on bargaining and tactics. Even the simplest of situations, involving two individuals with two alternatives apiece to choose from, cannot be exhaustively analyzed and catalogued. Their possibilities are almost limitless. For this reason, game theory is more than a "theory," more than a set of theorems and solutions; it is a framework for analysis. And for a social scientist the framework can be useful in the development of his own theory. Whether the theory that he builds with it is then called game theory, sociology, economics, conflict theory, strategy, or anything else is a jurisdictional question of minor importance.

Consider two individuals with two choices each, four possible outcomes. For each participant, rank the four outcomes from first choice to fourth, without yet using numbers to represent the intensity of preferences; eliminate ties, that is, assume that no two outcomes are equally attractive or unattractive for either of the participants. How many different 2 × 2 situations can we get? The answer is 78. Furthermore, in 66 of these situations the positions of the two participants are different; and there are a total of 144 different positions a man can be in vis-à-vis his partner.

This number is large enough to surprise most people; but if it seems manageably small, we need only to make allowance for some tied preferences and the number of distinguishable 2 × 2 matrices exceeds a thousand. Just give each participant three alternatives to choose among, rather than two, with nine outcomes that can result from the joint decision, and the number of distinguishable positions a man could be in vis-à-vis his partner is more than a billion. That is to say, if we prepare a table with three rows and three columns and put, in each of the nine cells, one of the numbers from one to nine for the player who chooses column, and similarly for the one who chooses row, there are more than a billion different ways of inserting those numbers, even after we eliminate all the duplications that result from arbitrarily rearranging rows and columns. (To be more exact: the number is $[9!]^2 \div [3!]^2 = 3,657,830,400$.)

No wonder there is no exhaustive catalogue of even the simplest kinds of interdependence that can exist between the decisions of two people. Add a third person, or add for each person his estimate of the other person's preferences, or add an opportunity for one person to make his choice conditional on the other's choice, and the number of different possibilities quickly becomes astronomical. Let the population explosion go to any imaginable extreme and form all the possible pairs of human beings on this planet; there will not be enough pairs to illustrate the full variety of the situations that can occur when two people contemplate between them a dozen possible outcomes they jointly determine by choosing, in a brief sequence of moves, among three or four alternatives each.

These numbers are not meant to daunt the theorist but to encourage him. Since a definitive catalogue of even the simplest situations and their analyses could not be physically provided nor humanly read if it could be, and since evidently not all differences are important differences, one needs a system, or some criteria, for handling whole classes of situations that, though different, need not be distinguished. One needs to identify the models that have the greatest generality or some unique interest. And one needs a few theorems that permit him to make general statements based on a few salient characteristics of a model, without having to examine all the possibilities.

### Some Illustrative "Moves"

The use of matrices and explicit preferences can be helpful both in discovering and in communicating distinctions that need to be made (and in recognizing false distinctions or inessential ones). How does one distinguish a threat from a warning? How does one distinguish the potency of a threat from its credibility? How does one distinguish a bluff from an insufficiently credible threat? When does a threat need to be coupled with a reassurance to be effective? In what situations can both parties be interested in threats, in what situations can only one party have an interest? When is misinformation of value to both parties, when is it of value to one party, and when harmful to both? What is the minimum communication system required for the effectiveness of a threat, of a promise, of a threat coupled with a promise; and what kinds of insurance against failure will enhance the credibility of a threat, what kinds will degrade it? What definitions break down, or have to be replaced by more complicated notions, if the number of relevant alternatives increases from two to three, or from three to some larger number?

It turns out that many of these concepts and distinctions can be operationally defined by reference to an explicit "payoff matrix" that shows the preferences of two parties among the several outcomes. It also turns out that some cannot, and it is useful to see explicitly why they cannot. Some concepts can be operationally defined, and quite simply represented, as a change in a single number or preference ranking in a single cell of a matrix; some can be defined as simultaneous changes in two or more of the payoffs—two payoffs of the same person in different cells, or one payoff for each of the players.

This is hardly high-powered theory, and surely does not yet involve mathematics, but it can lead to discoveries and it can reduce ambiguity in communication.

We can make threats that are bluffs or bets that are bluffs: does "bluff" have the same meaning in both cases? My dictionary says that to bluff is to frighten someone by threats that cannot be made good. What about "will not" be made good? Is there a difference? What is it if I make a threat that I want you not to believe will be made good? Am I bluffing if I try to make you underrate either my capability or my willingness to do what I said? As von Neumann and Morgenstern pointed out, in situations like poker one may not only bluff to win an occasional hand on poor cards but also, quite rationally, bluff to be occasionally caught bluffing, so that a partner may think one is bluffing when one is not and put more money in the pot. It is extraordinary how rich in alternative meanings some of these apparently simple concepts are; the surest way I know to identify the necessary distinctions, to get away from verbal ambiguities, even to discover significant motives and actions that one had not thought of, is to use some of the rudimentary paraphernalia of game theory in making a model that one can manipulate.

Another superficially simple concept is *immunity.* An important problem in a rebellious area is to get people to give information that they want to give but are afraid to. The same problem arises in getting blacks to testify when their rights have been violated, or hotels integrated whose owners are afraid of reprisal. Medical authorities have the same problem in getting drug abusers to seek medical advice, since disclosure of the addiction makes the patient subject to prosecution. Grand juries often have to grant a witness immunity from self-incrimination. (A committee can even give an immunity that a witness does not want, to deny him the excuse that otherwise resides in the danger of self-incrimination.) In elections the secret ballot is mandatory, not an optional privilege, so that no one can give evidence of how he voted and thus cannot be made to comply with a bribe or a threat. This concept of immunity is susceptible to formal analysis, and the analysis could lean on some of the concepts and techniques of game theory. The situation is a "game" of *n* persons, where *n* is typically three or more but can be as small as two; there are payoffs to be identified, channels of communication and a structure of information, a distinction between verbal communication and evidence, and a set of choices that go in a certain sequence. There are alternative ways of providing immunity, such as privacy, protection, and coercion. Privacy can be personal or statistical; the protection can be based on defense against third parties or deterrence of them; the coercion can be secret or it can be made visible to third parties to discourage countercoercion. These situations do not especially belong to economics, law, political science, criminology, strategic intelligence, or any of the traditional disciplines; it cuts across them.

Still another example is the interesting subject of locks, alarms, warnings, and safety catches. We usually do not need much theory to help us buy a lock for the garage door, but a lock on nuclear weapons is rich in its theoretical possibilities. There are many kinds of locks and many motives, and even a classification of them requires something that looks a little like game theory. A lock on radium in a doctor's office has, among its purposes, the anomalous one of protecting the thief himself. A lock on the bathroom door is intended to keep people out who prefer to stay out and is equivalent to a sign saying "occupied"; and in bathrooms in some new buildings, to keep children from locking themselves in, there is an anomalous lock that can be unlocked from either side of the door. A lock on an ammunition chest may be designed to keep the contents from being used by somebody, and a mechanism that destroys the contents when the box is violated is almost as good as one that keeps the thief out; if the lock is to keep someone from destroying our ammunition, though, a destruct mechanism merely eases his task. A lock that makes the ammunition explode when the mechanism is joggled will not protect the ammunition if it works secretly, but if the burglar knows that it will explode in his face it can deter him. Some locks are designed only to measure the urgency of entry and are designed to give way under stress; fire alarms and emergency brakes are protected by a piece of glass to which a small metal hammer is conveniently attached. Some locks are meant to catch the intruder by blocking escape, some to catch his identity by photograph, some merely to report his intrusion by giving an "alarm," and they are hidden or made conspicuous according to whether one wants to trap the burglar or to deter him. And some, like the time lock on a bank vault, are designed to keep the owners themselves from being able to open them, so that they are immune to coercion during times of day that the place is unprotected.

And so on. Similar problems arise in handling confidential information, the reaction to a radar alarm and the authority to launch warfare, systems to guard the legal rights of apprehended suspects, and disciplinary systems. What we are discussing is devices or institutions that can be construed as a "move" in an *n*-person game, where interesting values of *n* may be anywhere from one up to half a dozen and the game can profitably be described by reference to the payoffs, the information structure, and the strategies available to the participants. The garage door, as I said, may be an easy one, but designing an appropriate device for a nuclear weapon, a fallout shelter, or an ammunition convoy in Vietnam requires explicit attention to the rich array of alternatives, the tradeoffs and compromises, the probabilities of contingent events, the relative magnitudes of payoffs, and what needs to be communicated, what guarded against revelation. The richness of the problem, and the value of explicit analysis, is occasionally brought home to us on those occasions when we lose a credit card, lock ourselves out of a house, or can't find something we hid to keep it away from the children.

I am not trying to advertise something called "game theory" that will provide instant insight into these interesting problems, but rather to illustrate the kind of problem that stimulated the development of game theory and to show how ubiquitous these problems are.

### Voting Strategy as an Example

Voting schemes provide nice illustrations of the domain of game theory. Voting is notorious for inviting strategy—the calculation of how one ought to cast his ballot in view of how others may cast their ballots. Someone who dislikes public housing may vote in favor of a civil rights amendment he despises, knowing that only with the amendment can the bill itself be killed on a subsequent ballot. Voting also invites coalitions; and implicit coalitions can be exploited by designing "package" proposals to be voted all at once as a means of enforcing the coalition. "Packages" eliminate alternatives; a rule obliging the President to enact or to veto an appropriations bill in its entirety permits the Congress to exploit the President's preferences.

I am going to work through an example, and to keep it simple I shall restrict the number of voters to two. I can do that if I use a rule of unanimity. You and I are members of a two-man committee to determine the career of an employee who would normally be considered for promotion but has been charged with a blunder that he might be fired for. Our committee has to decide two things. First, is the man's overall record so excellent that, leaving the blunder aside, we ought to promote him? Second, is he guilty of this blunder? If his record is excellent and he is innocent he will be promoted; if his record is only ordinary and he is guilty he will be fired. If we find him guilty, but find his record excellent, he will be demoted but not fired; if we find him innocent but of ordinary record he will be kept but neither promoted nor demoted.

I have been through the evidence and reached the conclusion that, all things considered, the man ought to be demoted, but I'd rather keep him than fire him, even promote him than fire him. You are convinced the man ought to be fired; if you can't fire him you'd like him demoted, least all promoted. Under the rules we must vote on both issues, his record and his innocence. Under the rules, it takes two to find him guilty of the blunder, and two to award him an excellent. Under the rules, we do not vote whether to promote, keep, demote, or fire the man; we vote these two issues.

The normal procedure is to vote first on guilt or innocence and, having that out of the way, to proceed with whether his record is excellent or ordinary. If both of us prefer, however, to take his record up first, we may. So together we first vote on which question to take up first, unanimity being required to take up his record first.

Both of us are interested in the *outcome*, not in the abstract notions of innocence and excellence. And both of us have made no secret of our preferences.

We can sketch this problem in the form of a branching tree (Figure 4).

There are eight ways that the balloting can go in arriving at one of these four results. The first branching point at the top determines which issue is taken up first; the second determines the answer on that first issue and the third the issue voted last. The numbers in the sketch refer to how many votes it takes to determine the choice; at the top of the diagram the 2 means that it

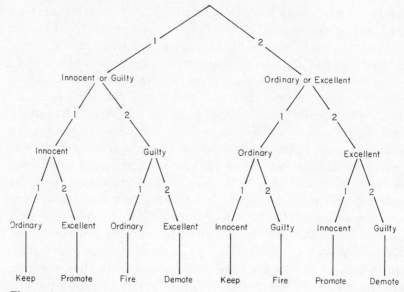

**Figure 4**

takes two favorable votes to elect the right-hand procedure (under which his record is voted before his innocence or guilt), the 1 means that it takes only one vote to have his guilt taken up first. It would take three unanimous ballots to reach the right-hand outcome where the man is promoted; either of us can bring about the outcome on the left because it takes only one vote for guilt to be considered first, one vote to find him innocent, and one vote to deny him an excellent rating. Under one procedure if I vote him guilty you can alone decide to have him fired; under the alternative procedure, if you vote him a good record I can get him promoted by finding him innocent. How should we expect each other to vote?

One way to work this problem is to start from the final votes and work up. At the far left (at the point reached if either of us votes for the normal procedure and if either of us votes him innocent) the final ballot (nominally on his excellence) is a choice between *promote* and *keep,* and it takes two to promote him. Evidently we'll both vote to keep him. At the final vote second from the left the choice is between firing and demoting, and it takes two to find his record excellent and thus to demote him; you prefer to fire him, and your vote would do it. Foreseeing this, at the preceding stage when we vote innocent or guilty, we know that the choice is between keeping him and firing him, so I shall vote him innocent, after which we shall both find his record ordinary. This means that if either of us supports the normal procedure on the first ballot the result will be that the man is kept.

Similarly, on the far right if we have found him excellent, we shall both vote to demote him; if instead we have found him ordinary I shall vote to keep him. So when we vote on his rating we know we are voting to demote or to keep him, and we both vote "excellent" in order to demote him at the next stage.

So, if we both vote to reverse the normal procedure and take up his record first, we can expect the man to be demoted. Since we both prefer his demotion to his merely being kept, we should both vote to reverse the normal procedure, then to find his record good, then to find him guilty.

There are several points to note. First, *the procedure makes a difference;* the man is demoted or merely kept according to which of the two questions we vote first. Second, one of the two procedures is *less satisfactory for both of us* than the other procedure, even though our interests do not coincide. Third, the reason why voting first on guilt or innocence leads to this less satisfactory outcome is that I must expect you to find his record poor after we both find him guilty. Because I do, I have to find him innocent. It is your power of decision on the final ballot that diverts me down another branch, to an outcome that we both like less than demotion. If you could promise in advance to vote his record good, I could go ahead and vote him guilty and we'd both be better off. The alternative procedure, down the right-hand branch, can be thought of as a way for you to give me that promise; by voting a good record in advance, you deny yourself the possibility to get the man fired after I vote him guilty, leaving me free to vote him guilty.

Each of us would have to reexamine his strategy if the other's preferences were switched. If you knew that I really wanted him promoted, for example, you would not dare to vote as you just did; nor would I if I knew that you wanted him promoted.

## A Matrix of Strategies

One technique of game theory is to identify all of these "strategies"—all of the different contingent plans that the voter may have for deciding along the way how to vote next. If I had to be absent, and sent a deputy to represent me, I could not simply tell him how to vote on each ballot. Each vote should depend on how the preceding ballot went. I can, however, if I'm willing to be sufficiently explicit, anticipate all possibilities and tell my deputy what to do in each case that could arise. I could say, for example, "Vote yes on the first ballot. If that loses, vote no on the next two ballots; but if it wins, vote yes on the next ballot and yes again if it wins or no if it fails."

This is a *sufficient* instruction; it tells him how to do everything I would have done as the situation unfolds. In the language of game theory, this is a "strategy." Every such contingent instruction, if it covers all possible contingencies, is a "strategy." In this voting problem, the number of different strategies is limited, and any advance plan or instruction that covers every contingency can be thought of as a selection of one strategy from among all the possible strategies. If we identify all of the alternative strategies, we can construct a matrix consisting of all possible plans that the two of us might have, and thus convert our dynamic sequential problem to a static simultaneous-choice equivalent, in which I mer)ely choose a strategy in advance, considering all the strategies open to you, and you do the same, and the outcome is the joint result of these two strategies.

To see how this is done, without cluttering the page with too large a matrix, suppose that we have already voted to reverse the usual procedure and to take up excellence first, and are about to decide on our remaining strategies. Since a no vote is decisive while a yes vote can carry or lose, I have one completely definite strategy: voting no on both ballots with the result that the man is kept, independently of how you vote. I also can vote no on the first ballot and yes on the second; if I want him fired, this may be a way of achieving my aim. If I vote yes on the first ballot there are four possible plans I could have for continuing: (1) to vote him guilty whether or not the first ballot finds his record excellent; (2) to vote innocent however the first ballot comes out; (3) to vote guilty if his record is found excellent, otherwise innocent; and (4) to find him innocent if his record is found excellent, otherwise guilty. I have, then, a total of six possible ways of playing the game when two ballots remain. You have the same alternatives, so there are thirty-six different ways our contingent plans can combine in reaching one of four possible outcomes. These are shown in Figure 5.

The numbers have to be explained. To represent my prefer-

|  | Your strategies | | | | | |
|---|---|---|---|---|---|---|
| My strategies | No No | No Yes | Yes No | Yes No/Yes * | Yes Yes | Yes Yes/No ** |
| No, No | 1 / 2 | 1 / 2 | 1 / 2 | 1 / 2 | 1 / 2 | 1 / 2 |
| No, Yes | 1 / 2 | 3 / 0 | 1 / 2 | 3 / 0 | 3 / 0 | 1 / 2 |
| Yes, No | 1 / 2 | 1 / 2 | 0 / 1 | 0 / 1 | 0 / 1 | 0 / 1 |
| *Yes, No/Yes | 1 / 2 | 3 / 0 | 0 / 1 | 0 / 1 | 0 / 1 | 0 / 1 |
| Yes, Yes | 1 / 2 | 3 / 0 | 0 / 1 | 0 / 1 | 2 / 3 | 2 / 3 |
| **Yes, Yes/No | 1 / 2 | 1 / 2 | 0 / 1 | 0 / 1 | 2 / 3 | 2 / 3 |

*Vote *yes*, followed by *no* if it carries, *yes* if it fails.
**Vote *yes*, followed by *yes* if it carries, *no* if it fails.

Outcomes:

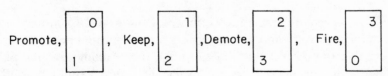

Promote, [0 / 1] , Keep, [1 / 2] , Demote, [2 / 3] , Fire, [3 / 0]

**Figure 5**

ences I have arbitrarily given a score of 3 to *demote*, 2 to *keep*, 1 to *promote*, 0 to *fire*. Since your preference order is *fire, demote, keep, promote*, I've scored you with 3 if he is fired, 0 if he is promoted, and so on. These numbers just remind us of our preference order, the magnitudes do not matter. (A little later we shall see where numerical values would make a difference.)

Neither of us has a "dominant" strategy, that is, a strategy that he would be satisfied to have chosen no matter what the other chose. Row 6 looks good to me unless you choose Column 3 or 4, in which case I'd rather have chosen Row 1. Column 5 looks good to you if I choose Row 2, bad if I choose Row 3 or 4, pretty good if I choose Row 5. There are some columns you might choose that leave me indifferent—Column 1, for example. There are some columns in which my score can be anything from 0 up to 3 according to what row I pick.

Though no row or column is an obvious "best" choice, we can still ask whether there is a pair of expectations we can have about each other that will lead us to choices that confirm those expectations. Is there a column such that if I expect you to choose it I will choose precisely the row that, if you expected it, would lead you to choose that column? Yes, Row 6 and Column 5 have that "equilibrium" property. If I expect you to choose Column 5, I am content with Row 6, and if you expect me to choose Row 6 you are content with Column 5. We cannot quite say that I "prefer" Row 6 when you choose Column 5, because I would do just as well in Row 5, but if you expected me to choose 5 you would choose Column 2. The intersection of Row 6 and Column 5 is an "equilibrium point," or an "equilibrium pair" of strategies. It has the property that if we both make the corresponding choices, each expecting the other to do so, each has behaved correctly in accordance with his expectations and each has confirmed the other's expectations.

Furthermore, the intersection of Row 6 and Column 5 is an "efficient" outcome, as economists use the term. There is no other cell in the matrix that can improve the outcome for one player without worsening it for the other. The same cannot be said for the cell in the upper left corner, which is also an equilibrium point but a weak one. (It is a "weak" one, a kind of "neutral equilibrium," because neither of us has an actual preference for that cell above any others in the corresponding row or column.)

If we draw up the corresponding matrix for the two-stage ballot under the normal procedure, with guilt or innocence being decided first, we get the matrix in Figure 6.

This matrix differs from Figure 5 in several ways. One is that you now have a dominant strategy: Column 3 in every row is as good as any other column and sometimes better. You can eliminate the other 5 from consideration. Since you can, I can assume you will, and I choose Row 1 or 2.

But though 3 dominates, your outcome is not especially favorable. Knowing your choice, I pick a row that gives me a score of 2 and you but 1. You cannot wish that you had chosen differently, all you can wish is that I could have expected you to. Then I might have chosen differently.

If Columns 3 and 4 could be suppressed, I would have a dominant strategy, Row 6, and you could choose Column 5 or 6, and both of us would be ahead. But in the matrix as it stands, the two of us cannot hold a consistent pair of expectations that would lead us to Row 6, Column 5. This pair of strategies has not the equilibrium quality; there is no line of reasoning by which we can reasonably expect each other to expect it.

### The Complete Matrix

The very first ballot, then, deciding the order in which to take up the two questions, can be construed as a ballot for deciding which of these two matrices to confront. We could of course construct a matrix corresponding to the whole three-ballot game. It would be hard to get on a single page, but we can at least ask what it should look like.

How many rows and columns would it have? A complete strategy has to indicate how to vote on the first ballot and how to vote thereafter in either of two cases. Since it takes two of us to reverse the normal procedure, one to keep it, a vote of no on the first ballot need only be coupled with a choice of a row (or column) in the matrix (Figure 6) corresponding to the left-hand branch. So there are six complete strategies corresponding to a vote of no on the first ballot. If I vote yes on the first ballot, my strategy must specify a row in each matrix, since I shall have to choose a row in whichever matrix the first ballot selects. There are, thus, 36 possible strategies containing a yes vote on the first ballot. Altogether,

Your strategies

|  | No No | No Yes | Yes No | Yes No/ Yes * | Yes Yes | Yes Yes/ No ** |
|---|---|---|---|---|---|---|
| **No, No** | 1 / 2 | 1 / 2 | 1 / 2 | 1 / 2 | 1 / 2 | 1 / 2 |
| **No, Yes** | 1 / 2 | 0 / 1 | 1 / 2 | 0 / 1 | 0 / 1 | 1 / 2 |
| **Yes, No** | 1 / 2 | 1 / 2 | 3 / 0 | 3 / 0 | 3 / 0 | 3 / 0 |
| ***Yes, No/Yes** | 1 / 2 | 0 / 1 | 3 / 0 | 3 / 0 | 3 / 0 | 3 / 0 |
| **Yes, Yes** | 1 / 2 | 0 / 1 | 3 / 0 | 3 / 0 | 2 / 3 | 2 / 3 |
| ****Yes, Yes/No** | 1 / 2 | 1 / 2 | 3 / 0 | 3 / 0 | 2 / 3 | 2 / 3 |

*My strategies* (row labels)

*Vote *yes*, followed by *yes* if it carries, *no* if it fails.
**Vote *yes*, followed by *yes* if it carries, *no* if it fails.

Outcomes:

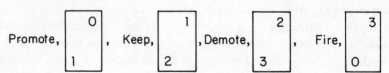

Promote, [ 0 / 1 ] , Keep, [ 1 / 2 ] , Demote, [ 2 / 3 ] , Fire, [ 3 / 0 ]

**Figure 6**

then, there are 42 strategies for me and the same number for you. This 42 × 42 matrix has 1,764 cells, each containing one of the four outcomes. What else do we know about it without taking the trouble to draw the matrix?

We know, without any more theory, that the outcome is bound to be asymmetrical; no outcome has the same rank in our two preference scales. We might guess, and with a little more theory we would know, that this large matrix shows an equilibrium pair of strategies corresponding to a yes on the first ballot for both of us and Row 6, Column 5, of the matrix in Figure 5. That is, the solution we arrived at by working backward from final outcomes corresponds to an equilibrium pair in our larger matrix.

Actually there is a further characteristic that game theory tells us to expect. There is at least one "dominated" row or column in the matrix—a row or column that is inferior to some other row or column in at least one cell and nowhere superior. If we strike out dominated rows and columns, compressing the matrix, we shall still find dominated rows and columns (because some that were originally not dominated are dominated after the eliminations). We can go on doing this until the residual matrix contains only cells with the *demote* outcome. Game theory is interested in which kinds of problems generate matrices that have various properties, like this one.

A few more things can be observed in this example. One is that a "dominant" strategy is not necessarily a good strategy *to have*. It is necessarily a good strategy *to play,* because no matter what the partner does the dominant strategy proves never to have been inferior to any other choice. But its mere availability can induce the other player to make a choice that condemns one to a poor outcome.

Another point, not illustrated in our matrix, is that in general a matrix need not show an equilibrium pair of strategies. It may show more than one; if it shows more than one they may differ, and they may differ by both payoffs' being lower in one cell than another or by one payoff's being lower, the other higher. (Game theory also tells us that if a matrix shows no equilibrium pair of strategies, one can be generated by a randomized choice, with suitable odds, among some or all of the strategies in the matrix; this procedure, though, requires that there be a suitable interpretation of the numerical values of the payoffs.)

## Collective Decisions

This voting example illustrates that a "gamelike" situation can be viewed as a *collective-decision* process—a process by which two or more individuals jointly decide on an outcome. The analysis also has ethical implications: we assumed the voters to be concerned with outcomes, not with strategies for their own sake; with consequences, not actions; with ends, not means; with justice, not truth. A voting scheme also illustrates how the organization of authority, leadership, and bargaining arrangements can affect the outcomes—can affect whether an outcome is efficient, can affect in whose favor the outcome discriminates. And evidently if we had been willing to enlarge our committee and have a majority-vote procedure, coalitions would have been important; communication might have been important to coalitions, and so might discipline. And it is evidently important what people know, or think they know, about each others' preferences.

The "legal" arrangements are important. If binding promises can be enforced, the alternative voting procedure is unnecessary; you just promise to vote the man excellent if I will join in finding him guilty. In fact, the first ballot can be thought of as a "bargain" that you have an incentive to keep because I have a credible incentive to vote for promotion if you back out of the bargain.

## Probabilistic Uncertainty and Numerical Preferences

The numbers in our matrices had only ordinal significance. To illustrate how the numerical values could assume importance, and how numerical values are assigned in game theory, suppose that any award of excellence or verdict of guilty is subject to a review procedure that we believe to have only a fifty-fifty chance of confirming our unanimous vote. If a man is found innocent and excellent there is a fifty-fifty chance that he will be kept or promoted; if a man is found guilty and excellent there are equal probabilities of 0.25 that he will be promoted, kept, demoted or fired.

To handle the problem we now need a more complicated set of preferences. It is not enough to know that I prefer demoting to keeping the man, keeping to promoting, and promoting to firing. We now have to know whether I'd rather keep the man or take a fifty-fifty chance between demoting and firing. And we may have to know whether I'd prefer a fifty-fifty chance between demoting and firing or a four-way split over the four outcomes. We can assume a few things, such as that if I prefer demoting the man to keeping him I prefer a fifty-fifty chance between demoting and keeping to the certainty of keeping him, and prefer any odds between demoting and keeping to any odds between promoting and firing.

Two points are worth mentioning. First, not only can these "critical odds" or "critical risks" be subjected to certain consistency postulates in a way that may permit us to go ahead and solve our problem, but it even turns out to be possible and convenient (though not necessary) to derive numerical values for the different outcomes from a limited number of expressed critical-risk preferences. These numbers can be operated on *as though* one were trying to maximize the mathematical expectation, that is, the expected value in a probabilistic sense. One can alternatively just postulate that a decisionmaker associates numerical values with all the outcomes and tries to maximize expected value; but the postulate need not be that heroic. It needs only to be that he can answer a few simple questions like those we asked earlier about the critical odds between a pair of outcomes that would make him just willing to settle for the certainty of a third that lies between the other two. If our man then obeys a few other "consistency" rules to avoid some kind of contradiction, we can often handle the problem. For convenience we can attach numerical values to outcomes, based on these critical odds, even calling these numbers "utilities" or something of the sort, but this is only a convenience for combining and compounding a limited set of expressed preferences in the form of critical odds.

The second point is that the need for numerical values arises only in the presence of uncertainties of this sort (and only when the number of alternative outcomes is at least three), when one has to place his bets in a probabilistic environment. (The uncertainty may be about another's choice or, in case of deliberate randomization or faulty control, about one's own.) If there is no such uncertainty, numerical values prove unnecessary (as they were in our original voting situation). And in the face of uncertainty one *has* to make choices of this kind, so it is not an outlandish assumption that one actually can. "Numerical utilities," though often thought unique to game theory, are by no means peculiar to game theory; they arise in the same fashion in any theory of decision under uncertainty.

These numerical values are arrived at separately for all the participants, and there is no intended interpersonal comparability among value scales. In some calculations it may appear that arithmetic is done on the numerical values of two or more players together, but it invariably turns out in game theory that an expression involving the "utilities" of two participants contains only *ratios of increments*, from which any units of measure would cancel out.

It is of some philosophical interest whether the value scales of two individuals are *assumed* inherently incommensurable, or instead we just mean that we don't yet *know how* to compare them. Game theory typically assumes the first position. Some writers treat this as a limitation of the theory and look forward to some way to compare the scales of value between people. I know of none, though, that has indicated how he would use such knowledge if it were available. Just as absolute-cost comparisons in international trade are unnecessary and usually meaningless—the notion of "comparative advantage" or "comparative cost" being sufficient to solve every problem of interest in international-trade economics—the notion of *comparative* ratios of *utility increments* (in which any absolute scales would cancel out) is sufficient in game theory. In fact, so far as game theory is concerned, there really are no "utility scales" to compare. There are only preference rankings among outcomes that have to incorporate numerical probabilities when some of the outcomes themselves are probabilistic. To say that a rational individual "maximizes utility" is a little like saying that nature "conserves" momentum or that water "seeks" its own level. These figures of speech save a lot of circumlocution; but when we forget that they are figures of speech and try to compare actual measures of utility, or to measure the "frustration" of water when a valve opposes it, it is time to abandon the metaphor and get back to operational statements.

### An Apotheosis of "Rationality"?

The question is often raised whether game theory restricts its empirical applicability by postulating mental giants with nerves of steel—perfectly rational amoral deciders who have access ex officio to the theoretical results of game theory.

The answer is: not quite. In principle there is no difficulty in imputing misinformation rather than true information, in supposing that calculation is costly or that people make mistakes or suffer from bad memories or display idiosyncrasies in their choices. In our voting scheme, for example, we can easily suppose that when a man votes on excellence he cannot remember whether or not a vote has already been taken on guilt or innocence; and in fact our review-board procedure can easily be interpreted as the likelihood that a vote will be recorded wrong or that one of the voters will shy away from the word "guilty" for unconscious reasons.[2]

But to handle these departures from perfection one has to specify them explicitly. And it greatly complicates the problem to depart from perfection, whether it be perfect memory or perfect absence of memory, perfect knowledge or perfect absence of knowledge, perfect calculation or perfectly random choice. The man with the perfect memory and the man without a memory are the easiest to handle in abstract analysis. To allow for an imperfect memory requires that we specify precisely how his memory misbehaves (and whether he knows how it misbehaves, whether his partner knows how it misbehaves and whether he knows whether his partner knows how it misbehaves, and so forth). Pretty soon we are tempted to give him either a perfect memory or no memory at all, or perhaps to provide him a simplified and idealized "imperfect" memory such that exactly half the time he forgets everything, knows that he does, and his partner knows it too.

But this is not a limitation of game theory; it is a limitation of any theory that tries to deal with the full multidimensional complexity of imperfect decisionmakers. Game theory usually does assume perfect knowledge or perfect absence of knowledge, because these are simple and unambiguous assumptions to make. Anything between the two extremes requires detailed specification, and game theorists can at least be forgiven for solving the simpler problems first and saving the more complicated ones for later.

Game theory usually supposes a few other things, such as that a man's ethics are what have recently been called "situation ethics"; he is concerned with *outcomes*, not intermediate processes. (In our voting example he is not seeking "truth" as to guilt or excellence, but defines justice in terms of what is done with the man.)[3] The decisionmaker is assumed not trying to be bold or novel for the sake of boldness or novelty, not trying to surprise us for the sake of surprise itself; he is not concerned with *why* his partner may choose a particular strategy, but what strategy his partner will choose. Nothing but the *outcomes* enter his value system. If a man has good will or malice toward his partner, a conscience or a bent for mischief, it is all assumed to be reflected in his valuation of the final outcomes. It is assumed that all the elements of his value system are displayed—everything that matters to him is allowed for—in the ranking or valuation of cells in the matrix.

How much a limitation this is depends, as in any theory, on whether an abstract, somewhat perfectionist bench mark can be helpful, and whether we can keep in mind that the result is only an abstract perfectionist bench mark. Newton's laws don't work if atmospheric resistance is present; purely inertial motion is hard to observe in the earth's gravitational field; some voters are shrewd parliamentarians, some are naive or inept. Game theory runs the same danger as any theory in being too abstract, even in the propensity of theorists to forget, when they try to predict or to prescribe, that all their theory was based on some abstract premises whose relevance needs to be confirmed. Still, game theory does often have the advantage of being naked so that, unlike those of some less explicit theories, its limitations are likely to be noticeable.

### Games, Theories, and Social Science

A word needs to be said about the name of this discipline, "game theory." The name has frivolous connotations. It is also easily confused with "gaming," as in war gaming, business gaming, crisis gaming—confused, that is, with simulations of decision or conflict.

The name arises from the observation that many parlor games have the key quality of interdependence among players' decisions. The best move in a chess game, the best way to bid or the best card to lay down in a bridge game, depends on what one's opponents are likely to do, even on what one's partners are likely to do. Furthermore, these games are usually well defined; there is an explicit and efficient set of rules; the information available to the players is specified at every point (even if in a probabilistic sense);

and the scoring system is complete. If we had a more general name for the subject now known as "game theory," it would be found that a great many parlor games fit the definition. It was this that led the authors of the first great work in the field to call their book, *Theory of Games and Economic Behavior*, and "game theory" stuck like a nickname.

Decades of usage have got professionals so used to the name that they occasionally forget that "game" is not only a technical term but a word in the English language. If they say that war is a *game*, elections are a *game*, industrial disputes or divorce negotiations are *games*, they usually have nothing playful in mind but are merely using a term that grew out of the recognition that some games, too, are *games*.

There is another problem of nomenclature: *game theory* already has the word "theory" in its name. We find it useful to draw distinctions between economics and economic theory, statistics and statistical theory, decisions and decision theory; but there is no accepted name for whatever the field is of which "game theory" refers to the theoretical frontier. Most game theory in fact has been substantially mathematical; some people prefer even to define it as the application of mathematics to this subject, and any bibliography of the discipline is dominated by accomplished mathematicians. Often the mathematicians have been more interested, for natural professional reasons, in mathematics than in law, social structure, diplomacy, economics, or sociology. Game theorists, and social scientists who deal with the subject of which game theory is the mathematical frontier, are out of touch with each other in a way that, say, economists and economic theorists are not, for a number of reasons including, often, the absence of a sufficient common interest to keep them in touch. The mathematical barrier is not the only one. There is an unusual dichotomy between the subtle, elegant, mathematical accomplishments of game theorists and the interests of social scientists.

Nothing in this essay begins to describe what mathematical game theorists actually do or even to give the flavor of it. For the social scientist, what is rudimentary and conceptual about game theory will be, for a long time, the most valuable. And it will be valuable not as "instant theory" just waiting to be applied but as a framework—one with a great deal of thought now behind it—on which to build his own theory in his own field.

Take the payoff matrix. This is hardly "theory," although a

good deal of theory underlies the definition of strategies and the interpretation of payoffs. Yet by itself, as a way of identifying alternatives and ordering choices, of laying out the structure of a situation to facilitate analysis, comparison, and communication, the payoff matrix may be, for the analysis of interdependent decision, what double-entry bookkeeping was for accounting, national-income accounts for economics, the truth table for logic, or even the equation for mathematics.[4]

# 11 | A Framework for the Evaluation of Arms Proposals

**T**HIS CHAPTER is an exploration of the different motives that can lead two countries to bargain about armaments. The purpose is to classify the alternative preferences about possession or nonpossession of weapons that the arms bargainers can have in mind, and to see what kinds of bargains are compatible with different preferences and what understandings and misunderstandings are likely.

I restrict the discussion to situations typically identified with arms control: the object is to reduce armament on the other side, and not, as in an alliance, to increase it. I discuss weapons that we prefer the other side not to have, and omit any weapons or systems of command and control that we might prefer they invest in for our joint safety. And I assume that the alternative to their investment in a weapon is not just some other weapon that we like even less. So I consider only weapons that each country prefers the other not to have.

To keep the analysis simple I assume that the choice is binary: to have it or not to have it. Some arms bargaining is in fact about all-or-none decisions, or decisions that are nearly so; ABM, biological weapons, weapons in orbit, MIRV, and many others have been approached as yes-no decisions. Other decisions are about quantities, numbers, sizes, distances, degrees, and durations; but even for them, the special case of dichotomous choice can be illuminating if not directly applicable. Often in these cases the negotiation eventually leads to a binary choice to adopt or not to adopt some specified limit or reduction or increment.

### Alternative Preference Configurations

The variety of preferences arises from the fact that one side, while deprecating possession by the other side, can have any of several motivations about possessing the weapon itself.

One is that our side prefers *not* to have the system under any circumstances, simultaneously preferring that the other side not have it. If our side has decided that ABM is a waste, whether or not the other side has it, that hundred-megaton weapons or bombs in orbit involve too much risk or bad publicity whether or not the other side invests in such weapons, we have a *dominant negative* preference. By dominant I mean that *not* having the weapon is preferred *irrespective of whether the other side has it.*

A second possibility is that one side prefers to have the weapon whether or not the other side has it. The Soviets, to take an example, may prefer to have a FOBS if we do not have one and prefer to have it if we do. We may prefer to have heavy bombers if the Soviets do, and prefer to have them if the Soviets do not. Either side may feel that way about sea-based missiles. This is the case of a *dominant positive* preference, where dominant again means that having it is preferred *irrespective of whether the other side has it.* (The term "dominant" is used this way in conventional decision theory. I am tempted to use a term like "unconditionally preferred," but there are ambiguities that can be avoided by using conventional terminology.)

Now a third case. The weapon may be one that we are not motivated to acquire if the other side does not, but that we would invest in if the other side did. Although the logic was not always clear, it was often asserted during the 1960s that ABM was the kind of weapon that the United States could not afford to be without if the Soviets had it, although the United States might not want to put resources into it unless the Soviets did. Sometimes the basis of this motivation is military effectiveness and strategy: a matching weapon may be needed if the adversary has it, but not be worth having otherwise. Sometimes it is psychology and diplomacy: our side must not appear incapable of developing the weapon, too stingy to procure it, or plain inferior for lack of it if the other side has it. Sometimes it is domestic behavior or politics:

the arms bargainer believes that political and bureaucratic pressures will be irresistible if the other side embarks on the program, but can be contained if the other side does not. This third case is one in which there is no dominant preference but a *contingent* one, a preference conditional on what the other side does. I omit the logically possible case that we want it if and only if "they" do not have it. It arises in other contexts, but seldom in disarmament negotiations. (The Appendix to this chapter discusses some neglected cases.)

ILLUSTRATIVE MATRICES

Each kind of preference can be depicted in a 2 × 2 matrix with a number in each of the four cells to denote the ranking of the outcome. Since each of the two countries can have the weapon or not have it, there are four outcomes: both have it; neither has it; we have it and they do not; they have it and we do not. (I am supposing that each side knows which among the four outcomes it likes best, which least, which second, and which third—not an innocuous assumption, considering all the interests and influences that go to make up a "side.") Sometimes it will not matter which is second-ranked and which third, or which third and which fourth, and tied rankings can take care of either order. I have found it mnemonically easier to let higher numbers denote higher rank and use 4, 3, 2, and 1 in that order to denote best, second best, third, and last choices. Thus, if one's most preferred outcome is that neither side have the system, the number 4 goes in the cell where the not-have row intersects the not-have column.

Figure 7 shows matrices corresponding to the three systems of preference for the country labeled "our side." The numbers have been inserted in the lower left corners of the cells to leave room for the other set of numbers—one number in each cell—for the "other side's" preferences.

I refer to the two countries as two "sides"—"our side" and "other side"—to avoid ambiguous words like "enemies" or "partners." I call a dominant preference in favor of the system a YES preference, and a dominant preference not to have the system a NO preference; the contingent preference I label IFF—if-and-only-if the other side has it, too. The two rows of the matrix represent the choice of our side and the two columns the choice of the other side. The number denoting the preference value of our side

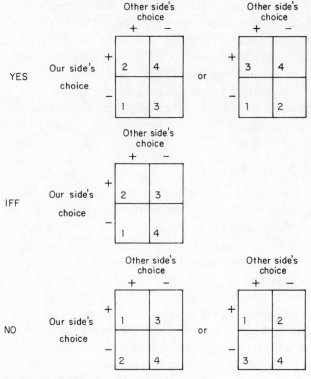

**Figure 7.** *Preference ranking.*

will be in the lower left-hand corner of the cell, the other side's in the upper right.

## Two Configurations of YES

There are two configurations of numbers consistent with the YES preference, and two for the NO preference. (There would be two for the IFF if I weren't omitting the weapon that we might want if and only if they did *not* have it. That possibility is considered in the Appendix.) The difference between the two NO preferences will usually not matter, but the difference between the two YES systems will. Note what the difference is: in both YES cases our side prefers to have the system if the other side does have it and also if the other side does not; but if the choice is between *both* having it and *both not* having it, in the first YES case, we prefer *both not*. In the second YES case we'd rather that both have it than have to do without it ourselves. Because that second case is stronger than a merely dominant preference, I label it the YES! preference.*

Having identified the four preference rankings for our side, we have the same four for the other side. There is no logical reason why the two should have similar preferences for any given weapon, although symmetry will occasionally suggest that the attitude of one side toward a particular weapon ought not to be wholly different from the attitude of the other side. We thus have 4 × 4 = 16 permutations. Four of these are symmetrical, both sides having the same rank ordering of the outcomes vis-à-vis each other. In the other twelve cases an IFF preference for our side will occur with, say, a NO preference for the other side; and, since any one of these asymmetrical combinations can be reversed, there are altogether sixteen different permutations and ten different combinations.

## SIXTEEN CASES

The sixteen permutations are shown in Figure 8. The four diagonal matrices are symmetrical: if we draw one of these four matrices from the point of view of the other side, reflecting the other side's choice in the two rows and our side's in the two columns, we get the identical matrix. The other matrices occur in pairs: the matrix corresponding to YES for us and NO for them has, from the other side's point of view, the configuration of the NO-YES matrix.

## RANKING ONLY

In these matrices preferences are only "indexed" and not "measured" by the numbers. Strength of preference is not shown. If we want to depict a first choice strongly preferred over the second, a

---

* The two NO cases parallel the two YES cases: each NO case is a YES case with the rows interchanged. The YES! case is unconditionally wanting it; the NO! case—we can label it symmetrically—is unconditionally not wanting it. The YES case corresponds to: "We want it but will do without it if you will." The NO case is: "We do not want it, but we are willing to get it on condition you do not." Note that it is not: "We do not want it but will get it if you will." That case does not occur here because it would correspond to a weapon that we wanted them to have—contrary to the arms-control assumption. The distinction between NO and NO! would be of interest if the reverse of IFF—they want it if and only if we do *not* have it—occurred on the other side. Because that case is being omitted, the two NO cases are merged in this discussion. In the interest of logical completeness, the reader can obtain that if-and-only-if-not case—IFFN—by interchanging rows in the IFF matrix.

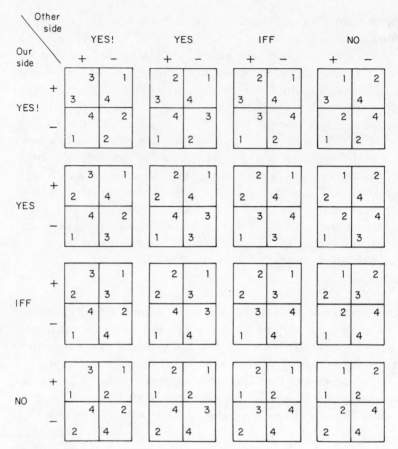

**Figure 8.** *Permutations of preference configurations.*

second choice barely preferred over the third, and a third moderately preferred over the last, we could impressionistically use numbers like 10, 4, 3, and 1 or, more extremely, 100, 10, 9, and 1. For some purposes that is necessary: sometimes it matters whether or not a preference between two outcomes is so weak as to be virtual indifference. In this essay we can get along with rank orderings and no cardinal quantities. (Evidently if we distinguished 4, 3, 2, 1 from 10, 3, 2, 1 we could end up with a dozen configurations for a single side and a gross of permutations to consider, although not all the permutations would be interestingly different.)

To avoid carrying along two sets of NO preferences and to avoid discriminating between them, I have replaced them by a

4-2-2-1 ordering in which the second and third ranks are both indexed by the number 2. Anyone who is uneasy about this suppressing of a possibly interesting distinction, or who is curious about the exhaustiveness of the classification altogether, is invited to read the Appendix, where the possible permutations are explored more completely.

## A Bargaining Matrix: YES versus YES

Begin with the combination of YES and YES, the second matrix on the diagonal from the upper left corner. This matrix is familiar to students of bargaining and conflict—and because of its symmetry it generalizes to multiparty situations. It has the following interesting characteristics.

First, each is unilaterally motivated to choose positively, whatever the other is expected to choose or has chosen. If they commit themselves to the weapon, we would elect to have the weapon; if they unilaterally promise not to have the weapon, we would welcome their promise but go ahead and get the weapon. But—if each of us makes that independent choice we both end up with a score of 2 instead of 3, with our second choice from the bottom rather than second from the top. Neither regrets his choice: had he chosen otherwise, he would have had the worst possible outcome, the other side having the system and himself not. If both should happen not to invest in the weapon, each has done "wrong," given what his preferences are, yet both are better off in terms of those very preferences than if both could change their minds!

This is the classic case in which something like "enforceable contract" can lead to a bargained result that is superior for both parties to what they can achieve independently. Though each prefers to have the system, whether or not the other does, each has a stronger preference that the other not have it. Each gains more from the other's foregoing it than from his own having it. There is room for a trade.

### TRADING WITH THE ENEMY

Here, then, is the case in which "trading with the enemy" is a good bargain. If we can reach agreement to abstain from this weapon we both get 3 instead of 2. But this is an agreement that has to be enforced. If the agreement cannot be monitored, and if the internal consciences or legal systems will not coerce compliance, each will not only decline to keep his part of the bargain but will expect the other not to.

It is not the case that every weapon that gives a side some relative advantage but is merely costly and to no avail if both sides have it corresponds to this YES-YES matrix. A weapon that yields a relative superiority can still generate a NO preference if it makes more likely the outbreak of war or has other deplorable side effects. There are, furthermore, weapons that one could prefer to have on both sides rather than on neither side; "invulnerable retaliatory forces" to supplement vulnerable ones might appear jointly desirable. I hesitate to name examples of YES-YES weapons because any example will be evaluated by the reader, and, if he evaluates the weapon differently from me, he may not find it a representation of the YES-YES matrix. But *suppose* that our side—whether or not you and I agree with this valuation—considers a fleet of warships in the Indian Ocean, or a forward-based missile system, or the deployment of a MIRV technology, worth having if the other side does not have it and perhaps even more worth having if the other side does have it, but nevertheless would consider any gains more than canceled out if both sides had it—no great relative advantage being achieved but some greater expense, some greater risk of war, some aggravation of diplomatic relations or some other undesirable consequence being entailed by joint possession of the weapon. Then we have the YES-YES situation and a basis for negotiated exchange if the result can be monitored and enforced.

## ALTERNATIVE AGREEMENTS AND UNDERSTANDINGS

An enforceable agreement is not the only kind of effective understanding that might be reached in this YES-YES case. Maybe one side can make a credible promise that it will abstain *if and only if* the other does. The second side then knows that its decision determines whether both have it or neither, and it can safely abstain. (A "credible promise" can be thought of as the deliberate incurring of some penalty on possessing the system if the other side does not, or on violating a promise, a penalty great enough to change the promising side's preference order from YES to IFF.)

A third way that restraint might come about is by each side's announcing that it will abstain as long as the other does. If both sides know each other's preferences and perceive that an enforceable agreement would be in their joint interest, they may perceive that a sufficient method of "enforcement" is simply each side's readiness to go ahead if the other does. Enforcement is by reciprocity. This requires that each be able to detect whether or not the other is proceeding with the weapon and to detect it in time not to suffer by being a slow second.

## Legislating IFF

An interesting kind of credible promise that might be available to the U.S. government would be a conditional legislative authorization. Suppose the Congress authorized procurement of a weapon system contingently—authorized appropriation of funds and procurement, with the authorization to take effect and the funds to be legally available only upon certification that the other side had unmistakably embarked on the program. In earlier times the British Parliament legislated contingent automatic procurement authorizations for naval tonnage, thus signaling to the other side—France in the late nineteenth century —that British procurement would be determined by French procurement.

## Two Qualifications about Agreement

Before leaving this case of YES-YES, two observations should be made.

First, while a weapon characterized by YES preferences is a clear opportunity for reciprocated restraint, achieved with or without a formal enforceable agreement as long as the choices can be monitored, it is not true that both sides, even with full understanding of each other's preferences, ought always to be willing to agree on restraint. Since either side can deny the other something it wants—at the cost of denying the same thing to itself—it may perceive a bargaining advantage with respect to some *other* weapon in making agreement on this case contingent on that other case.

Second, neither side can be sure of the other's preferences. This YES configuration can occur without its being plain on both sides. Other preferences can obtain with one of the parties mistakenly thinking that the situation is YES-YES. The consequences of mistaken estimates will be looked at later.

## Other Interesting Configurations

### RECIPROCATED IFF

A second configuration familiar in the study of bargaining is the symmetrical IFF matrix. This describes the weapon that each wants if and only if the other has it. It differs from the preceding case in that either side not only is willing to forego it on condition the other do likewise, but has no incentive to obtain it unless the other does.

There are two outcomes that are "conditionally satisfactory." As long as neither has it, and neither has reason to expect the other to acquire it, neither is motivated to go ahead. If both have it, neither is willing to dismantle it unilaterally. But if either side confidently perceives the situation to be IFF-IFF, it can confidently abstain or dismantle in the knowledge that the other side will do likewise.

Neither expects the other to be secretly preparing to jump the gun and race to be the first to get the weapon: the other side doesn't want to be the only side to have it. This weapon is one that is valuable only in the role of "counter-capability" to the other's possession of the same weapon.

This is an easy case for arms control. It is necessary only for the two sides to concert with each other and to reassure each other. If both confidently perceive what the situation is there should be no problem. Of course if each believes the other's preferences are in the YES! configuration, each may consider it a foregone conclusion that the other side will have the weapon and foresee no value in negotiating, and proceed with the weapon itself. (Without negotiating, they may never discover that they committed symmetrical errors in imputing wrong preferences to each other.)

Furthermore, it can be a tactical advantage to pretend that one's preferences are IFF when they are NO, if the other's preferences are YES: it offers some inducement for the other's restraint.

And, as when both had YES preferences, either side may consider it a bargaining advantage to threaten possession of the system, though its true preferences are IFF, to induce restraint on some *other* system that may be coupled with this one in negotiations.

Finally, as mentioned earlier, a YES configuration may be deliberately converted into an IFF decision by formal legislative commitment to contingent procurement.

(I leave it to the reader to think about the likely behavior in an IFF-IFF configuration if there is absolutely no way for either side to monitor the other's possession.)

## THE NO-NO CONFIGURATION

Ordinarily this would be a trivial case—a weapon that neither side wants, whether or not the other has it. There must be an infinity of ridiculous weapons that nobody is interested in having even if the other side is foolish enough to procure them. In isolation from other weapons, this is merely a logical category, empty of significance, that completes our matrix of permutations.

But in a wider context, as part of a logrolling package, one side might pretend that its preference was not NO but YES!; or it might, in aggressive bargaining, threaten to acquire the weapon despite its own preference not to have it. So the NO-NO case does not preclude bargaining.

## THE IFF-YES CONFIGURATION

This situation, if clearly recognized, leads easily to the same result as IFF-IFF. It is equivalent to a YES-YES situation in which one has arranged a credible promise to abstain if the other does. The one with the YES preference knows that its own choice determines the outcome, between both having the system and both not. Since it prefers that both not, it can abstain.

Problems arise if the IFF motivation is misperceived, or if the YES is misperceived to be YES! by the IFF side. Misperception can lead both to believe that the inevitable outcome is both having it. The IFF then gets it, confirming the mistaken belief of the YES side. If the YES side believes that the IFF motive is YES!, it may not even initiate the bargaining that would be invited by a symmetrical YES situation.

And, again, either side may perceive a bargaining advantage in coupling this weapon with another, exploiting the threat value of declaring an intention to acquire this one, and pretending its motivation is YES!

A frustrating situation can occur if possession of the weapon cannot be monitored. As in the symmetrical YES case, the YES country would prefer to own this weapon even if the IFF country did not; if possession cannot be monitored, the IFF country must assume that the YES country will procure it. Expecting that, the IFF country procures it, too.

Thus, with monitoring, the combination of IFF and YES can be as benign as symmetrical IFF; without monitoring, it can be as frustrating as symmetrical YES.

### YES-NO

If motives are transparent and there is no coupling with any other negotiable weapon, the outcome in this case is that the YES country goes ahead and the NO country does not. But if the NO country can successfully threaten to acquire the weapon or pretend an IFF or YES motivation, it can induce the YES side to forego it.

Alternatively, if the NO country is unable to misrepresent its motives or to threaten credibly that it will procure the weapon, it can bring in another weapon for logrolling: it offers a concession on the other, or threatens refusal on the other, to induce the YES country to abstain on this one.

### NO-IFF

This case does not differ significantly from NO-NO and nothing needs to be said.

### The YES! Configuration

Considered on its merits, the symmetrical YES! matrix is the trivial counterpart to the symmetrical NO matrix. There is no bargain confined to this weapon alone that we'd be interested in. While each prefers the other not to have it, neither is willing to abstain solely to induce the other to.

Interest arises only if this weapon can be coupled with another. Thus, among our sixteen permutations, seven preclude successful bargaining unless the weapon can be coupled with some other weapon or some other issue. The ramifications of this point are many.

First, it can appear a bargaining advantage to pretend one's motivation is YES! If coupling of two weapons were not possible, doing so would merely preclude agreement; but if one country's motivation is YES! on a particular weapon and the other's is YES on some other weapon the latter can refuse a bargain—or pretend a YES! motivation—on that second weapon in order to couple the two and overcome the first side's absolute preference for that first weapon.[1]

Second, the very possibility of a YES! preference can interfere with arms bargaining by being anticipated. It used to be commonly alleged that the Soviet Union's attitude toward active defense made no bargain on ABM possible: the Soviets would rather have ABM matched by ours than forego it on condition we do likewise. If that was a confident belief but a wrong one, and instead the situation was symmetrically YES (or IFF-YES or NO-YES), we could have missed an opportunity to bargain away ABM. If both sides are YES and believe each other to be YES!, discussion of the subject may seem so unpromising that the bargaining possibility is never discovered.

A third consequence of the YES! preference when the other side's is YES is a misunderstanding that spoils prospects for bargaining on other weapons. Suppose our preference is YES and we believe theirs is too, but theirs is really YES! Believing a bargain possible, we propose negotiation and are rebuffed; or we enter negotiation and discover that the other side insists on coupling this weapon with another that we believe irrelevant or inappropriate. We believe them to be holding out, jeopardizing a good bargain to get concessions on other issues. They may be quite unable to convince us that their preference is actually YES! and they are simply unprepared to forego the weapon merely on condition that we forego it. (We are unlikely to believe them if they tell us that, because that is precisely what they would tell us if indeed they were "just bargaining.")

### Misperceptions

Before we leave these permutations, some further results of misperception are worth noticing. Suppose both sides are IFF but believe each other to be YES: neither believes his own abstention will induce the other to abstain, but both believe agreement may be possible if they negotiate. To avoid appearing NO, which might leave the other side (believed YES) free to obtain the weapon with impunity, one side may exaggerate its interest as YES. Though in principle agreement is possible, there is no guarantee that the negotiations succeed. Each may overstate its case, get greedy, be inept, bog down in endless argument, or become domestically committed to the system. The negotiation having failed, each believes the other is going ahead, and so proceeds to get the weapon itself.

I consider it likely that each side was IFF on ABM but believed the other side to be YES, with a suspicion that it might be YES!, both believing that only a negotiated agreement could prevent ABM. Had the negotiations failed, both might have gone ahead with systems based on misperceptions—misperceptions that would have appeared to be confirmed, and would probably have been aggravated, by the negotiation itself. (Here is a case, by the way, in which the fiction that the "U.S. Government" had a "preference" can only be shorthand for a retrospective prediction about the policies that might have emerged from a multitude of interests and positions in different parts of the executive and legislative branches.)

Even NO configurations on both sides, if each believes the other to be YES, can lead to unnecessary negotiations to prohibit systems that neither side wants anyway. And if the negotiations fail, one or both may have got deluded into or committed to programs that, in the absence of bargaining, neither would have had any interest in.

### Natural Coupling, Tactical Coupling

Most of the foregoing discussion has looked at motivations, perceptions, and tactics in relation to a single weapon—ABM, strategic bombers, sea-based missile systems, or MIRV for examples. Some of the discussion has referred to the coupling of two or more weapons or issues in a bargain.

There are several kinds of coupling worth distinguishing; and at the risk of proliferating terminology I have to introduce some terms to call attention to the distinction.

One is between "natural" coupling and "tactical." Natural coupling occurs when two weapons are complementary. For example, it may be proposed that a natural package is not an agreement forbidding ABM on both sides—there being nothing about the other side's ABM that makes us want ABM—but rather between *their* ABM and *our* offensive missiles. Or, we might argue that MIRV technology on our side is "naturally coupled" with ABM on their side. We may propose that if they proceed with ABM we shall double our missile force or MIRV our land-based missiles. We propose therefore to abstain from some *offensive* capability if they abstain from some *defensive* capability. We do this on grounds that we have an IFF preference relation between our offensive capability and their defensive capability.

Similarly, we might take the position that the "natural coupling" is between our sea-based system and their ASW.

By "tactical coupling" I mean coupling, for bargaining purposes, two or more systems in which we and the other side have quite different interests. *They* may be concerned about forward-based bombers, *we* about ASW. The two have no natural relation. There is nothing about ASW that induces us to do anything about forward-based bombers. But there may not be a symmetrical agreement about forward-based systems that makes sense to both sides. And maybe we have nothing that quite corresponds to the particular ASW system that we deprecate on their side. So we propose—or they propose—that we restrain forward-based bombers and they restrain ASW.

This is what is usually called packaging or logrolling. It is different from natural coupling. In natural coupling there is a YES or IFF relation between the one weapon on their side and the other one on our side. In the case of tactical coupling there is a weapon that concerns us that does not seem promising for separate agreement, and another that concerns them that also does not seem promising for separate agreement; by combining the two we may reach an agreeable pair of restraints.

### Bargaining Chips

The idea of a "bargaining chip" seems to be some weapon or plan or intention that one side has, that is of less concern to that side than to the other side and therefore is eligible to be traded away. To be traded away means to be yielded or abandoned on condition that the other side make some appropriate concession. The term also is used to describe some project that a side merely pretends to be interested in, expecting a strong enough negative interest on the other side to make a trade possible.

Bargaining chips are not peculiar to arms bargaining, being familiar in tariff bargaining and other diplomatic bargaining and in fields like industrial relations. Because the term covers so wide an array of tactics, hardly any generalization can be offered about the wisdom or propriety of playing bargaining chips.

But to identify the situations to which the term can apply, it is useful to notice several different intentions that a country can have for a weapon, some of which correspond to this notion of bargaining chips.

(1) At one extreme is a weapon that a country is so interested in having that there is little likelihood it would bargain it away—a YES! interest. Of course if the other side has a strong enough negative interest and is willing to make enough coupled concessions, almost anything is likely to be negotiable. Still, some weapon plans are not expected to be part of any agreement or even to be discussed with a view to agreement. These will not be called bargaining chips.

(2) A second category consists of projects a side is strongly interested in but considers within the realm of bargaining, the other side's negative interest possibly outweighing this side's positive interest. This kind of YES project is within the arena of bargaining and recognized as negotiable—not brought to the table just to be traded away, but nevertheless subject to negotiation. This, as I perceive the current usage, would usually not be called a bargaining chip.

(3) The third category is YES projects that a country ordinarily would carry out but that are clearly of much more interest to the other side. These are the things that are taken to market, or brought to the bargaining table. There is nothing contrived or fictitious about them; they are genuine plans, but they are recognized in advance as strong candidates for being traded away.

(4) Fourth are the "pure bargaining chips"—things that a country has no real interest in but make a difference to the other side. These are the things, NO or borderline, that one side could innocuously do, or do at slight cost, that pose a risk or nuisance to the other side. They are not bona fide intentions, but they are trading assets because they threaten the other side.

If these projects are of no value to the side that puts them forward, why does the other side have to make concessions to get them put aside? There are at least two reasons. One is that the side putting forward the bargaining chips may successfully *pretend* a strong interest. The second is that it may more brazenly *threaten* to carry out the project unless the other side pays a price. Depending on accepted standards of behavior, this mode of bargaining may or may not be characterized as "blackmail" or by some such term that identifies the motive and deprecates the tactic.

(5) Finally, a country may project a NO weapon that it would deplore acquiring, hoping that the other sufficiently deplores it to bargain for its elimination. The side putting it forward wants *both* to get something for abandoning the weapon *and* to preserve itself

from having to acquire it. This case too, could be characterized by either pretense or blatant threat. Sometimes the ethical context of this tactic is judged according to whether it is employed cold-bloodedly for gain or instead is used to oppose—that is, to be bargained away against—something deemed improper that the other side proposes. (The threat to go through with a costly act of retaliation can be considered heroic or extortionate according to the way one judges the propriety of the other side's action that it is intended to deter.)

## ABSOLUTE AND CONTINGENT CHIPS

In negotiating, a side can put forward a projected weapon expecting to trade it away but without linking it to some particular concession of the other side. Alternatively, it can put forward a contingent project with an IFF motivation—a project that will go forward if and only if the other side proceeds with a particular project of its own. This automatically links the bargaining chip with the particular exchange that is intended—with a matching project on the other side. If the United States pretends a strong interest in ABM, believing the Soviets would pay some price in some currency to get the United States to abandon ABM, the proposal would be a bargaining chip of the general or absolute variety. But if the United States proposes ABM as a natural response to a Soviet ABM, or as a natural response to some Soviet offensive-weapon capability, implying not that we are YES toward ABM but IFF, with clear identification of what the IFF refers to on the other side, the project would be a "matched" or "contingent" bargaining chip.

Thus, the contingent chip gets linked or coupled with some weapon on the other side. There may not need then to be any further bargaining. With the absolute bargaining chip the bargaining is essential—one pretends a YES or a YES! motivation and needs to be induced to abandon it by some concession on the other side. In the contingent case the chip is matched with something in particular, and if that something on the other side is abandoned, by reciprocal announcement or unilaterally, the result may be achieved without negotiation.

## IFF AND YES BARGAINING CHIPS

A bargaining chip can be put forward in two quite different ways. Suppose the United States is only marginally interested in ABM, or even reluctant, but resolved on a tactic of pretending an interest or incurring a commitment, subject to progress in SALT. At some stage the U.S. negotiators have to suggest that the ABM program is *negotiable* and *contingent*. (There may be a pretense that it is not, but a pretense designed only to raise the bargaining price.) Inasmuch as there may be political and bureaucratic forces in favor of ABM as well as against it, the United States may be able to appear committed without having to pretend very hard.

Now there are two quite different commitments that the United States can appear to incur. One is to proceed with ABM if the Soviet Union does, and not otherwise. The second is to proceed with ABM unless agreement prohibiting ABM is reached with the Soviet Union. If successful, these two may come to the same thing; but the risks and procedures are different. If we commit ourselves, as a bargaining tactic, to match Soviet ABM there may be no need to reach formal agreement.

If instead we pretend a YES motive, we may commit ourselves to go forward unless an explicit agreement is reached. This tactic runs the risk that aborted negotiations leave us obliged, in consequence of a bluff, to go through with a program that we didn't want to go through with. But if the bargaining chip takes the IFF form, it is the other side's behavior, not the successful negotiation, that gets us off the hook.

## MOTIVATIONAL CONTEXT OF BARGAINING CHIPS

If the other side's motivation is known to be IFF we do not need the bargaining-chip tactic. We need only reassure them of our NO, and their IFF leads them to abstain. The bargaining chip is pertinent when the other side's motivation is believed to be YES.

If the bargaining-chip tactic succeeds the results are fine, as far as this agreement is concerned. (We might in the longer run prefer not to establish too much precedent for playing with chips.) We fail if his motivation is YES! In that case, if we bluffed an intent to proceed, we can be caught bluffing and back down or go ahead with a program we didn't want.

There is another danger. If we overplay our chip and pretend that our motivation is YES! to extract a high price, the other side may believe us! It may not even bother to bargain, and we end up committed to a program whose only purpose was to be traded away.

The risk of failure suggests that an IFF chip is safer than a YES or YES! chip. To become committed only on condition the other side proceed with some *action,* not committed in the absence of formal *agreement,* incurs less risk. A satisfactory result does not depend on a successful negotiation. If each side is IFF but thinks the other is YES, getting committed to a bargaining chip could mean that, if negotiations fail, both sides are committed to going ahead. If both sides are committed only to an IFF reaction, aborted negotiations can—may not, but can—leave both sides willing to wait and see.

### INTERNAL EFFECT OF BARGAINING CHIPS

There are two different ways that bargaining chips are put forward. One is pretense, the other commitment. There are many ways a government can get committed to something it clearly would not care to do, even while it is evident that the commitment was incurred for bargaining purposes. A legal way to do this, mentioned earlier, is to get legislation that obliges the government, in certain contingencies, to do what it might not ordinarily wish to do (and to get Congress to go home for the fall season, leaving the Executive Branch with its hands tied). There are other ways.

Many kinds of bargaining entail enough privacy for a pretense to be plausible or a commitment not to appear rigged. But it is hard for a democratic government to pretend an interest in, say, ABM, for the benefit of a diplomatic audience abroad, without deceiving the domestic audience. A corporation or a divorce lawyer or a land speculator can try to deceive the other party; and the Soviet government usually needn't broadcast an embarrassing public contradiction of the position it takes in negotiations. But the U.S. government often cannot help it. Bargaining chips are probably ineffectual for a government that cannot bluff without telegraphing its bluff. It is anomalous that in the last few years the bargaining-chip idea became a subject of popular discussion precisely because the Executive Branch put forward positions that it explained at home to be "bargaining chips."

There is nothing tactically wrong as long as the government can become committed, whether or not its hypocrisy is transparent. There is nothing tactically illogical in proposing to the home folks that one really wouldn't want ABM under any circumstances but needs to become committed to it. (If one can become convincingly committed.) But the pretense that typically makes bargaining chips so valuable is often unavailable to a government that must explain in a loud voice to a large audience that it didn't really mean what it said to its bargaining partner. And a democratic government risks losing some credibility at home—as the U.S. government probably did in making the argument so blatantly during SALT.

Precisely because the cold-blooded pretense is not easily available, a government may have to go through the motions of genuinely intending to go forward with the program, though part of the motive for the program was to generate a bargaining chip. The danger is that the government becomes genuinely committed, so committed that it forgets it didn't intend to go ahead, or so committed that it has to go ahead. It may become so committed that bargaining power within the government shifts in favor of those who want the weapon anyway. A government may believe it keeps the option of backing out of a commitment if the bargain doesn't come off, and discover that it lost the option.

## THE SYMMETRY OF BARGAINING-CHIP ANALYSIS

What has been said about "our side" and bargaining chips can usually be said about "the other side." The other side's interest in some weapon—a YES interest or an IFF interest—could be genuine, pretended, or contrived. By "contrived" I mean that, without necessarily pretending a genuine interest, the other side adopts a *policy* of proceeding with a weapon if we do, or of proceeding in the absence of negotiated agreement, or of proceeding unless we abstain from some other weapon or negotiate an agreement about some other weapon.

One difficulty in judging the other side's position with respect to some weapon is similar to the difficulty of knowing what our own side's position is. Within a government there are strong interests in favor of a weapon and strong interests opposed. Within a government there may be optimism about negotiation or pessimism. Within a government there may be a belief that the other side is already committed to procurement, so that an IFF motivation is a reason for proceeding with the weapon, not with negotiation. Within a government there may have been a tentative decision to proceed without full commitment, and no decisive determination yet of how strong the interest in the weapon is. To an observer not part of the government, there will be similar difficulties in judging the positions of both sides, although the USA and USSR clearly have governments that are different in their ability to pretend, to adopt conditional policies, to display or to disguise indecisiveness, to make up their own minds or to remain undecided, even to be incapable—when legislative as well as executive decisions are involved, or when allies have to be accommodated—of making up their minds or knowing what their own policies are.

### DOMESTICALLY ORIENTED "BARGAINING CHIPS"

Bargaining chips can be used to influence domestic decisions. One way is to initiate development or procurement of a weapon on ostensible grounds that, even if in the end it should not be procured, it enhances our bargaining position. Then by confusion, commitment, or default the program gets to go forward unless the other side manages to "obstruct" it with an agreement. Anyone who can sabotage the agreement can convert a bargaining position into a weapon program.

Another tactic is the opposite. A government that has decided against a weapon in which there is popular interest, in the Congress or elsewhere, or which it has promoted in the past but has changed its mind about, may need an excuse to abandon the weapon. Converting it into a bargaining chip and reaching agreement can legitimize a decision that could not so readily be taken unconditionally.

Negotiation of the Non-Proliferation Treaty probably provided instances of both of these tactics abroad.

### An Arms-Control Judgment on Weapons

The foregoing classification has at least a limited value, if only a limited value, in explaining or giving guidance on and clarifying the reasons why a person interested in sound strategy, including arms control, might favor or deplore a particular weapon program, or favor it only conditionally.

But this classification is abstract and somewhat uninformative because it does not relate either to the strategic characteristics of weapons or to budgetary, diplomatic, or domestic political considerations. It is not conclusive or comprehensive. Still, in clarifying and communicating one's attitude toward a weapon, even this classification can be useful.

People have opposed MIRV for Minuteman with a number of

different motivational permutations. There are those who felt that MIRV was positively bad on military-strategic grounds or military-industrial grounds, whether or not the Soviets had MIRV, but who also believed that the Soviets were not going to have MIRV anyway—a NO-NO configuration. There were those who believed it was not only bad on military-strategic grounds but, worse, would induce the Russians to acquire it themselves although they wouldn't if we didn't—a NO-IFF configuration. There were people whose configuration was IFF-YES who believed we should declare a willingness to abstain as long as the Soviets did, and others who with the same IFF-YES configuration felt that we should choose negotiating a MIRV ban. There were those who felt our own position should be IFF but believed the Soviet position to be NO and felt it therefore a mistake to go forward; others felt it was IFF on both sides, and we would force the Soviets into it if we got it ourselves. Others have felt that our position was IFF but the Soviets' was YES, and we should make clear to the Russians that we would if they did, although it was not necessary to negotiate. Some undoubtedly felt that the Russian position was YES! and there was no possibility of negotiating a MIRV ban, while others agreed that the Soviet motivation was YES! and that MIRV could be successfully coupled with other weapons in a larger package. And so forth.

Evidently these are different views of what our own preference should be, what the Soviet preference is, and what the diplomatic prospects are. This classification does not explain on what grounds one arrives at a NO, IFF, or YES preference. What this classification does is to clarify the arms-race considerations in one's position toward a particular weapon. That is, it clarifies one's position on whether we unilaterally want the weapon, unilaterally don't want it, conditionally want it, think our acquisition will affect the other side, think an enforceable agreement might be negotiated, or think this weapon might usefully be coupled with another.

This classification will not much help clarify a position that is based primarily on broader diplomatic considerations or domestic political ones. When the time came to vote on ABM in the Senate, the issue may have been the war in Vietnam, the military-industrial complex, the Nixon Administration, executive-legislative relations, the size of the defense budget, or promises given and positions taken that constrained what one could say or favor or vote on. But to the extent that one rests his position on what is usually called the "arms race," on the interplay or interaction of development and procurement and deployment of strategic weapons on both sides, this classification is useful.

## Appendix

Some readers may be troubled by a lack of symmetry in the two YES and NO configurations with a single IFF, uneasy about my collapsing the two NO configurations into a single compromise, curious about possible preference configurations that were neglected, or just interested in an exhaustive logical classification. In order to get on with some interesting cases I skipped the larger framework. This appendix is a long footnote to the first few pages.

There are altogether 24 different preference configurations for our side—for "having" or "not having" the system in question—if we confine ourselves to numbers like 4, 3, 2, and 1, thereby excluding ties and neglecting the sizes of intervals between "best" and "second best," and so on. (There are $4 \times 3 \times 2 \times 1 = 24$ different ways that we can distribute these four numbers in the four cells of our $2 \times 2$ matrix.) There is a like number of configurations for the same four numbers for the other side. And any one of our configurations can be paired with any configuration for the other side, for a total of $24 \times 24 = 576$ different matrices. I repeat: this is a minimum number because it neglects any preference systems we might want to represent by numbers like 10, 6, 2, 1, or 3, 2, 1, 1.

Abstracting from the difference between having and not having—dealing only with unspecified dichotomous choices—we can avoid quadruplication and get along with a quarter of that number, or 144. And by eliminating the duplicate cases in which one side's preference is matched with a dissimilar preference for the other, we can cover every combination with 78 different matrices. (Twelve symmetrical cases occur in which one side's preference ranking is the mirror image of the other's. Sixty-six asymmetrical cases occur twice each; IFF-YES and YES-IFF, for example. Twice 66 is 132; adding the 12 makes 144.)

Of the 24 configurations for our side there are 6 in which we uniformly prefer them to have it—whatever "it" is—and 6 in which we prefer them not to have it, 6 in which we want them to have it if and only if we do and 6 in which we want them to have it if and only if we do not. There are likewise 6 for the other side in which they have a dominant preference for our not having it. So if we restrict attention to weapons that we always prefer each other not to have there are $6 \times 6 = 36$ pairs of preference rankings to consider.

Among the 6 apiece, one is the IFF case in which each prefers to have it if and only if the other does not. We can call it IFFN. It is obtained from the IFF matrix by interchanging the rows. Logically the IFFN case cannot be excluded. But it rarely corresponds to weapons, and I suppressed it, getting 5 rather than 6 matrices in Figure 7. That would have led to $5 \times 5 = 25$ matrices in Figure 8.

I then chose to neglect differences between the two NO configurations. In a longer essay I would have to resurrect the distinction. The longer essay might have to consider preferences as shown in the two matrices in Figure 9. The other side has an IFFN configuration—a preference to have the weapon if and only if we do not. Depending on which of the two NO configurations we have, we may or may not see advantage in acquiring the weapon—visibly, irrevocably, and before the other side has it—inducing the other side to do without. In either case—NO or NO!—the other side

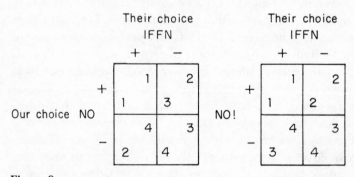

**Figure 9.**

will acquire the weapon if we do not. With NO, if someone is to have it, we'd rather it be us. With NO!, we'd rather let them go ahead and get it.

If we were dealing with bargaining situations other than those relating to weapons, the other form of the IFF configuration would undoubtedly be pertinent. There may be a number of contexts in which there is something that I would prefer to have only if you do not, and would prefer not to have if you do. It is hard to think of weapons that correspond to that preference. With a little imagination we can invent one. Consider any weapon such that if we both have it collision is inevitable and catastrophic. It is a positive advantage to have it as long as the other does not. I prefer you not to have it, whether or not I have it. If you do not, I can safely have it, and get an advantage; but if you have it I must avoid it to avoid collision. This situation meets my ground rule that we are discussing only weapons that I unconditionally prefer you not to have. It is the IFF case in reverse, that I labeled IFFN. If you are NO (but not NO!) you might preclusively acquire it to keep me from getting it.

By now it should be clear that two motivations led to my restricted set of matrices shown in Figure 8. One was the desire to stay within the realm of most familiar and plausible attitudes that a government could have toward its own possession of a weapon. This is a simplification that perforce neglects some interesting but unusual cases. The second was the desire to keep the number of matrices small enough to print legibly on a single page, and capable of being quickly scanned and comprehended.

The chapter could not be a complete treatment even of the important cases included, so some screening out of possibly interesting matrices was probably excusable. But any reader who is attracted to the examination of more complex motivations, either through curiosity about logical possibilities or through an imaginative contemplation of less mundane weapon systems, will want a richer set of matrices to contemplate, and he has my encouragement.

# 12 | The Strategy of Inflicting Costs

**T**HIS ESSAY was stimulated by a remark of Frederic M. Scherer on the notion "that a nation should weigh its own costs against the costs of its enemy" in choosing a strategy or in allocating resources to defense. He said the logic of it escaped him. I doubted that it did and began to develop a complacent defense of the proposition only to discover that indeed the logic—or at least an important part of the logic—had escaped me too; and where first I thought that economists like Scherer and me should neither disagree nor be in doubt about the proper formulation of so simple a principle, I no longer find the principle so simple.

Scherer argued that the proposition is valid only if the amount of resources a rival can allocate to defense is fixed—"an assumption unsupported by recent history," he says—or if an arms race is being waged as a "game of economic ruin." He doubts the advisability of the latter strategy, at least for the United States against the Soviet Union, and he goes on to criticize a good deal of recent defense analysis for its "zero-sum" orientation, its assumption of strictly opposing interests.[1]

The proposition that the enemy's costs in meeting some threat that we pose, or in responding to some measure we take, should be taken into account in deciding whether the measure is worthwhile, is not hard to defend in a zero-sum context; and one can set

268

Scherer straight by saying that the zero-sum context is all anyone had in mind. But though one can defend the letter of the proposition, it is not so easy to defend the spirit. Should we confine ourselves to the zero-sum context, where the answers are comparatively easy, evading the more interesting contexts where the answers may be harder? Should we defend the cost criterion in a way that increases our vulnerability to Scherer's charge that quantitative military analysis too readily assumes a zero-sum relation, even while our discussions of strategy are almost exclusively nonzero-sum?

We cannot justify zero-sum reasoning by assuming that the amount of resources an adversary will put into the contest is fixed. Even with a fixed budget the contest will almost surely be dramatically nonzero-sum. Deterrence, for example, is meaningless in a zero-sum context. So is surrender; so are most limited-war strategies; and so are notions like accidental war, escalation, preemptive war, and brinkmanship. And of course so are nearly all alliance relationships, arms-race phenomena, and arms control. The fact that war hurts—that not all the losses of war are recoverable—makes war itself a dramatically nonzero-sum activity whether budgets are rigidly fixed or not.

To get a zero-sum contest one needs a much more restrictive assumption than the one Scherer mentioned. The idea that we have some interest in an adversary's domestic economy, and that that interest is not simply opposite to his interest and measurable in the same currency as our military interests, is only one among many reasons—and surely not the most important reason—why military relations are nonzero-sum both in peace and in war. Furthermore, a "game of economic ruin" is not zero-sum if war itself is an alternative to progressive economic ruin, and if war is worse than economic ruin, or the threat of such ruin can be used to extort concessions.

Actually, it is hard to see how military relations can ever even approximate a zero-sum model unless things have reached the point where all but two extremes among the possible outcomes have become—for reasons of diplomacy, personality, technology, and geography, or some profound incompatibility between the two sides—practically unattainable and irrelevant to decision. There are of course tactical arenas within a nonzero-sum relation that can be dealt with, at least in a practical sense, as separable zero-sum local contests, but care is needed even at the tactical level.

### Separable Zero-Sum Components

There are indeed zero-sum military problems that can be separately analyzed. Cryptography is an example: one scrambles or enciphers tactical communications to keep secrets. The avoidance of predictable regularities is another: one tries not to be predictably unprepared on Sunday mornings. One randomizes the firing of hardened missiles so that they will not be simultaneously and predictably vulnerable during the moment the lids are off the silos before the missiles are on their way. Search and evasion will be randomized; depth and proximity fuses will be set on zero-sum principles; and scarce ammunition may be allocated among sites on strictly zero-sum criteria. These schedules and allocations relate usually to some fixed set of resources in circumstances where there is no thought of *influencing* enemy intention, even though the wider context may be a nonzero-sum campaign or bargaining process.

There is another way that a zero-sum situation can be embedded in a larger nonzero-sum context and yet be susceptible of isolated zero-sum analysis. This is if the payoffs are some kind of bargaining power, usable in some subsequent process of negotiation or coercion. A zero-sum contest can be fought to determine which side gets some advantage—some ammunition, some intelligence, some technology, or some part of the world that is significant for its later strategic role in some confrontation or bargain. It will be hard to classify such a contest as "zero-sum," though, if the two adversaries have different evaluations of the subsequent bargaining process. It will also be hard to classify it zero-sum if they can anticipate the later bargaining and make later behavior conditional on the conduct of the momentary contest. But if the thing fought over is uniquely recognizable as an advantage to the side that gets it and if any nonzero-sum use of the asset comes only later, the momentary contest can be treated as zero-sum.

There is a special case worth mentioning, though it is difficult to give it a contemporary interpretation. That is the case in which both sides agree to a "trial by ordeal"—to play a game of chess for the treasure, or to hold a tournament for a lady's favor. An agreement may be reached to avoid a potentially destructive nonzero-sum contest by letting some game (in the literal sense) determine the outcome. David and Goliath fought, according to Yadin, to make unnecessary a bloody battle between their armies; both sides agreed (though in the end Goliath's did not keep the agreement) to let the battle of champions determine which army would become slaves to the other.[2] Arbitration has this character; a zero-sum battle of wits determines the outcome, both sides being committed to abide by the result to avoid the potentially more destructive bargaining that would ensue if they were unable to wager their positions on some conventional procedure.

### Tactics: Zero- or Nonzero-Sum

It is often alleged that strategy is nonzero-sum while tactics tend to be zero-sum. There is a good deal to the notion; it often means merely that a mission, once ordered accomplished, should be accomplished efficiently. Bombing the civilian population of Japan was not a zero-sum strategy; but once it had been decided to light fires in Tokyo there was every reason to do it with a minimum of risk and effort, and each individual sortie could be scheduled from a zero-sum point of view.

On the other hand, a decision to take prisoners, to bomb civilians in order to destroy a military installation, or to suffer casualties in achieving an objective, are not zero-sum decisions. Furthermore, even though back at headquarters a particular engagement may be viewed as zero-sum, any operation carried out by live human beings is a multiperson, nonzero-sum game. Maybe some kinds of combat have become so mechanized that the individual combatant's valuation of his own life has little relevance to his choice; but the history of warfare tells us that tactical engagements have always been multiperson, nonzero-sum games in which fear disabled more combatants than weapons, and discipline counted more than numbers, weapons, terrain, or technology. General Rommel's order to his Panzer units to open fire before they were in range, because enemy soldiers ducking their heads were as good as enemy soldiers dead, was a recognition of the nonzero-sum character of local combat.

### Costs and "Suboptimization"

Still, the zero-sum contest is an interesting bench mark, a limiting case worth being acquainted with, and often a decent approximation in some localized arena of the larger contest. So it is worth while to get the cost principles straight for that situation, too. The principle says only that, in taking account of the consequences of some act or decision, any costs that the enemy is obliged to incur have a positive value to our side, just as the costs we incur in carrying out the act, or in consequence of the decision, must be valued negatively. And a corollary of this principle is that if substantial costs have to be incurred by the enemy and more modest costs incurred by us, and if as a result of incurring those costs the enemy keeps us from accomplishing anything locally, nevertheless his higher costs are a perfectly valid objective, or motive, for our going ahead with the action. We can even think of the local contest as a battle of costs.

Now, if the whole situation is strictly zero-sum, and if our analysis is intended to comprise the *whole* situation—if we are engaged in what Charles Hitch has called "grand optimization"—there is no need to bring in the concept of "cost," whether the enemy's costs or our own. The best overall strategy, worked out in detail, is just the best strategy, all things considered, and any relevant costs have already been implicitly taken into account. The fact that a particular measure on our part will "cost" an adversary some lives, ammunition, fuel, man-hours, or anything else is of no concern if we have made allowance in our overall model for the withdrawal of lives, fuel, man-hours, and so forth, from their alternative uses. Costs are intended to reflect the payoffs *left out* of our local analysis.

It is when we engage in "suboptimization," and the local contest for which we are suboptimizing uses resources that might have been allocated instead to other arenas, or resources that can be saved and used later in different arenas, that we need to make specific allowance for costs. If some particular measure is under consideration and we have allowed for all of its local tactical consequences but find that it either uses or saves some resources on our side, and that the adversary's accommodation increases or decreases some inputs on his side, the local payoffs do not tell the whole story. The extra resources are withdrawn from other fields of battle, resources saved are available to other fields of battle; it is all the same war, and we have to take account of what happens on those other fields. Costs are simply the measure of consequences, or payoffs, that occur outside the boundaries of our local problem.

They are the *external* economies that any partial or local analysis needs to take into account. If there is no economic linkage between our local problem and the rest of the whole problem—if all local resources are specific, if nothing can be added or withdrawn, if nothing can be saved for later use—then the local payoffs tell the whole story, and we need make no allowance, through "costs," for payoffs beyond our horizon.

To be sure, if all resources are so specific that to find out the "worth" of resources added or withdrawn elsewhere we have to examine in detail their impact on those other fields of battle, then we have to solve all the problems at once in order to solve our local problem, and suboptimization is infeasible. Suboptimization works only if there is little or no connection between the local problem and the overall problem, or if there is some convenient approximate way of making allowance for the impingement of the local problem on the bigger problem. If the enemy has an actual price system that works rationally or if he manages nevertheless by direct means to allocate his resources efficiently, and particularly if the situation allows the enemy time to adapt economically to the measures we confront him with, then we assume that increments of enemy resources can be allowed for as "costs" and "savings" without regard to how the individual items that comprise the resources are allocated elsewhere or precisely where they are drawn from.

That seems to be all. It could be illustrated by a set of a dozen zero-sum matrices, each dependent on the share of total resources allocated to it, the payoffs to each side being the sum of the payoffs in the individual matrices, with "optimization" achieved only when neither side could improve its position by reallocating resources among the different arenas. A shift in the parameters of one matrix might open opportunities for one side to improve its position by shifting resources into that matrix; if they are shifted from the other eleven matrices in a way that minimizes the reduction of payoffs in those other matrices, there is a calculable "cost" that is of interest to both sides. This "cost" will tend to be the same (for modest increments), whichever the matrix to which resources are being added, and it permits measurement of the impact of local decisions on other fields of battle. If we combine the twelve matrices into a single game we can drop the cost concept altogether; if instead it is convenient to analyze the twelve different subgames separately, the "cost" figures serve an essential purpose and make local optimization consistent with overall optimization.

The principle does not depend on there being a recognized live, rational zero-sum adversary. The traditional examples of external economies reflect the same principle. If decisions are decentralized to the managers of twelve fields belonging to the same farm, any managers who put up scarecrows, or plant extra seed, or protect the seeds so that it takes crows longer to get at them will affect the number of crows on each other's fields. These "adaptive" shifts of the "enemy" have to be taken into account in deciding whether the scarecrow, or the extra seed that draw crows from neighboring fields, is worth the cost.

Costs can of course be used incorrectly, and most of the exposures of the "fallacy" of this cost reasoning relate to some mistaken use. I have been asked whether I would buy a one-hundred-dollar nylon vest to protect myself from a five-cent bullet, as though the cost criterion says I should not—the factor of 2000-to-1 against me making it a bad investment—yet if I treasure my life I shall obviously buy the vest. In this example the cost criterion is merely backward; the relevant question is whether my adversary should buy a bullet knowing that I can nullify his investment with a bulletproof vest. He has wasted his money if the vest is cheap, made a splendid investment if my vest is expensive, and if asked what he accomplished by buying his bullet should have the good sense to say that he imposed a cost on me, not that he hoped to kill me and was frustrated.

### The "Exchange Rate"

We need some kind of "exchange rate" to tell, without extending our analysis into grand optimization, whether a cost imposed on the enemy is worth the cost to us of imposing it. Unless we and our adversary have comparable economies there is no reason why the appropriate exchange rate should equate percentages of gross national product or any other economic magnitudes on the two sides. We can say, as a kind of shorthand, that a cost is worth incurring if it imposes a "greater" cost on the other side; but then we must mean that "costs" have already been measured in the same currency as the payoffs in those other arenas. If we calculate "costs" for the two sides in any other way, such as money costs converted on a foreign currency market, percentages of GNP, or what the enemy's specific inputs would cost at our prices, there is no reason to suppose that a straightforward comparison of "greater" and "smaller" will tell us the story.

### The Incidence of Costs on Consumers

Suppose an enemy fuel shortage falls on consumers, and the enemy values the health and comfort of his people, deplores the death of infants, suffers in the suffering of his people, and takes those civilian values into account in his own planning, not for the military advantage they give him but just for their own sake. Then the relation between us is nonzero-sum. We may like his babies to be warm and healthy, prefer that they suffer, or not give a thought to it; but we are unlikely to be just as disposed to welcome the suffering of his people as he is to deplore it. In our cost calculations we should take no credit for the prospect that some children will be cold or sick because we damaged enemy fuel supplies.

In fact, the enemy may care less about his own people than we do—if by "enemy" we mean the directorate of the military opposition to us. Suppose the enemy neither likes nor dislikes his subjects—perhaps because he is a military occupant of another country and does not much care whether the citizenry suffers or prospers—and we do not care either, because our sole concern is military advantage. The game is still zero-sum; but if a local fuel shortage falls on the local citizens who will have less heat in their houses, or if a local fuel saving means only that less is requisitioned locally, there is no "cost" to be allowed for in our problem. The cost is passed along to somebody outside the contest. The costs we want in our analysis are those that reflect the flow of resources among the sectors of the contest, for all the sectors comprising the adversary relation between us; if other sectors are involved and can absorb or yield resources to the sectors engaged in the contest, then either those sectors matter and the situation is nonzero-sum, or they do not matter themselves and distort the price system. We have to correct for them. That makes it harder to ascertain the costs and to use the figures properly, but does not contradict the principle.

### The Nonzero-Sum Context

Let me turn now to the nonzero-sum adversary relation that usually characterizes war and military preparations. First let us remind ourselves of some of the reasons why wars and arms races are nonzero-sum. There is civilian damage—pain, disability, death, privation, lowered living standards, fear, and anxiety, both during the war itself and after the war. There are battle casualties; soldiers are people, and when they die there is not only a loss of military assets but also human pain and grief. There is, during military buildup, some influence of that buildup on the likelihood that war will occur; and military preparations affect the character of any war that ensues, including the capabilities of both sides for keeping it limited and for stopping it. Wars and military preparations affect precedents (like the use of gas or nuclear weapons) that affect the conduct of future war. The enemy in a war is often a potential ally or subject. (In colonial wars the killing of an enemy soldier is the loss of a colonial subject.) War involves hostages; much of the population of Western Europe was a potential hostage in German hands during World War II. Adversaries can furthermore gain or lose honor and prestige in a nonzero-sum fashion. War can induce political change; the monarchs of 1914 destroyed most of the system congenial to them. War can weaken both adversaries vis-à-vis other countries. There is a moral cost for some countries in the conduct of war. War is often a multiperson relationship; the generals' plot against Hitler's life and the shift in authority within Japan after Hiroshima remind us that nations are not the same as individuals or teams of like-minded individuals. Finally there is the point mentioned by Scherer, that the military expenditure of potential adversaries can affect the civilian welfare and political conduct of the country, affecting the likelihood of war itself.

We could go on, but there is no need to. Zero-sum adversary relationships are hard to find in any important area of human affairs; people in need of an example in a hurry sometimes point to war as one of the rare zero-sum social relationships, but this is pure thoughtlessness. About the only thing that could make war appear zero-sum would be a *belief* that war was zero-sum, a belief so obstinately held that the war would indeed be conducted that way. Designers who put chessmen on the dust jackets of books about strategy are presumably thinking of the intellectual structure of the game, not its payoff structure; and one hopes that it is chess they do not understand, not war, in supposing that a zero-sum parlor game catches the spirit of a nonzero-sum diplomatic phenomenon.

### Elasticities of Demand: A Comparative-Advantage Example

Because Scherer and others have already pointed out that costs imposed on the enemy may be passed along to his population, so that we gain less than we hoped or even lose if we prefer his civilians not to bear the cost, let me suppose a fixed enemy military budget and explore some of the ways the cost criterion gets complicated as we acknowledge that our interests and our opponent's are not strictly opposed. Consider that he has a given budget that he can allocate among two, or three, or more kinds of military resources for a war with us. We have to examine how our deployment of forces affects his deployment, and in what ways our choices can influence his choices and how we should evaluate his choices.

Begin with a simple model. He has a budget with which to buy missiles and sites. If he spends it mostly on missiles and concentrates on a small number of sites, he gets more missiles than if he went to the added expense of dispersing his missiles among more sites. At the same time, his missiles are more vulnerable if they are concentrated; and for "second-strike" purposes he prefers a dispersed force. His value system, we may suppose, contains two variables: the number of missiles that he can buy (with which he could launch an attack), and the number of missiles he could expect to have (or can threaten to have) left over in case we attack him. We can call these his "first-strike" force and his "second-strike" force. They are of course the same force, but they are evaluated differently according to who starts the war. A large vulnerable force has a comparative advantage in striking first; a smaller less vulnerable force has a comparative advantage in striking back. (Multiple-warheads raise the identical issue.)

How he disperses his missile force—how he uses money that might have been spent on missiles to buy more sites—will depend on how expensive the sites are. If sites are cheap he will buy a site for each missile (perhaps more, if we cannot tell empty sites from those that have missiles and must target as many sites as he buys). If sites are expensive he cannot much disperse his force without greatly reducing its size; beyond some point, even for a purely second-strike force, more dispersal becomes uneconomical.

To be explicit, suppose that his costs are a linear function of missiles and sites; missiles are procured at a constant price, sites are procured at a constant price. We have a given force with which we can attack all of his sites; and, not knowing the particular distribution of missiles among those sites, we would distribute our attacking missiles evenly if we attacked. Suppose our attacking missiles have independent probabilities of kill, so that the survival of a site is merely the survival probability in the face of one attacking missile, compounded by the number of missiles fired at the site. Let $X$ denote the number of missiles he buys, $Y$ the number of sites, and $M$ the size of our attacking force, with $P$ the survival probability of an individual site under attack by a single missile, $K$ his total budget (measured in units equal to the price of a missile), and $a$ the price ratio of sites to missiles. The expected number of missiles surviving our attack would be equal to:

$$XP^{M/Y}.$$

By substituting the budget equation, we get:

$$[K - aY]P^{M/Y}.$$

If he wants to maximize the expected value of his second-strike force, he merely maximizes that expression with respect to $Y$. If he wants to maximize some function of first- and second-strike forces, giving positive value to his first-strike force, we have to specify the function but then we can go ahead and solve his problem.

Now let me pose this question. Suppose we invent a new device, perhaps a new ingredient in the warhead of our attacking missiles, that if unanticipated by the enemy would increase the potency of each of our missiles against any site it is aimed at. It makes all of his sites more vulnerable, and hence his entire missile force. Never mind what it actually is; just imagine that it is available to us at modest cost. Suppose the enemy knows about it and can either see that we have it or assume that we have it. And suppose that this particular capability is one that is readily countered, but at a price. The enemy can defend himself against this measure with complete effectiveness but has to spend money to do so. Do we hope his countermeasure is cheap or expensive?

Now, the distinguishing characteristic of this particular measure is that it attacks *sites*, not missiles. Of course if it destroys a site it destroys the missiles on the site; that is the whole idea. The point is this: The enemy's countermeasure is associated with his sites, not with his missiles, so that the aggregate cost of defending his force against our new device depends on how many sites he has to protect, not on how many missiles he has to protect. His countermeasure, we suppose, is adding smoke screens, antiaircraft batteries, police dogs, duplicate generators, or some other active or passive defense to individual sites in such a way that the cost does not depend on how many missiles are on the site.

The point of this distinction is that it affects his allocation of resources between missiles and sites. That is, it affects the allocation of his budget between first- and second-strike forces. And *we care*. Furthermore, *we care in a way that is not strictly opposed to the way he cares.*

He may, for example, be mainly concerned to deter us with the best second-strike force he can buy and have little interest in either attacking us with his whole force or threatening to attack with his whole force. (He could even prefer to reduce our apprehension, and attach negative value to his first-strike force.) And *we* may prefer that he buy a second-strike rather than a first-strike force, that is, a force whose second-strike capability is relatively larger and whose first-strike capability relatively smaller.

We may not. It depends on whether we want to deter him or to attack him, and it depends on what we think raises or lowers the likelihood of our having to attack him or his having to attack us. However, if we mainly want deterrence, our preferences somewhat coincide with his. He wants a good second-strike force *even* at the expense of his first-strike force; we are willing to see him get a good second-strike force *if* it is at the expense of his first-strike force.

Now, do we want the price of his sites, as distinct from the price of his missiles, to be high or low? If we can raise the price of those sites by threatening them with a measure against which a costly countermeasure is available, do we want to make the threat? If he must assume we have the device, do we want the countermeasure to be expensive or inexpensive? And would we prefer to threaten him with a measure whose defense is associated with his missiles rather than his sites, so that they raise his cost per missile rather than his cost per site?

We can solve the problem explicitly and find out—at least we can if we specify his preference function as among first- and second-strike forces, and our preference function as between his first-

and second-strike forces. But offhand about the only conclusion we can jump to is that we would rather raise the price of his missiles than the price of his sites (if the aggregate costs in both cases are of about the same magnitude) because we anticipate that he will use more of the cheaper of the two inputs, and we know which one it is that we want him to use. Intuition, analogy, or quick mental arithmetic will not give us that answer about site costs. If some neutral country sells the site-defense countermeasure and we can influence its price policy, we do not yet know whether we want it cheap or expensive.

The key to our decision is what, in the familiar language of economics, we might call the enemy's "elasticity of demand" for missile sites. Whatever he spends on sites is unavailable to be spent on missiles. If we want to minimize his first-strike force, we want to minimize the money he spends on missiles, therefore to maximize the money he spends on sites. Will he spend more money on sites, or less, if the price of sites goes up? Is his demand for sites inelastic or elastic? We have to work the problem to find out.

In the specific form in which I set up the problem, if the enemy's exclusive interest is a second-strike force, it turns out that his demand for sites is slightly inelastic.[3] He spends somewhat more on sites if the price of sites goes up, less on missiles. To put it differently, the "income effect" of the price rise outweighs the "substitution effect," and, though missiles have become cheaper relative to sites, he now buys fewer missiles. ("Elasticity of demand" is strictly applicable only if the price of sites is fixed to the buyer, who chooses the quantity, at that price, that maximizes whatever it is that he wants to maximize. I shall use "elasticity" in a looser sense just to suggest the idea of a "revenue effect" and what happens to the budget available for other purchases.)

In this particular problem the answer happens to be independent of the initial costs of sites and missiles and independent of the budget; but this is a special case, and we would have to give a more qualified answer if we worked with a more complicated model—if, for example, missiles or sites were bought along rising or falling supply curves, if sites supported or interfered with each other, or if missiles did, or if the enemy's preference function were slightly different. It is easy to make a minor change in this model and reach the contrary conclusion—that we do not want sites to become more expensive to the enemy, we want the countermeasure sold cheaply; and we should avoid confronting the enemy with our own measure in the first place if we can, to keep him from finding missiles more attractive, relative to sites, than they used to be.

This kind of consideration cannot arise in the zero-sum confrontation. It furthermore can arise, as it did here, without regard to whether we care whether the enemy's people are better housed and fed. It can arise, as it did here, without our putting a positive value on his second-strike force. It requires only that our preferences not be strictly opposed to those of the enemy, or, in economic terms, that our indifference curves as between his first-strike and his second-strike capabilities not coincide with his in reverse.

### A Jointly Valued Capability

Consider another problem, where the answer should no longer surprise us after working through the first problem. Let there be some military capability that the enemy wants and that we want him to have. This is something we want him to buy not just because it uses resources that he would otherwise spend on things that we deplore even more; this is something it is positively in our interest that he have. We want him to have it even if it is free of charge, and we might even provide it if he could not buy it himself. It might be a device to avoid nuclear accidents, to minimize the false alarms that might cause him to launch war itself, to reduce nuclear fallout, to facilitate armistice, to permit the recovery of dead or wounded from the battlefield, to care for prisoners of war, to avoid the military destruction of fish and wildlife, or anything else. The point is, he wants it and we want him to have it; we have no military interest in denying it to him, and if it gives him any sort of local advantage in a zero-sum contest somewhere, that disadvantage to us is outweighed by its beneficial effects overall.

Suppose, now, there is some measure available to us with which we can destroy it. Or suppose we can affect the price he pays for it, causing it to be more expensive or less expensive. What should we do?

There is a lot to be said for being nice about it, if only to dramatize the common interest, to set a precedent for preserving assets of value to both sides, to induce him to avoid taking reciprocal measures that would hurt us as well as himself, and for other essentially diplomatic or bargaining reasons. Leaving those aside—just considering our influence on his allocation of resources—we have two interests here. First, we want him to possess that capability; even if we threaten to destroy it, we want him to take steps to defend it. Second, we want to divert resources from other capabilities that we do not like into this capability that we do like, not just because we like this capability but because we like it to draw resources from the rest of his budget.

Again it is something like elasticity of demand that is relevant. If we know that he will defend that capability at all costs, because it is important to him as well as to us, then we can safely threaten it, forcing him to defend it, knowing that the net effect will be fewer resources available to the part of his force that we do not like. We threaten—to pick an extreme example—to activate his warning system so that he would launch a successful first-strike against us—a first-strike that, though successful, he would rather not launch and would launch only in the mistaken belief that he was under attack. He anticipates our mischief and spends money to tranquilize his warning system, to make sure that we cannot provoke him into an attack that he would prefer not to launch, to make sure that we do not bring down on ourselves a war that we deplore as much as he. We watch him cut back his ground forces, or his first-strike capability against our strategic forces, or his second-strike capability against our civilian assets, or some other program that opposes our interests, in order to maintain the capability that, though we like it too, he likes very much.

But we must be careful. If we put the price so high that he prefers to do without it—if we threaten it in a way that makes its defense too costly for him—we divert no resources from other parts of his budget; we merely prevent his having something that we both badly want him to have. Or if the countermeasure is something that he can buy in varying quantities or degrees, raising the price or supply curve may cause him to buy less of it. If his "demand" is elastic he ends up with less of what we want him to have, more of what we do not want him to have, and we lose on both counts; if his "demand" is inelastic he ends up with somewhat less of what we want him to have, less also of what we do not want him to have, and we must weigh the one against the other.

The point of this example is twofold. First: to emphasize that there *are* military capabilities that we want the enemy to have—not just that we dislike less than we dislike other capabilities, considering his marginal rate of substitution, but that we value positively, which we want him to have, and would even buy for him if he did not procure it for himself. Second: that just as we might want to *lower* the price of a force that we prefer him *not* to have, to induce him to draw resources from other parts of his budget that we like even less, we could want to *raise* the price of things we prefer that he have, for the same reason. Here it is a case of wanting the income effect on the rest of his budget to outweigh the substitution effect for this particular item.

## A Diversionary Threat

Next consider the enemy's response to a new capability on our side to inflict damage on his civilians and their property. And suppose, just to clarify the principle, that what we threaten to destroy is of little or no military value. This could be because he cannot mobilize these civilian resources before or during war, or because they have low military value (a strong comparative advantage toward civilian value). Pain and life itself would have this quality, as would potential members of the labor force too young to work until the war is over; so would physical assets that would be more important after the war than during the war, and structures too specific in their civilian use to be transferable directly or indirectly into military strength. The idea is simply that, whatever the value of threatening such destruction, we get no military advantage from carrying out the destruction. Nor does the enemy suffer a significant military disadvantage. It is pure civilian loss, a kind of "side payment" that he makes but we don't get.

Aside from revenge, justice, and other moral and psychological satisfactions—and these could be negative—there appear to be two main purposes served by such a military threat directed against enemy civilian value. Both depend on influencing the opponent's behavior. One is *coercion* (that is, bargaining advantage) and the other is *diversion* (of resources from other uses). Coercion implies that he refrains from or performs some action as part of a bargain, according to which we carry out the destruction or not according to whether he refrains or not. Diversion implies that he anticipates our attack on his civilian value and does something to mitigate the effect. We may or may not want him to divert resources. If he does, it reduces our remaining coercive influence. But if we want him to divert resources—if that is the purpose—the result is brought about by coercion, by the threat that we will destroy civilian value unless he diverts resources to protect them. To the extent that he can attenuate our threat by shifting resources, he merely holds us to our bargain by carrying out his part.

Now, how do we feel about the costs to the enemy of countering our threat in some fashion? This will depend on how he counters it, and at the expense of what other capability. Two important possibilities are that he would defend his civilian assets and that he would procure a force of his own with which to threaten ours. If he defends his people, it could be at the expense of his battle-field forces—that is, the forces he could field in a "zero-sum contest" for territory or booty—or it could be at the expense of the force with which he threatens our civilian assets. (It could also be at the expense of some measures, of the kind suggested earlier, to which we attach positive value.) The diversion might also change the character of the forces he threatens us with, such as their first- or second-strike advantage, and change his expectation of the likelihood of war.

There are two limiting cases to consider: first, that the damage we threaten would *certainly* deter the enemy in all circumstances, so that we need no longer worry about how he allocates his military resources (and, if he could acknowledge the adequacy of our deterrence, he might as well disband his force); second, that though the damage we could do would severely reduce the net gain to the enemy from any war he might contemplate, it would certainly *not* deter him if on other grounds he had decided to have his war.

If he is certainly deterred, we have no interest in diversion. Our only interest is that diversion be incapable of spoiling our deterrence. We want the costs of an adequate defense to be prohibitively high.

If deterrence is clearly inadequate, our interest will be diversion. We want him to withdraw as much as possible from his other capabilities as the price of defending himself against our threat—at least, we do unless he withdraws resources from some capabilities that we prefer him to have. Assuming that he withdraws his resources from the battlefield, or from a first-strike stra-tegic force or from a second-strike force that does not shift in char-acter toward a first-strike force under the pressure of a smaller budget, we want the price of defense to be low enough to be at-tractive, high enough to be costly. Again, "elasticity of demand" is the analogy, although we are likely to be less interested in the "price" of a "unit of defense" than in the whole curve relating damage to investment in defense. If defense is too costly—if it is too ineffective compared with its cost—the enemy will not invest in it. We get nothing for our trouble. In fact, anticipating that he will not defend his civilian assets, we should not procure the threatening force in the first place. (Paradoxically, the enemy may prefer that his civilian assets be indefensible in the face of a threat not large enough to deter him. The indefensibility of his cities makes our threat purposeless, and we may not bother to buy it.)

He may instead react by developing a reciprocal civil-damage force of his own. If he does, we want it to be costly. We may not like this response, even if it is costly, and prefer not to provoke it. From his point of view, if he can afford either to defend his cities *or* to threaten ours but cannot afford both, defending and threat-ening may be equally attractive. From our point of view they are *not* equally attractive.

These considerations are important. Burton Klein pointed out in his study of German war economics that one of the main con-sequences of the strategic bombing of Germany in World War II was the sizable diversion of German resources into air defense—up to one-third of all German military production went into ac-tive defense against air attack at the climax of the war.[4] If the purpose was only to defend military strength, it was part of a zero-sum contest not related to what I have been discussing. But if the object was to preserve Germany and Germans, not just war potential, it was the diversionary principle expressed above. There is presently a corresponding question whether the United States should want the Soviet Union to invest, or not to invest, in ballistic-missile defenses.

Between the extremes of sure deterrence and no deterrence, the deterrent and diversionary motives can both be present. We might, for example, prefer a large Soviet investment in city de-fenses that, though inadequate to spoil deterrence altogether, would appear to the Soviet leaders a useful hedge against war, yet would take resources away from their offensive forces or their battlefield forces. One can hope that the threat provokes enough expenditure on the defense of civilian assets to constitute a substantial diversion without the defense being so effective that it greatly reduces deterrence. How to weigh the two considerations depends on what it takes to reduce deterrence. One probably has to pay some price in deterrence in order to achieve the diversion, because the enemy will not waste money on a futile defense; still, an opponent could find it worthwhile to spend money to reduce damage in a possible war, without the extent of such reduction necessarily affecting his willingness to launch war or to provoke it. If we manage to draw the enemy's "supply curve" of defense—the relation of damage-reduction to money spent on it—we want to be careful how we draw it; anybody who then shifts it upward may do us as much harm as if he shifted it downward.

## Adaptation and Costs

In zero-sum situations the enemy's adaptation to a new initiative on our part always reduces the value of that initiative. We see an opportunity or a new capability, take advantage of it, and get a certain score at his expense if he does not adapt; his adaptation takes away some of our advantage. The net advantage to us depends on how costly his adaptation is; but in zero-sum situations we always prefer that he be unadapted—that he not know of our new initiative, find adaptation too costly, or be institutionally unable to adapt. In nonzero-sum situations we can *prefer* that he adapt; and he can prefer to adapt, knowing that we prefer him to.

In fact, we can undertake moves that have no value for us unless he does adapt. The diversionary principle just discussed is one of these. Facing an enemy threat to our civilian values, we might be attracted to a completely defensive posture that virtually nullifies his threat. We might alternatively be attracted to a completely offensive posture because it *obliges* him to dismantle his offensive posture and devote resources to defense.

It is possible that our preferred posture in the face of an enemy offense is pure defense, but we like even better a pure enemy defense that is induced by a purely offensive posture on our side, and choose the offensive posture accordingly. If he does not adapt as we hope, we end up with offensive postures on both sides; that could be our last choice. In this case, unles he adapts as we expect, improving our position as he rectifies his own, our move is a bad one, for us and perhaps for him.

### Adaptive Cost-Avoidance: Comparative Advantage Again

Consider one more case, just to sharpen up the contrast between zero-sum and nonzero-sum calculations. The enemy is building a force, or about to buy a force, of one hundred "semi-hardened" missiles at a cost of $1 apiece. Our attack force can inflict 50 percent attrition on his one hundred missiles if we attack. He could alternatively buy hardened missiles, fully invulnerable, for $2.20 apiece. His goal is a force out of which fifty missiles could survive attack; and at these prices he gets it for $100 with the more vulnerable missiles while it would cost $110 if he bought fifty of the more expensive invulnerable variety. Suddenly we discover a device that increases the vulnerability of the semi-hardened type of missile; with this device, even though it costs us something and reduces the size of our attack force, the enemy's one-hundred-missile force would be 75 percent vulnerable and only twenty-five missiles would survive. What do we get for our money?

If he fails to adapt—if the device is our secret—we get a reduction by half of his surviving force in the event we attack. If he adapts by increasing his force of vulnerable missiles, we oblige him to buy twice as many (to reach an expectation that fifty will survive) and raise his costs by $100, the resources being detracted from somewhere. But he has another option: he can switch to the different type of missile and get a potential force of fifty surviving our attack for a cost of $110. For the sake of the example, suppose that his procurement is not too far along to permit the switch; perhaps the one type of missile is converted into the other by additional expenditure on the missile's environment of $1.20 per missile.

He switches, gets an estimated fifty surviving attack at a cost of $2.20 each, spending a total of $110, or $10 more than he originally planned. What did we get for our money—the money we spent on the device that caused him to switch his missile-procurement plan?

Mainly we got a qualitative change in his force—that is, a quantitative trade along two dimensions—together with a modest drain on his military resources elsewhere. He would have had a second-strike force of fifty and a first-strike force of one hundred; now, faced by our new device, he procures instead a second-strike

force of fifty and a first-strike force of fifty. Besides costing him
$10, we have cut his first-strike force by fifty.

We like it; and we like it quite out of proportion to the $10 cost
we inflicted on him.

In fact, our device may cost us so much that inflicting an extra
cost of $10 would be a poor bargain; but by cutting his first-strike
force in half without firing a shot we may achieve something well
worth the cost.

His cost increase can be a gross understatement of what we
gained by imposing on him the *incentive* to incur the cost. We
tilted his tradeoff line and were the beneficiaries of his shift in
procurement. (In the same way we might have sold him, or given
him, something that would have reduced the cost of the more expensive missile, and been the chief beneficiary of his savings. We
could actually have subsidized, with cash, his procurement of the
more expensive missile, and come out ahead.) Our gain is of the
same algebraic sign as his cost but bears no particular proportion
to it. We could have had the same result if the hardened missile
cost $2.01 or $3.99, except for the net cost to his other programs.
This net cost is really separable from the reduction in first-strike
force and has to be evaluated altogether separately. At $3.99 we
are more likely to enjoy the result (unless the resources come out
of that fail-safe system we were concerned about earlier); at $2.01
we are less enthusiastic; but the drain on his resources is separable
from the shift in first-second-strike composition.

Notice this, too. Had he been able to buy an even "softer" missile that was already 75 percent vulnerable and unaffected by our
new offensive device, but that cost, say, $0.55 and was not com-
petitive with the semi-hardened, our new capability would make
the semi-hardened a poor buy and his response might be to procure two hundred of the soft ones for $110. This we do not like; his
first-strike force is doubled at a net cost of $10, and, even if
he does not much care, we do. If both the "hard" and "soft" alternatives are available, minor shifts in the ratio of cost to sur-
vivability can make, from our point of view, major changes
in his force: at $0.53 per soft missile, with hard ones at $2.20,
he buys two hundred soft ones for $106, while at $0.57 per soft
missile he buys fifty hard ones for $110. To him, if second-
strike ability is what he wants, the decision is marginal; to us it is
systemic.

I am not now trying to illustrate, once again, that we may like or dislike what our initiative made him do, but that minor variations in his relative costs can make major differences in our evaluation of his response. A consequence of this is that no single measure of his cost—whether discounted, augmented, or changed in sign from the original estimate to make it a better measure of what we gain—can be used as a "correction" of his costs to reach their net worth to us. It is not just that the gain or loss to us is poorly measured by the cost inflicted on the opponent and needs to be corrected; it is that the gain or loss to us depends on the *particular* way that he reacts in a particular case, on the particular incidence of the new costs within his budget, on the particular price comparisons that determine his response. Two measures that identically raise *his* costs can induce changes in *our* payoffs that bear no relation to each other. No "exchange-rate" correction will take care of this. In the zero-sum case his marginal decisions are marginal to us, and we can use a single measure of "costs" to avoid tracing the ramifications of his response. In the nonzero-sum case there is no short cut; the ramifications have to be traced.

### Conclusion about Enemy Costs

What conclusion do we reach about the role of inflicted enemy costs in evaluating our own alternatives?

The main conclusion is that costs, in a nonzero-sum context, do not reflect the changes in payoffs outside the arena of our suboptimization. The reason is simple: the costs we inflict, or threaten to inflict, on the enemy can at most reflect the changes in his payoffs outside the local arena. They do not reflect the relevant changes in our payoffs because there is not the convenient perfect negative correlation between his losses and our gains once we drop the zero-sum restriction, that is, once we extend our analysis into the (almost universal) nonzero-sum contexts.

In the zero-sum case his costs reflect the gains to us that our local analysis would otherwise have left out of account. In the nonzero-sum case neither the magnitude of his costs, nor even the algebraic sign, reliably suggests the pertinent changes in our payoffs. Our gains may be greater than his costs suggest, less than they suggest, or opposite in sign to what they suggest, and will differ according to the particular choice we pose for him.

This strikes a blow at "suboptimization" of course. What makes partial analysis valid is often the dependability of enemy costs as a shortcut to all the ramifications outside the local contest. When costs are recognized as undependable—when they are no index to magnitude or even sign, neither an upper nor a lower limit to the effect on us of the adversary's adaptation, to what happens outside our local field of vision—we have to extend our field of vision.

And, as mentioned earlier, our attitude toward his adapting to our own behavior is different; instead of reducing our advantage it can raise it or offset it in a manner not communicated by his costs. As a corollary, our attitude toward secrecy and information can be dramatically different from what it is in the zero-sum case, as Martin McGuire has emphasized.[5] Taking the first move and letting the adversary adapt is never the right choice in a zero-sum situation; it often is in the nonzero-sum.

# 13 | Who Will Have the Bomb?

**T**HE QUESTION IS as interesting as the answer. What do we mean by "having" the bomb? Who has it now?

Does India have the bomb? Most of us would answer yes. Why do we answer yes? Because India exploded a nuclear device—call it a bomb. Do we know that India actually possesses another one? No. Does it matter? Probably not. Therefore, when we say that India has the bomb we do not mean literally that India possesses another nuclear explosive. In fact, it matters little whether India happens to have assembled a second device and has it all ready to explode.

But if we do not mean that India necessarily possesses an actual bomb when we say that India "has the bomb," what is it that we do mean?

We mean a mixture of things. First, India unquestionably possesses the technical knowledge with which to produce a nuclear explosive, having proven that by exploding one. Second, we expect that though India may not be rich in explosion-grade fissile material, India either has or can acquire enough explosion-grade fissile material to make some more explosive devices. And we may mean, too, that India has gone through the rites of passage—has celebrated its nuclear status by declaring to the world, by way of actual explosion, that it not only *can* explode a nuclear device but dared to and did.

What about Israel? Israel has not performed the ceremony of nuclear demonstration. (The Treaty on the Non-Proliferation of Nuclear Weapons [NPT] defines a "nuclear-weapon state" as one that "has manufactured and exploded" a nuclear weapon or explosive device prior to the cutoff date of January 1, 1967. Whether explosion is a test of possession or a test of willingness to explode, it is nonetheless part of the acknowledged definition. Mere Indian manufacture and display would not have fitted the definition.)

At the end of 1975 it became known that Israel wanted to purchase some American ground-to-ground missiles. Objections were voiced that the missiles might carry Israeli nuclear warheads and that indeed the missiles might be intended specifically for that purpose. To allay any such fears (or perhaps to confirm them), an Israeli spokesman indicated that Israel would be willing to incur a formal commitment not to install nuclear warheads on any such missiles. The proposal could hardly be construed as a ringing declaration that Israel already had, or could promptly acquire, the nuclear warheads that it would agree not to install; but it did remind us that, although a nation cannot get into the nuclear club without both making and exploding some nuclear device, not every nation that has access to nuclear weapons of its own construction will necessarily go through the initiation ceremony to join the club.

It can also remind us that the main significance of nuclear weapons is not their parade-ground display but the possibility of their being used. The inhibitions on using nuclear weapons are surely so strong that most governments would consider military use only in a grave emergency. And any government that was actually ready to use nuclear weapons would probably be a government that would not be much further inhibited by an explicit earlier promise not to.

To fabricate nuclear weapons under government auspices, there are two crucial ingredients. One is the fissile material, uranium or plutonium of sufficient enrichment or purity. The other is people with the requisite engineering knowledge and skill. With the growth of nuclear electric power, most countries of any size, possibly all of them, may eventually have within their national boundaries reactors that produce plutonium as an intended or an unintended by-product. (A good-sized power reactor produces plutonium in amounts equivalent to a couple of dozens of nuclear bombs per year.) The chemical separation of plutonium out of the spent reactor fuel is a process that will be within the industrial capability of most nations, even the industrially undeveloped nations, especially if foreign companies are available to do it on contract. And the actual design and fabrication of a nuclear bomb is authoritatively asserted to be a task that any nation with a moderate industrial capacity can do without outside aid. (Hans A. Bethe, Bernard L. Cohen, and Richard Wilson presented a statement to the National Council of Churches on January 28, 1976, in which they reassured us that it is impossible for a single person to make a bomb. "At least six persons, highly skilled in very different technologies, would be required to do so, even for a crude weapon.") The best universities on this side of the Iron Curtain, possibly on both sides, are perfectly willing to train nuclear scientists and engineers from any country that will pay their tuition. Countries that do not participate in the Treaty on Non-Proliferation may pursue a genuine or feigned interest in PNEs (Peaceful Nuclear Explosives), and there is no guarantee that in doing so they will observe the same technological secrecy that heretofore has appealed to the nuclear-weapon states. In another ten or fifteen years it is unlikely that many countries will lack the technology and the personnel needed for making nuclear weapons out of indigenously produced fissile materials.

So there we have it. In a terribly important and terribly dangerous sense they will practically all have the bomb. By "they" I mean governments. By "have the bomb" I mean that at any time one of those governments decides to explode a nuclear bomb it will be able to do so, with some lapse in time—and of course, for most of them, with some breach of treaty, contract, or widely accepted standards, and with some possibility of punitive action. But even the United States, or France, or China—that is, the weapon states—will be bound by strong inhibitions and sometimes by treaty; and even for the weapon states there would be some lapse of time between the decision to use nuclear weapons and their actual use, especially if the use were anything other than the firing of permanently alert strategic weapons.

Until recently, having or not having nuclear weapons appeared to be, and was treated as, a question of yes or no. From now on it will make more sense to describe a country's nuclear-weapon status not with a yes or a no but with a time schedule. The answer will be a chart, giving the number of weapons of certain energy yields and certain physical characteristics that could be available after elapsed hours, days, or weeks from the decisions to assemble them.

For many countries this is the way we describe armies. Does Switzerland have an army? In one sense the answer is no. Except in a military emergency or during the seasons of intensive training, Switzerland doesn't actually possess an army. What it has is a capacity to mobilize troops rapidly, and the best description of the Swiss army is not what one would get by an instantaneous census on a randomly selected day but a schedule relating manpower and firepower to elapsed hours from the moment of call-up. The governments of many countries in another decade or two will "have" nuclear weapons in much the way that Switzerland "has" an army.

Whether this is saying anything important or not will depend on whether the lead time to actual assembly of weapons in working order is measured in hours, days, months, or years. The longest delay might be measured in months if a country had taken no preparatory steps to acquire an inventory of weapons-grade uranium or plutonium. But if those preparatory steps, which would not need to be contrary to the Treaty on Non-Proliferation, had already been taken, either as continuing peacetime policy or after a crisis had begun to gather on the horizon, the rest of the mobilization would be a matter of weeks at most, more likely days, possibly hours. A useful comparison might be the time it would take the United States to airlift a division of troops overseas, or to mobilize the National Guard. Only a country that had deliberately eschewed any preparation that might enhance its capability for mobilizing nuclear weapons would need as long, from the moment of decision, as it would take the United States to pass a new draft law and train recruits and transport them with their gear to where they were needed.

There are two things to emphasize about this coming state of affairs, and it is important to emphasize them without making them seem to contradict each other or to detract from each other. The first is simply that unilateral access to indigenously produced nuclear weapons will have "proliferated"—if I may use that somewhat inappropriate word. In terms of actual military nuclear readiness, the prior possession or even prior detonation of a nuclear explosive is not going to be a great watershed. It will continue to be significant but not decisive. A government that has never even authorized the rehearsal assembly of a nuclear explosive device, fissile material and all, may be able to get its hands usefully on more bombs quicker than some other government that actually has a few in storage, or that has them in delivery vehicles that might not be in the right place or of the right kind at the moment it became urgent to get them ready.

The second thing to emphasize is that this does not make any less important, and perhaps not any less effective, the kinds of institutional arrangements and safeguards and treaty obligations and contractual commitments and precedents and traditions that for several decades have constituted the kinds of arms control that became known during the past decade as the anti-proliferation movement. The emphasis has to shift from physical denial and technological secrecy to the things that determine incentives and motivations and expectations. The fact that a government could get its hands on nuclear weapons doesn't mean that it would. For years there have been governments, maybe a score of them, that had jurisdiction over the physical facilities and the personnel with which to construct nuclear weapons. As far as we can tell, they either found it good policy to resist the temptation to mobilize those nuclear resources, or they were not tempted.

The most severe inhibitions are undoubtedly those on the actual use of nuclear weapons, not on the possession of them. We have no good measure of how strong those inhibitions are because, with the possible exception of two or three stages in the Korean War, there has not been a military emergency that came close to putting those inhibitions to the test. But the fact itself that the weapons have not been used in more than thirty years, even if not a measure of the strength of the inhibition, undoubtedly contributes to it. Of course this could be one of those traditions that, being absolute, is discredited at the first violation.

"Inhibition" has to be understood to include fear, especially the fear of retaliatory use of nuclear weapons against a first-user. It includes also a variety of sanctions and reprisals that may be directed at countries that violate treaties and contracts and understandings, and it includes the risk of disassociation on the part of protectors and allies that condition their help on a country's continued acceptance of non-nuclear status.

The worst of these fears and inhibitions would not apply to mere acquisition or display of nuclear weapons. But if the main purpose of *having* them would be to be able to *use* them, the disincentives to use them should detract from the advantages of their possession.

The decisive inhibitions, then, will always be those on the actual use of nuclear weapons. By far the worst consequences of their possession would be the use of them. Possession itself can be mischievous; and the stronger the perceived limitations on the usefulness of nuclear weapons, the stronger will be the considerations militating against acquisition.

There is a stronger way to phrase this. A government that would use nuclear weapons if it had them, and could get them, would get them. No inhibition on mere possession could survive a decision to use them. In ordinary times, when a country is not fighting for survival or for its vital interests, when it would not be using nuclear weapons if it had them, the incentives to possess them can be overridden by many kinds of inhibitions, including treaty obligations. And most of those inhibitions on possession per se should contribute to the reluctance to use them. But in an emergency, the ultimate safeguard has to be the reluctance to use them.

In these conditions—and we are probably talking mainly about the 1990s—possessing or not possessing some nuclear weapons, or having it known or not known that a country possesses some nuclear weapons, will not decisively differentiate countries as it may have done in the past. The difference will seem greatest when it doesn't matter much. When nothing is at stake except mere possession, those that have crossed the Rubicon will be sharply distinguished from those that have not. But when weapons really matter, and when capabilities to get weapons can be mobilized, the decisive considerations are likely to be similar for the countries that already have some and for the countries that don't quite have them yet. These considerations are the expected consequences of using them, not of just having them.

This does not mean that the weapon states and the nonweapon states will be in anything like the same nuclear status. Being able to produce some nuclear weapons on short notice would not make Panama look like the United States. But in an acute military crisis between Panama and a neighboring country, or between Panama and Cuba, or Panama and the United States, the nuclear aspects of the crisis should be not wholly dissimilar in the case of a Panama known by demonstration to have a few nuclear weapons and in the case of a Panama known to be without them but able to acquire them promptly.

The reactor fuel that is presently used for the production of electric power is not an explosive material. It is uranium that has been enriched in the isotope U-235 from the naturally occurring percentage of 0.7 percent to 2 or 3 percent (or, in reactors that use "heavy water" instead of plain water as the moderator, not enriched at all). Not only is this low percentage of U-235 incapable of an explosive chain reaction, it cannot at present be further enriched except by an expensive process in very large establishments embodying advanced engineering technology. There is no danger that anybody will steal the stuff to make bombs, any more than people can mine and refine uranium ore in the myriad locations in which it naturally occurs and proceed with the complex task of making a bomb. That stuff is harmless.

What has caused alarm in recent years, and serious discussion of hijacking and theft and the possibility of nuclear bombs in the hands of political terrorists or criminal extortionists, is what comes out of the reactor after it has "burned" the uranium fuel to produce steam to make electricity. Some of the U-238, which constitutes 97 percent or so of the uranium in the reactor fuel, is converted to plutonium in the fission process that produces heat. The plutonium is itself fissionable, and indeed a part of the plutonium that is produced within the reactor fissions right there in the reactor along with the U-235 and contributes some of the energy that goes directly into steam and electric power. When the spent fuel is removed from the reactor, as it periodically is for replacement with fresh fuel, there remains about a third of the U-235 together with plutonium. The amount of plutonium, measured in energy potential, is equivalent to something like a fifth of the U-235 that burned to produce the plutonium as a by-product.

Once this plutonium has been chemically separated from all the other materials present in the spent fuel it can be used directly to produce energy in either of two ways. It can be made into fuel assemblies and fed back into reactors like the one that produced it. And it can be used as the explosive material in a nuclear bomb. The chemical process by which it is extracted from the highly radioactive spent fuel is not an easy one; but it is far less demanding than is uranium enrichment, and can presently be done on a much smaller scale.

There is controversy about whether it is going to be economical to recycle plutonium as a reactor fuel. But the recycling may prove economical; governments may wish to promote the technology even if it is not currently economical, to enjoy a reduced dependence on foreign fuel supplies and to be abreast of the technology at the time when recycling does become economical; and the recycling of plutonium is an "innocent" way to acquire a national inventory of potentially explosive plutonium and the capacity to produce more in a hurry. And because not every step in this "nuclear fuel cycle" will be done at central locations under continuous heavy armed guard, there is a possibility of theft or hijacking of the kind of material of which nuclear bombs can be made.

There is also the possibility that a maverick government, not party to the Non-Proliferation Treaty and willing to flout the generally accepted rules, and not afraid of a nuclear or other boycott, might actually sell plutonium with no questions asked. It seems unlikely, but not out of the question.

So there is the possibility that persons or organizations other than national governments might acquire the wherewithal to produce an atomic bomb. Does this mean that future terrorists, for motives either personal or political, will hold cities hostage, rather than just airplanes full of people?

It has to mean that they could. But at this point we probably should be a little more careful in estimating how easy it may be to construct nuclear weapons in the years ahead.

As a national enterprise with government support it is not going to be difficult, ten or fifteen years from now, even in comparatively nonindustrial countries, to produce nuclear bombs. But compared with smuggling guns into an airport and shooting up an airplane full of passengers, the nuclear trick will be orders of magnitude more demanding. Remember the estimate given above: as a bare minimum, six highly skilled individuals possessing exactly the right skills, and very likely a good number of reliable employees to help with the job. Furthermore, in the absence of direct technical assistance they would have to do the job from the ground up. They must work together as a disciplined technical team over a protracted period, with access to computers, to a technical library, perhaps to metallurgical and other laboratory facilities, and probably to outside consultants. Even recruiting the initial six or more would be quite an enterprise, with some number of qualified people being approached who didn't want to participate, or who couldn't get away from what they were already doing, or who turned out to lack the skills that somebody thought they had. The people must either disappear or maintain contact with their normal lives and places of work while participating in the project. They will have wives or husbands. In addition to the menu of scientific and technological skills they must collectively provide, they have to be able to work productively together as a disciplined team, believing in the project and exercising skills in clandestine cooperation that may be as rare as the technical skills they bring to the enterprise. Unless they are simply paid huge amounts of money, they will probably want to be part of the organization that uses the bombs, or at least to have some veto over what is done with the enormous things they produce.

And so forth. Surely it can be done, and it needn't be quite as fantastically organized as it might be in a James Bond movie. But it is something altogether out of the league of the terrorists and separatist movements and liberation armies that have held our attention for the past seven or eight years. Perhaps the modern equivalent of the Jewish terrorist organizations that were active in Palestine in 1946 and 1947, with claims on money and Nobel Prizes, would be the kind of organization that might make itself into a small non-national nuclear power. But the potential number of such organizations is probably small compared with the number of nations that actually exist, and they might better be thought of as a special kind of mini-state. While they would be additional to the individual nations that we may already have counted as dangers to world peace, they would be very much like nations in the way they set their goals and conducted their diplomacy. At least, they won't be blowing up San Simeon with nuclear explosives.

## The Prospects for Nuclear Terrorism

The organizations most likely to engage in nuclear terrorism will be national governments. Passive terrorism on a grand scale we call "deterrence." When it is directed at us, rather than at our enemies, we call it "blackmail." At the small end of the scale of magnitude would be an organization possessing only a few weapons, or claiming to possess them or believed to possess them, weapons that might be clandestinely emplaced where they could do, or threaten to do, horrendous civilian damage in the interest of some political cause. But that is probably the image that would fit one of those small nations that might have a small supply of nuclear bombs or a small capability to produce some in a hurry.

Actually a suggestive model of nuclear terrorism is the one case in history that occurred. There was a government that felt a dreadful urgency to bring a bitter and costly war to an end and that had a couple of nuclear weapons of a kind that had never been fully tested. It considered announcements, demonstrations in uninhabited locales, use against military targets, and even a devastating attack on a population center. It couldn't be altogether sure that either bomb would work; a demonstration might be an embarrassing failure, and even if successful would half deplete the arsenal. Undemonstrated threats of some novel superweapon would suffer the usual problem of credibility. In the end it was decided that only a massive unexpected shock had any hope of causing the necessary changes in the Japanese government. And then an unopposed weather reconnaissance aircraft introduced nuclear terror into our world.

In quick succession the second one was dropped on another city, emptying the arsenal.

All of that was done by people who believed their cause was just; who believed they were saving lives, even Japanese lives, if the gamble worked; who thought they had considered all the options and received the best advice; and most of whom afterward were generally satisfied that they had done the right thing. Never again will a government, in using or considering the use of nuclear weapons, enjoy the luxury of knowing that it alone in all the world disposes of such dreadful things. Otherwise, the American model may not be a bad prototype for imagining what nuclear terrorism might someday be like. (This is another one of those predictions that we all hope can never be matched against experience.)

What is likely to be more widespread is the passive kind of terrorism that is called "deterrence." According to my dictionary, to deter is "to prevent or discourage (someone) from acting by means of fear, doubt, or the like." The Latin means to frighten *away from*. Compared with efforts to compel action through nuclear intimidation, encouraging *inaction* tends to be easier and quieter. Deterrent threats often go without saying. When they succeed they go untested. They do not involve deadlines. The terms usually do not involve quantities and degrees. (Don't do that, at all, ever!) There is no need for overt submission by the deterred party. Deterrence can be reciprocal. And the desired response—continued inactivity of some particular kind—is usually the kind of decision that a target government finds it easiest to agree on, and to implement.

The most passive deterrence of all would be just letting it be known, perhaps through an innocent leak of information, that a government or other organization simply had nuclear weapons, letting every potential addressee of this "deterrent threat" reach his own conclusions about what kind of misbehavior, if any, might provoke nuclear activity. A degree more active is the threat that specifies what action by what parties is under nuclear proscription, and what kind of nuclear response is to be anticipated. Especially if the threat is being extended, say, to cover a third party, the explicit statement is required, together with whatever ritual or preparatory actions are required to make the threat believable. A much more active, and undoubtedly more persuasive, deterrent threat could be directed at a type of misbehavior that involved overt preparation or some protracted operation, and would take the form of actually using a nuclear weapon against the victim the moment he begins his adventure, with repeated use as long as he keeps it up or as long as the bombs hold out. This method might appeal to a terrorist organization that chose to remain anonymous, or that acted on behalf of a friend or client that couldn't acknowledge the "help," or didn't want it.

Some of the more dramatic acts of terrorism that we have read about in recent years have been initiated by individuals or small groups that had more passion than perseverance, more interest in getting attention than in getting results. They did not appear to be well-articulated pieces of a grand strategy in furtherance of a major objective. Most of them do not seem to have involved careful planning by large numbers of thoughtful people. But an organization that had the brains and the money and the teamwork and the discipline to bring off the successful construction of a nuclear bomb would have plenty of time and plenty of reason to think carefully about how to use this potential influence, this dreadful threat that may be as diplomatically unwieldy as it is enormous. Furthermore, if they can make one bomb they can probably make two or more and will be motivated to plan what to do next if the threat succeeds. Or if it fails.

They may have the time, the money, the motivation, and the imagination to study strategy as well as bomb design. Although they may have an urge to engage in some apocalyptic histrionics, they were probably mobilized by some cause they believed in. So we should expect them to do a more professional job not only in the way they coerce the behavior they want but in selecting the behavior to be coerced and the victims who, directly or indirectly, can bring it about.

That means that the "nuclear blackmail" that might be practiced by a nongovernmental organization, by a front organization set up by some government, or even by a government would be more effective than the small acts of individual terrorism that may first come to mind. It would probably look more like diplomacy than terrorism. It might be attached to a cause that half the world, or the other half, considered a just cause. The strategists might be responsibly concerned to avoid harm to innocent bystanders (but equally aware of the long tradition of nuclear-weapon states, which threaten nuclear destruction to the people whose leaders misbehave.) And they might be no more transient in world politics than most liberation movements, governments in exile, or ethnic communities.

The most plausible "nuclear terrorism" on the part of a nongovernmental group may be the kind that is almost indistinguishable from the traditional nuclear deterrence practiced by the United States and some other countries. It would be a threat of nuclear reprisal against some overt military action or against abetment of some military enterprise. The victims would be selected for their complicity in the enterprise, and the targets would be related as directly as possible to the military enterprise itself. It could be on behalf of some victim country that enjoyed a good deal of sympathy, and it could be against the kind of military action that has already been the object of nuclear threats by the United States and the Soviet Union. A thirty years' tradition, acquiesced in by most American and Soviet spokesmen, that the appropriate targets of nuclear deterrent threats are people and their homes and their workplaces might make it especially easy for some smaller organization to look cleaner and more business-like by announcing targets that were obviously military—airfields, ports, troop concentrations, and the like—that symbolized the misdeed for which this was reprisal. Careful selection of both the deed to be punished and the target to be struck could endow the threat with credibility and sympathy. An especially effective threat would be one that demanded the nonperformance of an action, or the cessation of some initiated action, that depended on the cooperation of so many people with different interests that there was bound to be somebody around who could stop it or sabotage it or veto it or focus the blame in such a way that those who could still carry out the deed did not want to. (Examples are treacherous, but I propose the threat of a nuclear bomb on airfields in third countries that permit landing and refueling of aircraft bringing troops or weapons into a theater of military operations from a country that is considered an aggressor or an outsider.)

### Some Problems of Control

The chances are good that most countries, perhaps all of them, will accept safeguards against the diversion of nuclear energy from peaceful uses to nuclear weapons. The NPT requires the acceptance of International Atomic Energy Agency (IAEA) safeguards, but so do the several bilateral agreements under which countries that are not parties to the NPT have imported reactors and other facilities. And in his testimony March 9, 1976, to the Senate Committee on Government Operations, the Secretary of State reported some success in developing among the main nuclear suppliers a "common set of standards concerning safeguards and other related controls associated with peaceful nuclear exports."

No foreign government or international organization could physically prevent a government from making any use it wished to make of the nuclear equipment and material within its jurisdiction, except by launching a military attack against it. But not many governments, if any at all, will want to jeopardize their nuclear future by violating treaty commitments or bilateral agreements or commercial contracts in a way that will lead the main nuclear suppliers to embargo fuel, parts, reactors, technical assistance, and anything else the country needs to import for nuclear energy. In the absence of an emergency so serious that governments would abrogate treaties and risk being outlawed as nuclear renegades, the network of institutional arrangements of which the NPT is the centerpiece gives promise of being effective.

There remain at least two kinds of risks. One is the theft of explosive nuclear materials. Although most of the terrorist groups that might be moved to steal plutonium in some chemical form are not the kind that would know what to do with it after they had stolen it, a group that did know how to use the stuff might be able to launch a commandolike operation in a selected country or to offer a suitable amount of money, no questions asked, for high-grade nuclear explosive material. Someday it may be necessary to do a better job spoiling the black market for plutonium than has been possible with the black market for heroin. Maybe the intergovernmental cooperation will be a little more nearly unanimous.

A more serious problem will be a country's own armed forces. Two of the most common activities of military forces in many parts of the world are to fight among themselves—half the Army against the other half, or the Army against the Navy—and to depose civilian governments. Even in NATO four governments have been subjected to severe military revolts; in three the revolts succeeded, usually without united actions by all the armed forces. New regimes that impose themselves by force or by other illegitimate means often fear, and with reason, outside intervention. They are often in a mood to denounce or at least to question the international commitments of the regime they deposed. They have little reluctance to violate civil rights and property rights. Their first task is to disable opposition and to entrench themselves militarily and otherwise. And if there is plutonium as well as gold in the vaults of the national bank, it may be put to some potentially more effective use without qualms by the new government.

If the government has qualms, in the noise and confusion of a small civil war the IAEA monitoring system can at least be disturbed long enough to let somebody get away with the nuclear stuff. It might even be that when the troops are initially deployed to the presidential palace, to the national television station and the local airport, a fourth contingent will be sent to scoop up whatever fissile material is in a transportable form. This may be the strongest argument that a government would have for not allowing plutonium or highly enriched uranium to exist in readily usable form. It is hard to imagine keeping the location secret from senior officers in the armed forces, especially after they have taken power. But when Moslems are fighting Christians within the country, or officers fighting enlisted men, the Navy fighting the Army, or French paratroopers marching on Paris, even those who would find plutonium an embarrassment may have to race for it and fight for it simply to keep it from falling into the wrong hands.

Some dangers are better not talked about, but not this one. If the time comes to grab the plutonium, nobody is likely to neglect it merely because, thanks to the reticence of arms controllers, it never occurred to them to capture it. But even those who expect to seize power by force may have the good sense not to want dangerous nuclear materials to be up for grabs in the event of civil disturbance or military revolt.

It is a useful exercise to speculate on how different the course of events might have been in Lebanon in late 1975 and early 1976 if that country had had an indigenous capacity to reprocess reactor fuel and to extract plutonium, even a small pilot plant. Who would have guarded the facilities? Who would have destroyed them, from nearby or from afar, at the risk of spreading deadly plutonium locally to keep bomb material from falling into mischievous hands? What outside country might have invaded if the spoils of war would have included a nuclear-weapon capability, even only to deny that capability to some other greedy neighbor? What neutral outsiders might have been invited in by the President or the Prime Minister to guard or to abduct the dangerous stuff? And would all parties have willingly cooperated with the removal of such an awful prize, or would that have added merely one more armed group fighting its way to the cache? There may be some useful international understandings and procedures to be worked out for that kind of emergency. One thing is certain: in years to come there will be military violence in countries that have sizable nuclear power industries.

A tantalizing control problem will arise with respect to countries that do have, or are believed to have, nuclear weapons. The dilemma is this. Little as we like them to have nuclear weapons, if they are going to have them we would like them to have the best technical safeguards against accidental or unauthorized detonation, and possibly—though this is a tricky one—against military attack. At the same time, we shall not want to reward countries that make nuclear explosives by offering them our most advanced technology to safeguard against misuse, especially if some of the most effective safeguards would be in the design of the bomb itself. We have all heard of remote electronic locking devices; there may be some crucial design aspects that could keep a bomb from exploding unless it were in some predesignated condition and that would spoil the bomb if the mechanism were tampered with. There must be ways of making the bomb with the fissionable material recognizable, even after explosion, and ways of making it easier to locate if lost or to follow if carried away. And if the weapons were to be installed in missiles or aircraft or on board ship or were to be hauled around for emplacement as land mines, there may be American technology and experience in the fusing of weapons and other characteristics of the entire weapon system that would reduce the likelihood of unauthorized or inadvertent firing, or theft or capture.

The recipient of any such technical assistance would have to be a country that had never ratified the NPT or, having ratified, had withdrawn pursuant to Article 10 or had abrogated or denounced the treaty. Reading the treaty gives me no hint to its legal interpretation on whether help in bomb safety could be provided, but it is probably not the legal interpretation that would be controlling. Done bilaterally this would be a suspect activity. Broadcasting the technology would certainly violate the treaty. Discreet bilateral transfer might be accomplished but, at least to the recipient of this sensitive technology, such evident complicity might be interpreted as tacit cooperation or approval, especially if it were not yet acknowledged that the country to whom we slipped the prophylactics had taken the decision yet.

The resolution of this dilemma is probably to append this problem to the more general problem of physical security against loss or theft or sabotage of dangerous nuclear materials of all kinds. Ideas and experience relevant to the problem of bomb safety, even if not engineering designs, can probably be gotten across undramatically and without challenge if there is at least a reasonable pretense that the measures are of wide security application. (An alternative solution is to let the French do it.)

### And Now for the Good News

Think back twenty-five years [now more like thirty-five]. The Prime Minister had just flown to Washington to obtain assurances for his Parliament that President Truman would not let nuclear weapons be used in Korea. Russia had stunningly exploded a bomb, years before it was thought Russia would be able to. Our deterrent force was the propeller-driven B-36. Suppose I had been asked then to write something called, "Who Will Have the Bomb?" And suppose I had accurately answered that question for the ensuing twenty-five [thirty-five] years.

This is how I might have replied.

There are going to be thousands of nuclear bombs on air bases and hundreds, probably thousands, on aircraft carriers and smaller naval vessels in port and at sea. Nuclear weapons are going to be available to a variety of short- and medium-range ground-to-ground missiles, antiaircraft missiles, and even artillery. They are going to be in Germany, Greece, Turkey, Okinawa, and probably the Panama Canal Zone. Some will be intended for airplanes to be flown by foreigners, and these weapons will be physically located so that in a hurry they can be available to foreign aircraft.

We are going to fly B-47s over Western Europe and the adjacent ocean loaded with big nuclear bombs, and a little later on we are going to fly B-52s to the North Pole and back with them. There is going to be a "Cuban" missile crisis, and in the course of it B-47s alleged to be accompanied by nuclear weapons, possibly with the nuclear weapons on board, will be photographed on the runway at Logan Airport in Boston. There are going to be two military revolts in Greece while American weapons are located on Greek military bases; and Greece will be on the brink of war with another NATO country, Turkey, that is also going to have American weapons on its military bases.

The number of bombs produced in the United States is going to reach the tens of thousands, and they are going to be transported all over the United States and a lot of the world, in the custody of thousands or tens of thousands of people, most of them enlisted men. The French are going to supply nuclear weapons to their bomber force and then move into the production of tactical weapons. Dozens of nuclear-armed submarines belonging to at least four nations are going to be continuously cruising the oceans, the weapons as well as the boats presumably under the complete physical control of a few officers who will be hermetically sealed in their vessels for months at a time.

Some of you would think I was out of my mind. Some would think I was exaggerating to cause alarm. And some would think, sadly, that my prediction might be right. But on the next part you would surely agree that I was deluding myself.

Because then I go on to say that in twenty-five [thirty-five] years not a single one of these bombs will go off accidentally. Not a single one will be detonated by a demented military officer. Not a single one will be captured by foreign spies and used to defend Yemen against Egyptians or Cypriot Greeks from Turkish mainland forces. Not a single one will be captured by a domestic fanatic and used to avenge an assassination or to coerce the release of some prisoners. Not a single one will be known to have been sold by its guards or transport crews to foreign governments, to the Mafia, or to rich expatriate businessmen sought by the Internal Revenue Service and the Securities Exchange Commission.

A bomber will crash in Spain, rupturing a bomb and spreading its contents over some countryside and dropping another one in the water near a beach resort, but the Air Force will clean up the mess on land and our Ambassador will go swimming to reassure the Spaniards that their water is safe.

Nor will any awful things have happened with French or British or Russian or Chinese weapons, so far as we know.

And most important of all, there will have been no nuclear weapons fired in warfare.

# 14 | Thinking about Nuclear Terrorism

S OMETIME IN THE 1980s an organization that is not a national government may acquire a few nuclear weapons. If not in the 1980s then in the 1990s. The likelihood will grow as more and more national governments acquire fissionable material from their own weapon programs, their research programs, their reactor-fuel programs, or from the waste products of their electric power reactors.

By "organization" I mean a political movement, a government in exile, a separatist or secessionist party, a military rebellion, adventurers from the underground or the underworld, or even some group of people merely bent on showing that it can be done. My list is not a definition, just a sample of the possibilities. Two decades of concern about the proliferation of weapons have generated a familiar list of national governments that may have motive and opportunity to possess weapons-grade fissionable material and some ideas about how they might behave if they had it and what they might use it for. But there is also a possibility that somebody other than a government may possess the stuff.

Who they might be and how they might acquire it are related questions. Although not impossible, it is unlikely that an entity not subject to national-government regulation could independently obtain and enrich uranium for use in explosives or could produce plutonium as a reactor product and refine it for weapons use. There are undoubtedly corporations technically and financially able to do it, but not many with both the motive and opportunity to do it without being apprehended by an adversely interested party. Access to weapons or a weapon program, or to an authorized nuclear fuel cycle, or to an official research establishment licensed and authorized by some national government is currently the only way to do it. Identifying the opportunities and the access to those opportunities generates some answers to the question "Who?"

Theft of weapons is an obvious possibility. As far as we know, it hasn't happened. Despite the thousands in existence, including the thousands on foreign soil, and the large numbers of people who participate in the custody, maintenance, and transport of nuclear weapons, and despite earlier reports by the General Accounting Office that proper care in the transport of weapons has sometimes been lacking, I am not aware of any hint that theft has occurred in any country. And if there has been a theft, the thief certainly has not made a public announcement.

Nothing so flatly negative can be said about theft of separated plutonium or enriched uranium. An important difference between theft of the material and theft of a weapon is that nobody is likely to remove a weapon or a warhead in small pieces. A weapon, if stolen, is likely to be taken whole. Materials from some sources, on the other hand, would have to be secreted cumulatively over a protracted period.

Gift is a possibility. There may be things a nongovernment organization can accomplish that a national government would prefer not or dare not to try. Surreptitious or anonymous activities by agents of a government we can consider part of the *national* proliferation problem; but weapons entrusted to independent or uncontrolled parties who have at least some autonomy in what to do with them should be counted as part of the non-nation risk. The gift may be extorted; blackmail against a government possessing weapons or weapons material is one way of obtaining a "gift." Extortion would be especially pertinent if the recipients knew of a clandestine weapon program, and if they had a capability to hurt the government or the people concerned, but would target the nuclear capability elsewhere. In principle, we should add the possibility of purchase; but in matters of corruption, "bribery and extortion" are so often together that gift, blackmail, and purchase can be thought of as unilateral intentional transfers motivated by various inducements.

Defection of civilian or military officials, or units of national military forces, is an obvious possibility once a national government has weapons, especially weapons officially available for military use. Had nuclear weapons been in the hands of French forces in Algeria in 1958, the paratroopers and Secret Army Organization that challenged the Paris government might have made threatening use of such weapons or arranged their disappearance for use on some later occasion. When Batista went into exile from Cuba, or Somoza from Nicaragua, or the Shah from Iran, any official holding of nuclear weapons or the materials from which they can be made could have accompanied him, or could have left the country, or gone into hiding with other officials. The civil war that has ravaged Lebanon, the war that separated the two parts of Pakistan, the overthrow of Sukarno in Indonesia, and the turmoil in Iran from the first confrontations between officers loyal to the Shah and officers disobeying suggest the circumstances in which something could have happened to an official arsenal of nuclear weapons. Three other NATO countries besides France—Portugal, Greece, and Turkey—have undergone changes in government by violence or the threat of violence in such a way that any weapons could have reached "unauthorized hands," either at the time or on a later occasion.

It is worth speculating on what might have happened to Iranian nuclear weapons had the turmoil that began in 1978 broken out a dozen years later, when the Shah's originally planned nuclear power program would have been generating spent nuclear fuel from which plutonium could be reprocessed or weapons fabricated. The Shah or someone loyal to him might have taken weapons or material out of the country (or sent it out in advance) for the purpose of staging a comeback or defending wealth and personal security in exile. They might already have been entrusted for safekeeping to somebody abroad. Loyal troops without access to weapons might have taken steps to obtain them to keep them out of dangerous hands; disloyal troops might have sought to capture weapons for political use or, also, to keep them out of even more dangerous hands. The disintegrated regime presided over by the Ayatollah might have found it awkward and controversial to have nuclear-weapons material in the possession of some impermanent official—the President, say, who disappeared with his executioners in pursuit in July 1981. Or whoever managed to possess the material might have claimed authority under the

Ayatollah to withhold it from the President or Prime Minister, without any countermand from the Ayatollah. Indeed, it isn't clear to whom it might have been entrusted by whoever might have been in a position to do the entrusting during the near-anarchy of 1979–80. Other interested parties would undoubtedly have been willing to consider commando tactics to preempt the stuff, either because of its value in the right hands or because of its value in the wrong hands. Israel, the Soviet Union, and the United States of America come to mind, as does the PLO. What would have come out of the scramble is a guess that has many answers. And as with the jewelry, the cash, or the negotiable assets that the Shah or others that fled may have taken with them, it might never have been known how much nuclear material there had been and how much was missing. A prudent royal family would have exercised the same caution with nuclear material as with gold or Panamanian bank accounts.

These different routes by which weapons or material might get out of official hands tend to compound themselves. Whatever the likelihood that, say, the government of Iran would have sold nuclear weapons or given them away, or yielded them to blackmail by the PLO, weapons in the hands of militants or of disaffected naval or air forces might be subject to less inertia and less inhibition, or more subject to theft or capture or plain loss in the confusion of escape and evacuation. Whoever had such weapons or material would be unlikely to hold it or transport it in labeled containers. Just what do you do with a hundred pounds of plutonium when the building is under siege and you are in a hurry to reach the airport, or you have to leave town in disguise, and you don't exactly trust the "authorized" official to whom it is supposed to be surrendered under standard operating procedures?

For now this is all just rehearsal. In ten or fifteen years it may be a live performance.

### Getting It All Together

If weapons material is obtained in any of these ways from a nation that has a small or clandestine weapons program, or especially from one that has no weapons program at all, the material is not likely to be obtained in the form of completely assembled bombs or warheads. For reasons of custodial security, the weapons might be unassembled. If weapon development is a continuing process, a government might not commit scarce material to permanently assembled weapons of obsolescing design. A government unwilling to entrust weapons to its own armed forces might find it expedient, in dealing with senior military officials, to keep its arsenal of finished weapons in the future. A government preferring to keep a weapons option, but not to declare or leak a nuclear military capability, might reduce the lead time between weapon decision and completed weapon without marrying the fissionable material and the other components, except in laboratory rehearsal. So an organization that obtains the material may still face the task of constructing a portable explosive.

That fact makes strong demands on the organization. Highly qualified scientists and engineers are required. Some years ago Hans Bethe publicly calculated a minimum of six well-trained people representing just the right specialties. Unless they already possessed weapon designs, they would need access to computers and a library. They would need the discipline and loyalty to work in secrecy and in trust. And it would take time. Recruiting the team secretly would be difficult; even clandestine advertising could give the whole thing away. Mercenary engineers might feel uneasy about an enterprise that required them to leave no trace behind, an enterprise premised on willingness for large-scale violence and one not likely to give much thought to the welfare of mercenary engineers if secrecy were at stake. If the key people were sympathizers rather than mercenaries, they would want to participate in the planning of what was to be done with the weapons. In sum, it appears to require a group of significant size, high professional quality, and excellent organization and discipline to convert unauthorized or illicitly obtained materials into a usable weapon.

A consequence is that there would be time and opportunity to make plans, to assure that the weapons or the opportunity were not wasted, and to work out the technical and tactical problems of exploiting the weapons once produced. If the material were obtained for an existing emergency, there might be urgency in completing a weapon promptly and exploiting it at once; otherwise, a major consideration would be that exploiting the weapon early would eliminate secrecy, stimulate countermeasures, close the source of material if it remained open, and use up the unique occasion of "first revelation."

I conclude that people capable of all this will be able to do some pretty sophisticated planning. There will be time and motivation to think about how to use this unique capability. They may wait for the right occasion; they may patiently create the right occasion. They may be in no hurry. They may even hope it will not prove necessary to their cause actually to explode the weapon or weapons. And they are likely, having thought long and explored alternatives in detail before embarking on their plan, to be better prepared intellectually than their adversaries.

If they decide to claim possession of a nuclear bomb and, as at Hiroshima, do not wish to deplete their supply by an innocuous demonstration or to risk failure in an open test, they will have to be prepared to prove that they have what they claim. But they will have had the time, and probably the right people, to have considered how to authenticate their claim—what technical demonstrations are feasible, even which ambassadors to appoint in presenting their claim.

If they need to pre-position a few weapons and can best accomplish it before their victims have any inkling of what is up, there will be further reason to postpone revelation and more time to plan the campaign.

And a *campaign* is what they will plan, not an episode. Unlike most "terrorist" acts of recent years, the activity initiated by the announcement or demonstration of a nuclear weapon is not likely to culminate in a decisive outcome that terminates the episode. If a weapon were used to coerce, neither the success nor the failure of coercion would necessarily lead to the surrender or capture of the weapon. Even the explosion of a weapon might not be interpreted, with any confidence, as the exhaustion of the arsenal and the end of the threat. Acquisition of a nuclear-weapons capability may confer permanent status on the organization and create a permanent situation, not just initiate a finite event.

## Will They Be Terrorists?

The question is sometimes posed, Will terrorists come to acquire nuclear weapons? That question starts a series of thoughts: think of all the different terrorist organizations, from Quebec to Uruguay, Ireland to the Basque country, Rhodesia to Israel. Who among them might acquire weapons material during the coming decade or two? Who would know how to produce a weapon, or even to build an organization technically and institutionally capable of bringing such an enterprise to fruition? Who among them would trust each other enough to want such a thing?

Those questions probably focus on the wrong issue. The proper question is not whether an organization of the kind that we consider "terrorist" will get nuclear weapons in pursuit of its goals. It is whether any organization that acquires nuclear weapons *can be anything but* terrorist in the use of such weapons. Does possession of a nuclear weapon, or a few weapons, necessarily make an organization "terrorist"? Are the weapons themselves so terrorist, in any use that can be made of them, that they make their possessors supreme terrorists, whatever else they may or may not be?

Except for acquiring a weapon just to prove it can be done—a motive that I don't doubt appeals to some, but one that I doubt adequate to accomplish the feat—I find it hard to think of any use that would not be "terrorist." I also find it hard to think of any exploitation of nuclear weapons by a *national government,* other than one with a sufficient arsenal for battlefield use, that would not be terrorist. Even the language of "mass destruction" in categorizing these weapons suggests intimidation and reprisal rather than battlefield effectiveness.

The concept of "massive retaliation" is terrorist. My dictionary defines terrorism as "the use of terror, violence, and intimidation to achieve an end." And to terrorize is "to coerce by intimidation or fear." The passive form, known as "deterrence" (using the root of the word "terror"), need not connote bloodthirstiness, but there is a forty-year tradition that the appropriate targets for nuclear forces are cities or populations and that strategic nuclear forces induce caution and moderation in an adversary by threatening the destruction of the enemy society. I imply nothing derogatory or demeaning about strategic nuclear forces by emphasizing the traditional expectation that their primary use is to deter or to intimidate, and thereby to influence behavior, through the threat of enormous civilian damage.

It is worth remembering that on the only occasion of the hostile use of nuclear weapons, they were used in a fashion that has to be considered "terrorist." There was a nation that had a very small capability to produce nuclear bombs. The need was sufficiently urgent that it was decided to go ahead with "revelation" when only two were in hand. The hope was to stun the enemy into surrender, or to create such a tremor that the government itself would change into one disposed to surrender. The possibility of a harmless detonation in an unpopulated place was considered but rejected on grounds that the demonstration might fail (possibly through incomprehension by the witnesses) and in any event would deplete the stockpile by half. The weapons could not be wasted on a remote battlefield; and even military destruction in the Japanese homeland would be incidental compared with the shock of an anti-population attack. With a modest pretense at military-industrial targeting, the industrial city of Hiroshima was chosen. No warning was given that might have allowed interference with the demonstration. And so much was at stake—the possibility of continued warfare and the prospective loss of more millions of lives, mostly Japanese—that the demonstration's casualties might be justified as the price of persuasively communicating the threat and precluding any militarist refusal to take the threat seriously. When the response to the first bomb was not prompt enough, the second was dropped on Nagasaki, depleting the arsenal altogether. (Whether a third was ready for delivery, the victim government could not know.)

The bombs on Hiroshima and Nagasaki remind us that, from the point of view of those who use the weapons, use favors the right side. It may even be hoped that use will minimize the ultimate violence to the enemy.

To make the comparison more contemporary, we can contemplate the kind of use that might be made by a national government that had a few nuclear weapons, "few" meaning single numbers or teens, few not only by comparison with so-called nuclear powers, but too few for decisive use on the battlefield. It is generally expected that population threats, verbal or communicated by detonation, would be the obvious role for such weapons, and that even nominally "battlefield" use would be intended mainly for intimidation rather than local target destruction. A national government with only a few such weapons would not have any but a "terrorist" mode in which to use them. There are many ways to differentiate a national government from a nongovernmental entity, but the "terrorist" quality in any use of nuclear weapons does not seem the crucial differentiation.

If a government that exploited any genuine or pretended nuclear capability would appear to "descend" to the level of a terrorist organization by doing so, an organization other than a national government that possessed or could credibly claim to possess nuclear weapons conversely might "ascend" to the status of a government. It might seek its own permanence as a nuclear mini-state, even if lacking territory. Or it might claim a territory or seek a homeland, identifying itself as the rightful claimant to legitimate authority in some existing state. Considering the status and "prestige" that are supposed to go with the fearsome accomplishment of producing or otherwise acquiring nuclear bombs, and recognizing that something as vaguely defined as a Palestine Liberation Organization can achieve diplomatic recognition, observers should not have to tax their imaginations to suppose that an organization with the ability to acquire the wherewithal to produce nuclear weapons might proceed to set up its own foreign office and dispatch its own ambassadors to the governments with which it proposed to do business.

This idea is supported by the consideration that an organization that could have one bomb could well have more than one. So even violent use of a weapon might not exhaust the campaign. Furthermore, "successful" exploitation of a weapon, for a nongovernmental entity as for a national government, would likely achieve its purpose without explosion, without destroying the weapon itself. So the organization need not contemplate its own demise, as a nuclear mini-state, in the event of initial success.

### Modes of Utilization

It is hard to foretell what mode of exploitation might be adopted by some organization that comes into possession of nuclear weapons. It is especially hard because the people who would decide the strategy could have had weeks or months or longer to think and argue intensely about what their "nuclear strategy" should be. Most of us have not spent weeks or months attempting to *anticipate* that exercise. And because we have not identified our specific candidate, we have no vivid image of either its objectives or its limitations to help sharpen our imagination or to screen out the implausible. We can, however, generate a menu of some possibilities with which to acquire some notion of the range of surprises to which we may be subject someday.

Not the most dramatic but an effective way that a small nuclear-weapon capability might be exploited would be to announce it. Announce it nonbelligerently, and do nothing else. The announcement might require identifying who it was that had it, unless the organization or its affiliation was already well known. Alternatively the information could be allowed to leak; and if there was already conjecture that the organization was acquiring a nuclear capability, the "announcement" might take the form of merely not responding negatively (or convincingly) to inquiries. The fact of possession could be interpreted as an implicit threat. If the object were to gain attention and status, a believable announcement ought to do the trick. The announcement might be secret and limited to a few addressees, perhaps the target governments toward whom the weapons represented an implicit threat, perhaps a friendly government that might or might not welcome the news of such support.

Some effort to authenticate the claim would accompany the announcement. We have fictional and journalistic accounts of how this might be done—revealing details of theft or capture that only thieves or captors could know, inviting or kidnapping witnesses for a "show and tell," delivery of a weapon facsimile or a sample of weapons-grade material, open declaration by the distinguished scientists who had designed and assembled the weapons, or a "test" detonation. Depending on the risk of interception, the latter could be by surprise, at an unannounced time and place, or by "invitation" or advance tip-off.

An alternative passive, but more dramatic, mode might be to eschew announcement and proceed to demonstration. If the object were to strike a little terror, an anonymous blast might do; and although minor terrorist groups might claim authorship in the usual style, the authentic perpetrator should have no difficulty proving its claim.

In case it seems that mere announcement, unaccompanied by overt threats and demands, would lack the climactic quality one expects to find associated with a non-nation nuclear capability, it helps to reflect that announcement or, alternatively, leaks and undenied conjectures are what one usually expects of a national government. Except for the initial American revelation, mere announcement (or even letting another government do the announcing) has been the custom. Those who believe that Israel has nuclear weapons, whether in readiness or ready for quick assembly, must believe that "announcement by denial" is a believable tactic. (Whether they believe that Israel also made some explicit but discreet revelations, I don't know.) In any case, there is nothing about "mere" announcement that precludes becoming more explicit later. The way it is done would depend, too, on the manner in which some national governments might, between now and then, have conducted their own revelations or tests or first uses. An effective way to announce possession if the most likely target government had just announced that it possessed nuclear bombs would be to counter, "we do too."

In a more active mode, the organization could approach the target government, that is, the government whose behavior it hoped to influence by formulation of demands. It could do this secretly or openly. There are at least four combinations: open announcement coupled with secret demands; secret display or announcement associated with open demands; or both secret; or both open. There might be more than one target government; the "victim" might be different from the "target," the overt threat made against one government with the intent of intimidating another. A Libya that nominally threatened Israel might be aiming its terror at Americans.

The target might be a populace, not a government. Panic, evacuation, political pressure on a government, or mass civil disobedience or obstruction could be the response either to mere announcement or to a threat aimed obliquely or directly at the population. Winston Churchill was reportedly concerned, at least briefly, that the German bombing of London might cause disorderly evacuation—and those were pretty small bombs.

The most active mode of intimidation would be to detonate a weapon on a live target. Hiroshima represented intimidation: the object was not to eliminate that city; the true target was the emperor's palace in Tokyo. A weapon could disable a nation by destroying the center of the capital city; and a weapon or several might be used by surprise on a military installation or troop concentration. But even on a military target, nuclear weapons might be intended more to terrorize a populace or to intimidate a government than just to cause local blast and radiation damage. (A nuclear facility might be judged an appropriate target by an organization that wanted the drama of military use but wanted to target hearts and minds rather than bodies.) Detonation against some specific target is evidently more likely if there is a war on.

Not out of the question is the possibility that a weapon would be offered for sale. Whether a dedicated group of scientists and engineers would elect to turn a profit rather than perform diplomatic miracles strains my credulity, but only somewhat; a weapon obtained opportunistically from a military arsenal seems more compatible with mercenary utilization. Putting a weapon up to public auction would be a clever bit of mischief. It might be purchased by someone desiring the weapon, or ransomed by a government that could finance preclusive purchase. There might be the usual difficulty with kidnap ransom, namely, of showing up to collect the money or giving one's mailing address; but the father of Patty Hearst was ordered to deliver ransom to a third party—food for the poor—and that strategy, if the owner isn't after the money itself, takes care of half the problem. The other half is credibly surrendering the weapon.

An outside possibility is that an organization acquiring a nuclear weapon would surrender it with ceremony, not against ransom or on any conditions or concessions. It could be an effective anti-nuclear demonstration. Such a consummation seems incompatible with the deadly serious and dangerous task of designing and constructing a weapon; but a less professional organization that obtained a military weapon by theft or hijacking might be tempted to dramatize disarmament in that fashion. (Or they might announce a contest: now that they have it, what should they do with it?)

### Strategies for Terrorist Use

Nuclear weapons are enormous, discrete, unrenewable, and scarce. They are too valuable to waste or to entrust to any but the most reliable operatives. They are out of proportion to most of the things that terrorists demand in response to some finite threat, like something or somebody held hostage. Only recently has a single finite opportunistic terrorist threat—the Americans captured with the embassy in Teheran—been parlayed into a quasi-permanent source of intimidation. Assassination of a head of state is an act to compare to a nuclear threat or nuclear test, but assassination doesn't lend itself to a protracted strategy of coercion. Few terrorist incidents of recent decades therefore contain interesting suggestions for terrorist activity on a nuclear scale.

A characteristic of nuclear weapons, unlike live hostages, occupied buildings, hijacked ships or aircraft, or stolen precious objects, is that there is no inherent limitation on how long a nuclear threat can last and no necessity for surrender of the weapon at the end of a successful negotiation. In ancient times hostages were taken in large numbers as security against the good behavior of a tribe or a town or a nation. In recent times, with the ambiguous exception of Iran, terrorist hostages have been dynamically unstable assets, not capable of being held indefinitely in comfort and safety either for captives or captors. The ultimate mobility and security of the captors depends on release *from* as well as release *of* the hostages. We have to look back to the occupied countries of World War II, or eastward to more recent military occupations, to find instances of "steady-state" rather than "episodic" hostages.

An important distinction for the terrorist use of nuclear weapons, whether by a small nation or organization or by great nations like France, the United States, and the Soviet Union, is between deterrence and compellence. (I apologize for the *word* "compellence," which I introduced some years ago for this purpose, but not for the *distinction*, which has been understood since historical times.) By "deterrence" I mean inducing an adversary or a victim *not* to do something, to continue not doing something. The word takes the preposition "from." According to my dictionary, "to discourage or keep (a person) from doing something through fear, anxiety, doubt, etc." It is the more passive kind of coercion. By "compellence" I mean inducing a person *to do* something through fear, anxiety, doubt, etc. "Compel" takes the preposition "to." My dictionary contains no word specialized toward this more active kind of coercion, so I coined the word.

Deterrence is simpler. The command to do something requires a date or deadline; to keep on not doing something is timeless. Acquiescence to a compellent threat is visibly responsive; doing nothing in face of a deterrent threat is not so obvious. Acquiescence to a compellent threat invites another demand; complying with a deterrent leaves things unchanged and leads to no sequel. Compellent threats have to be spelled out: "go back" needs an indication how far; "give help" an indication of what and how much; while "don't" usually takes its definition from what exists. And if a compellent threat is met by inaction, no event or initiative triggers or mandates the execution, while violation of a deterrent threat, unless softly and gradually done, initiates the action. In military affairs the deterrent threat can often target the same activity that constitutes the violation, while a compellent threat must often find a target disconnected from the desired response: "don't advance or I'll shoot" makes the connection, while "send money or . . ." cannot usually target the money but must find some linkage elsewhere.

I propose that terrorist nuclear threats have a comparative advantage toward deterrence. The more familiar terrorist actions of recent years had the dynamics and disconnectedness of compellence. Organizations making nuclear threats, like nuclear nations, have a credibility problem; deterrent threats are more credible. One of the great advantages of deterrent threats is that they often do not need to be articulated. They are typically addressed to some obvious overt act. If you draw a gun on somebody approaching, he may stop whether or not you tell him to; if you want him to turn around, take the keys from his pocket, and throw them to you over his shoulder, you have to say something. Not only does the deterrent threat economize communication and minimize ambiguity, it permits one to create a threat without doing anything belligerent, without acknowledging, even while denying, that one is threatening.

It was easy to draw up a list of things that the U.S. government might have done but didn't do for fear of jeopardizing the hostages in Teheran. It is not so easy to draw up a convincing list of affirmative American actions that were coerced through the hostages, except for the final ransom.

A second distinction for terrorist nuclear strategy is between military and civilian targets. A nuclear threat, and especially a detonation, will frighten, terrorize, and intimidate, whatever the target indicated in the threat or attacked by a bomb. But if the unofficial mini-state aspires to international diplomacy and identifies its role as taking part in international conflict, especially military conflict, it may want to legitimize its possession of weapons, its campaign of intimidation, even its use of nuclear explosives, by nominally confining its attention to military targets. It may not want to discredit the side that it favors. If the organization considers itself immune to reprisal because it has no homeland and its location is unknown, it may not wish to make its intended beneficiary a target for reprisal. As in a conflict between

India and Pakistan, Argentina and Brazil, Israel and Syria, Cambodia and Vietnam, or South Africa and any black nation of the continent, terrorist organizations may not want to appear inhumane and terrorist, and may select military targets to attack or to threaten.

Similarly, the actions deterred may be military. Just as the United States would not consider nuclear threats except against some military "aggression," and all nations that make reference to nuclear weapons of their own do so in reference to self-defense or commitments in defense of allies, the terrorist organization may adopt the custom and confine its threats to the deterrence of military actions.

In doing so it need not look more terrorizing than France or the United States. By eschewing "massive retaliation" against homeland populations and avoiding threats of destroying "enemy societies as such," it may legitimize its nuclear role and appear less inhumane or destructive than the greater nuclear powers. Whatever it achieves for them, striking the posture may not cost them much.

In choosing the actions to deter and the targets to threaten, nuclear terrorists may enjoy the advantage of multiple victims. When an action they want to deter can be obstructed by any one of several deterrable actors, they may select their victims and targets for likely compliance. Let me use a historical instance as an example, one that does not have to be wholly invented. During the October War of 1973 the United States was denied by many European countries the privilege of refueling aircraft carrying ammunition and equipment for Israel. No nuclear threat was needed: it was megatons of energy to be withheld rather than delivered that deterred cooperation with the United States. But Portugal, justifying two decades of pretense that that country had anything to contribute in NATO, allowed use of airfields in the Azores. A pro-Arab terrorist organization, acting on its own or fronting for a government that had a few nuclear weapons, might have declared the resupply of Israel an aggressive intrusion into a military conflict, one that they would resist with their modest nuclear force. They could simply threaten to explode their weapon near a base on which U.S. planes were refueling unless the airlift ceased. Assuming they could prove possession, their ability to do what they threatened could be credible. The United States might be deterred. Alternatively, the Portuguese government might be deterred. Or third, civilian employees and others near the threatened site could be motivated to strike, to obstruct, to evacuate. If the threat were not heeded, and a weapon were detonated in the vicinity, the perpetrators would at least have caused minimal civilian damage in attacking a military operation. Whatever the political and diplomatic consequences of such a stunning event—and on that I am not even going to conjecture—it at least does not appear a wholly self-defeating threat, or even a self-defeating action, from the point of view of an organization wholly sympathetic to the Syrian-Egyptian cause.

Notice that if we go back and replay the scenario, allowing some Israeli nuclear counterthreat that might entail equally imaginative targeting, we have an indeterminate situation, one in which the fact that the nuclear organization is not a recognized nation does not make much difference. I have heard comparable scenarios conjecturing how a government like that of Libya, if it had a few nuclear weapons, might operate through a front organization, or might issue a threat anonymously, or might even detonate a weapon without acknowledging its role. I have heard scenarios in which some small nation's nuclear weapons are entrusted to the air force or navy and escape the control (or appear or are alleged to have escaped the control) of the national government. Whether the nuclear-armed entity in these stories is a nation or not does not make much difference.

Like governments in these scenarios an organization not a government would not necessarily condition its nuclear participation on a request from the government for whose benefit it appears to be intervening. The real purpose may not even be to help the "beneficiary."

Governments are of course more susceptible to nuclear reprisal, or almost any other kind of reprisal, than an unattached or anonymous organization. Countries can be denied exports, blockaded, diplomatically ostracized, or even subjected to non-nuclear attack if they appear about to create a nuclear inferno in a population center or to rupture a moratorium on the use of nuclear weapons that has survived since V-J Day. In contrast, an organization that needs only a small boat to dock in a metropolitan harbor, with a nuclear weapon on board and someplace to operate a two-way radio, can hardly be starved into second thoughts by denial of soybeans, military spare parts, or air traffic; and it evidently cannot be invaded or captured or we wouldn't have the problem in the first place.

The difference is undeniably important, but need not be decisive. Up to the point of actually exploding a weapon, a national government may be in no more danger of diplomatic or military counteraction than an organization that is not a government. Even a nation that actually used nuclear weapons against enemy troops or enemy population would not necessarily be subjected to nuclear reprisal. Fear of escalation, abhorrence of anti-population attacks, and an interest in enhancing rather than abandoning nuclear restraint could inhibit some of the potential nuclear retaliators, especially if other modes of reprisal or disabling attack were available. And if the nongovernment organization uses its nuclear status in military support of a particular country, the country so "helped" might not escape all blame. So the difference, though important, is not decisive.

## Safeguards against Non-National Weapons

Eventually we may need a domain of strategy for coping with these lesser nuclear threats, coming from either national governments or nongovernmental organizations. It is likely to be different from the principles and ideas that have been developed during the past three decades for the Soviet–American or NATO–Warsaw Pact confrontation, and at least as complicated. It will be especially complicated by the utter lack of symmetry between the United States and any such nuclear adversaries or clients as we have been talking about. I do not propose to outline any such strategy here.

But in preventing the acquisition of nuclear capabilities by non-national entities, there is at least one principle that I think is undeniable: the best way to keep weapons and weapons-material out of the hands of nongovernmental entities is to keep them out of the hands of national governments. Saying that doesn't get us very far, but it does remind us that this is the problem we have already worried about, or a large part of it. International war—war between nations that are enemies of each other—is only one relevant occasion when possession of nuclear weapons might make a terrible difference.

The main military activity of military forces around the world is overthrowing their own government or fighting other military forces in the same country—air force against navy, officers against enlisted men, East against West Pakistan, Moslem against Christian, royalist against anti-royalist. The risk that nuclear weapons, or the material from which such weapons can be assembled, would actually play a role in hostilities seems to be enhanced by the fact that military action in much of the world is so much characterized by internal disorder and loss of national control over military forces. There is just a chance, maybe only a prayer, that some governments or heads of government may appreciate the dangers, to their own country and to themselves, of acquiring a weapons capability. Aside from becoming a target for nuclear blackmail or nuclear attack by joining the ranks of declared nuclear nations, some governments might possibly recognize how divisive a small nuclear capability could be.

What should a wise head of government respond if offered immediate delivery of a few nuclear weapons? I think, "Not yet—let me think about where to put them." A prudent citizen might be appalled if a truck arrived unexpectedly and conspicuously delivered objects of great value that he had inadvertently won in some lottery, fearing that robbers would arrive before safeguards could be erected and he would be left in worse shape than before the goods arrived.

Ownership of nuclear weapons poses embarrassing questions for a head of state. Does he trust his senior officers sufficiently to put his weapons in military hands? Can he dare to display his distrust by keeping them from the military? Would he have to provide them to the competing military services or can he elevate one service as the sole nuclear force? Could he, as Secretary McNamara could not in the early 1960s, get enthusiastic military acquiescence in electronically safeguarded presidential control? And could he in some future war—a contingency that has to be considered possible, otherwise why nuclear weapons?—let an army be surrounded, immobilized, even captured, as suggested by the final stage of the October War, without authorizing some use of these supposedly awesome weapons? And what use might that be? And if he withheld the weapons, wouldn't he then regret having possessed them?

There is little that the United States can credibly do to increase the alarm any heads of non-nuclear governments might feel at the prospect of getting close to having the weapons. We have too evident an interest of our own. It must furthermore be exceedingly difficult to get a president, defense minister, minister for nuclear power, and chief of armed forces to sit together around a table and acknowledge that they may shortly be on opposite sides of a coup or civil war, or evacuating in disorder, and that they would therefore be wise not to encumber themselves with as competitive a prize as a nuclear arsenal.

I wish there were evidence that some heads of government shared my misgivings. I have never heard representatives of Pakistan or Iraq or Argentina explain that a positive interest in nuclear weapons should never be imputed to them because the weapons are far more dangerous than they are worth. We might not believe them if we heard them say it, but it would be good to know that it had occurred to them.

# 15 | The Mind as a Consuming Organ

LASSIE DIED one night. Millions of viewers, not all of them children, grieved. At least, they shed tears. Except for the youngest, the mourners knew that Lassie didn't really exist. Whatever that means. Perhaps with their left hemispheres they could articulate that they had been watching a trained dog and that *that* dog was still alive, healthy, and rich; meanwhile in their right hemispheres, or some such place (if these phenomena have a place), the real Lassie had died.

Did they enjoy the episode?

We know they would not have enjoyed the death of the dog that played Lassie. Did the adults and older children wish that Lassie hadn't died? Do the dry-eyed parents of a moist-eyed teenager wish their child hadn't watched? If he hadn't watched, what would have been his grief at breakfast, reading the news that Lassie was dead? And would he regret missing the final episode?

What about declaring that Lassie did not die and showing an alternative episode, one filmed after Lassie's death was screened, explaining that, Lassie being only fictional, the screenwriters thought it best, in view of the widespread grief (evidenced by some people's wanting to know where to send flowers), to rewrite the story. I don't think that works, but maybe a substitute screenwriter could be blamed for an inauthentic episode, Lassie's true creator having been hospitalized but, now having recovered, swearing that the real Lassie hadn't been going to die and that the dying episode was a counterfeit.

But there are rules that must not be violated. An important one is: no feedback from the audience. You cannot show two episodes and let each viewer choose, nor poll the audience to determine whether Lassie dies. Nor can the viewers simply imagine themselves a different episode in which Lassie is spared. The problem is not the lack of imagination, but discipline and authenticity. Fantasy is too self-indulgent. Daydreams escalate. Before I can spend the $10,000 that my opponent at poker bet because he thought that I was bluffing, I revise the figure to $100,000; then I put it in gold at forty dollars an ounce, spend a couple of years hiking home from a plane crash in northern Canada, phone my broker to sell and hit the eight-hundred-dollar market, and start plotting to invest my two million in something equally good. By then I realize that it is all counterfeit if I can make it up so easily.

There is no suspense, no surprise, no danger. Likewise there is no emergency in which Lassie can risk her life with which I can quicken my pulse as long as I know that I write the ending.

Engrossing fiction, whatever else it is, is disciplined fantasy. If you know your authors you can even choose, as people choose their opponent's skill in a chess machine, the risk of tragedy. Killing a character in whom the reader has made an investment puts the lives of the remaining characters in credible jeopardy, and some authors acquire a reputation for poignant endings.

There is something here akin to self-deception. Jon Elster's work on self-deception is persuasive. (See Chapter 4, note 3.) His interest is rational cognitive self-deception, reasoning one's way into a belief one knows to be false, inducing the belief through practice, or permanently removing something from memory together with the memory of the decision to remove it. Other phenomena that could be called self-deception are less permanent and less cognitive. Riding a safe roller coaster can give some people the same exhilaration as a genuinely risky trip. Their eyes and semicircular canals capture the communication channels. I don't know who I thought was being stabbed in the shower in *Psycho*, but after the movie my wife and I, who had arrived at the theater in separate cars, left one car behind and drove home together. I have not been able to determine whether it is the scare that I enjoy or the relief that comes after. Solomon and Corbit have discussed an "opponent process" that might generate net utility from the infliction of pain or fright; his parachutists enjoyed a high that lasted twenty-four hours after the jump.[1] I wonder whether someone thrown from an airplane, saved by a parachute that he didn't know he had, would be exhilarated by the experience. In skydiving and in horror movies the sensation of risk is controlled; self-deception is partial; the glands that secrete euphoric stimuli are encouraged to be deceived, but not the control centers that would make us sick.

A puzzle occurs to me. I have never been instructed in how to produce good daydreams. It could be that I haven't the talent to create fiction, for myself or for anybody else, and I rely on novelists to provide fully articulated fantasies with which I can identify in a participatory way. But perhaps I just don't know the rules of construction. Like a sculptor who finds challenge in the stone itself, artistic fantasy may require the challenge of self-imposed restraint. Perhaps I could be taught strategies of self-discipline to prevent that runaway inflation to which my favorite daydreams are so susceptible. There may be ways to introduce genuine surprise, perhaps by some random drawing from a library in my mind. The problem suggested by Elster's comments on self-induced beliefs, and on sneaking up on one's own insomnia, is that in the act of reining in one's daydreams to give them greater authenticity, one may not be able to hold reins and forget he's holding them.

It does not detract, as far as I can tell, from the suspense and credibility of the fiction I read that I chose the book, that is, chose an author I knew or knew something about the book by hearsay. (Douglas Hofstadter, in *Gödel, Escher, Bach*,[2] pointed out that by unconsciously estimating the pages remaining we spoil some of the terminal surprise of a novel, just as by checking our watch during an adventure film we can tell whether we are on another false summit or have reached the climax.)

I doubt whether these puzzles can be resolved by just thinking about them. The rules of argument for certain philosophical problems require idealizing a person as a reasoning machine, one that not only can think logically but cannot think illogically, that has no hallucinations and no chemical or electrical means of putting things into memory or taking them out. Whether that kind of person can do something that would be called "fooling himself," and the limits on what he may fool himself about, is an intriguing question. But it is not the only question, because that is not the only kind of person worth studying. What makes dreams, day-dreams, books, and films captivating, credible, and irresistible, with or without music or stimulants, requires more than reflection. Though we can often simulate by reasoning what can be done by reasoning, spellbinding requires other modes of study.

Maybe real dreams are more promising. Some work of Kilton Stewart indicated that people in the Malay Peninsula have developed techniques for taming their dreams, reshaping dreams in progress.[3] Apparently they do not make up their dreams in advance, but assume enough command to keep the dreams from getting out of hand. I cannot claim even to understand what that means, but I also don't understand the particular control that I had when that nice girl was being stabbed in the shower.

Lassie represents only one of the ways that, as consumers, we live in our minds. She was fiction and her medium was television; Rin Tin Tin was radio and movies. But novels, plays, puppets, and stories, impromptu or composed, new or familiar, are of the species. They are primarily for enjoyment. And they usually, but not always, capture the mind.

By capture I mean to engage it, to hold it, to occupy or to pre-occupy it so that one's thoughts are not elsewhere; to give the reader or viewer or listener a stake in the outcome; to make him identify in some fashion with characters in the story, if only by caring what happens. The engagement has dynamics; it progresses. Interruption is disagreeable, though a person can sometimes go on "hold" while the man in the projection room changes the reel.

The characteristic that interests me is the engrossment—not merely the surrender of attention but the participation, the sense of being in the story or part of it, caring, and wanting to know. Some fiction lacks that quality; irony and humor require a more conscious attention, and some plots are constructed to be admired rather than absorbed into. Some surprise turns of plot are intended to jolt the reader out of the story and into a relation with the author; and some science fiction is more like turning the leaves of a mail-order catalog than participating in a story.

There is also nonfiction that works like fiction. For many of us it is impossible to watch sports on television just to admire the performance. Not only do we end up caring how the game comes out, we are incapable of watching the game symmetrically. It is more fun to be engaged. And that Lassie phenomenon occurs: I cannot change the side I am on, especially not to be on the winning side, because changing sides discredits the notion that I have a side, just as I cannot mentally bring Lassie back to life without denying that Lassie is mortal and I care what happens to her.

It is this suspense and concern that qualifies certain live events to be considered as impromptu fiction. Snippets of football, like an eighty-yard punt return, can be good entertainment for a few minutes, but I have never known a TV channel to replay old games regularly; and people who look forward to a delayed broadcast do all they can to avoid overhearing the outcome in advance.

What puzzles me is how to relate these observations to a theory of what people are up to. Take the rational consumer in economic theory: what is he consuming?

What do I consume when I purchase *The Wizard of Oz?* Physically I buy a book, or a reel of videotape. But that is a raw material; I "consume" two hours of entertainment. But should I say that, like Dorothy, I consumed a trip to Oz? Or, to phrase it awkwardly, that I procured Dorothy's trip to Oz, in which I participated? I do not mean a sight-seeing trip—television can always show me places that I cannot afford to visit—but the adventure, with the risk and poignancy and excitement and surprise.

A way to try to make sense of the question is to ask what the substitutes are. If you lower the price of air travel I may travel less by bus, but if I see *Around the World in Eighty Days,* am I less likely to travel? Can I do without a dog if I have Lassie? Do I need as much romance, repartee, or fresh air and sunshine if I get plenty of it from nine until midnight on a screen in my living room? I am not sure what I should be expected to consume less of once I have seen two killings in *Psycho.* And since some consumer goods whet appetites, the notion of substitutes may not be the correct one.

There is no question but that part of what I get from a two-hour movie or two hours in a book is "two hours' worth" of something. I get two hours of time-out, of escape, of absentmindedness. Escape from what? Certainly from boredom. Escaping boredom is escaping the tedium of consciousness, of one's own company, of being here and now and oneself, not someplace else or somebody else.

And there is escaping things the knowledge of which makes one unhappy. If "truth" is what we know and are aware of, in the most engrossing fiction we escape truth. Whatever else it is, drama is forgetfulness. We can forget and forget that we are forgetting. It is temporary mind control. If memories are pain, fiction is anesthesia.

But is it more than that? Is it more than time-out? Do we consume the contents of the story or just the time? And what implication does this kind of consuming have for what we are doing with our minds the rest of the time?

There is a funny correspondence between the mind and the home computer. For years the mind has been likened to a calculating machine, and much "artificial intelligence" is an indirect way of studying the human mind. Texts in cognitive science treat perception, recall and recognition, and reasoning with the same schemata as are used in analyzing electronic machines and their software, with the same flow charts and terminology. But I have in mind what families bought last Christmas.

These are the machines you use to calculate the payback period of a new furnace or the answer to a child's geometry problem and, when you have done that, to shoot down enemy missiles or go spelunking in a cave full of reptiles. The computer is a tool *and* a plaything, and *that* is what makes it like the mind.

An important difference is that to switch a computer from tool to toy or toy to tool you usually have to insert a cartridge or disc, but the mind is able to go from work mode to fantasy like a computer that, halfway through an income-tax program, finds oil on your property.

But fantasy and fiction are not all that I have in mind. Aside from those two related forms of make-believe, most of the things that affect my welfare happen in my mind. I can say this, I suppose, because I am part of that minority of the human race that is comfortable most of the time, trained from childhood to be reflective and socially sensitive, and most of the day not required to be busily alert at tasks that entirely absorb one's attention. The things that make me happy or unhappy, at any level of consciousness that I can observe, are the things I believe and am aware of.

I like to be liked, I like to be admired. I like not to be guilty of cowardice; I like to believe that I shall live long and healthily and that my children will too, that I have done work I can be proud of and that others appreciate, that my life will be rich with challenge but I shall meet the challenges and have many accomplishments. That the talk I gave yesterday was a good one, and what I am writing today will be read and appreciated.

If I were hungry or cold or itched all over my body or had to work physically to exhaustion, those would be the conditions that determined my welfare. But I think I have stated the situation correctly for myself and for most of the people that I know.

An unavoidable question is whether I could be happier if only I could believe things more favorable, more complimentary, more in line with my hopes and wishes, than what I believe to be true. That might be done by coming to believe things that are contrary to what I know, such as that my reputation or my health or my childrens' health is better than it is, my financial prospects or my childrens' better than they are, and that I have performed ably and bravely on those occasions when I did not. Or it might be accomplished by improving the mix of my beliefs by dropping out—forgetting—some of the things that cause me guilt, grief, remorse, and anxiety.

Whether I would be happier, whether my welfare should be deemed greater, with those improved beliefs is one of the questions; another is whether, if I had the choice, I would elect a change in my beliefs. Set aside for the moment the question whether there is any way I could do that. The question whether I would choose to revise the contents of my mental library, so that even in my most rational thinking I would come to more positive conclusions, is independent of whether or not we know the technology by which it might be done. I admit that whether I would choose it might depend on the technology. There are cognitive psychotherapies that purport to improve the quality of a patient's beliefs by substituting more favorable correct beliefs for depressing wrong beliefs. But substituting still more favorable wrong beliefs would apparently require a different procedure.[4]

A third question is whether you would encourage me to manipulate my own beliefs in the interests of my own happiness, or permit me to if you had anything to say about it. Maybe for that question we have to be more explicit about technologies. There are animals that reportedly self-administer pure pleasure through electrodes in their brains, to the point of endangering their survival by not stopping to eat or drink. The nature of that euphoria we may never know until we try it; and whether it sounds like music, feels like a rocking chair, tastes like chocolate, reads like a novel, or is merely a pleasant absence of sensation may determine our attitudes. Currently it is considered all right to do it with stereo headphones but not electrodes.

Of course if we ever can select our favorite beliefs off some menu we shall have to be practical about it. I might want to forget I had cancer but not to forget showing up for treatment. I must avoid beliefs that collide with each other or with reality in such a way that I have to confront my own confusion and recognize my beliefs as unreliable, coming to doubt the beliefs I selected off the menu. Just as lawyers advise us to stick close to the truth because the truth is consistent and easier to remember, self-deceivers will be wise to pick sparingly from that menu.

A little later I shall invite you to think about that menu, about what you would like to find on a menu of beliefs and disbeliefs, of ways to insert things into memory and to remove things, to manipulate awareness and the ease or difficulty of recall, and in other ways to affect what is resident in your mind. But first let me recall some of the methods already available, that work well or ill according to who uses them and what for. Most of them we do not think of as mind control, although several fit that description. They would not be described as *belief* control, but that may be because we speak about beliefs as if they were little entities in the mind. That notion misses some relevant dimensions. We forget things all the time, in the sense that we do not *currently* have them in mind, are unaware of them. We can be using knowledge that is not in mind, aware of conclusions that derive from things we are momentarily unaware of. We don't usually call this forgetting; but when it is important to get things out of mind, and we make an effort at forgetting, doing things and thinking things that are incompatible with the awareness of what it is we are trying to forget, what we are doing deserves to be called "forgetting" even though it is temporary. People do say they went to a movie to forget tomorrow's examination.

The language of belief is confusing here. I have observed in myself, so often that it no longer surprises me, that if I give a performance before some audience, I am jollier at dinner and eat more if I am pleased with my performance. Disagreeable feedback spoils the evening. At my age the statistical record of my performance ought to reflect so many observations of good, poor, and mediocre performance that one more experience at either tail of the distribution could hardly affect a rational self-assessment. I try to remind myself of that on those occasions when feedback depresses me; but my welfare function apparently isn't constructed that way. It feels to me as if I am taking the audience reaction as evidence, and what makes me feel good or bad is the belief that my *average* career performance is high or low and will continue so in the future. I think it is plain bad reasoning. I am making a rudimentary statistical error, attaching weights that are distorted by vividness or recency and "forgetting" the bulk of my experience. I mention this as evidence that there are kinds and degrees of forgetting even despite our knowing better.

Before we compose that menu of mental self-controls and self-stimuli that we might wish we could choose from, an inventory of techniques already available is useful. I offer a suggestive list. I exclude from the list things that require a large investment in time, effort, or therapeutic care, like education, psychoanalysis, and hermitage, and those that entail irreversible surgery, like castration and lobotomy, and also those that cope with diagnosed pathologies and are based on prescription drugs or dietary supplements that require the attention of a physician. I am rather thinking of tranquilizers, caffeine, and sleeping pills.

First is sleep itself. Sleep is somewhat addictive: giving it up each morning is for many people one of the hardest things they do. Sleep can be escape from awareness of what is fearsome or hideous. Sleep with dreams can be enjoyable, but not reliably for most of us. Meditation and other modes of relaxation apparently offer escape from anxiety and mental torment for some people. Maybe the more generic term "unconsciousness" includes the state of apparent sleep that goes with blood alcohol and other anesthesia.

Different from sleep itself are things that bring on sleep, whether sleeping pills, white noise, rocking, alcohol, or breathing exercises. Sleep is an equilibrium state after we get there; getting there requires controlling stimuli. The distinction between sleep as a state and getting to sleep as a transition is sharp, even though some techniques for arriving at sleep, like relaxation, are also substitutes for sleep, and some of the things that induce sleep, like alcohol, help to sustain sleep.

Then we have tranquilizers—pills or alcohol—that are intended not only to relieve distress but to remove inhibitions, shyness, anxiety, specific phobias, and fear in general, so that one can perform and remain calm despite stimuli that might otherwise be disabling.

We have things that help us to remain alert. Caffeine in coffee and in tablet form prevents dozing and sleep, as do some prescription drugs. Unexpected stimuli, including noise and even pain, can help, and sometimes aerobic exercise. A useful distinction here is between staying awake and enhancing awareness.

There are techniques to enhance mental concentration. These may take the form of suppressing stimuli and intrusive signals. Insulation against noise is an example. Even fatigue sometimes helps concentration.

Sensory deprivation is a technique, the purposes and results of which I am not sure of. Generally it includes earplugs, masks over the eyes, avoidance of tactile sensation or stimulation of skin, and deliberate relaxation, as well as tanks of warm water. Classical and operant conditioning can affect what one likes, dislikes, fears, enjoys, remembers, or forgets.

Sensory enhancement is a possibility. Marijuana is sometimes reported to make colors more brilliant, music more profound, dance more sublime.

Drive enhancement of various kinds is apparently available to increase gustatory or sexual appetite. Aside from deliberate starvation, there are visual and olfactory stimuli, conditioning, imaginative self-stimulation, and the ubiquitous alcohol.

Hypnosis has been successful in affecting permanent change in desires, in the effectiveness of stimuli, in the treatment of addictions and phobias, and in what one forgets or is reminded of.

Subliminal stimulation can apparently have some effect, whether in stimulating, reminding, or providing information. Subliminal visual stimulation in connection with television never became the menace that some feared, but the technology remains a possibility. Cassettes are advertised that offer subliminal help.

Finally I would mention electrical and chemical control of memory and other mental processes. We should consider the possibility, which I believe not absolutely ruled out by current theories of information storage in the brain, that memories could be extinguished permanently by electrical stimulation or surgery. In science fiction this would be done by having the patient recall vividly the memory to be extinguished, in order that the memory itself or its location could be targeted, the exciting of the memory being the process that offers the target. If the act of recall produces merely a photocopy and not the original, nothing is accomplished; but there are enough ways to erase something erroneously in the memory of even good computers to suggest that deliberate memory extinction may not be forever beyond reach.

For an extreme therapy that differentiates the reasoning mind from the reactive one I propose this example. I love somebody whose face has been hideously disfigured in an accident. I know that it will be difficult to love her forever if I continuously see her as ugly as she is going to be. I was in the same accident; I'm in the same hospital; I haven't seen her yet, I've only heard about her facial disfigurement. My doctor visits and asks if there's anything I would like.

I ask to be blinded.

This is not self-deception in the Elster sense. Not only do I know that she is ugly; every day my blindness will remind me that she must be too ugly to love if I see her. It keeps me, however, from reacting to visual stimuli that I would not be able to accommodate.

There is something here like reaction to a mask. Might the doctor propose that, though there is nothing plastic surgery can do to restore the looks of the person I love, she can wear a mask? How does this relate to cosmetics? If I know that somebody looks prettier than she would if her face were clean of cosmetics, and if I prefer her looks with cosmetics, is it that the cosmetics make me think she is more beautiful, or do I just react to the sight that includes the cosmetics as well as the face?

Maybe the term "self-delusion" can be used for these processes, saving "self-deception" for the more purely intellectual.

Now to consider that menu of believings, forgettings, awarenesses, remindings, and other modes of mind control that we might be tempted to administer to ourselves if they were reliably available at moderate cost without side effects. We need to put a boundary on what we should let ourselves wish for. Wouldn't it be delightful if we could change our taste in foods and enjoy turnips as much as we enjoy smoked oysters? Think of the money we would save, to say nothing of calories and cholesterol! Instant wit, efficient memorization, bravery, poise, optimism, and immunity to disagreeable noises would look good in a Christmas stocking. The capacity to like, even love, one's work, colleagues, neighbors, spouse, and neighborhood would make rose-colored glasses a bargain. In contemplating the self-paternal self-deception that might interest us if only it were available, we shall get nowhere—or rather we shall get infinitely far too fast—if we let our wishes escalate the way our daydreams sometimes do.

A modest place to begin is phobias. We could wish for either of two things about phobias: that we didn't have them, or that we did. The usual definition of a phobia is a disabling or severely discomforting fear, persistent, illogical, and serving no prudential purpose. The more famous of them have Greek names. Most people who react with repugnance to enclosure, open space, rodents, reptiles, insects, viscera, blood, audiences, precipices, needles, and the dark, suffer directly from the sensation when it cannot be avoided and suffer the costs of avoidance when it can be. Phobias seem to be based upon memories of real or imagined scenes and events or associations of real or imagined scenes or events. Therapies like conditioning, hypnosis, relaxation, and stimulus control can weaken or extinguish the phobia, and there must be corresponding ways to enhance or aggravate them. Whether, for some phobias or most of them, there is something that could be "forgotten" that would extinguish the phobia, I do not know. But for at least some phobias some of the time it can help to forget the phobia itself. Just as closing one's eyes can sometimes eliminate a stimulus that produces vertigo or a reaction to blood or even darkness, forgetting a phobia can sometimes reduce one's awareness of the presence of the conditions that trigger the phobia. There are people who are suddenly stricken when reminded that they are in circumstances—enclosures, high places—to which their normal reaction is phobic. Thus, a modest minimum that might be achieved through specific forgetfulness would be occasional neutralization of a phobia by merely forgetting it. (Forgetting one's insomnia does make it easier to get to sleep.)

Acquiring a phobia can be useful. Some of the therapies offered to people who smoke attempt to produce a mental association of cigarettes with dirty lungs, lip cancer, and foul breath. If these are presented as realistic consequences of smoking and the smoker is expected to reflect on them and to decide never to smoke again, and actually never to smoke again, there is no need to characterize the aversion as a phobia.

But if the patient is unable to respond reasonably to the danger itself, through lack of self-control or absentmindedness, raising the fear an order of magnitude and putting the enhanced fear itself beyond reason permits the resulting fear to be both unreasonable and useful. The technique might work for particular foods that are to be altogether eliminated from one's diet; for plain overeating the corresponding phobia against food in general is not helpful, as demonstrated by extreme cases of anorexia. Cigarettes have the advantage that there is no minimum required level of smoking, and the response to the phobia can be absolute.

The idea of deliberately cultivating latent disagreeable thoughts suggests an important distinction. Some of the things we would like to believe and forget are beliefs and memories that directly affect our internal welfare, our state of hope and happiness, regret, anxiety, guilt, fear, compassion, or pride. If I am going to smoke anyway, believing that cigarettes cannot hurt me improves my welfare. That cigarettes are dangerous is a belief that, if available for adoption, I should adopt only if I thought I would act on it and quit the habit that worries me.

But the instrumental beliefs and the "consumable" beliefs cannot always be distinguished. There is evidence that people who believe themselves to be exceptionally at risk—people who after a severe cardiac episode are flatly told by their physicians that continued smoking will likely kill them—not only have a higher success rate in quitting than people who are merely advised to cut down or quit, but suffer less in quitting than the people who succeed on the more ambivalent advice. (I believe the difference is between the mental activity of the person who believes himself *to have quit* and that of the person who thinks of himself as *trying to quit*. For the latter there is suspense and the need to decide over and over on the occasions that invite one to smoke.)

What might our menu offer for daydreams? One possibility would be a mechanism to keep my mind from wandering. Often when I try to pay attention to a speaker I hear something that sends my mind on a detour. Paradoxically, the more stimulating what I listen to, the more I miss because of so many opportunities for my wayward mind to pursue a thought and, in doing so, to miss the next one.

The same thing happens when I think to myself. I am supposed to be working a problem and I wake up to discover that for some unmeasured period my mind has been playing, not working.

Mind wandering is not about beliefs but about mental behavior. But there is also make-believe. Children seem better at it than adults. That may be because children can do it together. I spend some time in pure reverie—what my dictionary calls "dreamy imaginings, especially of agreeable things"—in which I am the protagonist, but I don't usually admit it and would be mortified to recapitulate my daydream for somebody else, and haven't done it as a duet since childhood. Along one dimension the quality has certainly deteriorated, that of believing in the plot. I may be able to imagine vividly an audience that I hold spellbound, but the feeling that I am really doing it is a weak one. Children who make-believe out loud together seem to enjoy a higher quality of involvement. That may be partly because they are unabashed about it. Should we wish that the menu contain something to make our daydreams more real? I don't mean make the plot more realistic, just make the imagined experiences feel more like real experiences.

I can think of two different kinds of daydreams to which this notion of enhancement might apply. One is pure entertainment, unrelated to the activity one is engaged in or the environment in which one finds oneself. I do it sitting on a bus or on an airplane. The other one is, I am a little shy to admit, investing something that I am doing with a make-believe interpretation. People who run for exercise sometimes pretend to themselves that they are in a race or on some heroic errand. There is not much else to do while running, so any mental recreation is at low opportunity cost. A little anesthesia is welcome. Any arduous task ought to become a little less burdensome if one could dress it up with some make-believe. I refuse to answer whether I would order some instant make-believe if it were available on the market; I would certainly order it only if it came in a plain wrapper. Trying to improve the quality of our daydreams sounds shamefully childish; the childishness of our actual daydreams is, fortunately, known only to ourselves.

So we come to the final item under "daydreams" on our menu,

the daydream suppressant. If daydreams are a childish waste of time, a bad habit, might we like to be rid of the habit? Are daydreams only low-grade entertainment, as involuntary as preoccupation with something on a TV screen that the management won't turn off? If we cannot improve our daydreams, would we like them turned off? Whether we would like it may depend on what it is we are going to do instead. If we daydream to escape thinking about what we are supposed to be thinking about, eliminating the daydreams may just make us find some other escape. Until I know what that other escape is, I am not sure whether I would rather stick with my daydreams. If it means I will get my work done more expeditiously, I should welcome it. If I am facing a long bus ride and the alternative to daydreaming is studying the upholstery on the seat in front of me, or looking for the letters of the alphabet in the billboards we pass, it may be better to improve the quality of the dreams than to reduce the quantity.

The human mind is something of an embarrassment to certain disciplines, notably economics, decision theory, and others that have found the model of the rational consumer to be powerfully productive. The rational consumer is depicted as having a mind that can store and process information, that can calculate or at least make orderly successive comparisons, and that can vicariously image, imagine, anticipate, feel, and taste, and can simulate emotion in order to compare and choose. To decide whether to risk being caught in bad weather on an off-season mountaineering expedition, whether to face immediate embarrassment or to get a reputation for running away, whether to have another child, whether to change to a pleasanter occupation at reduced earnings, whether to forgo wine to save money for a stereo system or even just to choose a restaurant meal over the telephone, the mind has to be capable of somehow sampling the pleasures and discomforts, the joys and horrors, on the basis both of remembered experience and description and of creative extrapolation.

Just how one decides whether he's in the mood for broiled salmon or roast duck isn't the concern of the decision sciences, at least not unless the way it is done turns out to conflict in some fashion with the rest of the model of rational choice. It sometimes seems to me—to me as a consumer and not as an economist—that I choose dinners from menus a little the way I used to choose movies from "coming attractions": I mentally consume a morsel of broiled salmon, register the quality of the taste but erase the taste itself, do the same for the roast duck, and let the two sensations feed into an analog computer that signals my choice. But I can't be sure; if I watch myself and find that that is what seems to happen, it may be the result of the watching.

Now we probably believe, if we bother to think about it, that ultimately the roast duck I order is enjoyed in my brain. But not in my *mind*. We can say that I consume the roast duck, or we can say that I consume tastes and smells that I produce with roast duck; we could say that I consume chemical and electrical activity in the brain that is triggered by the sensory nerves of taste and smell, but unless our interest is the brain, that doesn't add anything. Still, there is mental activity; looking at the roast duck is not eating it, but it is part of the activity, and the visual aesthetics of the meal seem "mental" in a way that appeasement of appetite does not. Anticipating the roast duck, contemplating the first bite, has a "mental" quality.

If a gourmet host dawdled thirty minutes choosing the grandest meal of his career, looking at the raw meat shown him by the chef, discussing wine with the wine steward, watching it brought to the table and tastefully served; smiled at the friends assembled around him, delicately sampled the wine and nodded his approval, and watched the first course served impeccably onto everybody's plate—and died instantly of a heart attack—we'd be tempted to say that the last half hour of his life was perhaps the best half hour of his life. More than that, we might say it was the most enjoyable meal of his life, one of the best he had ever "consumed."

If he did not die but proceeded to the more conventional enjoyment, and two days later described this superb meal in mouth-watering details to a few of his gourmet friends, we might be tempted to judge that he enjoyed the meal as much in the telling as in the eating, much as a person who barely wins a bitterly fought tennis tournament enjoys the winning more in reflecting back on it than on the hot afternoon on which he nearly lost it.

These observations bring me to the notion of the mind as a *consuming organ*. We consume with our mouths and noses and ears and eyes and proprioceptors and skin and fingertips, and with the nerves that react to external stimuli and internal hormones; we consume relief from pain and fatigue, itching and thirst. But we also consume by thinking. We consume past events that we can bring up from memory; future events that we can believe will happen; contemporary circumstances not physically present, like the respect of our colleagues and the affection of our neighbors and the health of our children; and we can even tease ourselves into believing and consuming thoughts that are intended only to please. We consume good news and bad news.

We even—and this makes it a little like traditional economics—spend resources to discover the truth about things that happened in the past. People wish to know that children dead for many years died without too much pain or died proudly. It gets very compounded. If an estranged child makes a painful and urgent journey to arrive at a parent's bedside in time to become reconciled just before the parent dies, all that the parent gets is an hour's love and relief before leaving this world. Whatever the worth of a single hour of ecstasy, compared with vicariously enjoying Dorothy's trip to Oz, it is entirely a mental consuming. The days away from work and the airfare the child spent to be at the dying parent's bedside is a consumer expenditure, a gift to the parent. If the parent dies too soon and never knows that the child is on the way, the investment is largely wasted. If the trip succeeds, the child may consider it the most worthwhile expenditure of his consuming career. One hour's mental consumption.

Furthermore, others will want to know, and will care, whether the child made it to the bedside. There are some who care enough to make large expenditures to hasten the child's arrival or to prolong the parent's life long enough for the reconciliation to take place.

And finally, the whole story can be fiction. We can be gripped with suspense and caring as we wonder whether an entire lifetime is going somehow to be vindicated by an ecstatic discovery that, after barely an hour, will be extinguished by death.

So we have at least two distinct roles for our minds to play: that of the information processing and reasoning machine by which we choose what to consume out of the array of things that our resources can be exchanged for, and that of the pleasure machine or consuming organ, the generator of direct consumer satisfaction. Like a television set that can frighten small children or bring grief in the form of bad news, the mind can directly generate horror as well as ecstasy, irritation as well as comfort, fear and grief as well as enjoyable memories, reflections, and prospects. But that is partly because of still another characteristic of the mind: it doesn't always behave nicely.

Just as it may fail us when we need to remember, or panic when we need all our faculties, the mind can remember things that cause grief or that spoil our appetite. It remembers ugly things it insists on associating with beauty, or hums interminably a tune we'd like to get out of our minds. It is like a complex piece of machinery that has a mind of its own and is not disposed to be our obedient servant. Or possibly we just have not learned how to get the right service out of our mind. In our culture we stress the importance of the mind as an auxiliary instrument, the information storage and retrieval and articulating mechanism that performs intellectual tasks like communicating and reasoning, and we do not encourage learning to make our minds produce the thoughts and memories and exploratory previews that bring joy and comfort and to expunge the other kind.

The mind evolved as an organ of many uses and many capabilities, an imperfect organ whose imperfections along some dimensions are compensated or adapted to by the mind's development along others. The dimensions that we associate with analytical thought and speech, even the orderly filing system of our memory, are fairly recent in human evolution; they may not have achieved the autonomy that is assumed in some decision theories and philosophies. Consider whether a person can be said to have values and to know his values and to make choices in accordance with those known values. When it is time to make a decision, that is, when beset by certain stimuli that call for a response, the rational individual is supposed to be able to illuminate and scrutinize his preference map in order not only to calculate how to achieve a particular outcome but to remind himself which outcomes he prefers. His brain may not only selectively transmit information but selectively illuminate his preference map. We know that people are incapable of keeping their eyes from focusing on potato chips, sexy pictures, or animated cartoons; we know that both externally administered and internally secreted chemicals can suppress or anesthetize certain activities; we have little empirical basis for believing (and much for not believing) that the mind will neutrally and indiscriminately process information and scrutinize memory to permit a person to make a choice unaffected by momentary stimuli, whether related to food, fear, sex, affection, aesthetic pleasure, or attractive violence. The unconscious accommodation of one's beliefs to achieve a reduction in "cognitive dissonance" is often treated as a defective or undesirable process, one to be guarded against. Maybe it is to be welcomed like the reduction of other annoying dissonances. At least the mind is *trying* to help!

This is all apart from the fact that the mind is a wanderer, a source of fantasy, and an easy captive for puzzles, mysteries, and daydreams.

As far as I know, it's all the same mind. Marvelous it is that the mind does all these things. Awkward it is that it seems to be the same mind from which we expect both the richest sensations and the most austere analyses.

There is an interesting question of perspective. Like the question, Do creatures reproduce themselves by way of genes, or do genes reproduce themselves by way of creatures?—Do I navigate my way through life with the help of my mind, or does my mind navigate its way through life by the help of me? I'm not sure who's in charge.

# Notes
# Sources
# Index

# Notes

## 2. Command and Control

1. Richard E. Neustadt, *Presidential Power: The Politics of Leadership* (New York: Wiley, 1960), p. 9.
2. Marshall I. Goldman, "The Convergence of Environmental Disruption," *Science* 170 (October 2, 1970), 37–42.
3. Konrad Lorenz, *On Aggression* (New York: Harcourt, Brace and World, 1966), p. 109.

## 3. The Intimate Contest for Self-Command

Epigraph. *The Odyssey of Homer*, translated by R. Lattimore (New York: Harper and Row, 1965), p. 186.
1. Lewis Thomas, *The Lives of a Cell: Notes of a Biology Watcher* (New York: Viking, 1974), and *The Medusa and the Snail: More Notes of a Biology Watcher* (New York: Viking, 1979); Carl Sagan, *The Dragons of Eden* (New York: Random House, 1977).

## 4. Ethics, Law, and the Exercise of Self-Command

1. The richest, most varied, and most comprehensive approach to this subject that I have discovered is George Ainslie's "Specious Reward: A Behavioral Theory of Impulsiveness and Impulse Control," *Psychological Bulletin* 82 (July 1975), 463–496, and some of his later, unpublished work. An intriguing philosophical approach to these issues is Jon Elster's "Ulysses and the Sirens: A Theory of Imperfect Rationality," *Social Science Information* 41 (1977), 469–526, and his book with a similar name (see Note 3). In economics there are attempts to accommodate self-management or self-control within traditional consumer theory and, more recently, some efforts to break out of the tradition. A pioneer work was Robert H. Strotz, "Myopia and Inconsistency in Dynamic Utility Maximization," *Review of Economic Studies* (1955–56),

349

165–180. The best-known effort to fit this subject within the economics tradition is George J. Stigler and Gary S. Becker, "De Gustibus Non Est Disputandum," *American Economic Review* 67 (March 1977), 76–90; their formulation denies the phenomenon I discuss. On the edge of traditional economics are C. C. von Weizsacker, "Notes on Endogenous Change of Tastes," *Journal of Economic Theory* (December 1971), 345–372, and Roger A. McCain, "Reflections on the Cultivations of Taste," *Journal of Cultural Economics* 3 (June 1979), 30–52. Outside the tradition, and viewing the consumer as complex rather than singular, are Amartya K. Sen, "Rational Fools: A Critique of the Behavioral Foundations of Economic Theory," *Philosophy and Public Affairs* 6 (Summer 1977), 317–345; Gordon C. Winston, "Addiction and Backsliding: A Theory of Compulsive Consumption," *Journal of Economic Behavior and Organization* (December 1980), 295–324; and Howard Margolis, *Selfishness, Altruism, and Rationality* (New York: Cambridge University Press, 1982). Winston and Margolis recognize the referee, or superself, that I find lacking; whether the difference is one of perception or of methodology, I am not sure. The only genuinely multidisciplinary work of any great scope that I know of by an economist is Tibor Scitovsky's brilliant small book, *The Joyless Economy: An Inquiry into Human Satisfaction and Consumer Dissatisfaction* (New York: Oxford University Press, 1976).

2. Charles Fried, *Contract as Promise* (Cambridge, Mass.: Harvard University Press, 1981), p. 13.

3. There is stimulating discussion throughout Jon Elster, *Ulysses and the Sirens* (New York: Cambridge University Press, 1979). I am indebted to his work and to his comments on this chapter. Most of the legal discussion I have found deals with mental illness and informed consent; see Note 4.

4. Rebecca S. Dresser, "Ulysses and the Psychiatrists: A Legal and Policy Analysis of the Voluntary Commitment Contract," *Harvard Civil Rights–Civil Liberties Law Review* 16 (1982), 777–854.

5. Voluntary submission to polygraph testing is a perfect example. "In addition to its uses in prisons, the military, police work, FBI and CIA investigations, and pretrial examinations both for the prosecution and for the defense, the polygraph has also found its way into corporate America, where it is widely used for detecting white-collar crime and for screening potential employees. This year, it is estimated, half a million to a million Americans, for one reason or another, will take a lie detector test"; Alfred Meyer, "Do Lie Detectors Lie?" *Science* 82 (June 1982), 24. Refusal to submit "voluntarily," like pleading the Fifth Amendment or declining to make financial disclosure, is construed as an admission of having something to hide.

### 5. The Life You Save May Be Your Own

1. D. J. Reynolds, "The Cost of Road Accidents," *Journal of the Royal Statistical Society* 119 (1956), 393–408.

2. Selma J. Mushkin, "Health as an Investment," *Journal of Political Economy* (October 1962), supplement, p. 156. She cites an unpublished paper by E. E. Pyatt and P. P. Rogers.

3. Reynolds, "Cost of Road Accidents."

4. The "scaling" principle sketched here follows from modern decision (utility) theory as presented in R. Duncan Luce and Howard Raiffa, *Games and Decisions: Introduction and Critical Survey* (New York: Wiley, 1957), pp. 23–31, and especially reflects the authors' assumptions #4 (substitutability) and #2 (reduction of compound lotteries). It is consistent with the conclusions reached by Armen A. Alchian, "The Meaning of Utility Measurement," *American Economic Review* 43 (March 1953), 26–50, esp. 43. It can be simply construed from the "sure-thing" principle of Leonard J. Savage, *The Foundations of Statistics* (New York: Wiley, 1954), pp. 21ff. It is being used here, though, to cover an irreversibility in the "continuity" assumption (#3) of Luce and Raiffa. That continuity assumption implies that the certainty of any finite loss of income is equivalent to some probability of death; it does not say that the consumer can identify some finite loss of income, the certainty of which is equivalent to some specified probability of death. If though, he can identify a loss of income the certainty of which is equivalent to some specified probability of some specified larger loss of income, it may be possible to fill in these gaps in the consumers' utility map. Thus, we have a technique for making roundabout comparisons when the individual is unable to make a direct comparison. It may or may not be helpful.

5. This technique, whatever its strengths and weaknesses, does not treat the marginal utility of income as constant. It never "scales" income, or any other quantitative variable except pure probabilities.

## 8. What Is the Business of Organized Crime?

1. Mark H. Furstenberg, "Violence and Organized Crime," in *Crimes of Violence: A Staff Report to the National Commission on the Causes and Prevention of Violence* (Washington, D.C., 1969), 13:916, 925.

2. The President's Commission on Law Enforcement and Administration of Justice, *Task Force Report: Organized Crime* (Washington, D.C., 1967), p. 1.

3. Schur used the term in relation to the consumer as well as to the purveyor, and did not limit it to marketplace activities but let it include private deviance, such as homosexuality, as well. See Edwin M. Schur, *Crimes Without Victims* (New York: Prentice-Hall, 1965).

## 9. Strategic Analysis and Social Problems

1. Xenophon, *The Persian Expedition*, trans. Rex Warner (New York: Penguin Books, 1949), p. 236.

2. Ibid., pp. 136–137.

3. Thucydides, *The Peloponnesian War*, trans. Rex Warner (New York: Penguin Books, 1959), pp. 417–419.

4. Lynn Montross, *War through the Ages*, 3rd ed. (New York: Harper, 1960), p. 159.

5. H. D. F. Kitto, *The Greeks* (New York: Penguin Books, 1951), p. 197.

6. Caesar, *The Conquest of Gaul*, trans. S. A. Hanford (New York: Penguin Books, 1960), pp. 32–33.

7. H. H. Turney-Hight, *Primitive War* (Columbia: University of South Carolina Press, 1949), p. 215.

8. Ibid., pp. 217, 200.

9. Neil Hickey, *The Gentleman Wr      'hief* (New York: Collier, 1962), pp. 78–79.

10. *Pascal's Pensées* (New York: E. P. Dutton, 1958), p. 90.

11. Hickey, *Gentleman Was a Thief,* p. 135.

12. Erving Goffman, "On Face-Work," *Psychiatry: Journal for the Study of Interpersonal Processes* 18 (August 1955), 213–231.

13. Erving Goffman, *Asylums* (Garden City, N.Y.: Anchor Books, Doubleday, 1961), pp. 14–35, and *Herodotus,* p. 76.

14. Anatol Rapoport, *Fights, Games and Debates* (Ann Arbor: University of Michigan Press, 1960), chs. 10–13; *Strategy and Conscience* (New York: Harper and Row, 1964), chs. 6–15.

## 10. What Is Game Theory?

1. Impressive support for this approach is in Jerome S. Bruner, Jacqueline S. Goodnow, and George A. Austin, *A Study of Thinking* (New York: Wiley, 1957). In studying experimentally the process of "concept attainment" the authors use the term "strategy" to refer to a "pattern of decisions in the acquisition, retention and utilization of information that serves to meet certain objectives, i.e., to insure certain forms of outcome and to insure against certain others" (p. 54). Furthermore—and this is an interesting step beyond the restrictions of game theory—the authors do not demand that the subject be conscious of his strategy. "Psychology has been celebrating the role of 'emotional factors' and 'unconscious drives' in behavior for so long now that man's capacity for rational coping with his world has come to seem like some residual capacity that shows its head only when the irrational lets up ... Man is not a logic machine, but he is certainly capable of making decisions and gathering information in a manner that reflects better on his learning capacity than we have been as yet ready to grant" (p. 79).

2. A perfect example is in Bruner et al., *Study of Thinking,* in which the limitations on memory show up in the difference between "in the head" and "on the board" records. They even allow for the "comforting" quality of certain strategies. Their work is impressive evidence that one of the best ways to study "irrational" (or, better, "imperfectly rational") decisions is to look at specific departures from perfection rather than to start from no base line at all.

3. Lying, murder, abortion, suicide, violence and nonviolence, adultery, and presumably voting are to be judged by their consequences, not by reference to absolute laws (which, if plural, are bound to conflict occasionally), in "the new morality," which Joseph Fletcher characterizes as "a method of 'situational' or 'contextual' decision-making." Joseph Fletcher, *Situation Ethics* (Philadelphia: Westminster, 1966), esp. pp. 11–39, 64–68, 71–75. The question whether "deterrence" is evil if it threatens something awful (massive retaliation, capital punishment) and it works, so that what is threatened need not be done (and indeed is not expected to be done), is a question to which "situation ethics" will give a different answer from the more traditional ethics. In some of these questions the central issue is how the consequences of an action depend on the way it influences someone else's choice: thus, not only does

game theory typically assume a "situation ethics," but "situation ethics" needs game theory. (Fletcher, p. 188, even supports a game-theoretical attempt "to assign numerical values to the factors at stake in problems of conscience.")

4. *Bibliographical note:* The definitive survey of game theory for twenty-five years was R. Duncan Luce and Howard Raiffa, *Games and Decisions* (New York: Wiley, 1957); Martin Shubik's *Game Theory in the Social Sciences* (Cambridge, Mass.: The MIT Press, 1982), complements rather than supersedes it, and rests on twenty-five more years of work (much of it by Shubik himself). Both books are for professional social scientists. More for the general reader are Henry Hamburger, *Games as Models of Social Phenomena* (San Francisco: W. H. Freeman and Co., 1979), and Steven J. Brams, *Game Theory and Politics* (New York: The Free Press, 1975). A professional treatment of zero-sum games, with illustrative applications to military tactics, is Melven Dresher, *Games of Strategy: Theory and Applications* (Englewood Cliffs, N.J.: Prentice-Hall, 1961). For some of my own ideas, see Thomas C. Schelling, *The Strategy of Conflict* (Cambridge, Mass.: Harvard University Press, 1960). For applications to sociology and politics, the journal to watch is *The Journal of Conflict Resolution*. The original classic is John von Neumann and Oscar Morgenstern, *The Theory of Games and Economic Behavior* (Princeton: Princeton University Press, 1944); it is a stunning architectural achievement, even if not the best route of access for social scientists.

## 11. A Framework for the Evaluation of Arms Proposals

1. With two weapons, a side can have one or the other, neither or both; for the two sides together there are 16 outcomes. To identify all the bargaining possibilities we would need the preference rankings of both sides among 16 outcomes, or 32 rank numbers. The 2 × 2 matrices for the two weapons separately contain 8 numbers each, or 16 in total. Because those numbers expressed only rank order and not magnitude, there is no way to operate arithmetically to derive the rank numbers for the 4 × 4 matrix. Even if we had used cardinal numbers to express strengths of preference, numerical operations would require that the two weapons be so independent of each other that the possession of either weapon on either side did not affect the preferences of either country for the other—not a likely situation if the weapons are important, and especially unlikely if they are "naturally coupled" in negotiation.

## 12. The Strategy of Inflicting Costs

1. See Scherer's review of E. S. Quade, ed., *Analysis for Military Decisions* (Chicago: Rand McNally, 1964), in *The American Economic Review* 55 (December 1965), 1191–1192.

2. Yigael Yadin, *The Art of Warfare in Biblical Lands*, 2 vols. (New York: McGraw-Hill, 1963), II:267–269.

3. $X e^{(M \log P)/Y}$ is maximized at $Y^2 + MY \log P - (KM \log P)/a = 0$. Differentiating this equation yields:

$$-\frac{a/dy}{y/da} = \frac{KM \log P}{aY(2Y + M \log P)} < 1$$

More directly, one can maximize $XP^{aM/(K-X)}$ and differentiate the resulting equation for $dX/da$. That derivative is negative.

4. Burton H. Klein, *Germany's Economic Preparations for War* (Cambridge, Mass.: Harvard University Press, 1959), pp. 232–233.

5. Martin C. McGuire, *Secrecy and the Arms Race* (Cambridge, Mass.: Harvard University Press, 1965), pp. 212–232.

## 15. The Mind as a Consuming Organ

1. R. L. Solomon and J. D. Corbit, "An Opponent-Process Theory of Motivation," *Psychological Review* 81 (1974), 119–145.

2. Douglas R. Hofstadter, *Gödel, Escher, Bach: An Eternal Golden Braid* (New York: Vintage, 1980).

3. Robert E. Ornstein, *The Psychology of Consciousness,* 2nd ed. (New York: Harcourt Brace Jovanovich, 1977), pp. 142, 143.

4. Aaron T. Beck, M.D., *Cognitive Therapy and the Emotional Disorders* (New York: New American Library, 1976).

# Sources

Permission to reprint these essays has been received from the following publishers and is gratefully acknowledged.

**Chapter 1,** "Economic Reasoning and the Ethics of Policy," appeared in *The Public Interest* 63 (Spring 1981), 37–61, and in a slightly different version as "Analytic Methods and the Ethics of Policy," in Daniel Callahan, ed., *Ethics in Hard Times* (New York and London: Plenum Press), pp. 175–215.

**Chapter 2,** "Command and Control," is reprinted from James W. McKie, ed., *Social Responsibility and the Business Predicament* (Washington, D.C.: The Brookings Institution, 1974), pp. 79–108.

**Chapter 3,** "The Intimate Contest for Self-Command," appeared in *The Public Interest* 60 (Summer 1980), 94–118.

**Chapter 4,** "Ethics, Law, and the Exercise of Self-Command," is reprinted from Sterling M. McMurrin, ed., *The Tanner Lectures on Human Values IV* (Salt Lake City: University of Utah Press, 1983), pp. 43–79. The lecture was delivered at the University of Michigan in March 1982.

**Chapter 5,** "The Life You Save May Be Your Own," appeared in Samuel B. Chase, Jr., ed., *Problems in Public Expenditure Analysis* (Washington, D.C.: The Brookings Institution, 1968), pp. 127–162.

**Chapter 6,** "Strategic Relationships in Dying," is reprinted from Ernan McMullin, ed., *Death and Decision* (Boulder, Colo.: Westview Press, 1978), pp. 63–73; copyright © 1978 by the American Association for the Advancement of Science.

**Chapter 7,** "Economics and Criminal Enterprise," is reprinted from *The Public Interest* 7 (Spring 1967), 61–78. An earlier version was published as Appendix D, *Task Force Report: Organized Crime* (Washington, D.C.: The President's Commission on Law Enforcement and Administration of Justice, 1967), pp. 114–126.

**Chapter 8,** "What Is the Business of Organized Crime?," is from the *Journal of Public Law* 20 (1971), 71–84 (now the *Emory Law Journal*).

**Chapter 9,** "Strategic Analysis and Social Problems," is reprinted from *Social Problems* 12 (Spring 1965), 367–379.

**Chapter 10,** "What Is Game Theory?," was originally published in James C. Charlesworth, ed., *Contemporary Political Analysis* (New York: Free Press, 1967), pp. 212–238; copyright © 1967 by The Free Press, a Division of Macmillan Publishing Company.

**Chapter 11,** "A Framework for the Evaluation of Arms Proposals," is reprinted from Martin Pfaff, ed., *Frontiers in Social Thought: Essays in Honor of Kenneth E. Boulding* (New York: North-Holland Publishing Company, 1976), pp. 283–305. It is a revised version of "A Framework for the Evaluation of Arms-Control Proposals," *Daedalus* 104 (Summer 1975), 187–200.

**Chapter 12,** "The Strategy of Inflicting Costs," is from Roland N. McKean, ed., *Issues in Defense Economics* (New York: Columbia University Press, 1967), pp. 105–127; copyright © 1967 by the National Bureau of Economic Research, Inc.

**Chapter 13,** "Who Will Have the Bomb?," is reprinted from *International Security* 1 (Summer 1976), 77–91.

**Chapter 14,** "Thinking about Nuclear Terrorism," is reprinted from *International Security* 6 (Spring 1982), 61–77.

**Chapter 15,** "The Mind as a Consuming Organ," will appear in Jon Elster, ed., *The Multiple Self* (Cambridge: Cambridge University Press, 1984).

# Index

ABM, 243, 244, 255–256, 259–260
Abortion, 3, 17, 170–172, 174–175
Absentmindedness, 340
Affirmative action programs, 29, 46
Aircraft hijacking, 39–42, 48–49
Airplanes and airlines, 117, 145; hijacking, 39–42; safety, 10–16
Airport safety, 10–16
Alternative policies, 15–17, 37; in game theory, 219–221. *See also* Arms bargaining
Anesthesia, make-believe as, 333, 341
Anxiety about death, 130–131, 135–137
Argentina, 327
Arms bargaining, 243–244; alternative preference configurations in, 244–249; attitudes toward weapons in, 263–265; bargaining chips in, 257–263; coupling of weapons or issues in, 256–257; disarmament, 217, 219; IFF-IFF matrix, 252–253; IFF-YES matrix, 253–254; misperceptions in, 255–256; NO-IFF matrix, 254; NO-NO matrix, 253; YES! matrix, 254–255; YES-NO matrix, 254; YES-YES matrix, 249–252
Arrow, Kenneth, 93
Artificial intelligence, 333
Assassination, 320
ASW, 257

Atomic bomb. *See* Arms bargaining; Nuclear weapons
Authentic self, 107–109, 111–112, 152–153
Automobiles and auto industry, 48, 50–51, 54, 196, 206

Babysitters, 133–134
Ballot. *See* Elections and voting
Bargaining, arms. *See* Arms bargaining
Bargaining chips, 257; in arms bargaining, 257–263
Behavior, influence of. *See* Strategic analysis
Beliefs and disbeliefs, 334–336, 340
Berlin Corridor, 197
Bethe, Hans A., 293
Bets, 224. *See also* Gambling, organized
Binary choice, 243, 244
Biological weapons, 243
Birth control, 116
Black-market monopolies, 161–162, 173, 175–178
Black markets, 159–162, 169, 189; and competition, 175–178
Blindness, 257
Blue Cross, 73
Bluffs, 224
Bookmaking. *See* Gambling, organized
Boredom, 332
Brinkmanship, 197

357